Hybrid Political Ord
Politics of Uncertair
Governance in Lebai

Lebanon hosts the highest number of refugees per capita worldwide and is central to European policies of outsourcing migration management. *Hybrid Political Order and the Politics of Uncertainty* is the first book to critically and comprehensively explore the parallels between the country's engagement with the recent Syrian refugee influx and the more protracted Palestinian presence.

Drawing on fieldwork, qualitative case-studies, and critical policy analysis, it questions the dominant idea that the haphazardness, inconsistency, and fragmentation of refugee governance are only the result of forced displacement or host state fragility and the related capacity problems. It demonstrates that the endemic ambiguity that determines refugee governance also results from a lack of political will to create coherent and comprehensive rules of engagement to address refugee 'crises.'

Building on emerging literatures in the fields of critical refugee studies, hybrid governance, and ignorance studies, it proposes an innovative conceptual framework to capture the spatial, temporal, and procedural dimensions of the uncertainty that refugees face and to tease out the strategic components of the reproduction and extension of such informality, liminality, and exceptionalism. In developing the notion of a 'politics of uncertainty,' ambiguity is explored as a component of a governmentality that enables the control, exploitation, and expulsion of refugees.

Dr. Nora Stel is Assistant Professor in Conflict Studies at the Center for International Conflict Analysis and Management of the Department of Political Science at Radboud University Nijmegen. She studies the politics of knowledge and in/formality in the governance of and by displaced people.

Routledge Research in Ignorance Studies

Series editors:
Matthias Gross *is Professor and Head of the Department of Urban and Environmental Sociology, Helmholtz Centre for Environmental Research, UFZ, Leipzig, Germany.*
Linsey McGoey *is Senior Lecturer in Sociology at the University of Essex.*
Michael Smithson *is Professor in the Research School of Psychology at The Australian National University.*

This timely series brings together cutting-edge scholarship in the emergent field of studies on the flipside of knowledge. It addresses the blossoming interest – within an increasing number of disciplines – in the uses and deployment of strategic not knowing, the right to nonknowledge, of forgetting, of producing and keeping secrets.

From classical perspectives on the unknown to the most recent analyses in theology, brain research, decision making, economics, political science, and science and technology studies, this interdisciplinary series will serve as an indispensable resource for both students and scholars. The *Routledge Research in Ignorance Studies* series places the study of ignorance in historical and interdisciplinary context.

Sociology as Analysis of the Unintended
From the Problem of Ignorance to the Discovery of the Possible
Adriana Mica

Hybrid Political Order and the Politics of Uncertainty
Refugee Governance in Lebanon
Nora Stel

For more information about the series, please visit: www.routledge.com/Routledge-Research-in-Ignorance-Studies/book-series/RRIGS

'*Hybrid Political Order and the Politics of Uncertainty* is the first comprehensive analysis of how institutional ambiguity shapes refugee governance. Nora Stel offers a nuanced reading of the proliferating modes of uncertainty that emerge both strategically and tactically at the intersection of local, national and international governance in Lebanon. The book explores the other side of knowledge, its institutional production and its effects on subjectivity. It is a key text for those interested in what ignorance studies can offer to refugee studies.'

– Claudia Aradau, *Professor of International Politics at King's College London*

'Stel's book navigates the alleyways of uncertainty that mold the lives of Palestinian and Syrian refugees in Lebanon. Through case studies in a country hosting the largest number of refugees per capita in the world, the book tackles often misconstrued notions of ambiguity and informality in refugee policy and research. It distinctly shows how institutional ambiguity is deliberately used as an instrument to hold refugees in a state of exceptionalism and constant temporariness. The book is a remarkable addition to the field of critical refugee studies.'

– Nasser Yassin, *Director of the Issam Fares Institute for Public Policy and International Affairs at the American University of Beirut*

'In this important book, Nora Stel provides a novel analysis of Lebanon's multi-layered refugee governance that moves beyond simplistic notions of a "weak-state." Combining first-hand research among Palestinian and Syrian refugees with critical readings of extant scholarship and policy, her keen analysis not only details how ambiguity is strategically employed in all levels of the state bureaucracy, but the costs to those subject to it. The book thereby represents a highly original perspective on refugee governance in Lebanon and beyond.'

– Are Knudsen, *Senior Researcher at the Christian Michelsen Institute*

'*Hybrid Political Order and the Politics of Uncertainty* provocatively and persuasively demonstrates how informality, liminality and exceptionalism in Lebanese refugee governance is everything but accidental. Those continuing to view the country's institutional bedlam and injustices as "state failure" will have a hard time confronting Stel's lucid analysis. Theoretically sophisticated and informed by deep knowledge of Lebanon's intricate politics, the book flags the significance of intra-elite collaboration in disciplining both refugees and citizens. This has profound implications for understanding the Lebanese state.'

– Reinoud Leenders, *Reader in International Relations and Middle East Studies at King's College London*

'With this theoretically sophisticated and empirically rich book, Nora Stel makes a profound contribution to our understanding not only of refugee governance in Lebanon, but of institutional ambiguity and the politics of uncertainty. With eloquence and analytic intensity, Stel conceptualizes how marginalised spaces both make and are made by deliberate forms of ignorance, offering tremendous insights and inspiration to scholars working across multiple fields.'

– Tom Slater, *Reader in Urban Geography at the University of Edinburgh*

'Zooming in on Lebanon, this book has profound theoretical implications for our understanding of the causes of institutional ambiguity in the lives of refugees. Through her detailed desk review, ethnographic fieldwork and interviews, Stel points to the reasons why such institutional ambiguity emerges, whom it benefits and how it is navigated. The book thereby offers a much-needed perspective in today's world of systematic denial of rights behind the veil of uncertainty as a general mode of governance of populations.'

– Katarzyna Grabska, *Assistant Professor in Displacement Studies at the International Institute of Social Studies*

Hybrid Political Order and the Politics of Uncertainty

Refugee Governance in Lebanon

Nora Stel

Routledge
Taylor & Francis Group

LONDON AND NEW YORK

First published 2021
by Routledge
2 Park Square, Milton Park, Abingdon, Oxon OX14 4RN

and by Routledge
52 Vanderbilt Avenue, New York, NY 10017

Routledge is an imprint of the Taylor & Francis Group, an informa business

British Library Cataloguing-in-Publication Data
A catalogue record for this book is available from the British Library

Library of Congress Cataloging-in-Publication Data
Names: Stel, Nora, author.
Title: Hybrid political order and the politics of uncertainty :
   refugee governance in Lebanon / Nora Stel.
Description: Abingdon, Oxon ; New York, NY : Routledge, 2020. |
   Series: Routledge research in ignorance studies | Includes
   bibliographical references and index.
Identifiers: LCCN 2020008594 (print) | LCCN 2020008595 (ebook) |
   ISBN 9781138352544 (hbk) | ISBN 9780429434716 (ebk)
Subjects: LCSH: Refugees—Government policy—Lebanon. |
   Refugees, Palestinian Arab—Lebanon. | Syria—History—Civil
   War, 2011—Refugees—Lebanon.
Classification: LCC JV8748 .S74 2020 (print) | LCC JV8748
   (ebook) | DDC 325/.21095694095692—dc23
LC record available at https://lccn.loc.gov/2020008594
LC ebook record available at https://lccn.loc.gov/2020008595

ISBN: 978-1-138-35254-4 (hbk)
ISBN: 978-0-367-51861-5 (pbk)
ISBN: 978-0-429-43471-6 (ebk)

Typeset in Times New Roman
by Apex CoVantage, LLC

If you think you understand Lebanon, you have not been explained properly.[1]

Contents

Abbreviations

LCRP	Lebanon Crisis Response Plan
LPDC	Lebanese-Palestinian Dialogue Committee
NGO	non-governmental organization
PLO	Palestine Liberation Organization
UN	United Nations
UNHCR	United Nations High Commissioner for Refugees
UNRWA	United Nations Relief and Works Agency for Palestine Refugees in the Near East

Acknowledgements

This book has been in the making for quite some time. After the first seeds for my ideas about the political convenience of subjecting refugees to uncertainty had been planted by some critical Palestinian friends and interlocutors in 2013, many wonderful people provided me with the inspiration, support, courage, and means to develop these ideas into what eventually became a book project.

There were the various research institutes: The Maastricht School of Management, which always supported my research even when it went far beyond the school's core business. The Center for Conflict Studies at Utrecht University, my intellectual home during and beyond my doctoral research, where encouragement and questions never run out. The Issam Fares Institute at the American University of Beirut, where Nasser Yassin was always ready to anchor abstract ideas in real-life experiences. The Governance and Local Development Program at Gothenburg University, where Ellen Lust helped to fund my fieldwork and hosted me as a visiting scholar so that I had Nesrine Ben Brahim as an amazing analytical sparring partner. And the Centre for International Conflict Analysis and Management at Radboud University's Department of Political Science, where I am incredibly grateful to now have the chance to take the research underlying this book further.

There were the organizations funding my research, without which this book would have never seen the light. The Hendrik Muller Fonds. The Lutfia Rabbani Foundation, with its phenomenal vision, commitment, and warmth. The Niels Stensen Fellowship, whose flexibility, support, and faith in my work have been a beacon when the going got tough.

There were the many seminars, conference panels, and workshops – in Neuchâtel, Luxembourg, London, Malmö, Geneva, Utrecht, Prague, Manchester, Barcelona, Gothenburg, Nijmegen, Brussels, and New Haven – where I had the chance to sharpen my analysis through engaging with truly brilliant people. Jolle Demmers, Lauren Gould, Chris van der Borgh, Georg Frerks, Niels Terpstra, Luuk Slooter, Ralph Sprenkels, Lotje van Uhm, Toon Dirkx, Ali Aljasem, and Mario Fumerton have constituted an essential sounding board and support base every step of the way. Anja Franck and Rebecca Tapscott have both been indispensable to this book in first pointing out to me some of the many scholarly traditions of questioning failure as the main explanation for informality and limbo. Annika Lindberg and Lisa Marie Borrelli have been amazingly generous in including me in their exciting networks and activities, which has profoundly impacted my understanding of knowledge and power in the governance of migration. The critical and compassionate, intricate yet intuitive understandings of Lebanon developed by Estella Carpi, Sima Ghaddar, and Diana Allan have been crucial touchstones for my analysis. Lucas Oesch, Lorenzo Vianelli, and Léa Lemaire are pioneers in bringing together scholars working on uncertainty and displacement, efforts from which this book has benefitted tremendously. Leonie Ansems de Vries and Nadine Voelkner have broadened my horizons in thinking about epistemic politics. I have learned a lot from Jessy Nassar's analysis and conviction.

There are, most important of all, the hundreds of people who have acted as interlocutors in my research, sharing their time, thoughts, analyses, experiences, emotions. My debt to them is infinite, and to do justice to the insights they have conveyed to me is the core ambition of my analysis. Many people have advised me, thought with me, helped me out, guided me, and put up with me throughout my various fieldwork periods, and the book is beholden to all of them – Yaser, Fakhri, Jaber, Souhail, Rashid, Ahmad, Samir, Mahmoud, Soha, Reem, Erik, Ammeke, Nicolien, Annemijn, and many more. I am particularly grateful to the families that have hosted me during fieldwork, an experience that has enriched my life in endless ways. Without the perseverance, patience, and intelligence of my fieldwork partners, Asmaa Al Mohamad and Nadia Al Mostafa, I would have been utterly lost. It is an honor to have had you as my guides. The grounded intellect, unwavering sense of justice, and energetic certitude of Anke van der Meijden have prevented my postdoctoral research from failure. I am forever thankful to have had the chance to share part of my research experience with her.

There are the people who have been instrumental in turning analysis into an actual book. It is a privilege to publish under the auspices of Linsey McGoey, whose groundbreaking work on strategic ignorance has fundamentally changed my perspective on anything I can imagine to ever study. She and many of the people mentioned above have been so kind to read with me in compiling this manuscript, as have Reinoud Leenders and Jake Cassani. Their feedback has been of tremendous value to me. I am also thankful to the entire team at Routledge that made this book happen and to the seminal scholars whose work I have long admired who were so generous to endorse it.

Finally, there are the people who are always there to remind me that happiness is more important than success, that life is not work: my parents, my siblings, my friends. Felix and Peter. Erik. Writing a book has been harder than I thought it would be. Living with me must have been harder than you thought it would be. Thank you for being part of my life, for being my life.

Note

1 Lebanese saying cited on the first page of Pierre Jarawan's *Am Ende Bleiben die Zedern* (2016).

Introduction

Institutional ambiguity and the politics of uncertainty: a new perspective on refugee governance

A Spring evening in 2013. I am chatting with a leader of the local Palestinian youth movement on the corniche of Tyre, the ancient port city in South Lebanon. We had met before to discuss his interpretation of the relations between Lebanese and Palestinian authorities in informal refugee settlements in the area. Not particularly interested in this issue, my interlocutor instead reflects on the challenges he and his friends face in organizing their nascent movement. One of his frustrations, he says, is that the situation and status of Palestinians in Lebanon is 'totally clouded and unclear.' In fact, he adds, 'it is meant to be cloudy, we're not supposed to understand!'[1]

Five years later. I am behind my computer, talking about the Lebanese response to the Syrian refugee 'crisis' with an experienced and context-savvy inter-agency coordinator for an international humanitarian organization on Skype. Vexed about her attempts to comprehend Lebanon's legal and institutional framework for engaging with Syrian refugees, she sighs: 'So, like, it all does not make sense. At least not enough sense for us to be able to understand how they're doing it, why they're doing it and who in the government is doing it.'[2] Noting my bewilderment, she laughs, adding: 'If you're confused, don't worry, everybody is confused here.'

These remarks represent many similar reflections by the wide array of people with whom I discussed the way in which refugee communities in Lebanon govern and are governed. They are the point of departure for this book, which interrogates how uncertainty and ambiguity shape Lebanon's attempts to deal with the refugees it hosts.

Refugee governance and uncertainty

In 2018, 68.5 million people fled their homes, the highest number of refugees since World War II. The displacement of more than six million Syrians escaping their war-torn country is one of the most urgent refugee crises that the world currently faces. As with other refugee flows, the great majority of Syrian refugees seeks shelter and safety in Syria's neighboring countries. Facilitating such 'reception in the region' has become the cornerstone of the international community's response to displacement. European policies outsource the governance of migration by investing in development in 'the region' and 'deals' with regional host countries. Many of such regional host countries that are affected by the arrival of large numbers of refugees, however, already struggle with a range of political, socio-economic, and institutional challenges.

This intersection of existing institutional predicaments and refugee crises means that regional refugee governance is often ad hoc, piecemeal, and chaotic. Considering the centrality of regional shelter in most refugee experiences as well as in international refugee policy, understanding this 'mess,' as a human rights lawyer called it, is of great importance.[3] Yet, there has been comparatively little research and even less theorization of regional host states' treatment of refugees (Norman, 2017). To remedy this situation, this book turns to Lebanon. Lebanon hosts the highest per capita number of refugees worldwide. Sheltering approximately 200,000 Palestinian refugees and around 1.5 million Syrian refugees, it is heavily implicated in both the world's most protracted and, arguably, most urgent refugee 'crises' respectively. Like many regional host countries, moreover, Lebanon grapples with a war-torn past, political instability, social and ecological tensions, and severe economic problems.

The experience of refugees in Lebanon is accordingly determined by insecurity and uncertainty. Lebanon's refugee governance appears to be overwhelmingly fragmented and inconsistent. This is evident in the stories of refugees themselves, who describe the situation they face as 'a lot of chaos' (Lebanon Support, 2016: 23). It surfaces in the accounts of the humanitarian organizations that try to aid refugees. They point out the constant fear and unpredictability that refugees face in the absence of a coherent legal framework and stable policy and the resultant bureaucratic discrepancies (Amnesty International, 2015) and express many of their own challenges in assisting refugees as following from the 'exceptional complexity' and arbitrariness of Lebanese refugee governance.[4]

Uncertainty is a recurrent theme in the studies of analysts as well. These highlight the emergence of a 'legal limbo' (Turbay, 2015: 23) and a 'no-policy-policy' (El Mufti, 2014); the prevalence of 'impromptu decisions' (Al-Masri, 2015: 12) that is typified by 'ad hoc changes and discretionary applications' (Bidinger et al., 2014: 37); and, as a consequence, the 'sea of insecurity' in which refugees find themselves (Yassin et al., 2015: 38). It is even a central tenet in the experiences of state officials tasked with refugee governance. They acknowledge 'that the absence of policies has created a state of chaos because of varied standards and decisions.'[5]

This book seeks to explore and understand this overwhelming experience of uncertainty by all major stakeholders involved in refugee governance in Lebanon. To describe such governance uncertainty, I develop the notion of 'institutional ambiguity,' which revolves around the key aspects of informality, liminality, and exceptionalism. The aim here, however, is to go beyond rendering visible the institutional ambiguity that shapes refugee governance and explain how such ambiguity emerges and why it prevails. The book seeks to understand how institutional ambiguity operates and is reproduced, what its effects are, and who benefits and who suffers from its consequences.[6] In particular, it aims to empirically capture and analyze the strategic dimensions of institutional ambiguity, which are conceptualized as a 'politics of uncertainty.'

As a property of refugee governance, it is assumed that the logics of institutional ambiguity will be determined by 'refugeeness,' the experience of forced displacement to another country, on the one hand, and by 'governance,' the organization of public authority, on the other hand. I thus turn to these respective literatures to venture an answer to the aforementioned questions.

Refugees

Ever since the 'birth' of 'the refugee' as an object of politics, policy, and knowledge production (Malkki, 1995), uncertainty has been a key theme in the field of critical refugee studies (Nassar and Stel, 2019). Together with mobility, uncertainty is increasingly recognized as the defining feature of refugee life. Yet while the interface between uncertainty and migration is widely acknowledged, its theorization is still rudimentary. Where there is an explicit engagement with uncertainty, scholars working in critical border and refugee studies traditionally tend to focus particularly on the 'radical uncertainty' produced by the conflict that generated displacement and by the process of displacement itself (Horst and Grabska, 2015).

Analyses of the refugee-sovereignty nexus that think through the international state system and the production of refugees as 'two sides of the same coin' (Betts, 2014: 1), however, engage more explicitly with the 'protracted uncertainty' that emerges for refugees in host country settings after displacement (see, for instance, Brun, 2015; Gibney, 2014; Horst and Grabska, 2015; Hansen, 2014; Stepputat and Nyberg Sørensen, 2014; Zetter, 2007). Protracted displacement, Grabska and Fanjoy (2015: 76) note, often turns into protracted uncertainty 'when plans for the future cannot be made because the past and the present are marked with precariousness and unpredictability.' Here, by far the most attention has been paid to the ways in which refugees experience and navigate such uncertainty (see, for instance, Brun, 2015; El-Shaarawi, 2015; Eule et al., 2018: 51; Hasselberg, 2016; Kramer and Balaa, 2004; Marston, 2003; Norman, 2017).

Key publications have, nevertheless, been calling for an acknowledgement of uncertainty as not just a lived experience but also a potential disciplinary strategy (Ansems de Vries and Guild, 2019). Biehl (2015) has done pioneering work in outlining how refugees in Turkey are not merely living in uncertainty, but are governed through it. Norman (2017) shows how in Egypt the absence of formal refugee policy is often mistaken for neglect, whereas it in fact reflects a deliberate policy of ambivalence. El-Shaarawi (2015: 39, 46), while not investigating these policies and politics herself, flags the importance of seeing the uncertainty that refugees face as not merely 'profoundly personal,' but also 'inextricable from refugee policy and politics on both the state and international level.'

These political dimensions of uncertainty, however, often remain underexplored. Chimni (2003) describes how in India the absence of a legal framework has resulted in a situation in which there are 'only ad hoc mechanisms in place' to deal with refugees. This legal limbo, which he calls a form of 'strategic ambiguity,' has resulted in 'arbitrary executive action' and makes refugees 'dependent on the benevolence of the state' (Chimni, 2003: 443). Why exactly such ambiguity is strategic and for whom, however, is not pursued. Ilcan, Rygiel and Baban (2018) explore the 'architecture of precarity' designed to govern Syrian refugees in Turkey, but the agency and interests behind the production of such precarity, which they see as generating vulnerability and ambiguity, are not investigated. In fact, precarity and the resultant ambiguity are seen as symbolizing 'the *failure* of policies to address the displacement,' obscuring the possibility of uncertainty constituting a governance strategy in its own right (Ilcan, Rygiel and Baban, 2018: 66).

Mostly, then, refugee studies acknowledges the 'governing effects' of uncertainty. A subsequent investigation of the agency behind such outcomes is often lacking. Recent work, however, increasingly questions if and how decisions and mechanisms that are assumed to be 'ordering' are in fact – and at times strategically – reproducing institutional ambiguity. The sub-field of refugee studies concerned with the study of asylum and immigration systems has been groundbreaking in conceptualizing the partially strategic nature of the 'disjuncture, uncertainty, and ambiguity' defining refugee governance (El-Shaarawi, 2015: 40). Calavita's (1998: 53) seminal study reveals the ways in which immigration laws 'actively "irregularize" people by making it all but impossible to retain legal status over time.' Summarizing this innovative reading of institutional dysfunction, Whyte (2011: 21) argues that, in governing refugees, uncertainty is not an 'unfortunate byproduct,' but rather 'fundamental to the system's functioning as a technology of power.' Furthering this paradigm shift, Griffiths (2013: 263) suggests that 'disorder should be understood as a technique of power, with governance through uncertainty constructing certain immigrants as expendable, transient and ultimately, deportable.'

Scholars like Anderson (2014), De Genova (2002), Rozakou (2017), and Whyte (2011) demonstrate how authorities seek to create institutional ambiguity to minimize accountability and maximize discretionary power in dealing with irregular, often forced, migrants by 'deliberate nonrecording' that allows, as Kalir and Van Schendel (2017: 1) put it, for exploitation and 'state-produced social oblivion.' My central argument departs from this body of work that does not see institutional ambiguity as just a contingency of state failure, but rather explores it as a possibly 'intentional state practice' or a 'conscious strategy' to abandon, expel, exploit, or discipline particular societal groups (Kalir and Van Schendel, 2017: 2; Whyte, 2011: 18).

Governance

Governance broadly refers to processes to organize collective representation and accountability and the provision of public goods. This is not, and has never been, a privilege of the state, but regards a set of interactions involving multiple societal actors (Rose, O'Malley and Valverde, 2006: 85; Rose and Miller, 1992). Following Foucault (1983), to govern means to determine the field of action of others. It thereby refers to a 'more or less systematized' mode of power (Lemke, 2000: 5). More specifically, in this book, governance refers to acknowledging specific issues, groups, or spaces, producing frameworks to regulate them, and enforcing these frameworks. Policies – sets of instructions issued by a specific governance actor on how to reach a particular governance goal that can range from laws to decrees or other executive decisions – and the related implementation processes are a crucial aspect of governance.[7]

In this book, the particular governance issues that are under scrutiny regard refugees' status, spaces, and representation. These domains of governance are selected because they fundamentally determine the parameters of refugees' presence in a host country and thereby predispose other aspects of refugee life, such as security, mobility, and access to services. Refugee status refers to whether refugees are legally acknowledged as refugees, but also to their residency status and the related registration and recording procedures. Refugee spaces pertain to the arrangements for refugees' shelter and tenure and the associated legal frameworks and political decisions, often with encampment as a central contention. Refugee representation on the one hand concerns the mandates allocated by the host country considering who is responsible for dealing with what aspects of refugees' presence. On the other hand, it relates to the question of who speaks for refugees and acts on their behalf and the internal organization of refugee communities.

Governance is mostly understood as an attempt to minimize ambiguity by creating rules and regulations and ensuring their implementation in a standardized manner, with bureaucratic organizations acting as 'ambiguity-reducing machines' (Best, 2012: 91). Yet, uncertainty and unpredictability are a fact of life everywhere. This is often the inescapable effect of 'bureaucratic muddling through' and 'fuzziness' (Davenport and Leitch, 2005: 4) or of 'policy flaws' caused by 'decision accretion' (Smithson, 1989: 239). Ambiguity is then either an inevitable manifestation of an inherently 'unknowable world' or 'residual,' surviving despite efforts to minimize it (Best, 2012: 92, 91). But ambiguity can also be the result of concerted efforts. Foucault has long recognized the disciplinary power of uncertainty. In critical management studies, 'strategic ambiguity' is defined as 'the deliberate use of ambiguity in strategic communication' to allow for multiple interpretations (Davenport and Leitch, 2005: 2). Legal scholars have also pointed out the centrality of 'legal ambiguity' in structuring governance, which, Oomen et al. (2019: 7) note, is often purposefully invoked and expanded.

The notion of strategic ambiguity assumes that uncertainty serves purposes, that it is politically convenient and therefore strategically deployed (Aradau, 2017: 339). Such convenience can regard general public interests: political decision-makers may need to deal with limited capacities and resources or to broker consensus, for which ambiguity can be advantageous. Navigating 'competing interests' often results in 'negotiated compromises that are purposively vague' so as to facilitate 'unified diversity' (Davenport and Leitch, 2005: 3).

Ho (2001: 400) even calls 'institutional indeterminacy' the 'lubricant' on which governance runs. Ambiguity also allows governance actors to be flexible and adaptive. Policy-makers' insistence on 'clarity and rule promulgation' can be counter-productive, because passing legislation 'often requires ambiguous language and contradictory goals to hold together a passing coalition' (Matland, 1995: 147). Strategic ambiguity can also follow from private interests, producing the maneuvering space in which political decision-makers maximize their own influence at the expense of others. Finally, strategic ambiguity can serve more specific political objectives concerning the governance of particular groups, spaces, or issues (Nassar and Stel, 2019).

Uncertainty, evidently, is more profound for some people than for others and more apparent at some times and in some places. The 'governing effects' of uncertainty that are fundamental in refugee studies, then, are a core concern in the literature on hybrid political order as well. This field of study, further discussed in Chapter 1, focuses on the question of how governance operates 'beyond government' (Risse, 2013) or under 'split sovereignty' (Hoffman and Kirk, 2013) when state authorities are unable or unwilling to take on the extensive range of exclusive governance activities assumed by the Weberian ideal-type. Uncertainty is mostly taken for granted and assumed to be a structural feature of these contexts. The question of how public and political authorities operate in such hybridity and whether their behaviour challenges, extends, or exacerbates it is only rarely addressed.

This book builds on and extends the notable exceptions to this situation. Chabal and Daloz's (1999) book on 'disorder as a political instrument' produced a paradigm shift in debates about patronage and neopatrimonialism. It agendized the importance of recognizing 'disorder' as a 'different order' in which political actors can capitalize on an existing 'state of confusion, uncertainty, and sometimes even chaos' by perpetuating and aggravating it (Chabal and Daloz, 1999: xix). Administrative 'inefficiency,' minimal institutionalization, and the relativity of formal rules then become cause as much as consequence of hybrid forms of political order. Das and Poole's (2004) influential reading of state power as operating through unpredictability and 'unreadability' has further theorized the disciplining effect of inaccessible information and opaque decision-making. Tapscott's (2017: 263) ground-breaking work on institutionalized arbitrariness further conceptualizes this utility of fostering unpredictability and uncertainty as a mode of governance.

Contingent and strategic uncertainty

Work on refugees and governance thus tends to regard uncertainty as overwhelmingly contingent, either upon the refugee condition defined by unexpected displacement and temporary settlement or upon a hybrid governance context determined by 'weak institutions' and a lack of capacity and resources. Yet in both literatures, there are increasingly influential alternative readings of uncertainty as well. These contend that such exclusively structural analyses are insufficient as they overlook important elements of agency, interests, and responsibility in the emergence, institutionalization, and reproduction of governance uncertainty. They suggest that disorder does not have to be the antithesis to dominance, as often intuitively assumed, but can be an instrument of it (Cullen Dunn, 2012: 2). As is the case with the governance of security, refugee governance practices do not just tame unknowns, but also enact and utilize them (Aradau, 2017: 329).

This book works with this idea of strategic ambiguity – with uncertainty consistently recurring and demonstrably serving interests – in exploring the institutional inconsistency that permeates refugee governance in Lebanon. It does so by synthesizing and sophisticating the core tenets of these emerging literatures in, first, a heuristic device – institutional ambiguity – and, second, an explanation of the agential aspects of the production and reproduction of institutional ambiguity – the politics of uncertainty. Crucially, the book does not contend that institutional ambiguity is only, or even predominantly, strategic. As proposed by structuration theory, agency and structure, strategy and contingency, constitute a dialectic (Giddens, 1984). I put analytical premium on the strategic aspects of the emergence and endurance of institutional ambiguity because these are conceptually underdeveloped and, perhaps therefore, empirically striking and as such offer the most significant room for contribution.

The idea that uncertainty and insecurity were not simply incidental or circumstantial but also partially strategic surfaced in many of the accounts that underlie my analysis. Refugees keenly felt the repressive aspects of ambiguity. The frustrated remark of a Palestinian youth leader with which I opened this chapter was what got me thinking about the politics behind uncertainty in the first place. Humanitarians and civil society representatives also routinely pointed out the interests underpinning vague and absent policies and arbitrary implementation dynamics. A project manager for a non-governmental organization (NGO) working with refugees in the Bekaa and North Lebanon was convinced that 'the whole thing has been intentionally left informal, non-regulated; or regulated but not enforced.'[8]

Even Lebanese state representatives described the treatment of refugees in the country as trapping them in an 'institutional void': a ministerial advisor referred to the agency behind the non-policy towards Syrian refugees, saying that 'someone refused to organize the presence of the Syrian displaced.'[9] As previously presented in Nassar and Stel (2019), analysts working on refugee governance in Lebanon similarly emphasize the strategic aspects of the legal, spatial, and political uncertainty faced by refugees, calling 'the absence of policy and governance' a 'strategy of exploitation'[10] and suggesting that governance appears to be 'clearly aimed' at 'maintaining nebulousness' (Ghanem, 2016: 54). In light of this situation, the book's core research interest is to understand how institutional ambiguity operates as a partly strategic governance modality to deal with refugee 'crises' in Lebanon.

Institutional ambiguity

Ambiguity refers to plurality of definition, meaning, and interpretation. Ambiguity produces uncertainty in the sense that, as Tapscott (2018) defines it, governance policies and practices are 'experienced as meaningfully unpredictable by those for whom they are of political consequence.' I use institutional ambiguity to synthesize a vast array of concepts used across disciplines. It is a tool to capture the institutionalization, with which I mean the recurrence and (tacit) acceptance, of ambiguity as operating on three main axes: informality, liminality, and exceptionalism. These three dimensions of institutional ambiguity, as apparent in the following operationalization, extensively overlap and constitute each other to produce a broader environment of inconsistent, partial, and negotiable institutionalization.

Informality

I understand formal governance as those issues, spaces, and populations that are recognized and addressed in official state policies (Yassin, Stel and Rassi, 2016). Informality, then, regards those governance concerns that are not acknowledged, regulated, and/or made implementable by the state. Importantly, this does not mean that these issues, spaces, and populations are not governed. They are likely to be taken on by non-state governance actors, or even by state governance actors, but in an unofficial, de facto capacity rather than a de jure fashion. Informality is thereby closely related to illegality, extra-legality, and the criminalization of refugees (De Genova, 2002; Zaiotti, 2006). The absence of formal refugee or residency status infamously contributes to stripping refugees from the 'right to have rights.' Informal governance also analytically associates with bureaucratic invisibility and illegibility as it can render refugees (or other categories of people) administratively nonexistent (Griffiths, 2013; Janmyr and Mourad, 2018; Kalir and Rozakou, 2016).

Informality makes governance irregular and personalized and thereby more unpredictable but also more pliable and negotiable for those able to navigate and instrumentalize 'a shifting and ill-defined' boundary between public and private (Chabal and Daloz, 1999: 149). Like liminality and exceptionalism, it is not a binary category. Refugee status, for instance, might be denied, but other (temporary and exceptional) administrative categorizations can be devised to nevertheless allow a form of regulation. Refugee shelter arrangements, to give another example, might be acknowledged formally by some state institutions, whereas they are not recognized by others. Refugees' representation structures, similarly, could be acknowledged and regulated by state institutions, but be partially informal nevertheless if the relevant directives and decisions are not implemented or enforced.

When explored from the perspective of a politics of uncertainty, it is particularly 'planned illegality' (Chiodelli, 2012) and the imposition of informality – under which refugees are 'led to break the law in order to survive' (Agier, 2008: 12) – that is at stake. If formally governing something means that the state makes itself responsible for it, then the governance inaction that renders refugee governance informal is an act of abandonment. In this way, my understanding of such potentially 'purposeful informality' (Polese, Kóvacs and Jancsics, 2018: 208) closely resonates with the idea of informality as an expression of sovereignty. Informality, then, is not a challenge to the state as much as it is produced by the state itself. Following Roy (2005: 149), state agencies themselves 'determine what is informal and what is not' and 'which forms of informality will thrive and which will disappear.' Even in hybrid political orders rife with capacity problems, formal recognition, regulation, and enforcement are never just a bureaucratic or technical issue. They involve significant political choice and struggle. To study informality, then, means confronting how the state is not simply an apparatus of planning, but a system that 'produces the unplanned and unplannable' (Roy, 2005: 156 in Nassar and Stel, 2019).

Liminality

Liminality engages with the notion of temporal uncertainty. As Agier (2008: 30) so imperatively noted, the word 'refuge' itself 'denotes a temporary shelter, while waiting for something better.' Neither refugees nor the states hosting them know if and when refugees may return. Liminality is thus a default cornerstone of refugee life, but it is also a characteristic of hybrid order, where suspension and undeterminedness can be important ingredients of political capital. In the context of thinking through a politics of uncertainty, then, liminality is closely related to exceptionalism in that it is something that can be extended and instrumentalized by placing specific issues, communities, or spaces 'in between' (Menjívar, 2006: 999) or 'outside' (Griffiths, Rogers and Anderson, 2013: 5) time, putting them forever 'on hold' (Agier, 2008: 47). This turns crisis from an opportunity for transformation into an instrument to maintain the status quo (Hage, 2015: 1).

Liminality regards the constantly reinforced transitional and temporary nature of governance practices. It refers to a 'permanent impermanence' (Brun, 2015: 19), a 'stuckedness' (Hage, 2009) that characterizes the increasingly protracted nature of most refugee situations and results in ad hoc arrangements and a 'dominance of the short-term' (Chabal and Daloz, 1999: 161). Liminal arrangements are unstable and place people in limbo. They preclude integration and institutionalization and reinforce transience. This 'liquid' appropriation of time, as Bauman (2007) theorized, reflects and enables the pervasiveness of uncertainty. Temporal uncertainty denotes a dual ambivalence with regard to time as it 'simultaneously threatens imminent and absent change;' 'stickiness' and 'suspension' on the one hand and 'frenzy' and 'rupture' on the other (Griffiths, 2014). Thus, as a component of institutional ambiguity, liminality captures the simultaneous processes of stasis and transformation.

An extensive literature concerned with the governmentality of waiting indicates the disciplinary power of making people wait without 'purpose, fairness or progression,' rendering their experience of time and life simultaneously meaningless and endless (Brun, 2015: 19; see also Anderson, 2014; Griffiths, Rogers and Anderson, 2013; Jefferson, Turner and Jensen, 2019). At the same time, work on deportation and deportability refers to the implications of acute and unexpected change imposed on people that is similarly enabled by the conditionality inherent in 'permanent temporariness' (Cullen Dunn, 2014: 304; see also Franck, 2017). This can add up to what Tazzioli (2017) has conceptualized as 'containment through mobility,' a situation in which people are temporally pinned down through spatial relocation.

Building on foundational work regarding the 'strong relationship between power, the state and management of time,' liminality refers to more than just indecisiveness or even stalling, but regards time as a potential instrument of control (Rutz, 1992 in Griffiths, Rogers and Anderson, 2013: 29). This disciplinary effect of time can be a result of neglect or inherent in bureaucracy, but 'time traps' can also reflect strategy and design (Eule et al., 2018: 151, 160–161). Being made to wait as well as being subjected to acute and dramatic institutional ruptures are reflections of power relations and bureaucratic domination. Protracted temporariness and 'ageing' emergencies are not inevitable (Carpi, 2015a). They are, the United Nations High Commissioner for Refugees (UNHCR) has well-noted (2004: 2 in Milner, 2014: 153), 'the result of political action and inaction.'

Exceptionalism

The idea of a 'state of exception,' coined by Agamben (2005) and extended, adapted, and nuanced by many others, has its roots in critical refugee studies. It denotes a central paradox of governance by marking specific groups or issues as outside normal legal and political regimes, but inside specific surveillance and repression mechanisms. Exclusion, 'outsideness,' and 'othering' in one realm are complemented by extreme discipline in other domains (El-Shaarawi, 2015: 40; Hanafi and Long, 2010; Salter, 2008) – dynamics that are routinely legitimized through securitization processes (Nassar and Stel, 2019). Crucially, then, the analytical value of exceptionalism as a component of institutional ambiguity does not lie in its sometimes assumed establishment of a nigh totalitarian order by an apparently cohesive sovereign. Rather, what exceptionalism signifies is the arbitrary definition and application of regulations and mandates. Exceptionalism, Carpi (2017: 121) established, is not a 'product of fate,' but rather of experimentation (Turner, 2005: 318). It can be imposed and lifted, defined and redefined, resulting in unpredictably changing rules of the game. As Cons (2007: 21) concludes, exceptionality is not a neat in/out binary. Instead, it 'produces an overwhelming sense of uncertainty, insecurity and confusion' that allows and facilitates exploitation and enhances the discretionary power of authorities (Cons, 2007: 21).

This materializes through legal and spatial governance practices. Legally, exceptionalism denotes the political and administrative distinctions between different categories of people – refugees and citizens, for instance – and the ways in which arbitrariness becomes a routine everyday experience for populations that are placed outside any such categorizations in legal 'gray' areas (Menjívar, 2006). This makes them dependent on the goodwill of those holding power over them. The idea of exceptionalism compellingly reveals that legal suspensions or voids tend not to be 'filled by an ethics of care and responsibility,' but are rather signals 'that a particular class of persons exists only at the mercy of the state' (Chimni, 2003: 465). The exceptionalism invoked by discourses of crisis[11] and 'perpetuated emergency' allows for governance actors to shirk responsibility while retaining authority (De Genova and Tazzioli, 2016; Janmyr and Knudsen, 2016: 391). It produces for particular groups the 'experience of a fragile and uncertain relationship to the law and to states' (Agier, 2008: 11; see also Cons, 2007: 24).

Spatial exceptionalism is especially apparent in encampment policies. These often materialize refugees' informality and simultaneously entrench it. Refugee camps both signpost and ensure the temporary nature of refugees' presence, 'warehousing' them for protracted periods of time in 'suspended spaces' without ever acknowledging this de facto permanence (Janmyr and Knudsen, 2016: 391). Refugee camps and detention and deportation centres, as well as 'sensitive spaces' such as borderlands and frontiers more broadly, are spaces taken outside the legal order, but nevertheless, and thereby, integral to the political order (Agamben, 2005; for reflection and critique, see Agier, 2011; Diken, 2004; El-Shaarawi, 2015; Hanafi, 2008; Hanafi and Long, 2010; Malkki, 1995; Ramadan, 2009; Ramadan and Fregonese, 2017). As with legal exceptionalism, this entails simultaneously claiming control and denying responsibility in and for these spaces (Cons, 2007; Tapscott, 2017, 2018). Refugee settlements, 'ambiguous spaces' of concurrent inclusion and exclusion (Oesch, 2017), thereby become sites of abandonment, spaces that are 'knowingly neglected' (Davies, Isakjee and Dhesi, 2017: 18) or ambiguously and precariously outsourced, generating complex governance assemblages and layered forms of sovereignty.

The politics of uncertainty[12]

My interpretation of a politics of uncertainty starts out from an anthropological understanding of uncertainty. This suggests that uncertainty can best be understood through the analysis of the empirical manifestation of particular governmentalities in specific, and subjective, technologies and experiences (Samimian-Darash and Rabinow, 2015). The notion of a politics of uncertainty acknowledges that institutional ambiguity will be part of any governance practice. In particular, it will be in place by the general settings of hybrid political order and will be extended through the behaviour of authorities that pursue the overall aim of staying in power (or gaining power) and governing 'cheap and efficiently' in such settings (Tapscott, 2017: 268). What the idea of a politics of uncertainty adds is accounting for the possibility that institutional ambiguity also follows from more specific attempts to manage 'problematic' populations, here refugees. It posits that a combination of inaction and ambiguous action reproduces informality, liminality, and exceptionalism towards a specific population, following more specific interests that go beyond the generic objective of accumulating and preserving power.

Institutional ambiguity often results from inaction in the realm of formal political decision-making (Barber, 2017). Governance inaction manifests itself in a lack of official acknowledgement, regulation, and enforcement of particular issues; the extent to which matters relating to, in my case, refugees are recognized and addressed in policies and the degree to which such policies are subsequently followed up on. In the context of the politics of uncertainty, inaction is only analytically salient if it regards an issue that formally falls within the jurisdiction of the governance actor in question – if, in other words, an authority could have acted but did not (McConnell and 't Hart, 2014).

The notion of inaction closely resonates with work on 'standoffish policy-making' (Mourad, 2017; Slater and Kim, 2015), street-level bureaucrats' 'shirking' behaviour (Lipsky, 1980 in Eule et al., 2018: 212), the 'politics of doing nothing' (McConnell and 't Hart, 2014), and the structural violence of 'political abandonment' (Davies, Isakjee and Dhesi, 2017; Davies and Polese, 2015; Gupta, 2012). 'Policy-as-indifference,' a term coined by Norman (2019), can function as a form of de facto outsourcing. As El-Shaarawi (2015: 47) notes, for instance, 'passive non-response' towards the arrival of Iraqi refugees marginalized them and made them disregard Egypt as a place of permanent settlement. A 'not-dealing-with' modality of governance, as Kalir and Van Schendel (2017: 6) have called it, is also evident in processes of 'active' non-recording and suspension of official decision-making.

Although passivity can stem from a lack of capacities and resources, these different conceptualizations of governance inaction all demonstrate that it may be a choice as well. Although passivity is often depicted as apolitical or indicating neutrality, McConnell and 't Hart (2014) convincingly argue that 'doing nothing' is at heart a political activity. Inactivity, then, just as much as political action, Davies, Isakjee, and Dhesi (2017: 19) show, 'can be wielded as a means of control, coercion and power.' Following the logic of nonperformativity, inaction may often be cloaked, and even facilitated, by apparent proactiveness (Ahmed, 2004, 2006; Norman, 2005: 196; Pinker, 2015: 99). The very pronunciation of a decision may then serve to in fact deter the actual implementation of the same decision, with a 'tacit interest' working to 'contradict the stated aim or goal of the inquiry' (McGoey, 2007: 219).

In addition to governance inaction, the politics of uncertainty is constituted by ambiguous action that retains and exploits informality, liminality, and exceptionalism. At times, governance actors' approach of issues related to refugee status, space, and representation is primarily determined by inertia and avoidance, but such inaction is never total or predictable. In many instances issues will be recognized, decisions on how to regulate them will be made, and efforts towards implementing such regulations will be proposed. Yet, such recognitions, decisions, and proposals are often 'equivocally phrased' (Best, 2012: 92): partial, inconsistent, or vague. Policy objectives, instruments, and planning are routinely unclear. Documents or papers, often regarded as the summit of rational, accountable statecraft, are in practice mostly as 'tenuous and provisional as the political relationships with which they were entangled' (Pinker, 2015: 119; see also Hull, 2012). Interestingly, even the proliferation of policy can work as a form of policy ambiguity. Eule et al. (2018: 41) show that migration policies are often highly changeable. This makes them unstable and far less coherent and unified than usually assumed by both those implementing them and those subjected to them.

Statements, circulars, mandates, and directives can leave excessive room for contestation, interpretation, and discretion through implicit formulations, contradictory communication, and incomplete or fragmented operationalizations. They produce confusion, but, through that, opportunity and room for maneuver as well. Such ambivalence or anticipation may be inevitable components of governance, but, as the field of critical policy studies emphasizes, they are also shaped and manipulated in both the formulation of policies – their wording and identification of priorities, instruments, and implementers – and the varied decisions constituting the subsequent implementation and inevitable interpretation and negotiation of policies. Anthropologists of the state have increasingly shown how, as a result, 'state power is reproduced through practices that are less than coherent or fully rationalized, emerging rather as shifting, illegible, decentred, contingent, or capricious' (Pinker and Harvey, 2015: 17).

Inaction and ambiguous action will always be part and parcel of governance. Policy-making always lags behind societal needs. And when policies are formulated, they are always at least partly ambiguous: Objectives and instruments are often very general and mandates and responsibilities regularly vague. Laws usually designate what cannot be done, but, as Eule et al. (2018: 86) point out, 'rarely encompasses the full range of possible actions we *may* undertake.' This means that state officials always have substantial discretionary power that is located both in policies themselves and in limited institutional oversight (Eule et al., 2018: 81). Even if policies are relatively clear-cut, policy implementation – with its shifting and complex contexts and various, often competing, actors and the contending and complementary interpretations and interests associated with them – will inevitably produce unintended outcomes, diffuse much of the clarity that might be part of carefully formulated policies, and result in institutional ambiguity.

What I am interested in here, however, is strategic institutional ambiguity. To purport that institutional ambiguity is at least partly strategic is to assume that it serves interests, which may be actively pursued or indirectly determine decision-making. These can regard political objectives to gain and hold onto power, or particular concerns regarding the governance of certain groups, spaces, and issues. These different functions of institutional ambiguity will importantly overlap. Concerns related to generic making-do in challenging circumstances and brokering compromises among various stakeholders will be informed by political concerns to amplify power and complemented by yet different incentives related to managing specific crises or to subdue, exploit, or remove specific groups. Institutional ambiguity will always be both contingent and strategic, and when strategic, it serves both more pragmatic and generic governance interests and more political and specific ones. My focus in this book, however, will be predominantly on the latter type.

The functionality of a politics of uncertainty has two dimensions. These, as accounted for in Chapter 6, crucially intertwine and interact. For those doing the governing, institutional ambiguity serves to create room for interpretation and maneuver. This flexibility or leeway grants governing actors bargaining power. It also generates limited transparency and a form of 'diffuse' (Hull, 2012: 115) or 'deniable' (Davenport and Leitch, 2005: 4) responsibility that ultimately produces unaccountability and impunity for governance actors. This is a general form of arbitrary governance that maximizes power generically (Tapscott, 2017), but it simultaneously produces effects on the level of those being governed that might be politically convenient as well.

Informality, liminality, and exceptionalism generate vulnerability, hampering refugees' access to livelihoods and protection (Ilcan, Rygiel and Baban, 2018; Saghieh, 2015). This contributes to their controllability, exploitability, and deportability, but institutional ambiguity also disciplines more directly. For those being subjected to it, institutional ambiguity produces uncertainty, confusion, and ambivalence. Unpredictability, or destabilization of expectations, undermines agency and results in demobilization. This is by no means absolute. The 'governed' also govern themselves and subvert and resist forms of uncertainty that they face (Hasselberg, 2016). Although power is not unidirectional, it is fundamentally asymmetrical. The concern of this book, therefore, is with the ways in which uncertainty constrains and limits the people that face it. Informality, liminality, and exceptionalism undermine people's ability to plan and act and trap them in precariousness by producing anxiety, instability, and passiveness (Nassar and Stel, 2019). Cullen Dunn (2014: 300) has captured the disciplinary power of uncertainty in the term 'absolute zero' to denote how pervasive and enduring institutional ambiguity can paralyze people, draining them of energy and impeding them to act as coherent subjects. For people to meaningfully or constructively relate to a governance actor, for instance, there must be an understanding of what or who this actor is and what its prerogatives and responsibilities are (Tapscott, 2017).

As further conceptualized in Chapter 6, institutional ambiguity amounts to a politics of uncertainty when it operates as a precondition for the control, exploitation, and expulsion of refugees that serves the actors that produce it through lacking or ambiguous governance. Institutional ambiguity serves to control refugees, because it makes them 'insecure, passive and pessimistic' (Griffiths, 2013: 280). It prevents them from planning, organizing, and mobilizing as they have no way to credibly anticipate the consequences of any action (Eule et al., 2018: 93). Crucially, in the case of refugees, authorities will not seek to discipline them in the traditional Foucauldian sense that assumes citizens that ultimately need to be included in the governance fold. Rather, the form of control aspired to regarding refugees – especially in contexts such as Lebanon where integration is widely seen as entirely undesirable – is one premised on exclusion, distancing, and demobilization, a form of control that allows for exploitation as well as eventual expulsion.

'Chronic uncertainty' and the 'ontological insecurity' it produces can physically and mentally destabilize people to the extent that they are made passive and innocuous (El-Shaarawi, 2015: 40, 46–47, 52; Griffiths, 2014: 2005; Whyte, 2011: 21). The destabilization of expectations, the undermining of rights, the fragmentation of networks, and the production of existential challenges related to shelter, security, and health that follow from institutional ambiguity make refugees dependent on and exploitable for Lebanese strongmen, mediators, and brokers who – as Chapter 1 will show – are closely connected to the Lebanese authorities that are at the root of institutional ambiguity. The extra-legality and social vulnerability manufactured through institutional ambiguity, finally, renders refugees 'deportable.' Existential destitution 'encourages' refugees to consider return or further flight even if these options are entirely unsafe and legal limbo facilitates deportation in a more direct sense.

Studying ambiguity and uncertainty: methods and approach

To understand how institutional ambiguity operates in the context of Lebanese refugee governance and, more specifically, how and why it emerges and is maintained, extended, navigated, and contested, requires a specific methodological and analytical approach.

The empirical analysis central to this book draws on two case-studies that represent two different research projects of which relevant information about data generation will be provided in more detail in the respective chapters. The Palestinian case-study reflects a longer-term study into the local governance dynamics in informal Palestinian refugee settlements in South Lebanon (Stel, 2017). The pertinence of systematic uncertainty and the political drivers of this reality here surfaced in an inductive way as one of the main factors explaining why Palestinian authorities and Lebanese local governance representatives interacted the way they did.

This realization that institutional ambiguity is a key aspect of refugee governance in Lebanon was subsequently explored more deductively in the research constituting the Syrian case-study. This entailed a more targeted exploration of the causes, characteristics, and consequences of the informality, liminality, and exceptionalism that – desk research quickly revealed – determined Lebanon's response to this new refugee 'crisis' in perhaps even starker degrees.[13] Key research questions here were: How does institutional ambiguity manifest itself, nationally and locally, for different groups of stakeholders? Who benefits from such ambiguity or is empowered by it (economically, politically, socially) and who is disadvantaged or marginalized as a result of it? How is it reproduced, navigated, and defied? What are the root causes of institutional ambiguity, and how do these relate to questions of capacity and political will?

The selection of these two case-studies thus followed from an empirical imperative to better understand Lebanon's governance of subsequent and mutually reinforcing refugee 'crises.' My book, however, also aspires to further our theoretical understanding of the (re-)production of institutional ambiguity and to help sophisticate the analytical toolkit available to study this issue. Following Ragin's (1994) perspective on research as a dialogue between evidence and ideas, then, my empirical cases are not only a means to extend a theoretical idea and my conceptualizations are more than merely the instrument to understand an empirical phenomenon. The interplay between empirical and conceptual questions allows for a constructive and innovative engagement with both.

From a theoretical perspective, therefore, my focus on refugee governance in Lebanon functions as an extreme case-study into institutional ambiguity and the politics of uncertainty at large. Exploring the governance of refugees, a category of people facing particular uncertainty, in Lebanon, a country that, as a hybrid political order, is known to be particularly ambiguous in terms of politics and institutions, provides a unique window to capture and analyze the politics of uncertainty that might be at work more subtly in many other instances. By deliberately focusing on exceptional levels of uncertainty, institutional ambiguity as an empirical phenomenon becomes visible and researchable.[14]

The mutually reinforcing empirical and theoretical ambitions at the heart of this book pose the not-insignificant question of how to study inaction and ambiguous action. How to locate and make sense of things that are either not there – in the case of inaction – or inherently vague – in the case of ambiguous action? In analyzing the strategic aspects of institutional ambiguity, the imperative is to establish how institutional ambiguity follows from specific decisions in policy formulation and policy implementation and to tease out the interests driving these decisions. But how to get at motivations that are often unconscious or disguised? Institutional ambiguity, by its very nature, ironically defies – and, when part of a politics of uncertainty, is meant to defy – understanding and thereby analysis.

I engaged with this fundamental challenge by drawing on methodological and analytical strategies developed in the field of ignorance studies, that is introduced in more detail in Chapter 6, which purports that not-knowing can be considered an 'active accomplishment' and is often strategically feigned, maintained, or imposed (Gross and McGoey, 2015: 5; see also Cons, 2007; Lindberg and Borrelli, 2019; Nassar and Stel, 2019; Stel, 2019). Such an approach to capturing the politics of uncertainty is inspired by postcolonial and feminist theory that signaled the ways in which class, gender, and race 'produce absences of knowledge' (Croissant, 2014: 11) and takes cues from critical organization and management studies (Davenport and Leitch, 2005; McGowan, 2003). It entails two crucial exercises: First, to explicitly seek out inconsistencies, contradictions, and 'silences' in people's discourses and behaviours rather than discard them (Stel, 2019); and, second, to specifically explore such tensions and gaps in the data not as 'measurement errors' or 'thin data,' but as research findings in their own right that offer a relevant window onto the broader institutional context in which they are generated (Mazzei, 2003: 357). Rather than precluding understanding, silences and ambiguities in the data can convey important clues about the nature of governance and authority in the settings in which they were generated (Jaworski, 2005: 2; Pinder and Harlos, 2001: 333; Randazzo, 2015: 3; Zerubavel, 2006: 8). What is knowable, after all, is not decided on individually but 'enculturated,' negotiated socially and enforced politically (Poland and Pedersen, 1998: 298).

This approach harnesses work on 'metadata' (Fujii, 2010), unspoken thoughts or tacit understandings implicit in rumors, inventions, denials, evasions, and silences. It engages with the idea of 'infrapolitics,' 'political action [that] is studiously designed to be anonymous or to disclaim its purpose' (Scott, 1990: 199). Fundamentally, it asks: Who does (not) – or claims (not) to – know what and why is this so? Inspired by a rich literature dealing with fieldwork in 'difficult' settings, it reiterates that distilling 'reliable' data and 'valid' analyses is not simply a matter of deducing truthfulness or accuracy and distinguishing 'fact' from 'fiction' but rather of systematically exploring what so-called lies and falsehoods communicate about social reality and political institutions (Carpi, 2015b: 2). More practically, it asks a specific set of questions from the data: What is not being said? (mobilizing work on gaps and silences); What is not being done? (addressing the matter of inaction); What is sensitive? (drawing on studies of taboo, evasion, and denial); What is taken for granted? (inspired by Bourdieu's notion of 'doxa'); and What is inconsistent? (pertaining to contextuality in terms of timing, setting, and audience)

As outlined in Olivier de Sardan's (2016: 121) 'anthropology of gaps, discrepancies and contradictions,' such an approach demands qualitative, triangulated, and contextual data and iterative, critical, and reflexive analysis. It requires a study of policy practices rather than policies as such, of de facto behaviour and effects in addition to de jure stipulations. My analysis is based on elaborate desk research as well as extensive fieldwork. The Palestinian case-study draws on 12 months of ethnographic fieldwork in two informal Palestinian refugee settlements in 2012, 2013, and 2014, during which observational notes were systematically generated; 40 informal meetings, five group interview sessions, and 232 individual in-depth, semi-structured interviews were conducted; and complementary documentary material was collected (Stel, 2017). The Syrian case-study makes use of two bodies of data. The first was collected during six months of long-distance data generation in 2017 and 2018 that produced 34 in-depth interviews and 18 informal discussions with national stakeholders. The second resulted from three months of fieldwork in early 2018[15] that revolved around the governance of two specific informal Syrian refugee settlements in the Bekaa Valley. This fieldwork entailed 35 semi-structured, in-depth interviews and various informal meetings with local stakeholders and the collection of relevant documents. In both case-studies, these data were generated and reflected upon in close collaboration with local fieldwork partners.

My data mostly derives from interviews with political authorities and state representatives working nationally and locally, (self-proclaimed) political and communal refugee representatives, humanitarian 'professionals,' activists and representatives of 'civil society,' and a range of experts from academia, journalism, and think thanks.[16] This book, then, does not reflect a traditional street-level bureaucracy in that it offers only limited access to the internal understandings and individual deliberations of state officials.[17] Rather, by soliciting the reflections and experiences of political authorities and state representatives as well as their humanitarian 'partners' and the refugees they are supposed to govern, the book offers a multi-dimensional analysis that draws on not only the implicit or explicit considerations of decision-makers themselves, but also on reflections on their stated and unstated interests by a multitude of stakeholders.

Despite my aspirations for comprehensiveness, my research questions are necessarily bounded. Thus, in situating my analysis and argument, four important disclaimers with regard to demarcation are warranted. First, my analysis centres on ambiguity in the governance of refugees in host countries. The uncertainty produced by the process of displacement itself, well-documented in refugee studies, lies beyond the scope of my argument. Second, my interest specifically regards the role of political governance actors in the institutionalization of ambiguity. Although I focus on governance by the state, in the context of Lebanon's hybrid political order that is introduced in Chapter 1, this comprises a much broader mediated assemblage that includes officially non-state political and 'traditional' authorities. Nevertheless, my analysis does not explicitly consider the role of the Lebanese public and civil society in shaping such governance. Similarly, I recognize that humanitarian agencies also routinely keep refugees in the dark about procedures and criteria, so as to prevent them from 'gaming the system,' and are heavily implicated in forms of 'epistemic disorientation' (Atme, 2019; Carpi, 2014, 2015a; Cullen Dunn, 2012; Ferguson, 1994; Schmidt, 2019; Tazzioli, 2019). Yet while this is apparent throughout the case-studies and while Chapter 6 discusses the complicity of the humanitarian sector in the broader governmentality that the politics of uncertainty denotes, the focus of this book is on strategic ambiguity in the political regime.

Third, not discarding the fundamental importance of such projects, my analysis here does not aim to 'give voice' to refugees in a direct way. My quest to interrogate the strategic dimensions of ambiguity started out with the lived experiences of refugee communities that hosted me during my initial fieldwork, who understood the uncertainty they faced as a disciplinary strategy. Yet, although these experiences are prevalent throughout my analysis, the primary focus of the book does not regard the coping mechanisms of refugees. Instead, inspired by political anthropology approaches to 'study up' (Nader, 1972), I depart from these perceived disciplinary effects of uncertainty and trace them through the governance arenas in which they originated (Hasselberg, 2016: 94). Going beyond the experience of uncertainty to teasing out the politics of uncertainty contributes to validating refugees' implicit political understandings of institutional ambiguity and helps us to critically question our reading of the broader (dis)order that contributes to shaping their lives.

Fourth, I am acutely aware that my analysis and its implications can be read as first and foremost a critique on Lebanon's engagement with the refugees it hosts. This, as I further substantiate in the book's final chapter, would be a mistake. I recognize the enormous feat of hosting such a large number of refugees as Lebanon has faced, above all by the Lebanese population – of which the poorest segments welcomed the largest numbers of refugees – but also by many if not most state officials who do the best they can under extremely restraining circumstances. My analysis is certainly critical of particular practices and aspects of Lebanon's refugee governance. This perspective, however, should be carefully situated in the relevant geopolitical context. Problems in regional host states can never be understood in isolation from the political hegemony of Western policy actors in the global migration regime. Western states have contributed to causing or failed to prevent and solve the devastating conflicts that have produced the Palestinian and Syrian refugee crises. They condone and encourage the type of regional refugee governance that is the object of study in this book in their ruthless attempt to outsource migration management and safeguard their own countries from the predicaments they think hosting refugees entails. Clearly, governance of forced migration in the 'Global North' prefigures and parallels the maleficent inaction and ambiguity here explored for the Lebanese case (Stel, 2018).

Thus, while my argument, for instance, suggests that limited political will is as important as capacity deficits in explaining the informality, liminality, and exceptionalism that characterize refugee governance in Lebanon, this should not be taken to mean that Lebanon – or any other host country where institutional ambiguity is particularly significant – is entirely or even primarily responsible for the 'mess' it finds itself in.[18] The parameters that incentivize these modes of governance have geopolitical and (neo-)colonial drivers. Ultimately, as De Waal (2014) surmises: 'The agenda for poor and troubled countries is set by rich and powerful countries' and these 'are attuned principally to their own requirements of crisis management.' Such 'crisis management' by the Global North crucially encourages and props up the regional politics of uncertainty as explored in this book.

Outline

The book departs from a two-fold argument. It suggests that, on the one hand, the twin notions of institutional ambiguity and the politics of uncertainty offer a fruitful new perspective on refugee governance in Lebanon and, on the other hand, that studying Lebanon's refugee governance from this perspective can critically enhance our understanding of the ways in which political authority operates in a more general sense. Chapter 1 has the dual aim to advance in further detail the notion of hybrid political order and the forms of arbitrary governance that flourish within it, outlining the more contingent and structural roots of institutional ambiguity. It introduces the particulars of the sectarian, neopatrimonial, and oligopolistic incarnation of such hybridity in Lebanon.

This is followed by four empirical chapters engaging with the two case-studies central to the book, first discussing the national policy and local governance dimensions of Lebanon's response to the arrival of Syrian refugees, in Chapters 2 and 3 respectively, and then analyzing the Lebanese engagement with the more protracted Palestinian refugee presence in the country, in Chapters 4 and 5, that has crucially affected the governance of Syrian refugees. In these chapters, I demonstrate how institutional ambiguity is evident in the governance of Syrian and Palestinian refugees' status, spaces, and representative institutions and how this manufactures refugees' vulnerability in these three realms and enables authorities to control, exploit, and render deportable refugees.

This outline follows from my structurationist take on the analysis of politics in which agency – someone's capacity to initiate change in her or his circumstances – and structure – the rules of social life – are mutually constituting entities. Whereas Chapter 1 introduces and analyzes the structures and context that induce ambiguity, the book's empirical chapters focus on the political actions that shape and reinforce it. Chapter 6 brings these perspectives together. It relates the analytical framework presented in this Introduction with the empirical insights mustered in the case-study chapters and extends the idea of the politics of uncertainty as introduced here by drawing on the emerging field of ignorance studies. It suggests we can further understand the strategic aspects of the inaction and ambiguous action that produce institutional ambiguity by exploring these as forms of feigned, maintained, and imposed 'not-knowing.' This allows for a stronger analytical linkage between means – institutional ambiguity – and ends – control, exploitation, and expulsion – in Lebanese refugee governance dynamics. It furthers a nuanced reading of the agency behind institutional ambiguity that stays far away from conspiracy theories of masterminded chaos without succumbing to systemic platitudes.

The book's concluding chapter extends the insights arrived at beyond the specifics of the empirical contexts studied. It explores what my case-studies have to say about practices and processes of power, order, and political authority more broadly. Speaking to the academic literatures underlying my framework in the fields of refugee studies, hybrid governance, and ignorance studies, it explicates the empirical and conceptual contributions and political implications of my analysis.

Notes

1 Author's interview – Tyre, 7 May 2013.
2 Author's interview – Skype, 14 December 2017.
3 Author's interview – Skype, 16 March 2018.
4 Author's interview with international development manager – Skype, 19 December 2017.

5 An advisor to the Ministry of Interior and Municipalities, cited in Frangieh and Barjas (2016).

6 The book thereby synthesizes, revisits, and extends earlier work on the interface between institutional ambiguity and refugee governance in Lebanon published in Stel (2015, 2016, 2017) and Nassar and Stel (2019).

7 My understanding of policy implementation was greatly facilitated by a review by Meike Frotzheim.

8 Author's interview – Skype, 19 December 2017.

9 Statement of advisor to the Minister of State for Displaced Affairs, livestream of event at the American University of Beirut – 23 November 2017.

10 Author's informal discussion with project evaluation specialist – Skype, 21 August 2017.

11 I do not take the 'crisis' frame applied to the presence of refugees in the country by the Lebanese government for granted. When I refer to the Syrian or Palestinian refugee crises, I acknowledge but do not validate this dominant state discourse. Crisis denotes first and foremost the predicaments of refugees themselves.

12 This term previously appears in other work in different fields (Jones, 2014; Petersen, 1996; Power, 2004; Schedler, 2013), but my conceptualization here is distinct from these earlier applications empirically as well as politically.

13 The locus of fieldwork in the Palestinian case-study was located in South Lebanon and that of the Syrian case-study in the Bekaa. In both studies, however, local manifestations of institutional ambiguity were systematically linked to district/ provincial and national governmentalities, which allows me to speak of an encompassing politics of uncertainty instead of isolated local incarnations of institutional ambiguity.

14 This raises the question as to which of the institutional ambiguity detected is on account of the refugee status of the governance subjects I focus on and which of it stems from the hybridity of the Lebanese governance setting central to my analysis. This issue is addressed throughout the book and further taken up in the concluding chapter. In a nutshell, I argue that the politics of uncertainty leveled against refugees in Lebanon is an extreme and particular version of the politics of uncertainty that Lebanese citizens face, which in turn reflects governance more broadly and helps shed new light on how deliberate forms of institutional ambiguity work as a governance modality more universally.

15 This part of the fieldwork was conducted by a fieldwork partner. This denied me the opportunity of field 'immersion' that I initially and ideally sought. The subsequent intense coordination with my fieldwork partner on the ground – who, having lived in the country for years and having professionally worked on refugee issues for a long time, did bring extensive immersion to the table – has added a layer of reflexivity to data generation and analysis that helped navigate the ever-present question of whether confusion and uncertainty simply reflect researcher ignorance or indeed signal institutional ambiguity (Gershon and Raj, 2000: 10).

16 Interviews conducted for the Palestinian case-study (in 2012, 2013, and 2014) were not recorded, and citations from these interviews throughout the book are thus based on notes. Interviews for the Syrian case-study (held in 2017 and 2018) were mostly recorded and, unless indicated otherwise, quotes from these conversations are verbatim.

17 See Kalir, Achermann, and Rosset (2019), Lindberg and Borrelli (2017), and Mencütek (2019:14) for further deliberations on physical and psychological access to state officials.

18 Here the distinction between rulers and ruled, artificial and problematic though it may be, is essential. An important asset of the idea of a politics of uncertainty is that it

allows to at least tentatively locate some of the agency behind pervasive institutional ambiguity. Yet, such responsibility can – in hybrid settings where accountability is convoluted – not be extended to the broader population of a particular country, even if these are nominal democracies and even if over time people become implicated in institutional ambiguity through their everyday negotiation of it.

References

Agamben, Giorgio. 2005. *State of Exception.* Chicago: University of Chicago Press.

Agier, Michel. 2008. *On the Margins of the World: The Refugee Experience Today.* Cambridge: Polity Press.

Agier, Michel. 2011. *Managing the Undesirables: Refugee Camps and Humanitarian Government.* Cambridge: Polity Press.

Ahmed, Sara. 2004. 'Declarations of Whiteness: The Non-Performativity of Anti-Racism.' *Borderlands* 3, no. 2.

Ahmed, Sara. 2006. 'The Non-Performativity of Anti-Racism.' *Meridians: Feminism, Race, Transnationalism* 7, no. 1: 104–126.

Al-Masri, Muzna. 2015. *Between Local Patronage Relationships and Securitization: The Conflict Context in the Bekaa Region.* Beirut: Lebanon Support and United Nations Development Program.

Amnesty International. 2015. *Pushed to the Edge: Syrian Refugees Face Increased Restrictions in Lebanon.* London: Amnesty International Publications.

Anderson, Ruben. 2014. *Illegality, Inc. Clandestine Migration and the Business of Bordering Europe.* Oakland: University of California Press.

Ansems de Vries, Leonie and Elspeth Guild. 2019. 'Seeking Refuge in Europe: Spaces of Transit and the Violence of Migration Management.' *Journal of Ethnic and Migration Studies* 45, no. 12: 2156–2166.

Aradau, Claudia. 2017. 'Assembling (Non-)Knowledge: Security, Law and Surveillance in a Digital World.' *International Political Sociology* 11: 327–342.

Atme, Cybele. 2019. 'Finnovation. The Case of Financializing Humanitarian Interventions in Lebanon.' MSc thesis, University of Amsterdam.

Barber, Stephen. 2017. *Westminster, Governance and the Politics of Policy Inaction.* London: Palgrave Macmillan.

Bauman, Zygmunt. 2007. *Liquid Times: Living in an Age of Uncertainty.* Cambridge: Polity Press.

Best, Jacqueline. 2012. 'Bureaucratic Ambiguity.' *Economy and Society* 41, no. 1: 84–106.

Betts, Alexander. 2014. 'International Relations and Forced Migration.' In *The Oxford Handbook of Refugee and Forced Migration Studies*, edited by Elena Fiddian-Qasmiyeh, Gil Loescher, Katy Long and Nando Sigona, 60–73. Oxford: Oxford University Press.

Bidinger, Sarah, Aaron Lang, Danielle Hites, Yoana Kuzmova, Elena Noureddine and Susan M. Akram. 2014. *Protecting Syrian Refugees: Laws, Policies and Global Responsibility Sharing.* Boston: Boston University School of Law.

Biehl, Kristen Sarah. 2015. 'Governing Through Uncertainty: Experiences of Being a Refugee in Turkey as a Country for Temporary Asylum.' *Social Analysis* 59, no. 1: 57–75.

Brun, Catharine. 2015. 'Active Waiting and Changing Hopes. Toward a Time Perspective on Protracted Displacement.' *Social Analysis* 59, no. 1: 19–37.

Calavita, Kitty. 1998. 'Immigration, Law, and Marginalization in a Global Economy: Notes from Spain.' *Law & Society Review* 32, no. 3: 529–566.

Carpi, Estella. 2014. 'The Political and the Humanitarian in Lebanon: Social Responsiveness to Emergency Crisis from the 2006 War to the Syrian Refugee Influx.' *Oriente Moderno* 94: 402–427.

Carpi, Estella. 2015a. 'Adhocratic Humanitarianisms and Ageing Emergencies in Lebanon: From the 2006 War in Beirut's Southern Suburbs to the Syrian Refugee Influx in Akkar's Villages.' Paper presented at the annual Middle East Association Conference, Denver, 22 November.

Carpi, Estella. 2015b. 'Dealing with Reality and Falsehood in the Field.' *Alegra Lab*, 5 February.

Carpi, Estella. 2017. 'Rethinking Lebanese Welfare in Ageing Emergencies.' In *Lebanon Facing the Arab Uprisings*, edited by Rosita Di Peri and Daniel Meier, 115–133. London: Palgrave Macmillan.

Chabal, Patrick and Jean-Pascal Daloz. 1999. *Africa Works: Disorder as Political Instrument*. London: The International African Institute (in Association with James Curry, Oxford and Indiana University Press, Bloomington and Indianapolis).

Chimni, B.S. 2003. 'Status of Refugees in India: Strategic Ambiguity.' In *Refugees and the State. Practices of Asylum and Care in India, 1947–2000*, edited by Ranbir Samaddar, 443–468. New Delhi: Sage Publications.

Chiodelli, Francesco. 2012. 'Planning Informality: The Roots of Unauthorized Housing in Arab East Jerusalem.' *Cities* 29: 99–106.

Cons, Jason. 2007. 'A Politics of Sensitivity: Ambiguity and Exceptionality Along the India-Bangladesh Border.' In *SARAI Reader 2007: Frontiers*, edited by Monica Narula, Shuddhabrata Sengupta, Jeebesh Bagchi and Ravi Sundaram, 20–29. New Delhi: Centre for the Study of Developing Societies.

Croissant, Jennifer. 2014. 'Agnotology: Ignorance and Absence or Towards a Sociology of Things That Aren't There.' *Social Epistemology* 28, no. 1: 4–25.

Cullen Dunn, Elizabeth. 2012. 'The Chaos of Humanitarianism: Adhocracy in the Republic of Georgia.' *Humanity* 3, no. 1: 1–23.

Cullen Dunn, Elizabeth. 2014. 'Humanitarianism, Displacement, and the Politics of Nothing in Postwar Georgia.' *Slavic Review* 73, no. 2: 287–306.

Das, Veena and Deborah Poole, eds. 2004. *Anthropology in the Margins of the State*. Oxford: James Curry.

Davenport, Sally and Shirley Leitch. 2005. 'Circuits of Power in Practice: Strategic Ambiguity as Delegation of Authority.' *Organization Studies*: 1–22.

Davies, Thom, Arshad Isakjee and Surindar Dhesi. 2017. 'Violent Inaction: The Necropolitical Experience of Refugees in Europe.' *Antipode* 49, no. 5: 1263–1284.

Davies, Thom and Abel Polese. 2015. 'Informality and Survival in Ukraine's Nuclear Landscape: Living with the Risks of Chernobyl.' *Journal of Eurasian Studies* 6: 34–45.

De Genova, Nicholas P. 2002. 'Migrant "Illegality" and Deportability in Everyday Life.' *Annual Review of Anthropology* 31: 419–447.

De Genova, Nicholas P. and Martina Tazzioli. 2016. 'Europe/Crisis: New Keywords of "the Crisis" in and of "Europe".' *Near Futures Online*.

De Waal, Alex. 2014. 'Policy to Research to Policy in Difficult Places.' *Humanity Journal Online*, 4 December.

Diken, Bülent. 2004. 'From Refugee Camps to Gated Communities: Biopolitics and the End of the City.' *Citizenship Studies* 8, no. 1: 83–106.

El Mufti, Karim. 2014. *Official Response to the Syrian Refugee Crisis in Lebanon, the Disastrous Policy of No-Policy*. Beirut: Civil Society Knowledge Center.

El-Shaarawi, Nadia. 2015. 'Living an Uncertain Future. Temporality, Uncertainty, and Well-Being Among Iraqi Refugees in Egypt.' *Social Analysis* 59, no. 1: 38–56.

Eule, Tobias G., Lisa Marie Borrelli, Annika Lindberg and Anna Wyss. 2018. *Migrants Before the Law: Contested Migration Control in Europe.* Cham: Palgrave Macmillan.

Ferguson, James. 1994. *The Anti-Politics Machine: Depoliticization and Bureaucratic Power in Lesotho.* London: University of Minnesota Press.

Foucault, Michel. 1983. 'The Subject and Power.' In *Michel Foucault: Beyond Structuralism and Hermeneutics*, edited by Hubert L. Dreyfus and Paul Rabinow, 208–226. Chicago: The University of Chicago Press.

Franck, Anja. 2017. 'Im/mobility and Deportability in Transit: Lesvos Island, Greece, June 2015.' *Tijdschrift voor Economische en Sociale Geografie* 108, no. 6: 879–884.

Frangieh, Ghida and Elham Barjas. 2016. 'Interior Ministry Advisor: Lebanon Refugee Policy Based on Set of "No"s'.' *Legal Agenda*, 8 November.

Fujii, Lee Ann. 2010. 'Shades of Truth and Lies: Interpreting Testimonies of War and Violence.' *Journal of Peace Research* 47: 231–241.

Gershon, Ilana and Dhooleka Sarhadi Raj. 2000. 'Introduction: The Symbolic Capital of Ignorance.' *Social Analysis: The International Journal of Social and Cultural Practice* 44, no. 2: 3–14.

Ghanem, Nizar. 2016. *Local Governance Under Pressure. Research on Social Stability in T5 Area, North Lebanon.* Arezzo: Oxfam Italia.

Gibney, Matthew. 2014. 'Political Theory, Ethics and Forced Migration.' In *The Oxford Handbook of Refugee and Forced Migration Studies*, edited by Elena Fiddian-Qasmiyeh, Gil Loescher, Katy Long and Nando Sigona, 48–59. Oxford: Oxford University Press.

Giddens, Anthony. 1984. *The Constitution of Society: Outline of the Theory of Structuration.* Los Angeles: University of California Press.

Grabska, Katarzyna and Martha Fanjoy. 2015. '"And When I Become a Man": Translocal Coping with Precariousness and Uncertainty Among Returnee Men in South Sudan.' *Social Analysis* 59, no. 1: 76–95.

Griffiths, Melanie. 2013. 'Living with Uncertainty: Indefinite Immigration Detention.' *Journal of Legal Anthropology* 1, no. 3: 263–286.

Griffiths, Melanie. 2014. 'Out of Time: The Temporal Uncertainties of Refused Asylum Seekers and Immigration Detainees.' *Journal of Ethnic and Migration Studies* 40, no. 12: 1991–2009.

Griffiths, Melanie, Ali Rogers and Bridget Anderson. 2013. 'Migration, Time and Temporalities: Review and Prospect.' COMPAS Research Resources Paper.

Gross, Matthias and Linsey McGoey, eds. 2015. *Routledge International Handbook of Ignorance Studies.* London and New York: Routledge.

Gupta, Akhil. 2012. *Red Tape: Bureaucracy, Structural Violence, and Poverty in India.* Durham: Duke University Press.

Hage, Ghassan. 2009. *Waiting.* Melbourne: Melbourne University Press.

Hage, Ghassan. 2015. *Alter Politics: Critical Anthropology and the Radical Imagination.* Melbourne: Melbourne University Press.

Hanafi, Sari. 2008. 'Palestinian Refugee Camps in Lebanon: Laboratories of State-in-the-Making, Discipline and Islamist Radicalism.' Unpublished document.

Hanafi, Sari and Taylor Long. 2010. 'Governance, Governmentalities, and the State of Exception in the Palestinian Refugee Camps of Lebanon.' *Journal of Refugee Studies* 23, no. 2: 134–159.

Hansen, Randall. 2014. 'State Controls: Borders, Refugees, and Citizenship.' In *The Oxford Handbook of Refugee and Forced Migration Studies*, edited by Elena Fiddian-Qasmiyeh, Gil Loescher, Katy Long and Nando Sigona, 253–264. Oxford: Oxford University Press.

Hasselberg, Ines. 2016. *Enduring Uncertainty: Deportation, Punishment and Everyday Life*. New York and Oxford: Berghahn Books.

Ho, Peter. 2001. 'Who Owns China's Land? Policies, Property Rights and Deliberate Institutional Ambiguity.' *The China Quarterly* 166: 394–421.

Hoffmann, Kasper and Tom Kirk. 2013. *Public Authority and the Provision of Public Goods in Conflict-Affected and Transitioning Regions*. London: Justice and Security Research Programme.

Horst, Cindy and Katarzyna Grabska. 2015. 'Introduction: Flight and Exile – Uncertainty in the Context of Conflict-Induced Displacement.' *Social Analysis* 59, no. 1: 1–18.

Hull, Matthew S. 2012. *Government of Paper: The Materiality of Bureaucracy in Urban Pakistan*. Berkeley: University of California Press.

Ilcan, Suzan, Kim Rygiel and Feyzi Baban. 2018. 'The Ambiguous Architecture of Precarity: Temporary Protection, Everyday Living and Migrant Journeys of Syrian Refugees.' *International Journal of Migration and Border Studies* 4, no. 1–2: 52–70.

Janmyr, Maja and Are Knudsen. 2016. 'Introduction: Hybrid Spaces.' *Humanity: An International Journal of Human Rights, Humanitarianism, and Development* 7, no. 3: 391–395.

Janmyr, Maja and Lama Mourad. 2018. 'Modes of Ordering: Labelling, Classification and Categorization in Lebanon's Refugee Response.' *Journal of Refugee Studies* 31, no. 4: 544–565.

Jaworski, Adam. 2005. 'Silence in Institutional and Intercultural Contexts.' *Multilingua* 24, no. 1–2: 1–6.

Jefferson, Andrew, Simon Turner and Steffen Jensen. 2019. 'Introduction: On Stuckness and Sites of Confinement.' *Ethnos* 84, no. 1: 1–13.

Jones, Toby C. 2014. 'Toxic War and the Politics of Uncertainty in Iraq.' *International Journal of Middle Eastern Studies* 46, no. 4: 797–799.

Kalir, Barak, Christin Achermann and Damian Rosset. 2019. 'Re-Searching Access: What Do Attempts at Studying Migration Control Tell Us About the State?' *Social Anthropology* 27, no. 1: 5–16.

Kalir, Barak and Katerina Rozakou. 2016. '"Giving Form to Chaos": The Futility of EU Border Management at Moria Hotspot in Lesvos.' *Society and Space*.

Kalir, Barak and Willem van Schendel. 2017. 'Introduction: Nonrecording States Between Legibility and Looking Away.' *Focaal – Journal of Global and Historical Anthropology* 77: 1–7.

Kramer, Sander and Julia Balaa. 2004. 'Managing Uncertainty; Coping Styles of Refugees in Western Countries.' *Intervention* 2, no. 1: 33–42.

Lebanon Support. 2016. *Formal Informality, Brokering Mechanisms and Illegality. The Impact of the Lebanese State's Policies on Syrian Refugees' Daily Lives*. Beirut: Lebanon Support.

Lemke, Thomas. 2000. 'Foucault, Governmentality, and Critique.' Paper presented at the Rethinking Marxism conference, Amherst, 21–24 September.

Lindberg, Annika and Lisa Marie Borrelli. 2019. 'Let the Right One In? On European Migration Authorities' Resistance to Research.' *Social Anthropology* 27, no. 1: 17–32.

Lipsky, Michael. 1980. *Street-Level Bureaucracy: Dilemmas of the Individual in Public Services*. New York: Russell Sage Foundation.

Malkki, Liisa M. 1995. 'Refugees and Exile: From "Refugee Studies" to the National Order of Things.' *Annual Review of Anthropology* 24: 495–523.

Marston, Greg. 2003. *Temporary Protection, Permanent Uncertainty: The Experience of Refugees Living on Temporary Protection Visas*. Melbourne: Center for Applies Social Research.

Matland, Richard E. 1995. 'Synthesizing the Implementation Literature: The Ambiguity-Conflict Model of Policy Implementation.' *Journal of Public Administration Research and Theory: J-PART* 5, no. 2: 145–174.

Mazzei, Lisa A. 2003. 'Inhabited Silences: In Pursuit of a Muffled Subtext.' *Qualitative Inquiry* 9, no. 3: 355–368.

McConnell, Allan and Paul 't Hart. 2014. 'Public Policy as Inaction: The Politics of Doing Nothing.' Paper presented at the Australian Political Studies Association annual conference, Sydney, 28 September–1 October.

McGoey, Linsey. 2007. 'On the Will to Ignorance in Bureaucracy.' *Economy and Society* 36, no. 2: 212–235.

McGowan, Rosemary A. 2003. 'Organizational Discourses: Sounds of Silence.' Paper presented at the Silence and Voice in Organizational Lifestream conference, Lancaster, 7–9 July.

Mencütek, Zeynep. 2019. *Refugee Governance, State and Politics in the Middle East*. London: Routledge.

Menjivar, Cecilia. 2006. 'Liminal Legality: Salvadoran and Guatemalan Immigrants' Lives in the United States.' *American Journal of Sociology* 111, no. 4: 999–1037.

Milner, James. 2014. 'Protracted Refugee Situations.' In *The Oxford Handbook of Refugee and Forced Migration Studies*, edited by Elena Fiddian-Qasmiyeh, Gil Loescher, Katy Long and Nando Sigona, 151–162. Oxford: Oxford University Press.

Mourad, Lama. 2017. '"Standoffish" Policy-Making: Inaction and Change in the Lebanese Response to the Syrian Displacement Crisis.' *Middle East Law and Governance* 9: 249–266.

Nader, Laura. 1972. 'Up the Anthropologist: Perspectives Gained from Studying Up.' In *Reinventing Anthropology*, edited by Dell Hymes, 284–311. New York: Pantheon Books.

Nassar, Jessy and Nora Stel. 2019. 'Lebanon's Response to the Syrian Refugee Crisis – Institutional Ambiguity as a Governance Strategy.' *Political Geography* 70: 44–54.

Norman, Karin. 2005. 'The Working of Uncertainty: Interrogating Cases on Refugees in Sweden.' *Social Analysis* 49, no. 3: 195–220.

Norman, Kelsey P. 2017. 'Ambivalence as Policy: Consequences for Refugees in Egypt.' *Égypte/Monde Arabe* 1, no. 15: 27–45.

Norman, Kelsey P. 2019. 'Inclusion, Exclusion or Indifference? Redefining Migrant and Refugee Host State Engagement Options in Mediterranean "Transit" Countries.' *Journal of Ethnic and Migration Studies* 45, no. 1: 42–60.

Oesch, Lucas. 2017. 'The Refugee Camp as a Space of Multiple Ambiguities and Subjectivities.' *Political Geography* 60: 110–120.

Olivier de Sardan, Jean-Pierre. 2016. 'For an Anthropology of Gaps, Discrepancies and Contradictions.' *Anthropologica* 3, no. 1: 111–131.

Oomen, Barbara, Moritz Baumgärtel, Sara Miellet, Elif Durmus and Tihomir Sabchev. 2019. 'Strategies of Divergence: Local Authorities, Law and Discretionary Spaces in Migration Governance.' Paper presented at the IMISCOE international conference Understanding International Migration in the 21st Century: Conceptual and Methodological Approaches, Malmö, 26–28 June.

Petersen, Alan R. 1996. 'Risk and the Regulated Self: The Discourse of Health Promotion as a Politics of Uncertainty.' *Journal of Sociology* 32, no. 1: 44–57.

Pinder, Craig C. and Karen Harlos. 2001. 'Employee Silence: Quiescence and Acquiescence as Responses to Perceived Injustices.' *Research in Personnel and Human Resource Management* 20: 331–369.

Pinker, Annabel. 2015. 'Papering Over the Gaps: Documents, Infrastructure and Political Experimentation in Highland Peru.' *The Cambridge Journal of Anthropology* 33, no. 1: 97–112.

Pinker, Annabel and Penny Harvey. 2015. 'Negotiating Uncertainty: Neo-Liberal Statecraft in Contemporary Peru.' *Social Analysis* 59, no. 4: 15–31.

Poland, Blake and Ann Pedersen. 1998. 'Reading Between the Lines: Interpreting Silences in Qualitative Research.' *Qualitative Inquiry* 4, no. 2: 293–312.

Polese, Abel, Borbála Kóvacs and David Jancsics. 2018. 'Informality "in Spite of" or "Beyond" the State: Some Evidence from Hungary and Romania.' *European Societies* 20, no. 2: 207–235.

Power, Michael. 2004. *The Risk Management of Everything: Rethinking the Politics of Uncertainty*. London: Demos.

Ragin, Charles C. 1994. *Constructing Social Research: The Unity and Diversity of Method*. London: Sage Publications.

Ramadan, Adam. 2009. 'Destroying Nahr el-Bared: Sovereignty and Urbicide in the Space of Exception.' *Political Geography* 28: 153–163.

Ramadan, Adam and Sara Fregonese. 2017. 'Hybrid Sovereignty and the State of Exception in the Palestinian Refugee Camps in Lebanon.' *Annals of the American Association of Geographers* 107, no. 4: 949–963.

Randazzo, Chalice. 2015. 'Hearing Silence: Toward a Mixed-Method Approach for Studying Genres' Exclusionary Potential.' *Composition Forum* 21: 1–20.

Risse, Thomas, ed. 2013. *Governance Without a State? Policies and Politics in Areas of Limited Statehood*. New York: Columbia University Press.

Rose, Nikolas and Peter Miller. 1992. 'Political Power Beyond the State: Problematics of Government.' *The British Journal of Sociology* 43, no. 2: 173–205.

Rose, Nikolas, Pat O'Malley and Mariana Valverde. 2006. 'Governmentality.' *Annual Review of Law and Social Science* 2: 83–104.

Roy, Ananya. 2005. 'Urban informality: Toward and Epistemology of Planning.' *Journal of the American Planning Association* 71, no. 2: 147–158.

Rozakou, Katerina. 2017. 'Nonrecording the "European Refugee Crisis" in Greece: Navigating Through Irregular Bureaucracy.' *Focaal – Journal of Global and Historical Anthropology* 77: 36–49.

Rutz, Henry J. 1992. *The Politics of Time*. Arlington: American Anthropological Association.

Saghieh, Nizar. 2015. 'Manufacturing Vulnerability in Lebanon: Legal Policies and Efficient Tools of Discrimination.' *Legal Agenda*, 19 March.

Salter, Mark B. 2008. 'When the Exception Becomes the Rule: Borders, Sovereignty, and Citizenship.' *Citizenship Studies* 12, no. 4: 365–380.

Samimian-Darash, Limor and Paul Rabinow, eds. 2015. *Modes of Uncertainty: Anthropological Cases*. Chicago: University of Chicago Press.

Schedler, Andreas. 2013. *The Politics of Uncertainty: Sustaining and Subverting Electoral Authoritarianism*. Oxford: Oxford University Press.

Schmidt, Katharina. 2019. 'Developmentalising Humanitarian Space The (Anti-)Politics of International Aid for Refugees in Jordan.' MSc thesis, University of Amsterdam.

Scott, James. 1990. *Domination and the Arts of Resistance: Hidden Transcripts*. New Haven and London: Yale University Press.

Slater, Dan and Diana Kim. 2015. 'Standoffish States: Nonliterate Leviathans in Southeast Asia.' *TRaNS – Trans, Regional, and National Studies of Southeast Asia* 3, no. 1: 25–44.

Smithson, Michael. 1989. *Ignorance and Uncertainty: Emerging Paradigms*. New York: Springer-Verlag.

Stel, Nora. 2015. 'Facilitating Facts on the Ground: The "Politics of Uncertainty" and the Governance of Housing, Land, and Tenure in the Palestinian Gathering of Qasmiye, South Lebanon.' Governance and Local Development Program working paper no. 5, Yale University.

Stel, Nora. 2016. 'The Agnotology of Eviction in South Lebanon's Palestinian Gatherings: How Institutional Ambiguity and Deliberate Ignorance Shape Sensitive Spaces.' *Antipode* 48, no. 5: 1400–1419.

Stel, Nora. 2017. 'Governing the Gatherings: The Interaction of Lebanese State Institutions and Palestinian Authorities in the Hybrid Political Order of South Lebanon's Informal Palestinian Settlements.' PhD dissertation, Utrecht University.

Stel, Nora. 2018. 'Exporting Institutional Ambiguity in Refugee Governance: How Lebanon's Politics of Uncertainty Mirrors EUrope's Politics of Exhaustion and Abandonment.' Paper presented at the European International Studies Association's conference A New Hope: Back to the Future of International Relations, Prague, 15 September.

Stel, Nora. 2019. 'Ignorance Studies: How to Study What Is Not Known?' In *The Sage Encyclopaedia of Qualitative Research Methods*, edited by Paul Atkinson, Sara Delamont, Alexandru Cernat, Joseph W. Sakshaug and Richard A. Williams. London: Sage Publications.

Stepputat, Finn and Ninna Nyberg Sørensen. 2014. 'Sociology and Forced Migration.' In *The Oxford Handbook of Refugee and Forced Migration Studies*, edited by Elena Fiddian-Qasmiyeh, Gil Loescher, Katy Long and Nando Sigona, 86–98. Oxford: Oxford University Press.

Tapscott, Rebecca. 2017. 'The Government Has Long Hands: Institutionalized Arbitrariness and Local Security Initiatives in Northern Uganda.' *Development and Change* 48, no. 2: 263–285.

Tapscott, Rebecca. 2018. 'A Theory of Arbitrary Governance.' Paper presented at the Development Studies Association annual conference Global Inequalities, Manchester, 27–29 June.

Tazzioli, Martina. 2017. 'Containment Through Mobility: Migrants' Spatial Disobediences and the Reshaping of Control Through the Hotspot System in the Mediterranean.' *Journal of Ethic and Migration Studies* 44, no. 16: 2764–2779.

Tazzioli, Martina. 2019. 'Debit Cards, Refugee Subjectivities and Data Circulation: The Circuits of Financial-Humanitarianism in the Greek Migration Laboratory.' Paper presented at the Royal Geographic Society annual conference, London, 30 August.

Turbay, Marcela Guerrero. 2015. 'The "Politics of Representation": Syrian Refugees in the Official Discourse in Lebanon (2011–2015).' MA thesis, Erasmus University Rotterdam.

Turner, Simon. 2005. 'Suspended Spaces: Contesting Sovereignties in a Refugee Camp.' In *Sovereign Bodies: Citizens, Migrants and States in the Post-Colonial World*, edited by Thomas Blom Hansen and Finn Stepputat, 312–332. Princeton: Princeton University Press.

United Nations High Commissioner for Refugees Executive Committee. 2004. 'Protracted Refugee Situations.' Standing Committee meeting 10 June, EC/54/SC/CRP.14.

Whyte, Zachary. 2011. 'Enter the Myopticon: Uncertain Surveillance in the Danish Asylum System.' *Anthropology Today* 2, no. 3: 18–21.

Yassin, Nasser, Tarek Osseiran, Rima Rassi and Marwa Boustani. 2015. *No Place to Stay? Reflections on the Syria Refugee Shelter Policy in Lebanon*. Beirut: United Nations Human Settlements Program & the Issam Fares Institute for Public Policy and International Affairs at the American University of Beirut.

Yassin, Nasser, Nora Stel and Rima Rassi. 2016. 'Organized Chaos: Informal Institution Building Among Palestinian Refugees in the Maashouk Gathering in South Lebanon.' *Journal of Refugee Studies* 29, no. 3: 341–362.

Zaiotti, Ruben. 2006. 'Dealing with Non-Palestinian Refugees in the Middle East: Politics and Practices in an Uncertain Environment.' *International Journal of Refugee Law* 18, no. 2: 333–353.

Zerubavel, Eviatar. 2006. *The Elephant in the Room: Silence and Denial in Everyday Life*. Oxford: Oxford University Press.

Zetter, Roger. 2007. 'More Labels, Fewer Refugees: Remaking the Refugee Label in an Era of Globalization.' *Journal of Refugee Studies* 20, no. 2: 172–192.

Chapter 1

The Lebanese state

Twilight institutions and the making of hybrid order

You have political leaders in this country, they don't have the sense of governance. They have the sense to make consensus on how they can maintain their power-sharing platform. But that's it. That's it. This is very simple. It is simple as it is. I cannot add more and I don't have to add more and there is nothing to add. Because all the intelligent solutions are here; they don't want to adopt intelligent solutions. They want to keep creating problems and problems and problems and problems and talking and talking and talking. That's it. And if someone like me, for example, came in and has an official position, they can propose a first solution, a second solution, third solution, fourth solution . . . And it will not work.[1]

In this book, I want to shed light on the ways in which Lebanese authorities strategically uphold and extend institutional ambiguity to deal with so-called refugee 'crises.'[2] This assumes that ambiguity follows from both state structures and the behaviour of the people constituting these structures. It does not assume that state agencies are the only organizations implicated in the institutionalization of ambiguity. Businesses, transnational networks, and humanitarian regimes will all have a stake in this process. My concern with states follows from my interest in thinking through the relation between ambiguity and political forms of power. But most of the organizational logics explored in this book for state agencies might be fruitfully extrapolated to other societal realms. In fact, the notion of stateness that is put forward in this chapter sees the state as a hybrid, mediated assemblage that encompasses much of what traditional, formal approaches to the state would consider to lie beyond it.

To understand the political work that institutional ambiguity might do for Lebanese state agencies in their governance of refugees then requires two things: first, to establish a way to conceptually understand 'the state'; and, second, to make sense of the empirical specificities of the Lebanese state in light of such a conceptualization. Drawing on and contributing to debates on hybrid order and twilight institutions, the chapter's first two sections address these issues respectively. The final section subsequently reflects on the structural, systemic features of institutional ambiguity in Lebanon, considering the peculiarities of its state system and political arrangements. This chapter thereby sets the scene for the case-study chapters that will follow and that will focus on the more agential dimensions of Lebanon's governance of the Syrian and Palestinian refugee presence in the country.

Conceptualizing the state beyond the illusion of sovereignty

Many regional host states for refugees are considered 'weak' or 'fragile.' In working towards a better understanding of the political functionality and institutionalization of ambiguity, however, such a pathological approach to governance is hardly helpful. Discarding any reality that does not live up to an abstract European ideal-type as 'failed' reifies rather than interrogates disorder. Drawing on work on 'the anthropology of the state' (Sharma and Gupta, 2006; see also Das and Poole, 2004; Gupta, 1995, 2012; Hansen and Stepputat, 2001; Joseph and Nugent, 1994; Klem, 2012; Kosmatopoulos, 2011; Olivier de Sardan, 2008; Trouillot, 2001), I thus take 'fragility' as the starting point instead of the conclusion of my attempt to think through the political work that institutional ambiguity does. In this chapter, the premise is that, as a result of the legacies of colonialism and war as well as current geopolitical realities, sovereignty in the states that host the majority of the world's refugees is contested (Bacik, 2008; Fregonese, 2012). No single political authority can impose its will and use violence with impunity. This makes governance complex and unpredictable per definition.

In the shifting assemblages of formal state agencies, political parties, 'traditional' authorities and 'strongmen,' civil society organizations, religious institutions, and private enterprises, it appears as if 'the state does not exist and the state is everywhere' at the same time (Ismail, 2006: 165). As further explored in the next section, in Lebanon too, 'the state' [al dawle] seems to simultaneously represent everything and nothing. References to the state are often very generic, without an indication to a specific actor, institution, department, ministry, or person. It could refer to a municipality, the government, the army or police, the national electricity company, or all of those at the same time. For refugees especially, the state is often an external, largely unknown, and unspecified 'they,' a vague, faceless, address-less entity.

This paradox of simultaneous presence and absence can be unpacked by distinguishing between a 'state system' and a 'state idea' (Abrams, 1988; Migdal, 2001). The state system then refers to the collection of actors, practices, and institutions that legally make up the state as understood in a colloquial sense, constituting a material reality. The state idea is the socio-political construct that gives these actors, practices, and institutions a perceived coherence and collective intention and thereby conjures the state as an ontological structure. This tension between systems and ideas is relevant to the structural aspects of institutional ambiguity. When investigating ambiguity, dichotomous distinctions between 'state' and 'society' or between 'state' and 'non-state' are useless. What is at stake is not mapping who or what is inside or outside the state, but rather the shifting overlap and dynamic co-constitution of different forms of political authority by a variety of governance actors.

The notion of hybrid sovereignty is helpful in this exercise (see the work of Balthasar, 2015; Bierschenk and Olivier de Sardan, 1997; Hoffmann and Kirk, 2013; Kingston, 2004; Raeymaekers, Menkhaus and Vlassenroot, 2008; Risse, 2013; Risse and Lehmkuhl, 2007; Scheye, 2009; Van Overbeek, 2014; Wickham-Crowley, 1987; Wiuff Moe, 2011). The idea of hybridity emphasizes the multiplicity and interactive nature of governance and stresses the symbiotic relation between what are often thought of as bounded political actors or separate institutional fields. If 'state' and 'non-state' are recognized as mutually constitutive, distinctions like public and private and formal and informal become a moving target. These constructed boundaries can be claimed and denied by authorities and the people these authorities purportedly govern (although, as we will see, most often more successfully by the former than by the latter). The matter at hand, then, is not to define or pinpoint 'the state,' but rather to explore the empirical manifestations of the state system's inherently 'elusive, porous, and mobile' interfaces with other forms of political authority (Mitchell, 1990: 77).

If a 'political order' is the sum of institutionalized power and governance relations that one can empirically grasp at a given time and place, then hybrid political orders are countries that do not have a sovereign authority or one single focal point of governance (Boege et al., 2008; Boege, Brown and Clements, 2009; Hagmann and Hoehne, 2009; Kyed, 2017). Sovereignty is never absolute, but some 'orders' are more hybrid than others.[3] This regards the extent to which state systems have been able to co-opt governance functions. Hybridity often reflects the effects of colonial divide-and-rule legacies and neocolonial institutional imposition. It operates on various fronts. Hybridity regards a multiplicity of political authorities (inside and beyond the formal state system), a plurality of political institutions (with de facto practices often holding as much sway in political decision-making as de jure policies) and changeable political dynamics (where protracted communal power bases are combined with volatile alliances) (Stel and Van der Molen, 2015). In short, hybrid orders refer to a situation characterized by 'contradictory and dialectic co-existence' of governance actors in which 'diverse and competing authority structures, sets of rules, logics of order, and claims to power co-exist, overlap, and intertwine' (Boege et al., 2008: 17). The idea of hybrid order or hybrid sovereignty thus puts the tight, complex, and changing relations among different governance actors centre stage. This brings into focus the political heterogeneity and non-synchronicity that is essential to understand the structural components of institutional ambiguity.

Under hybrid sovereignty, governance, the organization of public goods and political decision-making, thus takes place inside but also beyond the state system. Various political authorities that are simultaneously part of and parallel to the state system compete for and negotiate over the power to govern. These 'twilight institutions' are authorities that command significant governance capacity and legitimacy, but are outside or only partially included in the formal state system (Lund, 2006). They often draw on the state idea in organizing and legitimizing their provision of security, welfare, and representation, casting their governance activities in 'languages of stateness' (Hansen and Stepputat, 2001; Stel, 2016). From the perspective of fragility, these authorities compete over governance power with the formal state system. In reality, however, their 'twilight' nature means that they more often partially co-opt – or are co-opted by – the state system, which governs in a mediated or negotiated manner (Menkhaus, 2006; Hagmann and Péclard, 2010; Scheye, 2009; Stel, 2015, 2017). In hybrid orders, various governance actors are 'doing the state' together (Migdal and Schlichte, 2005: 14). To work with hybridity, essentially, is to approach the state as a strategic field in which relationality – actors' embeddedness in multiple and dynamic networks – is the constitutive element.

As my account of Lebanon's political order that follows shows, I do not mean to romanticize hybridity or mediation. Elite collaboration in practice does little for accountability, and competing regimes of violence undermine human security in many ways. But a conceptual premium on relationality allows for a more nuanced understanding of neopatrimonialism. Neopatrimonialism revolves around the idea of 'state capture,' the notion that the 'public' state system is appropriated by the 'private,' or communal, interests of authorities that initially operated beyond this formal state system but have come to occupy it. The state system is then perceived as an empty shell that is nevertheless the 'ultimate prize' for political elites because of the redistributable resources it brings with it and the inherent legitimacy it can tap into in the form of the state 'idea' (Chabal and Daloz, 1999). From a hybridity perspective, this 'capture' is a more iterative process, where various forms of authority compete and negotiate over who can wield political power when and where and over whom. Rather than 'traditional' or 'communal' authorities that take over the state, which suggests an endpoint, twilight authorities that operate simultaneously inside and outside the state system constantly redefine and reallocate the power of the state agencies making up this state system.

In hybrid orders, to be able to govern, the state system is made up by more or less implicit partnerships and arrangements with a diverse range of local intermediaries and rival sources of authority that it partially subsumes. It requires and nurtures this assembled and multi-layered institutional power among social, political, and economic authorities. Where the idea of competition between 'state' and 'non-state' that is central to notions of fragility suggests its own form of predictability, the reality in which the state system – simultaneously or alternatingly – governs through as well as against other political authorities makes for a more complicated governance landscape in which ambiguity is a built-in feature. 'Rules of the game' or 'social contracts' will be more elusive in such settings, where governance will be subject to constant change and reinterpretation that are part of the mediation or negotiation of political authority.

Crucially, this is a matter of scale and degree. The analytical value of focusing on the hybridity of sovereignty and political order does not lie in pointing out that such hybridity exists – because it does everywhere and at all times – but in the analytical space it opens up to explore how it functions and what its effects are. My conceptualization of institutional ambiguity should be situated in this analytical space. In studying the institutionalization and the political use of ambiguity, bringing to the fore the hybridity of specific political orders is helpful because it reveals the structural and systemic aspects of uncertainty. It reveals how the inherently undefined nature of the interfaces between the 'twilight' actors operating in the assembled and shifting configurations of power underpins institutional ambiguity. These systemic drivers of ambiguity provide the context in which the agential aspects of ambiguity – the ways in which political authorities reproduce informality, liminality, and exceptionalism through inaction and ambiguous action – that I put centre stage in my further analysis emerge.

This book specifically explores how state agencies, the political authorities that are part of the formal state system, produce and reproduce institutional ambiguity in governing refugees. This may seem counter-intuitive considering the prior acknowledgement that to speak of hybridity is to problematize state agency. To discuss any state system as a coherent and unitary institutional actor is to reify the state idea that political actors may project, but which does not accurately describe reality on the ground. But that political decision-making in hybrid political orders is crucially located beyond the formal state system does not undermine the utility of a focus on state policy-making and implementation (or the lack of it) for understanding how institutional ambiguity works.

State agencies and institutions matter even if this is in entirely different ways than the dominant state 'idea' would claim. In Lebanon, specifically, Mouawad and Baumann (2017: 69) have shown, 'the state lies at the intersection of multiple societal and elite dynamics [and] informal networks and social service allocation structures are embedded in public institutions.' From a hybridity perspective, the formal state system operates as an arena as well as an instrument of governance for a wide array of political authorities that have their institutional reach inside and beyond the state system. The policy-making and implementation behaviour of state agencies is the product of the negotiation, contestation, and mediation of various political authorities. It thereby offers a helpful entry point into hybridity and the way hybridity constitutes ambiguity.

Doing the state in Lebanon

When Lebanese talk about their state, the perceived absence of this state is often invoked in the exclamation 'Where is the state?!' [*wayn el-dawle?!*] (Mouawad and Baumann, 2017; see also Kosmatopoulos, 2011) My interlocutors often spoke of an 'empty state'. This has to do not so much with the physical absence of the state – material manifestations of the presence of state agencies are abundant – but more with its elusiveness. Where does the state end and sectarian parties begin? What can and will the state do and for whom and under which conditions? Where to find information on which rules apply where? Analysts, too, have been skeptical, seeing Lebanon as 'a poster child of a failed state' (Joseph, 2011: 152). In the wake of the infamous Lebanese Civil War (1975–1990), the term 'Lebanoniza-tion' was coined to indicate the destructive fragmentation of a country (Migdal, 2001: 136).[4]

Lebanese sovereignty has been eroded externally, through a perverse colo-nial legacy that hardened existing sectarianism. After being part of the Ottoman Empire for four decades, the territory that now constitutes Lebanon was made part of the French Mandate until it gained independence in 1943. Since then Lebanon has faced almost continuous external intervention by regional sectarian power brokers and geopolitical alliances that turned it into the 'battleground of the Mid-dle East' and have made its independence nominal at best (Hirst, 2010).[5] The country was invaded by Israel in 1982, which occupied parts of South Lebanon until 2000, and was under de facto Syrian occupation, so-called tutelage, from 1976 until 2005. It has seen various armed conflicts since then, such as the 1996 Israeli 'Grapes of Wrath' campaign, the 2006 war between Israel and Hezbollah, and the 2007 Nahr el-Bared clashes.

Lebanese sovereignty has been internally contested as well. Lebanon estab-lished a unique system of sectarian consociationalism to share power among the 18 different recognized sectarian communities in the country – of which the Sunni and Shia Muslims and Maronite Christians have historically been the largest and most influential. These various sectarian communities reflect religious or cultural distinctions between Lebanese groups and each have their regional strongholds; political parties; social institutions like schools, clinics, and charities; and armed militias. The country's inter-sectarian power-sharing formula that was meant to unite these different groups while protecting their autonomy at the same time stip-ulates that Lebanon's President should be a Maronite Christian, the Prime Min-ister a Sunni Muslim, and the Speaker of Parliament a Shia Muslim and includes corresponding sectarian quota that guide the allocation of all public positions.

Resulting from trade-offs between the French mandatory power and the domi-nant, predominantly Maronite Christian, Lebanese elites at the time, this system was designed to accommodate much of the patriarchal and feudal patronage net-works that predated it. The parameters for this, in Hudson's (1968) words, 'pre-carious republic' were agreed upon in an unwritten 'National Pact' in 1932 that also stipulated the exact divisions of power based on the national census that was held that year, which has been the country's last census until today.[6] The 1989 Ta'if Agreement that officially ended the Lebanese Civil War expresses the vision to move away from political sectarianism but in fact merely updates the division of power between Muslim and Christian seats in Parliament and the relative influ-ence of the positions of the President, Prime Minister, and Speaker of Parliament.

As noted, Lebanon's limited sovereignty does not mean the Lebanese state is failed, weak, or absent. Both the state idea and the state system are at the heart of Lebanese governance. The state system is imperfect but omnipresent. As Hermez (2015: 513) sums up:

> The state installs traffic lights, is involved in tenders for infrastructure con-struction projects, builds and maintains roads, holds elections, passes laws,

manages prisons, arrests criminals, and, most invasively, maintains military and police checkpoints that, however ineffective, structure daily life and the zones of possibility for action, and force people to maintain relations – a level of social and political capital – to bypass this state of affairs if need be.

The state idea resonates fiercely in Lebanon as well. Lebanese citizens may be ambivalent towards and skeptical of the state, but they do believe in and look for its 'ideal face' (Obeid, 2010; see also Carpi, 2019; Hazbun, 2016). Despite the fact that their own behaviour often undermines this belief, political parties also routinely pledge allegiance to the notion of a 'strong state of institutions' (Ghaddar, 2016), feeding the notion of the Lebanese state as forever anticipated and 'awaited' (Mouawad, 2015 in Carpi, 2019).

Hybrid sectarianism

This omnipresence of the state system and idea in Lebanon indicates that what defines the Lebanese state is not weakness, but rather hybridity. It is not the absence of stateness, but the elusiveness of what the state is and the unpredictability of its institutional manifestations and operations that determines governance in Lebanon. Lebanon's political system is 'an unusual hybrid' (International Crisis Group, 2015: 16). It is centred on a 'fetishised sectarian balance' that facilitates endemic patronage and an oligarchic and clientelistic distribution of state resources and positions (Perdigon, 2015). The country's system of sectarian consociationalism is premised on the existence of clear communal boundaries, elite coordination, and balance of power. It reflects but also entrenches the historical centrality of politicized sectarian allegiance. Access to the welfare, security, and representation that the Lebanese state nominally should offer all its citizens is thus mediated through sectarian identity and the related political networks.

This amalgamation of sectarian authority and parliamentary democracy that consociationalism institutionalized makes for a particular hybrid order that combines not just different power structures, but also different logics of rule. The Lebanese President is elected for a six-year term. The government, or Council of Ministers, acts as the state's executive, developing laws, policies, and decrees. Lebanon's legislative is a unicameral parliament that is elected every four years by popular vote. While Members of Parliament can advance proposals for new laws and policies to the government, Lebanon's executive has been dominant in the country's policy-making. As a result of sectarianism, El-Ghali and Baalbaki (2017: 10) note, 'most policy issues are usually settled outside parliament.' When Lebanon's so-called troika – the President, Prime Minister, and Speaker of Parliament – agree, parliament will pass any decision without debate. This led a public administration expert consulting for various Lebanese ministries to conclude that 'In Lebanon, we don't have policy-makers, let's be very clear. Because we don't have policies. We have decision-makers.'[7] When I asked him about the difference between a policy and a decision, he answered: 'In a policy you have a sustainability and in decision-making you have always changes.' This explains why the Lebanese policies that are there tend to be ambiguous, or 'partial, temporal and provisional,' as Mencütek (2019: 52) observes (see also Verdeil, 2018).

Since Lebanon's legislative does not serve as an effective check on the executive, accountability is nominal at best. Various studies show that corruption is rife and that disciplinary mechanisms have been cosmetic and ineffective (Kisirwani, 1997; Leenders, 2004, 2012; Office for the Minister of State for Administrative Reform, 2011). That formal accountability is extremely wanting is further demonstrated by the fact that, while officially independent, Lebanon's judiciary is entirely under the control of the executive. This is acknowledged by leading politicians and religious leaders and by judges themselves. The late Prime Minister Rafik Hariri infamously stated: 'I have interfered, I do interfere and I will continue to interfere in the work of the judiciary because this is how it is done in this country' (quoted in Takieddine, 2004: 24 in Knudsen, 2009: 63).

Political decision-making in Lebanon thus depends on an intricate process of inter-sectarian negotiation that requires broad consensus, which is almost never attainable. Lebanon's state system, consequently, has operated more like a 'vetocracy,' where rule through veto produces endemic deadlock. Since Syria withdrew from Lebanon in 2005, competition among two broad inter-sectarian alliances has defined Lebanese politics. The March 8 bloc, led by Lebanon's Shia parties and their Christian allies, is considered pro-Syrian and is supported by Iran. March 14, conversely, headed by the main Sunni party and its Christian partners, allies with Saudi Arabia and its Western supporters, and is considered anti-Syrian.

While this alignment was initially based in respective resistance to and support for Syrian tutelage over Lebanon, it gained new pertinence in light of the Syrian War, in which – despite Lebanon's official policy of disassociation – the different Lebanese alliances supported opposing sides in the conflict. This extreme polarization has generated institutional paralysis. As Batruni and Hallinan (2018: 1) conclude, 'political quagmires' and 'maximal delays' define Lebanese governance. Pressing issues routinely get 'neglected or shelved' (Mencütek, 2019: 135). Although 45 parliamentary sessions were exclusively convened for this purpose, for instance, it took 30 months to appoint a President. Forming a government after elections often takes as much as ten months. Between 2007 and 2008, there was an, inherently severely curtailed, caretaker government for 18 months. The country went without a national budget for a decade since the withdrawal of Syria in 2005. Reflecting on such paralysis, a previous advisor to the Lebanese Minister of Social Affairs noted:

> In Lebanon everything is possible! I will tell you something: . . . we stayed between 2005 and 2017, which means twelve years, without a budget in Lebanon. How can it be? It happened. In Lebanon, it happens. So we can have no policy, actually, because we have a minimal state. So this is part one,

we always had a laissez-faire, laissez-passer type of a minimal state that let everything ongoing [sic], especially on the economic side. Secondly, actually there was . . . we don't have a united position inside the government. So we have one government, but actually it is not one government, it's maybe five, six governments inside the government.[8]

Passing a law, the ultimate institutionalization of decision-making, requires active participation of parliamentary committees and a national assembly vote. Considering the extreme polarization described earlier, this is often impossible in Lebanon. Reflecting on the 'reality and problems of the public administration' in Lebanon, the Office for the Minister of State for Administrative Reform (2011: 7) concluded that 'in terms of policy making and planning public administrations in general lack strategic planning which is based on clear visions as well as long and medium-term plans resulting thereof.' Rather than through laws, then, Lebanon is governed through decrees, which, unlike laws, can be approved by the government without direct involvement of parliament and are hence a more common policy modality. Even decrees, however, are often too ambitious. When this is the case, decisions are made by 'ministerial decision,' which only demands the approval of a single minister, not the whole government, and thus constitute the most realistic form of policy-making in the country.

In its 'government monitor,' the Lebanese Center for Policy Studies (2019) showed that in its first hundred days, the government that was installed in February 2019 published 522 legislative texts in the Official Gazette: 25 laws, 347 decrees, and 150 ministerial decisions. The great majority of these were administrative measures. Of the 32 regulatory measures, only one could be classified as a reform, a 'legislative or institutional change that goes beyond day-to-day policy management.' In Lebanon, then, the main legislator is in fact not the legislature but the executive (Knudsen, 2009: 69). As one government advisor explained: 'Policies are seen as political and need consensus, decrees are seen as operational and don't – this is why there are few policies, but many decrees.'[9] Paralysis extends beyond policy-making, moreover. As Mencütek (2019: 132) shows, even those laws, decrees, and decisions that are made are often not acted upon due to lack of commitment, consensus, or resources.

In Lebanon perhaps more than elsewhere, policy then is, as El-Ghali and Baalbaki (2017: 6) note in their exploration of Lebanese decision-making, 'whatever governments choose to do or not to do.' Hybrid sovereignty dictates what Lebanese state agencies do and not do and how they (not) do it. It cements short-term thinking and crisis management, having politicians focused on avoiding or navigating specific breakdowns rather than on developing shared meta-policies for the issues that cause such breakdown. The public good in Lebanon has become defined as avoiding the outbreak of violent conflict, and this results in the institutionalization of ambiguity. Lebanon's political parties embody and reproduce such ambiguity.

Twilight parties

Lebanon's main parties are the Party of God (or Hezbollah) and Hope (Amal) for the Shia community, the Future Movement (Mustaqbal) among Lebanon's Sunnis, the Progressive Socialist Party for the country's Druze, and the Free Patriotic Movement, the Lebanese Forces, and Kataeb (the Lebanese Phalangist Party) among Maronite Christians.[10]

Crucially, political parties in Lebanon do not operate on a political program. They organize to serve the interests of sectarian elites. Most parties have programs or manifestos, but these do not appear to meaningfully influence their actions. Indeed, political parties avoid commitment to any specific policy in their programs, limiting themselves to generic and uncontroversial positions (Hassan, 2019). As the Lebanese Center for Policy Studies has shown time and again, in Lebanese elections national parties run with and against the same parties in different places depending on the sectarian demographics of these localities (Atallah, 2018). Even members of the same party rarely hold the same policy views (Atallah and Diab, 2018). Members of Parliament are often not aware of the official position of their party – as manifested in either a program or the statements of the official party leader or spokesperson – on specific policy domains and disagree as often as they agree with members of the same party on policy matters. In terms of political principle or policy, political parties in Lebanon lack coherence entirely.

As vehicles of sectarian clientelism, however, they are consistent and effective. Political parties in Lebanon encompass clan and family allegiances, religious institutions such as the confessional family status courts, and geographic and economic patronage networks (Sensenig-Dabbous, 2009: 2). They are a mix between the reinvented power of the semi-feudal sectarian patrons, so-called *zuama*, that held sway before the Civil War; the political institutionalization of the militias that challenged and co-opted these traditional elites during the war; and various post-war business tycoons – with different parties being dominated to a different extent by each of these traditions and logics.[11] Most Lebanese parties are intimately related to militias that claimed to serve and protect sectarian communities during the Lebanese Civil War. The war produced a far-reaching breakdown of the state system. This, Ramadan and Fregonese (2017: 10) show, resulted in 'further hybridizations between state and nonstate actors, with elements of the government, army, and armed militias contesting and at times collaborating to control territory and infrastructure.'

Much of Lebanon's institutional ambiguity reflects the entrenchment of uncertainty during and due to armed conflict. Embodying both cause and effect of the 'cantonization' of Lebanon during the war, political parties are the institutional front office of much broader territorial and institutional sectarian strongholds with related religious and welfare institutions, civil society organizations and nongovernmental organizations (NGOs), international alliances, and armed groups. Party structures overlap with sectarian communal organizations that encompass civil society organizations, businesses, and militias. In essence, then, they serve as communal, rather than strictly political, representatives. This makes sense in light of the fact that, as Catusse and Karam (2010: 15) note, the Arabic word for party [*hizb*] is associated, or even interchangeable, with notions of 'clubs', 'clans,' 'militias,' and 'confessions.'

Therefore, while political parties are in formal terms merely political organizations that represent the interests of their electoral constituencies throughout the state system, in practice they simultaneously operate an institutional structure parallel to the state system to serve their sectarian constituencies. In my analysis, Lebanese political parties are not confined to the narrow institutional vehicle of the formal party, but encompass the political manifestation of larger communal-sectarian networks. In this way, sectarian communities and the state system meet in Lebanon's political parties. Ultimately, it is these parties that are 'doing the state' in Lebanon.

Political parties in Lebanon are formal electoral representatives that shape state governance. They are also parallel governance actors in their own right, commanding their own institutions in terms of welfare, security, and representation. This makes them twilight institutions in the sense that they simultaneously operate inside and beyond the Lebanese state system. When developing the idea of 'twilight institutions,' Lund (2006: 689) conceived of such institutions as being engaged in 'an ambiguous process of being and opposing the state.' That they are simultaneously governing in the name of the state and autonomously from it explains, for example, the paradoxical instances in which Lebanese political parties are seen as, and present themselves as, representatives of 'the people' against the government, despite the fact that their own representation in said government is the very reason they can claim that such representation might have any effect.

Lebanese political parties have strong interscalar institutions, with neighborhood dynamics that are intricately and tightly linked to national and geopolitical decision-making and 'elite-level bargains' (Belhadj et al., 2015: 7). The 'political boss class,' Ghaddar (2016) shows in her analysis of the 'machine politics' in the 'alleyways' of Lebanon's third largest city, Sidon, 'dominates the entire political process in Lebanon, from the presidency and cabinet all the way down to neighborhood ward.' Studies into local Lebanese security arrangements show that political party representatives are usually the first to respond to any incident and that state security agencies, such as the army and police, only intervene when they have a 'political green light to do so' (Belhadj et al., 2015: 9; see also Carpi, 2016; Mazzola, 2019: 15).

As a Lebanese analyst (cited in Belhadj et al., 2015: 9) summarized:

> Those who should be seen as doing the job on the ground are the mandated, uniformed institutions, even if the process of how and where they show up is wired through the parties. This status quo serves the parties and the state; there is consensus.

Such dynamics are not limited to security issues. A former official of the Lebanese-Palestinian Dialogue Committee, for instance, explained that municipal employees usually 'redirect' any sensitive issue to the relevant local party functionary, noting that the hands of a mayor, for instance, are often tied, and pointing out that there are 'ceilings of decision-making' that civil servants cannot breach without consulting with the dominant party cadres in the region.[12]

The formal state system is represented on various institutional levels. Under the Ministry of Interior, there are provincial governors [*muhafaza*], district governors [*qaemaqam*], and municipalities [*baladiyat*], and the respective administrations as well as *mukhtars* (village or neighborhood officials responsible for basic personal status documentation). Other ministries also have their respective local-level bureaucracies. Despite routine lip service to principles of decentralization, however, such local state structures suffer from lack of capacities and resources. Local authorities often feel abandoned by the national state, and the literature on the Lebanese system abundantly refers to the gaps between different levels of governance and the failure of nominal decentralization (Ghanem, 2016; Harb and Atallah, 2015).

This produces yet another one of the paradoxes that seem to define Lebanon: As a result of lacking policies and funds, local state agencies are simultaneously abandoned and curtailed (Mourad and Piron, 2016) – a dynamic that will feature throughout the book's empirical chapters. Interaction through formal state channels is often lopsided, with national state agencies dictating what needs to be done locally without providing sufficient means or responding to local demands. This does not mean that the analyses and needs of local political authorities are not accommodated nationally. Rather, the intricacies of local governance predicaments and local political dynamics are communicated 'upwards' via the parallel institutions of political parties and their subservient sectarian and communal networks. The more closely state agencies and political party structures are intertwined, as is the case, for instance, in the security sector, the more efficient such informal 'decentralization' is.

Because the relative power of each political-sectarian party determines the nature and functioning of state agencies, Lebanon is often said to lack a unified state, rather constituting a multitude of states, as different parties rule different regions or cities in the country. While this may ring true for many practical purposes, these different local 'party states' all operate according to the same overarching logic of hybrid sectarianism that was described previously. Various Lebanese regions certainly have different cultures, and the relative influence of particular institutions – clans, religious authorities, 'civil society' – may differ accordingly, but, as the 2019 October Revolution drove home, the centrality of sectarian-political parties that co-opt and coordinate these various power poles is a constant.

In all of Lebanon, political parties are in many ways the central hub in the hybrid order that is constituted by the complex interconnections among diverse actors, ranging from state agencies to civil society organizations and NGOs and to clans, militias, and organized crime. Political parties, at once parasitic on the state and constitutive of it, are at the heart of Lebanon's hybrid political order. They function as a 'fluid frontier' between what are formally state and non-state institutions and actors (Hagmann and Péclard, 2010: 549). If the Lebanese state is a mediated one (Stel, 2015, 2017; Mazzola, 2019), then Lebanon's political parties, as the politically institutionalized vanguard of sectarian communal organizations, are the central mediators (Stel and Van der Borgh, 2017). Combining functions of representation, provision, and brokerage, parties constitute de facto centripetal forces in Lebanon's hybrid sovereignty.

Fregonese's (2012: 659) theorization of Lebanon as 'a constellation of hybrid sovereignties' highlights the crucial positions that political parties hold in Lebanon's hybrid political order. Fregonese (2012: 657) identifies Lebanon's political parties as the main institutional hub of the 'tight circular connections between state and nonstate actors' that define hybridity. Hezbollah, often considered the most 'successful' and thereby perhaps quintessential Lebanese party,[13] in Fregonese's (2012: 668) words, is 'simultaneously a political party, . . . an armed resistance movement, a provider of social services, and a provider of infrastructure: it is simultaneously part of the state, nonstate, and state-like.'

To varying degrees, this applies to other political parties as well. Hazbun (2016: 1057) shows how the Lebanese Phalangists and the Future Movement first developed autonomous political and business networks. As these parties entered government, such networks were 'integrated into state structures to form hybrid state institutions . . . by displacing existing institutions and figures or else by creating parallel state institutions that could work around rival (hybrid) state institutions' (Hazbun, 2016: 1057). A representative of one of the dominant parties in South Lebanon explained that when he referred to 'the state,' he meant 'our people in the state' through which decisions can be made.[14] Political parties thus do not just shape policy-making inside the state system, they also mediate the interpretation and implementation of any law, decree, or decision from outside the state's institutional structure.

This twilight nature of Lebanon's political parties and the institutional brokering it enables is especially important when it comes to the governance of noncitizens such as refugees. In contrast to formal state agencies, political parties, which are formally related to state agencies through their elected representatives but also have a separate institutional governance structure, are well-positioned to engage with those populations that are excluded from the formal mandate of the state. As will become evident in the empirical chapters of this book, refugee populations that are ignored by or distance themselves from formal state policies and agencies often are accommodated by the sectarian-political institutions that are associated with Lebanon's political parties. This works both ways. Communities without citizen or residency status depend on informal parallel governance by, among others, parties. Parties, by dealing with the sensitive reality of refugee governance that has been excluded from state mandates through legal vacuums and policy deficiency, reinstate their centrality as de facto power brokers in Lebanon's broader hybrid political order. What is crucial here is, of course, that these same political parties have imposed informality, liminality, and exceptionalism on refugees by excluding them from Lebanese laws and policies in the first place.

Although Lebanon's political parties are often called communal, in essence they are elitist.[15] They serve themselves rather than their so-called constituencies. Lebanon's 'social contract' is sectarian rather than national. The provision of 'public goods' is mediated through the sectarian elites and their parties. This also means that to ensure consensus, Lebanon's political system is premised on elite deal-making rather than on broad popular representation (El-Husseini, 2004). As shown by Atallah (2016), Lebanon's electoral law, which results in infamous gerrymandering, 'allows the elite to select their constituency rather than voters electing their representatives.' Public policy in Lebanon, El-Ghali and Baalbaki (2017: 21) note in their meta-study on Lebanese governance, is determined by the preferences of the ruling elite rather than by the demands of their 'constituencies.' Surveying Lebanon's legislative processes over the last years, the Lebanese Center for Policy Studies has empirically evidenced that Members of Parliament are hardly aware of citizens' concerns and do not legislate on citizens' priorities (Atallah, 2018).

Despite sectarian and geopolitical polarization, Lebanon's consociational system revolves around the creation and protection of elite consensus across sects. Political rivalry and scheming should not obscure the fact that the interests of Lebanon's post-war 'elite cartel' converge on the issue of protecting the status quo (El-Husseini, 2004). Consociationalism, after all, is premised on the idea of mutual deterrence. The fact that all political-sectarian leaders need their peers to 'control' their respective constituencies makes for a tense equilibrium. The resilience of the current institutional ambiguity that defines Lebanon's political decision-making system stems from such shared elite interests. The International Crisis Group (2015: 14) writes:

> Perpetuation of a shaky equilibrium inherited from post-civil war arrangements has become the desirable status quo. Informal agreements negotiated on the margins of any formal, institutional framework have become factions' primary tool to overcome state paralysis and preserve their mutual interest in sustaining the system. Given their ad-hoc nature, such arrangements, susceptible to shifting domestic and regional dynamics, are imperfect, easily reversed, temporary stop-gaps, not durable solutions.

The twilight nature of political parties and their utility as vehicles for the realization of elite interests also has an economic dimension. Several, often dynastic families dominate business as well as politics (Chabaan, 2016; Diwan and Haidar, 2019; Nahas, 2012). In Lebanon, the political class is 'embedded in the private sector,' as 'most businessmen are former state officials and most politicians have some businesses' (Lebanese political analyst cited by Stel and Naudé, 2016: 264). The Lebanese political system is not just one of sectarian clientelism, it is essentially oligopolistic. In Lebanon, the combination of neoliberal capitalism and sectarianism has produced a situation of extreme inequality in which privatization is just another way to allocate spoils among Lebanon's governing elites. Instead of providing public goods, the Lebanese state 'allowed the existence of informal markets' to provide services (Uzelac and Meester, 2018: 37). The fact that such 'informal markets' are directly controlled by those associated with the country's sectarian elites has led commentators to talk about a 'mafiocracy' (El Mufti, 2012). Party leaders often do not claim official positions in government for themselves, but instead install trusted aides so that they are free to act as 'super-ministers', as an observer cited by the International Crisis Group (2015: 14) called them, 'whose power is greater but unofficial' and spans the state system, the private sector, and often civil society as well.

Uncertainty by consensus is thus not straightforward 'state capture.' The inherent heterogeneity and fragmentation of hybrid orders prevents any such unitary co-optation. Rather, it aligns with the understanding of hybridity that revolves around the twilight nature of political parties as outlined earlier. In Lebanon, state agencies are often associated directly with the party of the person who is heading it. In my interviews, for instance, the Ministry of Foreign Affairs, ran by the political leader of the Free Patriotic Movement who also happens to be the son-in-law of the President (affiliated with the same party), was discussed as a direct extension of that party, with interlocutors talking about 'the ministry of foreign affairs and other political parties'[16] or 'the ministry of foreign affairs and its constituents.'[17] At the same time, as a consequence of the sectarian quota system, ministries or other state departments are far from politically coherent, as different functions and positions within each agency have to be distributed across different sectarian groups and hence parties, which produces built-in centrifugal logics.

The systemic features of institutional ambiguity

Putting into conversation the notions of hybridity and ambiguity allows me to get at the structural dimensions of institutional ambiguity. It also contributes to debates on hybrid order by opening up the black box of hybridity. Linking hybrid order and institutional ambiguity enables us to go beyond the observation that orders are hybrid and gives us new analytical tools to study how and why they are hybrid. So how does Lebanon's hybrid political order that orbits around twilight governance actors institutionalize ambiguity? How does hybridity produce systemic uncertainty and unpredictability in Lebanon?

Under hybridity, the provision of services, the organization of security, and practices of representation, consultation, and accountability are highly informal in that they are importantly determined beyond the state system. In Lebanon, sectarian elite competition has produced overwhelmingly 'messy frameworks' and 'informal and uncodified institutions' and 'public,' 'private,' and 'communal' realms are institutionally entangled (Leenders, 2004: 16, 21; see also Nahas, 2012: 126). The contestation of such shifting boundaries has produced 'highly unpredictable and ambiguous outcomes' (Leenders, 2004: 16).

In addition to informality, the hybridity of Lebanon's political order also produces systemic liminality. Where institutional frameworks exist, they are routinely

'put on hold, often "temporarily," but without alternative regulations and procedures serving to guide routine operations' (Leenders, 2012: 120). Rules, regulations, and decisions are always subject to reconsideration and reinterpretation, but
this is particularly the case where such regulations are predominantly informal
and routinely politicized. Hage (2015: 11) describes Lebanese politics as being
in a 'permanent critical state' that puts a premium on short-term perspectives and
shrinks the space for long-term planning and imagining alternative orders. This
means that all forms of order that are arrived at are temporary and conditional,
which makes governance unstable and open-ended. Indeed, Carpi (2019) conceptualizes the Lebanese state as not just producing liminality but as inherently
liminal itself.

This form of liminality, in turn, constitutes exceptionalism. Entire state agencies – such as the Council for Development and Reconstruction that we will
encounter later – are subsequently created with the aim to 'circumvent the stalemates built into the political arrangement' and are thereby allowed to operate
beyond formal regulations (Leenders, 2012: 209). Because political-sectarian
leaders and their parties operate as twilight institutions that function inside as
well as beyond the state system, the application of the rule of law becomes a
matter of discretionary power. Reflecting on Lebanon's 'self-defeating survival
strategies,' the International Crisis Group (2015: 16) concluded: 'The constitution is violated at will; law-breaking is the norm and often goes unpunished; a
politicised judicial system guarantees impunity for the well-connected and human
rights abuse against vulnerable populations.' This does not herald the irrelevance
of formal rules and regulations, but it signifies how their implementation becomes
provisional and unpredictable.

In his seminal book on Lebanon's post-war political settlement, Leenders (2012)
shows in striking detail how institutional informality, liminality, and exceptionalism are built into the Lebanese state system as a result of fundamental hybridity.
Meticulous analyses of the bureaucratic operations of key state agencies – such as
the Ministry of Health, Middle East Airlines, and the Beirut Port Authority – and
of the quarry, reconstruction, and electricity sectors reveal that institutional ambiguity in terms of both regulation and implementation is the defining characteristic
of the Lebanese state system. Procedures and mandates for these various agencies
and sectors, are 'opaque, contradictory, ambiguous, or . . . nonexistent' (Leenders,
2012: 82–83). Such institutional ambiguity can follow from the hyper-presence
of institutions, the over-bureaucratization of procedures, as well as the absence of
policies and administrative structures (Halkort, 2019: 318).

Analyses of the workings of Lebanon's various security agencies, which are
perhaps the most potent state institutions the country has, arrive at similar conclusions. In his critical account of the often assumed capacity deficit of Lebanese
security agencies, Van Veen (2015: 6) warns 'that it would be a severe analytical
mistake to regard the inability of Lebanon's main state security organizations to
ensure either national or citizen-oriented security as a case of organizational dysfunction.' Instead, he argues, the organizational dysfunction of these agencies 'is

precisely the type of functionality desired by significant parts of Lebanon's elite and serves their purposes well' (Van Veen, 2015: 6; see also Nashabe, 2009). Mazzola's (2019) dissection of the linkages between senior state security officers and sectarian patrons similarly shows how the formal boundaries of the state system are deliberately blurred so that political elites can co-opt or constrain security agencies to create space for their own forms of provision and mediation.

This institutional ambiguity lies at the core of Lebanon's political settlement. The unwritten National Pact that premised Lebanese independence, the Lebanese constitution, and the Ta'if Accord that marked the end of the Civil War, Leenders (2012: 124) points out, are 'riddled with ambiguities about routine decision making.' The Lebanese constitution is 'deliberately vague and ambiguous,' for instance, when it comes to setting a number of ministries, demarcating the number of state positions someone may simultaneously occupy, stipulating deadlines for forming governments, or providing regulations for political parties (Batruni and Hallinan, 2018: 4; Sensenig-Dabbous, 2009: 2). The foundational agreements of Lebanese politics are similarly equivocal about the exact division of power of Lebanon's 'troika,' so that the President, Prime Minister, and Speaker of Parliament 'capitalize on any ambiguities' and interpret their mandates in their own favour (Leenders, 2012: 129). This inevitably places elites at loggerheads with each other and produces yet more deadlock and, to deal with this, improvised deal-making that entrenches exceptionalism.

Institutional ambiguity in this way serves three inter-related interests that validate the idea of a more strategic politics of uncertainty. First, as described earlier, it is instrumental in the intra-elite competition that defines Lebanese politics. But, second, it also serves shared elite interests in that institutional ambiguity precludes transparency, ensuring impunity for the endemic corruption of Lebanon's political class. Institutional ambiguity thus undermines accountability and serves the interests of Lebanon's elites. The underlying logic of allotment – allocating the spoils of public office – that follows from sectarian consociationalism means that governance is selective. The same institutions can be used to pave the way for some and obstruct the road for others. This points to the third aspect of the political utility of institutional ambiguity: It cements the relevance of Lebanon's elitist political parties as political mediators. To navigate Lebanon's 'minefield of administrative ambiguities,' citizens inescapably depend on the institutional peddling provided by the sectarian-political patrons who create and keep in place these ambiguities (Leenders, 2004: 1).

The structural interface between hybrid order and institutional ambiguity can be understood through the idea of aleatory sovereignty. Aleatory sovereignty emerges at the interface of multiple forms of power and makes governance unpredictable and apparently random. It refers to situations where 'there are so many interwoven projects, logics, goals, and anxieties of rule operating at once' that for most people these will be impossible to comprehend (Cullen Dunn and Cons, 2014: 102). In Lebanon, citizens, political authorities, and any other social organization will have to navigate such 'shifting landscapes of unpredictable power'

(Cullen Dunn and Cons, 2014), but to protect their interests and guard and extend their positions within hybrid settings, political authorities will not merely navigate institutional ambiguity. They may also use and extend it, seeking to 'maximize their returns on the state of confusion, uncertainty, and sometimes even chaos' that they are faced with (Chabal and Daloz, 1999: xix).

The twilight nature of the authorities that successfully navigate hybridity allows them to capitalize on what Tapscott (2017) calls fluid jurisdictions by constantly redefining what is and what is not the state's responsibility or mandate. This makes it unpredictable if, where, and how state agencies might intervene and which rules and regulations will be upheld when and for whom. Authorities can then sometimes outsource authority while claiming it back at other moments. This is further exacerbated by the strategic cultivation of ill-defined and overlapping mandates and hierarchies and the existence of parallel institutional structures. If societal organizations, other political actors, and citizens cannot meaningfully know what does and does not fall under state jurisdiction, they cannot coherently make claims on state agencies, which enhances state agencies' discretionary power. This will be particularly pertinent for refugees as they are not merely withheld many formal entitlements that citizens, at least nominally, have, but will also lack the socialization that allows Lebanese to at least to some extent navigate Lebanon's peculiar hybridities.

Institutional ambiguity is structurally premised. Hybrid sovereignty incentivizes the strategic extension of uncertainty through inaction and ambiguous action. The plurality and dynamism inherent in hybrid orders will often preclude decisive and explicit political action as this is mostly not politically opportune. Instead, inaction and ambiguous action will be more strategic to amass, maintain, and expand power in an aleatory governance field. The institutionalized nature of such inaction in Lebanon is broadly recognized (Baumann, 2019: 2; Salamay and Payne, 2008: 466). For Borgmann and Slim (2018: 12), a 'culture of denial' has defined Lebanon historically and 'substitutes for effective policy decisions.' Lebanon's post-war amnesia, Mourad and Piron (2016) similarly point out, means that a lot of social cleavages have to be ignored and hence cannot be acted upon if the genie of civil war is to be kept in its bottle.

Hybrid political order does not merely encourage inaction. It also puts a premium on ambiguous action. Like the original National Pact, most 'rules of the game' in Lebanon's hybrid political order are unwritten (El Mufti, 2012). The Lebanese policies that are written down are often vaguely formulated. This is a logical consequence of the ambiguity and non-committal of the programs of Lebanon's political parties, which, Hassan (2019: 2) shows, are routinely made up of positions that allow 'flexibility' and 'contradictions' on policy positions. Such ambiguity in policy positioning prevents key stakeholders, ranging from citizens and civil society to international donors, from holding the government accountable (Atallah, Dagher and Mahmalat, 2019: 1). In fact, inaction in one realm produces ambiguity in another realm. This is illustrated by Lebanon's information economy. For a state that depends on quota to maintain its illusion of power-sharing, statistics, or any other form of demographic information, are remarkably hard to come by. Evidence-based policy-making, El-Ghali and Baalbaki (2017: 18) reveal, hardly takes place or is at least not institutionalized. The rotation of bureaucrats that is dictated by sectarianism, moreover, undermines institutional continuity and learning. Looking specifically at the Lebanese response to the Syrian refugee crisis, Uzelac and Meester (2018: 26) conclude that in many cases data is either not produced or of questionable quality, 'making it subject to various interpretations and contentious debate.'

Institutional ambiguity, then, is a defining trait of the Lebanese state. It is a structural characteristic of sectarian hybridity and follows from and facilitates the 'twilight' nature of the parties through which the country's sectarian socio-political and economic elites have organized themselves. Hybrid order produces institutional ambiguity directly, by structurally entrenching it, and indirectly, by incentivizing political actors to reproduce it. It is well-recognized that institutional disarray serves the interests of elites as an instrument to trump competitors. My book builds on this observation and extends it by arguing that institutional ambiguity is not just a generic cause and consequence of inter-elite competition, but can also serve as a more concerted elite strategy to govern particular societal groups. Looking at refugee governance, in the upcoming chapters I show how under hybrid political order, political authorities do not utilize institutional ambiguity only to navigate hybridity and uphold and extend power within it, but can and will leverage it in ways that enable the control, exploitation, and expulsion of refugees.

Notes

1 Author's interview with former advisor to the Minister of State for Displaced Affairs – Skype, 22 January 2018.
2 My book, as such, is concerned with the relations between refugees and the Lebanese state. Although 'state' and 'society' are of course crucially related, this is to say that I do not focus on the societal and private relations between Lebanese and Palestinian and Syrian refugees, which have often been far more hospitable (Serhan, 2019: 243).
3 Or hybrid in different ways. While this is often assumed, hybridity is certainly not exclusively applicable to 'non-Western' countries or conflict-affected settings. Bergh (2009: 45), for instance, shows that the hybrid political order notion needs neither a post-war nor a peace- or state-building context to be valuable. Processes of decentralization, privatization, and the proliferation of civil society also generate contexts the hybrid political order lens might help to illuminate (Hagmann and Hoehne, 2009: 49).
4 A detailed discussion of the causes, dynamics, and consequences of the Civil War is beyond the scope of this book. Please refer to Fisk (1990), Hanf and Salam (2003), Hirst (2010), and Traboulsi (2007).
5 Such interventions regard regional powers such as Saudi Arabia and Iran, but also Western states such as the United States and multi-lateral bodies such as the United Nations.
6 A 2011 demographic study by Statistics Lebanon found that 27 percent of the population are Sunni Muslim, 27 percent Shia Muslim, 21 percent Maronite Christian, 8 percent Greek Orthodox, 5 percent Druze, and 4 percent Greek Catholic, with the

remaining 7 percent belonging to smaller Christian denominations and other religious groups (Mencütek, 2019: 131). Such studies, however, are not formally acknowledged and do not impact the sectarian-consociational quota that are in effect.

7 Author's interview with former advisor to the Lebanese Minister of State for Displaced Affairs – Skype, 22 January 2018.

8 Author's interview – Skype, 9 April 2018.

9 Author's interview with former advisor to the Lebanese Government – Skype, 19 February 2018.

10 These parties are not officially limited to these sectarian communities and mostly convey a discourse of nationalism, but in practice serve as vehicles for sectarian interests.

11 A disaggregated analysis of each party – its institutional legacy, its engagement with ambiguity, and/or its positioning vis-à-vis refugees – is beyond the scope of this book, which posits that, without denying such crucial variations, the shared interests among Lebanon's political elites are crucial in understanding the ways in which institutional ambiguity functions to govern refugees.

12 Author's interview – Beirut, 23 July 2013.

13 Hezbollah is often considered the exception to the Lebanese rule. Its exceptionalism, however, lies in its 'foreign politics,' not in its parallel institutions. These are more extensive than those of other parties, but apart from its armed forces, not qualitatively different.

14 Author's interview – 27 July 2013.

15 This elite is fairly circumscribed. Leenders (2004: 4–5) shows that out of the 243 posts (ministers, prime ministers, vice ministers, and ministers of state) that were assigned in the period from 1989 until 2003, 177 posts were distributed among 49 persons who obtained these positions at least twice (and, he writes, in some cases, up to seven times) or held two posts simultaneously.

16 Author's interview with former advisor to a Lebanese Ministry – WhatsApp, 12 January 2018.

17 Author's interview with refugee protection expert of an international humanitarian organization – Skype, 18 January 2018.

References

Abrams, Philip. 1988. 'Notes on the Difficulty of Studying the State.' *Journal of Historical Sociology* 1, no. 1: 58–89.

Atallah, Sami. 2016. *Can Municipalities Take on the Refugee Crisis?* Beirut: Lebanese Center for Policy Studies.

Atallah, Sami. 2018. *Addressing Citizens' Concerns Is Not on the Parliament's Agenda.* Beirut: Lebanese Center for Policy Studies.

Atallah, Sami, Georgia Dagher and Mounir Mahmalat. 2019. *The CEDRE Reform Program Needs a Credible Action Plan.* Beirut: Lebanese Center for Policy Studies.

Atallah, Sami and Mohamad Diab. 2018. *Lebanon's MPs Don't Know Where Their Parties or Political Allies Stand on Key Issues.* Beirut: Lebanese Center for Policy Studies.

Bacik, Gokhan. 2008. *Hybrid Sovereignty in the Arab Middle East.* New York: Palgrave Macmillan.

Balthasar, Dominik. 2015. 'From Hybridity to Standardization: Rethinking State-Making in Contexts of Fragility.' *Journal of Intervention and State-Building* 9, no. 1: 26–47.

Batruni, Catherine and Markus Hallinan. 2018. *Government (Non-)Formation in Contemporary Lebanon: Sectarianism, Power-Sharing, and Economic Immobilism.* Beirut: Civil Society Knowledge Center and Lebanon Support.

Baumann, Hannes. 2019. 'The Causes, Nature, and Effect of the Current Crisis of Lebanese Capitalism.' *Nationalism and Ethnic Politics* 25, no. 1: 61–77.

Belhadj, Souhaïl, Chris van der Borgh, Rivke Jaffe, Megan Price, Nora Stel and Michael James Warren. 2015. *Plural Security Provision in Beirut*. The Hague: Knowledge Platform for Security and Rule of Law.

Bergh, Sylvia. 2009. 'Traditional Village Councils, Modern Associations, and the Emergence of Hybrid Political Orders in Rural Morocco.' *Peace Review: A Journal of Social Justice* 21: 45–53.

Bierschenk, Thomas and Jean-Pierre Olivier de Sardan. 1997. 'Local Powers and a Distant State in Rural Central African Republic.' *The Journal of Modern Africa Studies* 35, no. 3: 441–468.

Boege, Volker, Anne Brown and Kevin Clements. 2009. 'Hybrid Political Orders, Not Fragile States.' *Peace Review: A Journal of Social Justice* 21: 13–21.

Boege, Volker, Anne Brown, Kevin Clements and Anna Nolan. 2008. 'On Hybrid Political Orders and Emerging States.' *Berghof Handbook* no. 8: 1–21.

Borgmann, Monika and Lokman Slim. 2018. *Fewer Refugees, More Refugeeism*. Beirut: Umam Documentation and Research and Institut for Auslandsbeziehunger.

Carpi, Estella. 2016. *Crisis and Control: (In)Formal Hybrid Security in Lebanon*. Beirut: Netherlands Organization for Scientific Research, International Alert, and Lebanon Support.

Carpi, Estella. 2019. 'Winking at Humanitarian Neutrality: The Liminal Politics of the State in Lebanon.' *Anthropologica* 61: 83–96.

Catusse, Myriam and Karam Karam. 2010. 'A Return to Partisan Politics? Partisan Logics and Political Transformations in the Arab World.' In *Returning to Political Parties? Partisan Logic and Political Transformations in the Arab World*, edited by Maryam Catusse and Karam Karam, 11–59. Beirut: Lebanese Center for Policy Studies.

Chabaan, Jad. 2016. *I've Got the Power. Mapping Connections Between Lebanon's Banking Sector and the Ruling Class*. Giza: The Economic Research Forum.

Chabal, Patrick and Jean-Pascal Daloz. 1999. *Africa Works: Disorder as Political Instrument*. London: The International African Institute (in Association with James Curry, Oxford and Indiana University Press, Bloomington and Indianapolis).

Cullen Dunn, Elizabeth and Jason Cons. 2014. 'Aleatory Sovereignty and the Rule of Sensitive Spaces.' *Antipode* 46, no. 1: 92–109.

Das, Veena and Deborah Poole, eds. 2004. *Anthropology in the Margins of the State*. Santa Fe: School of American Research Press.

Diwan, Ishac and Jamal Haidar. 2019. 'Clientelism, Cronyism, and Job Creation in Lebanon.' In *Crony Capitalism in the Middle East – Business and Politics from Liberalization to the Arab Spring*, edited by Ishac Diwan and Adeel Malik, 119–145. Oxford: Oxford University Press.

El-Ghali, Hana A. and Noor Baalbaki. 2017. *Perspectives on Policy-Making: Insights into the Role of the Parliament in Lebanon*. Beirut: Westminster Foundation for Democracy, American University of Beirut Policy Institute, and Issam Fares Institute for Public Policy and International Affairs.

El-Husseini, Rola. 2004. 'Lebanon: Building Political Dynasties.' In *Arab Elites: Negotiating the Politics of Change*, edited by Volker Perthes, 240–266. London: Lynne Rienner Publisher.

El Mufti, Karim. 2012. 'Lebanon Downhill, a Mafiocracy in Action.' *The Beirut Enterprise*, 15 July.

Fisk, Robert. 1990. *Pity the Nation: The Abduction of Lebanon*. Oxford: Oxford University Press.

Fregonese, Sara. 2012. 'Beyond the "Weak State": Hybrid Sovereignties in Beirut.' *Environment and Planning D: Society and Space* 30: 655–674.

Ghaddar, Sima. 2016. *Machine Politics in Lebanon's Alleyways*. New York: The Century Foundation.

Ghanem, Nizar. 2016. *Local Governance Under Pressure. Research on Social Stability in T5 Area, North Lebanon*. Arezzo: Oxfam Italia.

Gupta, Akhil. 1995. 'Blurred Boundaries: The Discourse of Corruption, the Culture of Politics, and the Imagined State.' *American Ethnologist* 22, no. 2: 375–402.

Gupta, Akhil. 2012. *Red Tape: Bureaucracy, Structural Violence, and Poverty in India*. Durham: Duke University Press.

Hage, Ghassan. 2015. *Alter Politics: Critical Anthropology and the Radical Imagination*. Melbourne: Melbourne University Press.

Hagmann, Tobias and Markus Hoehne. 2009. 'Failures of the State Failure Debate: Evidence from the Somali Territories.' *Journal of International Development* 21: 42–57.

Hagmann, Tobias and Didier Péclard. 2010. 'Negotiating Statehood: Dynamics of Power and Domination in Africa.' *Development and Change* 41, no. 4: 539–562.

Halkort, Monika. 2019. 'Decolonizing Data Relations: On the Moral Economy of Data Sharing in Palestinian Refugee Camps.' *Canadian Journal of Communication* 44: 317–329.

Hanf, Theordor and Nawaf Salam, eds. 2003. *Lebanon in Limbo: Postwar Society and State in an Uncertain Regional Environment*. Baden-Baden: Nomos Verlagsgesellschaft.

Hansen, Thomas Blom and Finn Stepputat, eds. 2001. *States of Imagination: Ethnographic Explorations of the Postcolonial State*. Durham: Duke University Press.

Harb, Mona and Sami Atallah, eds. 2015. *Local Governments and Public Goods: Assessing Decentralization in the Arab World*. Beirut: The Lebanese Center for Policy Studies.

Hassan, Nizar. 2019. *Where Do Lebanese Political Groups Stand on Policy Questions? An Analysis of Electoral Platforms*. Beirut: Lebanese Center for Policy Studies.

Hazbun, Waleed. 2016. 'Assembling Security in a "Weak State": The Contentious Politics of Plural Governance in Lebanon Since 2005.' *Third World Quarterly* 37, no. 6: 1053–1070.

Hermez, Sami. 2015. 'When the State Is (N)ever Present: On Cynicism and Political Mobilization in Lebanon.' *Journal of the Royal Anthropological Institute* 21: 507–523.

Hirst, David. 2010. *Beware of Small States: Lebanon, Battleground of the Middle East*. London: Faber and Faber.

Hoffmann, Kasper and Tom Kirk. 2013. *Public Authority and the Provision of Public Goods in Conflict-Affected and Transitioning Regions*. London: Justice and Security Research Programme.

Hudson, Michael C. 1968. *The Precarious Republic: Political Modernization in Lebanon*. Boulder: Westview Press.

International Crisis Group. 2015. *Lebanon's Self-Defeating Survival Mechanisms*. Brussels: International Crisis Group.

Ismail, Salwa. 2006. *Political Life in Cairo's New Quarters: Encountering the Everyday State*. Minneapolis: University of Minnesota Press.

Joseph, Gilbert M. and Daniel Nugent, eds. 1994. *Everyday Forms of State Formation: Revolution and the Negotiation of Rule in Modern Mexico*. Durham: Duke University Press.

Joseph, Suad. 2011. 'Political Familism in Lebanon.' *Annals of the American Academy of Political and Social Science* 636: 150–163.

Kingston, Paul. 2004. 'States-Within-States: Historical and Theoretical Perspectives.' In *States-Within-States: Incipient Political Entities in the Post-Cold War Era*, edited by Paul Kingston and Ian S. Spears, 1–13. New York: Palgrave Macmillan.

Kisirwani, Maroun. 1997. 'Accountability of Lebanese Civil Servants: An Overview of Disciplinary Mechanisms.' In *Lebanon Beyond 2000*, edited by Amin Saikal and Geoffrey Jukes. Canberra: Australian National University, Centre of Middle Eastern and Central Asian Studies.

Klem, Bart. 2012. 'In the Wake of War: The Political Geography of Transition in Eastern Sri Lanka.' PhD thesis, University of Zurich.

Knudsen, Are. 2009. 'Widening the Protection Gap: The "Politics of Citizenship" for Palestinian Refugees in Lebanon, 1948–2008.' *Journal of Refugee Studies* 22, no. 1: 51–73.

Kosmatopoulos, Nikolas. 2011. 'Towards an Anthropology of "State Failure": Lebanon's Leviathan and Peace Expertise.' *Social Analysis* 55, no. 3: 115–142.

Kyed, Helene Maria. 2017. 'Hybridity and Boundary-Making: Exploring the Politics of Hybridization.' *Third World Thematics* 2, no. 4: 464–480.

Lebanese Center for Policy Studies. 2019. *The Government Monitor No. 4: 1 Reform in 100 Days*. Beirut: Lebanese Center for Policy Studies.

Leenders, Reinoud. 2004. 'In Search of the State: The Politics of Corruption in Post-War Lebanon.' Unpublished essay.

Leenders, Reinoud. 2012. *Spoils of Truce: Corruption and State-Building in Postwar Lebanon*. Ithaca and London: Cornell University Press.

Lund, Christian. 2006. 'Twilight Institutions: Public Authority and Local Politics in Africa.' *Development and Change* 37, no. 4: 685–705.

Mazzola, Francisco. 2019. 'Mediating Security – Hybridity and Clientelism in Lebanon's Hybrid Security Sector.' In *Hybrid Governance in the Middle East and Africa: Informal Rule and the Limits of Statehood*, edited by Ruth Hanau Santini, Abel Polese and Rob Kevlihan. London: Routledge.

Mencütek, Zeynep. 2019. *Refugee Governance, State and Politics in the Middle East*. London: Routledge.

Menkhaus, Ken. 2006. 'Governance in the Hinterland of Africa's Weak States: Toward a Theory of the Mediated State.' Paper presented at the annual meeting of the American Political Science Association, Philadelphia, 30 August–2 September.

Migdal, Joel S. 2001. *State in Society: Studying how States and Societies Form and Constitute One Another*. Cambridge: Cambridge University Press.

Migdal, Joel S. and Klaus Schlichte. 2005. 'Rethinking the State.' In *The Dynamics of States: The Formation and Crisis of State Domination*, edited by Klaus Schlichte, 1–40. Aldershot: Ashgate.

Mitchell, Timothy. 1990. 'Society, Economy, and the State Effect.' In *State/Culture: State-Formation After the Cultural Turn*, edited by George Steinmetz, 76–97. Ithaca: Cornell University Press.

Mouawad, Jamil. 2015. 'The Negotiated State: State-Society Relations in Lebanon.' PhD dissertation, School of Oriental and African Studies.

Mouawad, Jamil and Hannes Baumann. 2017. 'Wayn al Dawla? Locating the Lebanese State in Social Theory.' *Arab Studies Journal* XXV, no. 1: 66–90.

Mourad, Lama and Laure-Hélène Piron. 2016. *Municipal Service Delivery, Stability, Social Cohesion and Legitimacy in Lebanon: An Analytical Literature Review*. Beirut: Issam Fares Institute for Public Policy and International Affairs.

Nahas, Charbel. 2012. 'The Lebanese Socio-Economic System, 1985–2005.' In *The Arab State and Neo-Liberal Globalization: The Restructuring of State Power in the Middle East*, edited by Laura Guazzone and Daniela Pioppi, 125–157. Reading: Ithaca Press.

Nashabe, Omar. 2009. 'Security Sector Reform in Lebanon: Internal Security Forces and General Security.' The Arab Reform Initiative, unpublished document.

Obeid, Michelle. 2010. 'Searching for the "Ideal Face of the State" in a Lebanese Border Town.' *Journal of the Royal Anthropological Institute* 16: 330–346.

Office for the Minister of State for Administrative Reform. 2011. *Strategy for the Reform and Development of Public Administration in Lebanon*. Beirut: Office for the Minister of State for Administrative Reform.

Olivier de Sardan, Jean-Pierre. 2008. *Researching the Practical Norms of Real Governance in Africa*. London: Africa Power and Politics Programme.

Perdigon, Sylvain. 2015. '"For Us It Is Otherwise": Three Sketches on Making Poverty Sensible in the Palestinian Refugee Camps of Lebanon.' *Current Anthropology* 56, no. 11: 88–96.

Raeymaekers, Timothy, Ken Menkhaus and Koen Vlassenroot. 2008. 'State and Non-State Regulation in African Protracted Crises: Governance without Government?' *Afrika Focus* 21, no. 2: 7–21.

Ramadan, Adam and Sara Fregonese. 2017. 'Hybrid Sovereignty and the State of Exception in the Palestinian Refugee Camps in Lebanon.' *Annals of the American Association of Geographers* 107, no. 4: 949–963.

Risse, Thomas, ed. 2013. *Governance Without a State? Policies and Politics in Areas of Limited Statehood*. New York: Columbia University Press.

Risse, Thomas and Ursula Lehmkuhl. 2007. *Governance in Areas of Limited Statehood – New Modes of Governance?* Berlin: Freie Universität.

Salamay, Imad and Rhys Payne. 2008. 'Parliamentary Consociationalism in Lebanon: Equal Citizenry vs. Quotated Confessionalism.' *The Journal of Legislative Studies* 14, no. 4: 451–473.

Scheye, Eric. 2009. *State-Provided Services, Contracting Out, and Nonstate Networks*. Paris: Organization for Economic Co-Operation and Development.

Sensenig-Dabbous, Eugene. 2009. *The Lebanese Political Party System*. Bucharest: Middle East Political and Economic Institute.

Serhan, Waleed. 2019. 'Consociational Lebanon and the Palestinian Threat of Sameness.' *Journal of Immigrant and Refugee Studies* 17, no. 2: 240–259.

Sharma, Aradhana and Akhil Gupta, eds. 2006. *The Anthropology of the State: A Reader*. Malden: Blackwell Publishing.

Stel, Nora. 2015. 'Lebanese-Palestinian Governance Interaction in the Palestinian Gathering of Shabriha, South Lebanon – A Tentative Extension of the "Mediated State" from Africa to the Mediterranean.' *Mediterranean Politics* 20, no. 1: 76–96.

Stel, Nora. 2016. 'Languages of Stateness in South Lebanon's Palestinian Gatherings: The PLO's Popular Committees as Twilight Institutions.' *Development and Change* 47, no. 3: 446–471.

Stel, Nora. 2017. 'Mediated Stateness as a Continuum: Exploring the Changing Governance Relations Between the PLO and the Lebanese State.' *Civil Wars* 19, no. 3: 348–376.

Stel, Nora and Chris van der Borgh. 2017. 'Political Parties and Minority Governance in Hybrid Political Orders: Reflections from Lebanon's Palestinian Settlements and Kosovo's Serbian Enclaves.' *Journal of Intervention and State-Building* 11, no. 4: 490–510.

Stel, Nora and Irna van der Molen. 2015. 'Environmental Vulnerability as a Legacy of Violent Conflict: A Case Study of the 2012 Waste Crisis in the Palestinian Gathering of Shabriha, South Lebanon.' *Conflict, Security and Development* 15, no. 4: 387–414.

Stel, Nora and Wim Naudé. 2016. '"Public-Private Entanglement": Entrepreneurship in Lebanon's Hybrid Political Order.' *Journal of Development Studies* 52, no. 2: 254–268.

Takieddine, Suleiman. 2004. 'An Independent Judiciary for a Better Justice.' In *Options for Lebanon*, edited by Nawaf Salam, 23–50. London: I.B. Tauris.

Tapscott, Rebecca. 2017. 'Local Security and the (Un)Making of Public Authority in Gulu, Northern Uganda.' *African Affairs* 116, no. 462: 39–59.

Traboulsi, Fawwaz. 2007. *A History of Modern Lebanon*. London: Pluto Press.

Trouillot, Michel-Rolph. 2001. 'The Anthropology of the State in the Age of Globalization: Close Encounters of the Deceptive Kind.' *Current Anthropology* 42, no. 1: 125–138.

Uzelac, Ana and Jos Meester. 2018. *Is There Protection in the Region? Leveraging Funds and Political Capital in Lebanon's Refugee Crisis*. The Hague: Clingendael Institute.

Van Overbeek, Fons. 2014. *Studying "the State" in Bukavu: A System, an Idea, and a Process*. Wageningen: Wageningen University.

Van Veen, Erwin. 2015. *Elites, Power, and Security: How the Organization of Security in Lebanon Serves Elite Interests*. The Hague: Clingendael Institute.

Verdeil, Éric. 2018. 'Infrastructure Crises in Beirut and the Struggle to (Not) Reform the Lebanese State.' *Arab Studies Journal* XVI, no. 1: 84–112.

Wickham-Crowley, Timothy P. 1987. 'The Rise (and Sometimes Fall) of Guerrilla Governments in Latin America.' *Sociological Forum* 2, no. 3: 473–499.

Wiuff Moe, Louise. 2011. 'Hybrid and Everyday Political Ordering: Constructing and Contesting Legitimacy in Somaliland.' *The Journal of Legal Pluralism and Unofficial Law* 43, no. 63: 143–177.

Chapter 2

The governance of Syrian refugees in Lebanon

No-policy-policy and formal informality

When you see the level of bureaucracy and complications that the Syrians have to go through in order to request legal status, you understand that this is intentional because the authorities can simplify the residency process and have a better distribution of capacities and resources. Due to these complications and ambiguity in the process, it's become very difficult for lawyers to assist Syrians and guide them through the process. One of the biggest fears of every Syrian in Lebanon is to hand over their passport to the General Security, because they never know if or when they would get it back.[1]

This first empirical chapter turns towards Lebanon's response to the Syrian refugee arrival, focusing on the political and policy dynamics that have shaped Lebanon's national response to the Syrian refugee 'crisis.' After providing a brief historical contextualization of the relations between Lebanon and Syria, the chapter proceeds with three sections. It first traces the evolution from a 'no-policy-policy' to a situation of 'formalized informality,' describing the emergence of institutional ambiguity in Lebanon's governance of Syrian refugees. The subsequent section turns to the consequences of this institutional ambiguity and chronicles the manufactured vulnerability that followed in its wake. The chapter's third section engages with the partially strategic drivers of institutional ambiguity. By means of a series of in-depth vignettes, it demonstrates how the institutional ambiguity that has shaped much of Lebanon's national response is at times, at least to some extent, the manifestation of a politics of uncertainty.

The data that underlie the analysis presented in this chapter comprise extensive desk research and 34 in-depth, semi-structured interviews and 18 more informal conversations with people involved in the development of Lebanon's response to the arrival of Syrian refugees.[2] These conversations with state officials, ministerial consultants, humanitarian professionals, and researchers, journalists, and activists revolved around both the formal and informal decision-making dynamics to address this 'crisis,' exploring questions such as: How and why were certain national decisions on how to (not) engage with the refugee presence made? How can watershed moments be explained? and What are the rationales and interests that drive fragmentation, ambiguity, and inconsistency and how have these evolved?[3]

Context and history

The Syrian conflict internally displaced 6.5 million people and forced more than 6 million others to flee abroad, overwhelmingly to neighboring countries. The number of Syrian refugees in Lebanon is extremely contested, as will be discussed in detail in one of the vignettes presented later in this chapter. In Spring 2018, there were 995,512 registered Syrian refugees in Lebanon and an estimated half million refugees that are not registered with the United Nations High Commissioner for Refugees (UNHCR) (Janmyr, 2018).[4]

The socio-economic, cultural, and political histories of Lebanon and Syria are closely intertwined. Until independence in 1943, the two countries were part of the same province in the larger Ottoman Empire and under the same French colonial system. In more recent history, the de facto occupation of Lebanon by Syria has intensified their economic and political entanglement. After intervening in the Lebanese Civil War in 1976, the establishment of the Arab Deterrent Force, which consisted of 90 percent Syrian soldiers, allowed a Syrian military presence in Lebanon that lasted until 2005. The 1990 Ta'if Agreement that ended the Lebanese Civil War in 1990 describes the 'fraternal' connection between the two countries as 'a special relationship that derives its strength from the roots of blood ties, history, and joint brotherly interests' (Atallah and Mahdi, 2017: 11). In practice, this meant Syrian hegemony over Lebanon, which was extended throughout domestic and foreign politics.

After the killing of previous Prime Minister Rafiq Hariri in 2005, there were massive public protests against the Syrian presence in Lebanon, which was seen as responsible for, or at least complicit in, this assassination. Protesters demanded Syria's compliance with United Nations Security Council Resolution 1559, adopted the previous year, that requested Syria to withdraw from Lebanon to enable free and fair presidential elections. The uprising indeed led to the withdrawal of Syrian troops in Lebanon and ended the post-war *pax Syriana* characterized by overt Syrian tutelage in Lebanon. The Syrian regime nevertheless continued to wield significant influence over the country in the post-2005 period through its political allies. These developments, moreover, divided Lebanon's political landscape into two distinct alliances determined by their relation to Syria: March 8 and March 14, referring to the respective pro- and anti-Syrian rallies that were held on these dates in 2005.

Syria's engagement with Lebanon was never only political, but had important economic aspects as well. These economic ties outlived the Syrian military presence in Lebanon. After independence, 'good neighborliness' resulted in various bilateral treaties between the countries, such as the 1964 Treaty of Brotherhood, Cooperation, and Coordination, that ensured labour privileges for Syrians in Lebanon and an 'open border' between the countries. Since the 1970s, vast numbers of Syrian workers have done most of the work in Lebanon's construction and agriculture sectors. In the years before the outbreak of the Syrian War, Lebanon counted between 300,000 and 400,000 Syrian migrant workers (Fakhoury, 2017: 684).

Thus, apart from many forms of socio-cultural proximity and genuine hospitality for refugees, in contemporary Lebanon a 'vivid memory of humiliation, killings and arbitrary power over Lebanese citizens' importantly feeds resentment vis-à-vis anything Syrian (Meier, 2014: 4). The sense of socio-economic and cultural superiority that is broadly felt among Lebanese towards Syrians, which was fueled by decades of associating 'Syrians' with menial labour, further affects governmental and societal engagement with them. Many Lebanese consider the majority of Syrians presently in the country as guest workers overstaying their welcome rather than 'genuine' refugees (Ghanem, 2016: 48).

The emergence of institutional ambiguity

In combination with the hybridity described in the previous chapter, the described Lebanese ambivalence towards Syria and Syrians resulted in extensive institutional ambiguity in the way in which Lebanon has governed the presence of Syrian refugees. This section outlines how this institutionalization of informality, liminality, and exceptionalism has emerged throughout two distinct phases – 'no-policy-policy' before and 'formal informality' after the formulation of the October 2014 'policy' – and how both phases were underpinned by the same fundamental forms of inaction and denial in terms of refugee status, refugee shelter, and refugee representation.

No-policy-policy

There was no plan or response mechanism in place when Syrian refugees started to arrive in Lebanon in 2011. In 2010, the Prime Minister's Office had formed a committee to develop a framework for a national response plan to deal with emergencies. But the committee's draft plan, spearheaded by the Ministry of Social Affairs, was never actually approved or implemented (Helou, 2014: 41). Instead, in 2011, the Prime Minister's Office requested the High Relief Commission to deal with the Syrian refugees who were located predominantly in North Lebanon at that time. This initiative included a joint registration process of refugees by the Ministry of Social Affairs and the UNHCR, but was never taken beyond the North and was abandoned when the refugee presence escalated to different regions (Helou, 2014: 114).

In 2012, after a civil society campaign that urged the government to come up with a 'roadmap' or 'masterplan' to deal with the refugee crisis and under increasing pressure from the UNHCR, the government formed an Inter-Ministerial Committee, comprising the High Relief Commission and all relevant ministries, to coordinate the response to the Syrian refugee 'crisis.' However, according to a policy advisor who has worked for various ministries, the Inter-Ministerial

Committee was 'not founded through any official documentation' and 'functions without a clear response strategy or a contingency plan' (Helou, 2014: 42). In December 2012, for instance, then Prime Minister Mikati presented a 'Response Plan to the Crisis of Displaced Families from Syria' at a donor meeting, but this plan was never formally adopted (Helou, 2014: 122).

As a result, Lebanon's initial engagement with Syrian refugees was characterized by what analysts have called a 'no-policy-policy' (see Ghaddar, 2017; Hamdan and Bou Khater, 2015: 35; Mencütek, 2019: 130; El Mufti, 2014; Nassar, 2014 in Nassar and Stel, 2019). Initiatives were developed by various ministries, such as the Ministry of Interior's 2013 'Security Plan,' but these were not official public policies (Mourad, 2017: 54). The 2013 'Lebanon Roadmap of Priority Interventions for Stabilization From the Syrian Conflict,' to give another example, provided an outline for the government to deal with the effect of the refugee crisis on Lebanese citizens, but it disregarded the situation of refugees and was mostly not implemented (Hamdan and Bou Khater, 2015: 23 in Nassar and Stel, 2019: 47). This inaction extends to the fact that the refugee presence has not been addressed by the Lebanese Parliament and has been eschewed by the National Dialogue, the platform through which Lebanon's main political elites seek to deal with 'intractable issues' (Fakhoury, 2017: 687).

Several intertwined factors underlie this initial no-policy-policy. First, Syrian refugees arrived in Lebanon when it was facing one of its decision-making stalemates (Hamdan and Bou Khater, 2015: 34; Janmyr, 2016: 59). In 2011, Lebanon faced a presidential vacuum, and its political elites were extremely divided, making the necessary consensus on any policy formulation impossible. To further complicate things, this polarization was exactly about the Syrian War and its geopolitical as well as domestic implications, with some parties supporting the Syrian regime and others the resistance. In this context, any formulation of an approach towards the growing refugee crisis proved impossible. Instead, the government focused on proclaiming the country's neutrality in the Syrian War and formulated a dissociation policy in the 2012 Baabda Declaration.

Second, this focus on dissociation from the war and the lack of engagement with the associated refugee crisis also stemmed from the widespread belief that the refugee presence would be temporary. Part of this assumption must have been wishful thinking from the beginning, but with the Palestinian experience of decades of contentious refugee presence in mind, acknowledging any possibility of yet another protracted refugee situation was a political taboo. Stressing, even actively ensuring, the temporary nature of the Syrians' presence was crucial (Janmyr and Mourad, 2018a: 556; Yassin et al., 2015: 32).

Third, apart from a policy-making vacuum, there was also a lack of a legal framework on how to deal with the Syrian people fleeing to Lebanon. Lebanon has not ratified the 1951 Convention relating to the Status of Refugees and the 1967 Protocol relating to the Status of Refugees. Although it has signed a number of relevant international human rights law instruments and the Lebanese constitution reinstates the country's commitments to these human rights principles, which include the right to seek and enjoy asylum, in practice this is not adhered to (Janmyr, 2016; Stevens, 2017). In addition, Lebanon has ratified regional agreements on refugee issues only with such far-reaching reservations that it basically constitutes non-committal, and it does not have national laws to regulate the presence of refugees. Instead, Syrian refugees were dealt with according to the 1962 law on entry and stay of foreigners, but the implementation of this law was, according to Helou (2014: 41), undermined by a lack of capacity and institutional structure.[5]

Formal informality

With the adoption of a 'Policy Paper on Syrian Refugee Displacement' in October 2014, the phase of 'no-policy-policy' apparently came to an end (Nassar and Stel, 2019). On 24 October 2014, the Inter-Ministerial Committee tasked with coordinating the response to the Syrian refugee 'crisis' presented a 'policy paper' that was approved by the Lebanese government and backed by a confidence vote of the parliament. This one-page document puts forward three main goals: first, to reduce the numbers of refugees (through regulating entry and encouraging return 'by all means' (Uzelac and Meester, 2018: 19)); second, to extend security measures, including municipal registration and municipal policing capacities and practices; and, third, to assuage the impact of the 'crisis' by channeling the humanitarian response to host as well as refugee communities and restricting refugees' access to the labour market.

   In line with these priorities, the Lebanese government also got involved in developing a joint framework with the United Nations (UN) to coordinate the state's response with the humanitarian response. The resultant Lebanon Crisis Response Plan (LCRP) articulates three strategic priorities: ensuring humanitarian support for Syrian refugees and vulnerable Lebanese; building the capacity of the service delivery systems needed for this; and supporting Lebanon's overall stability (Nassar and Stel, 2019: 47). While the LCRP has a strategic dimension and aims at a comprehensive approach, it remains donor-driven, and the ministries involved have mostly not integrated the LCRP directives into existing policy and practice (Hamdan and Bou Khater, 2015: 30). Moreover, the LCRP itself is paradoxical because it remains unclear which laws actually underpin it and because it is inconsistent in terms of refugees' status and the related obligations of authorities (Janmyr, 2018; Mencütek, 2019: 169).

   The October 2014 policy paper was operationalized by means of a number of decisions and decrees that significantly reduced refugees' eligibility for admission, residency, and regularization. With regard to entry, in the first three years of the crisis, if they entered Lebanon through an official border crossing, all Syrians received an entry coupon free of charge that could be renewed every six months upon payment of a fee of US$200. However, this fee, clearly unaffordable for most refugees, was routinely avoided by Syrians. They would return to Syria simply to cross the border again and receive another free entry coupon.

Regulations that came into force on 5 January 2015, however, significantly restricted the number of refugees who are able to enter Lebanon.[6] From then on, Syrian nationals seeking to enter Lebanon would be admitted only if they adhered to one of the nine new visa categories that appear to have been specifically formulated to bar Syrian refugees (Nassar and Stel, 2019: 47): the one visa category that regards displaced people explicitly excludes those fleeing the conflict in Syria. All visa categories, moreover, require Syrians to produce elaborate and specified documentation, which they cannot afford and have trouble to obtain, before being allowed entry. The consequence of the new regulations, then, is that no new refugees can enter the country legally and that Syrians already present in Lebanon can no longer cross the border to avoid the status renewal fee (Hamdan and Bou Khater, 2015: 25).

For Syrians who entered Lebanon before these regulations were in place or who entered despite them, renewing or regularizing residency status has been made extremely difficult since October 2014 as well (Uzelac and Meester, 2018: 19). Syrian refugees in Lebanon can renew their legal residency with the General Security through two avenues: they either present a certificate of UNHCR registration and a pledge not to work signed by a notary in addition to a demonstration of financial means or they can opt for staying under the auspices of a Lebanese sponsor, in which case they have to present a pledge of responsibility of this sponsor (Janmyr and Mourad, 2018a: 553).[7] Because the UNHCR was forced to suspend registration in 2015, all refugees who failed to register with the UNHCR before that date are automatically excluded from the first avenue.

The new regulations put in place after October 2014 are thus extremely restrictive and, as discussed in further detail in the chapter's next section, have forced Syrians into destitution and illegality. They are also highly ambiguous. The Lebanese government's 'unprecedented policy involvement' after October 2014 did not actually produce more clarity (Mencütek, 2019: 149). Although the October 2014 policy paper marks a departure of inaction that typified the previous period, in many ways it signified the consolidation of earlier uncertainty. The various decisions and circulars that operationalized the policy were not transparently communicated to either the public or humanitarian partners. They were enforced in a manner that made Lebanon Support conclude that this policy in reality formalizes the exceptionalism that was produced under the first phase of 'no-policy-policy' (Lebanon Support, 2016 in Nassar and Stel, 2019: 47).

Lebanon's governance of Syrian refugees is not determined by law but by 'ministerial decrees, orders, and circulars' (Fakhoury, 2017: 687; Hamdan and Bou Khater, 2015: 34; Human Rights Watch, 2016; Janmyr, 2016: 66; see also Nassar and Stel, 2019: 48). In fact, the specific operational decrees that have put the October 2014 policy in practice are considered illegal by many experts. These decrees were issued by the General Security rather than by the government itself. After a lawsuit raised by the non-governmental organizations (NGOs) Legal Agenda and Frontiers Ruwad, a Lebanese lawyer involved in the process explained, the Lebanese court ruled that in issuing these regulations, 'the General Security was trespassing, or transgressing over the prerogatives of the government, because this was a matter for the government; refugee policy is a government matter, not a security agency matter.'[8] This ruling, however, has apparently remained without consequences. Thus, although hallowed as a fundamental shift in the government's response, the October 2014 policy, Mourad (2017: 251) notes, did not genuinely aim to 'render Syrians "legible" to Lebanese authorities but rather has served to make ambiguity and arbitrariness a central characteristic of policy.'

Legal and policy experts stress the incoherent formulation of the October 2014 policy and its operationalizing decrees as well as the piecemeal fashion in which they were communicated. The criteria for specifying the 'humanitarian cases' that provide the exception under which Syrian refugees can occasionally be granted entry under the October 2014 policy (through the category referring to 'displaced persons'), for instance, have not been made public and are thus at the complete discretion of specific officials if applied at all (Al-Masri, 2015: 13; Janmyr and Mourad, 2018a: 553). The same goes for the 'petition for mercy' that people who have irregularly entered the country can plead (Nassar and Stel, 2019: 48). This petition, and the accompanying fee of US$600, should regularize refugees' status, but Bidinger et al. (2014: 36) note: 'The success of such petition is entirely uncertain, as there are no policies or guidelines for the exercise of discretion by the GSO [General Security Office], and applicants cannot be represented by counsel in their proceedings.'

When I asked a lawyer and legal activist how, after years of 'no-policy-policy,' the relatively straightforward October 2014 policy impacted her work with Syrian refugees, she retorted my assumption of increased clarity. She explained that although the policy paper may have clarified some principles, the implementation mechanisms were far from clear. This was, for her, evident in the regulations that were issued by the General Security to establish specific entry and residency conditions. She indicated: 'I don't think that the regulations are clear! They're not written in the form of a legal decision, it has no signature, no date. It's just a table with several categories and no clear criteria. It looks quite unprofessional.'[9] She continued: 'Refugees are facing a lot of difficulty to understand in which category they fit, especially as these categories are not adapted to their situation.'

If the policies are far from clear, their implementation is even less coherent (Nassar and Stel, 2019; see also Frangieh, 2017; Mencütek, 2019: 154; Norwegian Refugee Council and International Rescue Committee, 2015: 6; Sanyal, 2018: 67; UNHCR, 2015: 12). Interpretations vary widely for each General Security office and even per officer within each office, Lebanon Support's (2016: 22) in-depth report on 'the incoherence, informality, and insecurity in the renewal process' concludes. A humanitarian regularly liaising with the General Security similarly noted that:

Everybody, every person could explain it [residency requirements] in his own way. So every office . . . sometimes explains the points differently. So they ask from people things the other offices didn't . . . don't ask from the people renewing through the same way the same things. So they ask for different papers or different things.[10]

A lawyer working with Syrian refugees explained that refugees are routinely held off and their procedures are delayed until relevant documents are no longer valid.[11] Amnesty International (2015: 15) notes that, when investigating the case of refugees who were turned back because their documents were only valid for a certain number of days after being stamped, it 'could not find any information on official deadlines related to documents for renewing residency.' Although denied by the General Security itself, such instances of discretionary refusal of residency renewal have also been extensively documented in cases where refugees provided all the relevant information (Janmyr, 2016; Janmyr and Mourad, 2018a: 553).

A Syrian interviewed by Lebanon Support (2016: 23) summarized: 'The people who work at General Security don't know anything about the laws.' Each General Security officer demands a different set of documents, and the chances of any document being accepted depend on the 'mood' of the officer in question (Lebanon Support, 2016: 23). The prevalence of such confusion, interlocutors working in the humanitarian field indicated, is constantly communicated to the General Security. But the General Security has apparently made little effort to clarify matters and systematic problems have been denied with reference to local capacity problems. Thus, the core tenet of the notion of a no-policy-policy – the absence of a coherent legal framework and a comprehensive and operationalized plan of action – is in essence still in place even after the October 2014 policy was issued. In 2015, Hamdan and Bou Khater (2015: 34) found that:

> The Government of Lebanon's response is not sufficiently clear and few brief documents state the policies and plans endorsed. Until now, the state response mainly consists of irregular decisions pertaining to different sectors without adequate coordination or synergies among them.

Writing in 2017, Atallah and Mahdi (2017: 38) conclude:

> The lack of political will and administrative capacity to respond to the crisis led to the absence of a national legal and policy framework for the refugee response. Micro-level policies are not part of a national framework, and local communities have the discretion to govern refugees as they see fit. Although the Lebanese Crisis Response Plan frames the international response to the Syrian humanitarian crisis by sector, a national strategy is required to outline the Lebanese state's national legislation toward Syrian refugees by defining the legal framework and jurisdiction of various actors responding to the crisis.

A 'set of nos'

Through these two distinctive phases, first a 'no-policy-policy' based on policy inaction and then a 'formalization of informality' that reflects policy ambiguity, the Lebanese government effectively leveled a regime of institutional ambiguity on Syrian refugees in the country. This institutional ambiguity is underpinned by what a senior advisor of the country's Ministry of Interior called a 'set of nos:' no refugees, no camps, no representation (Frangieh and Barjas, 2016; Mourad, 2017; Nassar and Stel, 2019). These 'nos' have served to make the status, spaces, and representational institutions that shape refugees' life informal, liminal, and exceptional.

Considering the first 'no,' the Lebanese government has refused to avoid recognizing Syrian refugees as refugees. Instead, it considers them 'displaced persons,' 'guests,' or 'de facto refugees' (Janmyr, 2016; Mourad, 2017). Indeed, the October 2014 policy is often referred to as the 'Zero Refugees' policy (Borgmann and Slim, 2018: 25). The convenient absence of a national and regional legal framework for refugees and the Lebanese state's non-ratification of the relevant international conventions has allowed Lebanon to deny formal refugee status to Syrians fleeing war. This allowed Lebanon to avoid commitment to refugee protection – because even if Lebanon is not a signatory to the 1951 Refugee Convention, however, it acknowledges that this does not absolve it from the obligations that host states have under international customary law (Nassar and Stel, 2019: 47). Widening the protection gap for refugees that is created in the absence of formal refugee status, the complex and arbitrary residency regime has subsequently stripped most 'de facto' refugees from legal residency status as well.

The second 'no' underlying Lebanon's response to the Syrian refugee presence in the country regards the decision not to allow refugee camps. Whereas the UNHCR has set up camps in Jordan and the government did so in Turkey, Lebanon prohibited the establishment of camps. There was initial covert support for sheltering Syrian refugees in formal camps by some political parties and humanitarian organizations, but the Lebanese government was too 'traumatized' by the Palestinian refugee experience to consider this option seriously (Carpi, Younes and AbiYaghi, 2016: 11; see also Dionigi, 2016: 22).[12] Refugee camps were regarded as a testimony and precursor of the long-term nature of displacement. The government, moreover, saw them as potential terrorist safe havens (Nassar and Stel, 2019: 47). This refusal to allow formal camps was a way to uphold the increasingly delusional idea that the refugee crisis would be short-term.

A third, less distinctive but equally profound 'no' that dictates Lebanon's governance of Syrian refugees is the credo of 'no representation.' This regards representation on the side of Syrian refugee communities. Nationally, Lebanon's dissociation policy ensured that the Lebanese government would not have to formally deal with representatives of either the Syrian regime or the opposition, which, for better or worse, left the Syrian refugee population in the country without any political representative. Locally, as detailed in the next chapter, there has been a clear directive from the Lebanese government to prevent any form of political mobilization or organization among refugee communities. 'No representation' also concerns the Lebanese side. In the early days of the crisis, the Ministry of Social Affairs and the High Relief Council led the response in the North, but an interlocutor working for these agencies at the time explained, further leadership by these agencies was subsequently politically blocked.[13] Instead, since then, a variety of agencies took on various tasks in an ad hoc fashion and without clear mandates, resulting in competition, overlap, and policy and implementation gaps and, ultimately, a lack of representation – a reality that is further discussed in the vignette about Lebanon's Minister of State for Displaced Affairs in the chapter's last section.

The LCRP, the formal joint approach of the Lebanese state and the humanitarian community to address the Syrian refugee crisis, does not in any way include direct Syrian representatives. Instead, it apparently assumes that the UNHCR acts on behalf of the refugees it is formally not allowed to recognize as such. But the basis on which NGOs and the United Nations (UN) are allowed to operate in Lebanon is itself ambiguous. Janmyr (2018: 395) describes the UN's presence as hardly formalized and its legal mandate as 'largely undefined.' UNHCR's operational space in Lebanon is in fact crucially curtailed by the absence of a host country agreement that regulates division of tasks and responsibilities between the UNHCR and the Lebanese government. This absence is despite the fact that host country agreements are routine aspects of the UNHCR's modus operandi in other countries and that the government has signed such agreements with some other UN agencies (Mourad, 2017: 255; Helou, 2014: 44).

There is a Memorandum of Understanding regarding the UNHCR's operations in Lebanon. But this Memorandum was signed, in 2013, by the General Security, not by the government, which limits its validity. It has, moreover, been heavily criticized, even been called a 'mistake' by UNHCR staff, for adopting 'a Lebanese perspective on refugees' that securitizes refugees and legitimized and institutionalized the notion of Lebanon as a 'non-asylum country' (Janmyr, 2018: 395, 2016: 63). In 2012, the UNHCR therefore drafted a more comprehensive Memorandum, stipulating specific procedures that were left undetermined in the 2003 version (which was designed to deal with individual asylum cases but not with a mass arrival of refugees). This new Memorandum was to be endorsed by the government (rather than the General Security). So far, however, it has not been signed and the UNHCR, Mencütek (2019: 142) concludes, continues to operate on a 'shaky legal authorization ground.' This ambiguity turns the UNHCR into a 'useful tool' for the government, which, as Uzelac and Meester (2018: 46) note, makes it 'vulnerable to government policy changes, pressures limiting the reach of its protection mandate and opportunistic attacks by Lebanese politicians for short-term political gains.'

These three fundamental 'no's' on behalf of the Lebanese government reveal that while there may be a lack of de jure policies to govern the presence of Syrian refugees in Lebanon, there are clear guiding principles, de facto policies, that underlie the country's engagement with refugees. These 'many unwritten agreements and unspoken rules of the game that determine the management of this crisis,' as an advisor to the Prime Minister's Office involved in the refugee response called them, put a premium on inaction and ambiguity.[14] As explored further in the next chapter, shirking formal engagement opens up room for more convenient informal engagement. Lebanese officials are of course well aware that there are in fact refugees in Lebanon, that despite the absence of formal camps there are hundreds of informal refugee settlements across the country, and that there are ample structures through which refugees organize and mobilize even if formal political parties and local committees are prohibited. Officially renouncing these realities, however, enables authorities to govern them with far more leeway.

Manufactured vulnerability

The fundamental denial and inaction ingrained in the 'set of nos' that dictates Lebanon's governance of Syrian refugees has distinct consequences. The institutional ambiguity produced by Lebanon's 'no-policy-policy' and 'formal informality' has contributed to extreme precariousness among Syrians. In terms of status, Syrian refugees are by and large forced into illegality.[15] In 2017, an estimated 74 percent of Syrian refugees in Lebanon did not have valid legal residency documents (UNHCR, United Nations Children's Fund and World Food Program, 2017), and 83 percent of Syrian children born in Lebanon since 2011 have not been registered (Yassin, 2018: 55).

This lack of official residency status is a root cause of refugees' vulnerability. Because illegally residing in the country is a criminal offense under Lebanese law, it makes refugees vulnerable to arrest and detainment (Atallah and Mahdi, 2017: 25). International Alert documented that approximately 1,000 Syrian refugees are arrested each month by the General Security because of 'documentation issues' and one-quarter of all Syrians held in Lebanese prisons are there on the basis of 'violations related to documentation' (Slavova, 2017: 2). This is even more marginalizing because the same 'illegality' that gets refugees arrested hampers their access to justice and complaint procedures (Slavova, 2017: 2). As the International Crisis Group (2015: 11) notes, lack of legal status makes refugees 'easy prey' for corrupt security officials and often results in forms of extortion by authorities, such as when refugees are forced to pay for identity cards issued by municipalities (see also Barjas, 2016; Uzelac and Meester, 2018: 21).

Without official residency status, refugees' access to services is also limited. Refugees are, for instance, regularly denied at hospitals when they do not have a legal residency and are not insured. That is if they can even reach a hospital. For refugees who do not have legal residency status, freedom of movement is severely circumscribed, as there are many checkpoints, both regular and ad hoc ones, in place where they risk arrest (Sanyal, 2018: 68). This constrained mobility also blocks refugees' access to livelihoods, with all the socio-economic implications and abuse this entails (UNHCR, United Nations Children's Fund and World Food Program, 2016: 1). In 2017, economic vulnerability among refugees increased, with over half of them living in extreme poverty (UNHCR, United Nations Children's Fund and World Food Program, 2017: 1). Despite the high levels of financial support that Lebanon has received in the past years, more than 50 percent of Syrian refugees live in extreme poverty and more than 75 percent live below the poverty line (Uzelac and Meester, 2018: 7).

Institutional ambiguity also marginalizes refugees in terms of shelter (Nassar and Stel, 2019). The absence of any shelter policy resulted in an unsystematic assemblage of de facto settlement and residency approaches (Yassin et al., 2015: 15). Because there are no formal refugee camps, Syrian refugees in Lebanon are all, as it is euphemistically called, 'self-settled.' The large majority of them, around 80 percent, lives in mostly substandard housing in urban or peri-urban settings. The remainder live in so-called informal tented settlements. Around 2,000 unofficial, mostly small-scale refugee camps are located predominantly in the Bekaa Valley and North Lebanon's Akkar region. In both cases, refugees are paying for their residency. Considering that they are largely barred from legal employment and severely exploited in the informal sector, this has meant additional vulnerability, for instance in the form of often enormous debts that most refugees have been forced to accrue.

The combination of lacking refugee and residency status and an absence of formal refugee protection spaces in the form of camps, moreover, makes refugees extremely vulnerable to extortion and abuse by the landlords from which they rent apartments, garages, land, or tents. Approximately 82 percent of refugees do not have written lease agreements with their landlords and tenancy arrangements are unstable (Amnesty International, 2015: 16; REACH and UNHCR, 2014: 26). Refugees mostly pay excessive rent for the substandard housing they inhabit, facing fundamental problems with construction, safety, and sanitation – and, in informal settlements, floods and fires (Thorleifsson, 2016: 1075). In informal settlements, apart from exploitation by landlords and employers, refugees are 'highly vulnerable to attack and harassment from local police or host populations,' which means they often hardly dare to leave these de facto camps, where they feel they are 'held captive' (Clarke, 2017: 19; Shawaf and El Asmar, 2017: 22). Self-settled refugees, because they are spatially dispersed, are less visible and accessible to humanitarian organizations, which further increases their predicament (Jacobsen, 2006 in Dorai, 2016; Janmyr and Mourad, 2018a: 554; Yassin et al., 2015: 38). This informal, liminal, and exceptional spatial reality that refugees in Lebanon face also leads to an ever imminent threat of eviction, as further explored in the next chapter.

The extremely curtailed and deliberately informalized forms of representation available to Syrian refugees in Lebanon further exacerbate their vulnerability. As detailed in the next chapter, lack of legal status and dispersed settlement combined with the divide-and-rule approach of Lebanese authorities have fragmented, paralyzed, and ultimately delegitimized forms of refugee representation that go beyond specific localities. The lack of representative structures and the low degree of organization among Syrian refugees is typical for the Lebanese situation (Mourad and Piron, 2016: 37). As Clarke (2017: 19) describes, in Lebanon, unlike in, for instance, Jordan, the informal leaders among Syrian refugee communities 'have not formed their own dense and hierarchical leadership networks.' They have been unable to mobilize the broad following or provide the mutual support and protection that would allow them to act and speak in the name of refugees vis-à-vis authorities. This has meant that, effectively, there is no way for refugees to collectively contest or mobilize against abuse. Instead, refugees are at the mercy of often exploitative local authorities and strongmen and rely on patronage networks with Lebanese and humanitarian agencies to address the many predicaments they face (Al-Masri and Altabbaa, 2016; Amnesty International, 2015; Lebanon Support, 2016; Mourad and Piron, 2016: 37).

Following Saghieh's (2015) work, the term 'manufactured' indicates that the described vulnerability is more than a contingency of the messy policy-making that characterizes the Lebanese response to the Syrian refugee arrival (see also Akesson and Coupland, 2018: 21). Rather, vulnerability is used to enable control, expulsion, and exploitation (Nassar and Stel, 2019). As ALEF (2018) noted in its reflection on the Brussels II donor conference that was held in April 2018, the regulations and decisions put forward are 'not only failing to patch the gaps in protection but often creating more of them.' While the October 2014 policy was allegedly supposed to formalize the refugee presence, in reality it 'widened the gap between refugees and the government' and forced refugees to 'live outside of the law' (Ghaddar, 2017). The residency regime installed through the October policy was, as Uzelac and Meester (2018: 18) conclude, 'made to be broken.'[16] Considering the implausibility of imposing high renewal fees on refugees largely precluded from working, it was always unlikely to produce its official objective of regularizing refugees in the country. Policy then becomes not only performative (Sanyal, 2018: 70), but, as we will see in the next sections, 'nonperformative.'

Imposed informality, liminality, and exceptionalism serves to generate politically convenient vulnerability. Lebanon's 'set of no's' creates fear, insecurity, and anxiety amongst refugees not merely through the direct disempowerment it produces, but also through the exceptional complexity and arbitrariness it generates. The next section explores the strategic dimensions of the institutional ambiguity that helps produce refugees' vulnerability.

A politics of uncertainty

In the prior section, I documented how institutional ambiguity and the marginalization it has helped produce stem from policy inaction and ambiguous policy-making and implementation. These forms of ambiguous (non-)policy often have structural causes. They are the systemic side effect of the generic institutionalized arbitrariness that helps to avoid responsibility and accountability and to maximize flexibility and discretion that was the focus of Chapter 1.

They reflect Lebanon's paralyzed and polarized political system, especially at the time when the first Syrian refugees arrived, which explains why many policies and initiatives that were drafted or discussed never formally saw the light of day (Fakhoury, 2017: 693).

But much of the furthering of institutional ambiguity and the vulnerability it generates is strategic to the specific context of the Syrian refugee situation as well. The default institutional ambiguity that is inherent in hybridity is further utilized and extended to serve particular interests in governing refugees. Concerted decisions were made and implemented by Lebanon's governing elites to eliminate, contain, and make use of the refugee 'crisis' (Stevens, 2017). In some cases, then, the generation and extension of institutional ambiguity served to prevent refugees' mobilization, facilitate their exploitation, and encourage their return. Political actors created or failed to redress legal and policy vacuums, thereby sowing confusion. The gaps that follow from such inaction and the maneuvering space left by such ambiguous action can then be opportunistically navigated according to intertwined political and socio-economic interests. As a development officer affiliated with an international development organization hypothesized when discussing the mass illegality of Syrian refugees in Lebanon:

> I mean by essentially removing from them the status of legality you make them much more insecure and precarious which then also presumably means that they won't do any of the things that the Lebanese government fears. For example, to mobilize politically as Palestinian refugees did. So, you know, by I guess stripping them of that legal security you create a persistent sense of fear and vulnerability that makes that population easier to control and manage.[17]

The three pillars of Lebanon's initial 'no-policy-policy' towards Syrian refugees as described earlier – political division and deadlock, a conviction that the crisis would be short-lived, and the lack of an appropriate legal framework to guide decision-making – are not simply systemic. As mentioned, former ministerial representatives and consultants and humanitarians that were involved in the early days of the response recall how in 2011, there was a coordinated response by the government (in the form of the High Relief Committee and the Ministry of Social Affairs) and the UN to address the arrival of refugees in North Lebanon, with the Ministry coordinating refugee registration. Six months into the crisis, however, according to these sources, a new cabinet decided not to expand this government-led response to the Bekaa province, which was by then also facing a large influx of refugees. Instead, it encouraged the UNHCR to take over. When I asked for the rationale behind this decision, an interlocutor who was working for various ministries and was closely involved in the response in North Lebanon during those days emphasized the complexities of political antagonism, the lack of funding, and the lingering hope that the Syrian refugees would soon return home. Yet, the government's decision not to engage further was, according to her recollections, first and foremost a form of denial. She said:

> When an expansion [of the government-led response from North Lebanon to the Bekaa] was requested it was rejected because they didn't want to acknowledge that 'yes we do have Syrians in other places and yes this might actually be a refugee crisis.' It was just a matter of politics.[18]

Similarly, the lack of a legal framework to deal with refugee issues is not an inevitable given, but reflects a political position, an 'unwillingness to host refugees,' according to Janmyr (2018: 394). Lebanon, Mencütek (2019: 34–35) concludes, 'intentionally avoid[s] developing concrete national refugee legislation and asylum institutions.' No-policy-policy, formal informality, and the set of nos do not just reflect circumstances, but choices as well. They bring to light limited capacities and resources, but also allocation decisions and a fundamental political reluctance to act (Dionigi, 2016: 10, 17). In the following section I present three vignettes related to the set of nos introduced previously that serve to illustrate in more detail the ways in which a politics of uncertainty partly shapes the governance of the Syrian refugee crisis in Lebanon.

Non-registration and blurred categorization: playing the 'numbers game'

Knowing who is who and who is where, in other words rendering legible a population, is usually assumed to be the basis for formulating policy. With regard to Syrian refugees, indeed, the Lebanese government, in the 'Lebanon Partnership Paper' that was published after the Brussels II conference, 'acknowledges the importance of having accurate data and statistics on the refugees present on its territory.' In practice, however, state authorities seem to have gone out of their way to avoid such legibility by abstaining from refugee registration. No official records of refugees are kept (Mencütek, 2019: 136). This is not simply due to a lack of capacity, but also reflects political will.

As described earlier, in 2011 there was a joint registration of Syrian refugees by the Ministry of Social Affairs and the UNHCR under the auspices of the High Relief Council. This process, however, was short-lived and only regarded North Lebanon. According to an advisor working for a Lebanese ministry, the Ministry of Social Affairs abandoned this because it was found to be too sensitive considering that registration was seen as acknowledging the potentially long-term stay of refugees.[19] Apparently, there was another attempt at centralized registration of refugees by the same ministry in 2015, but this initiative was never actually implemented. While the relevant office in the ministry was created, a civil society representative who closely followed this initiative explained, it was never seriously supported or capacitated.[20] Since 2017, there has been persistent talk of a national census of Syrian refugees in Lebanon, to be implemented by the Ministry of Interior, but so far this has not occurred either.

Thus, the General Security has monitored the entrance of Syrians at official border crossings and keeps track of Syrians' residency status, but the many people who entered 'illegally' elude these 'registrations.' Since 2014 municipalities are supposed to register the Syrian refugees present in their area, but, as the next chapter will show, such local registration is neither systematically controlled nor formally accumulated in a central database or overview. Central and official registration, instead, was left to the UNHCR. When, in 2015, UN-registered refugees counted more than the symbolic threshold of one million refugees, however, the government ordered the UNHCR to stop registration.[21] The fact that the Lebanese state has not only refrained from registration itself, but has also barred other organizations from doing so shows once more that Lebanon's non-registration of Syrian refugees is not merely due to resource problems, but reflects a choice for inaction.

Non-registration means that the Lebanese state does not have formal knowledge on the Syrian refugee population on its territory: 'Hundreds of thousands of people have become invisible to the authorities, absent from the state's registers, and outside of the state's purview' (Frangieh, 2017). The UNHCR states that in early 2018 there were 995,512 Syrian refugees in Lebanon. Yet this number does not include refugees that arrived after the UNHCR was ordered to stop its registration.[22] According to the 2017 LCRP, the country has 'welcomed around 1.5 million refugees' from Syria. Considering that the LCRP is coproduced by the UN and the Lebanese government, the Lebanese state thus admits the existence of some 500,000 non-registered refugees (Janmyr and Mourad, 2018a: 556).

The lack of definite and reliable statistics when it comes to the presence of Syrian refugees in Lebanon was a constant in my interviews. A Lebanese consultant working on Lebanon's engagement with Syrian refugees lamented:

> Everyone from the officials [is] saying different numbers about the number of refugees. If you go to hear the ministers or to hear the President or even the Prime Minister, you will listen to different numbers. There is no one number that you can present about the number of Syrian refugees in Lebanon.[23]

Officially, then, no one knows how many Syrian refugees there are in Lebanon. The crux here, however, is the word 'officially.' My interlocutors were confident that an official central database was no prerequisite for state (security) agencies to be able to know what they needed to know about refugees. They stressed that regardless of the lack of official registration, information on refugees is gathered in various ways – ranging from registration at the border, status renewal procedures with the General Security, surveillance at checkpoints and through raids by the State Security and police, and municipal registers. A former representative of the Minister of State for Displaced Affairs described this simultaneous formal ignorance and informal awareness as 'it's like what we know and what we don't know at the same time; so it's not officially said, but it's known.'[24]

This shows that registration is not about generating information but about allocating entitlement. State authorities avoid formal registration not because they have no interest in information about refugees, but because they have an interest in being able to formally deny such information in order to shirk responsibility. Non-registration has helped to avoid any impression of the government bestowing formal refugee rights and status on Syrians.

As noted before, Syrian refugees in Lebanon are not recognized as official refugees by the government, but they face intricate alternative classification and labeling dynamics. The 'complexities and uncertainties' involved in these dynamics, Mencütek (2019: 151) notes, 'itself serve as a means of restrictive governance in Lebanon.' The multiplicity of these different labels and the overlap between the various categorizations means that the legal, institutional, and political status of refugees becomes conditional and often arbitrary. Janmyr and Mourad (2018b) conclude: 'The blurring of categories makes conditions for refugees precarious.' The latest LCRP, for instance, includes a statement that 'Lebanon reserves its sovereign right to determine their [Syrians'] status according to Lebanese laws and regulations.' As Janmyr (2018: 397) notes, however, considering the absence of laws and regulations for refugees in Lebanon, 'it is unclear exactly on what basis . . . the government seeks to assert status determination.' Authorities can thus shift between the different readings and interpretations as they please.

The political 'utility' of non-registration goes beyond shirking responsibility (Janmyr and Mourad, 2018a: 556). Not having an undisputed number of refugees also generates leeway for state authorities to pursue different interests vis-à-vis different audiences. The fact that the Lebanese government does not formally register refugees and does not provide stable and legally valid categories for Syrian refugees allows Lebanese authorities to play a 'numbers game.' One former advisor to the Ministry of Social Affairs voiced his surprise regarding the fact that:

> During all these meetings that all these ministries and agencies had [on how to deal with the refugee crisis] at no moment the central administration of statistics was invited. They were absolutely never invited to attend any of these meetings. And [they] never asked or any donor provided them any kind of money so that they can do the survey.

When I asked him why, his simple conclusion was that 'they want to keep [things] fluid, for political reasons.'[25] An advisor to the Prime Minister's Office explained how the registration stop since 2015 and the withdrawal of UNHCR registration of refugees that he claimed were 'commuting' between Syria and Lebanon meant that 'for the first time the number dropped to below one million. Registered.'[26] Only to add that: 'We still believe there are a few hundred thousand not registered and unofficially present in the country.' Such ambiguity allows state representatives to point towards the official UNHCR registration when it suits them and disregard these same registered numbers in favour of a much higher 'unknown' number of 'actual' refugees at other times.

For internal Lebanese consumption, numbers on the lower spectrum of the estimate are routinely used to testify to the impact of the government's more tough response since 2014. The October policy of that year, after all, made it a priority to decrease the number of Syrian refugees in the country by all possible means, and the subsequent entry and residency regimes have clearly sought to realize this goal. Thus, as several humanitarian experts have explained, Lebanese state officials use the minimal UNHCR-registered number to insist that there are fewer than a million refugees in the country in their public political discourse. A former representative of the office of the Minister of State for Displaced Affairs explained that the Minister, as well as other state agencies, is aware of the fact that there are many non-registered refugees. She said:

> The reality is that there are plenty of non-registered Syrian refugees that entered based on a tourist visa or medical visa or any other kind of visa and are now either, like, without residency or illegally across the borders. So they are there. Yeah. We don't see them on paper, but they are there.[27]

This, however, she reflected, does not stop some politicians from claiming that 'their policy of halting registration to decrease the number . . . showed a good result.'

In engagements with humanitarian agencies and donors, state officials stress high numbers of refugees to illustrate the need for continued aid. The same officials that claim there are fewer than a million Syrians in Lebanon when addressing domestic media, acknowledge that there are de facto some 1.5 million refugees in the closed-door planning meetings they have with the humanitarian community. A protection officer working for a Lebanese human rights organization explained that when she confronted state officials that she engaged with in inter-agency coordination meetings with the unlikeliness of their claim that there were as many as three million Syrian refugees residing in the country, they told her outright: 'You can't know that.'[28] Lack of solid numbers problematizes the development of a solid rationale for allocating aid and thus enhance the discretionary power of state officials (Atallah and Mahdi, 2017: 39). At a conference on 'refugees and social cohesion,' a ministerial advisor admitted that 'yes, we exaggerate the numbers to get more aid as well as for politics reasons.'[29]

In practice, then, the government accepts the number of 1.5 million refugees mentioned in the latest LCRP when it comes to emphasizing the burden Syrian refugees constitute to Lebanon's society and infrastructure, but denies it when it comes to identifying those in need of refugee protection (Janmyr, 2018). The utilization of such discrepancy, a development expert offered, was enabled by the creation of what she called an 'ambiguous space' in which 'different claims could be made also by the government in terms of how many refugees are actually in the country' that could not actually be disputed despite their contradictory and often unlikely nature.[30] In response to my question of why no inclusive, central registration system was in place, a policy advisor to the Minister of State of Displaced Affairs explained that there was no political will to work towards such undisputed registration:

> Now, let me tell you frankly. Not having one figure will open the door to more manipulation. At all levels. To minimize or to maximize. That's it. It's very clear. . . . It's a game of minimization and maximization. And this is a manipulation. And now we're near the election. Maybe they want this to manipulate more.[31]

Such 'minimization and maximization' and the strategically ambiguous numbers game it reflects allows the government to shirk responsibility and enables the vulnerability that makes refugees controllable, exploitable, and deportable.

The 2017 fee waiver for refugees' residency status renewal: creating a 'window of flexibility'

As described in the previous vignette, non-registration and vague categorization allow for a strategic 'numbers game' that demonstrates the utility of informality and illegality. The following vignette shows that even measures that are ostensibly taken to further regularization in practice often exacerbate institutional ambiguity.

In February 2017, the Lebanese government waived the US$200 fee for renewing residency status in what was widely seen as an attempt to remedy the mass illegality of Syrian refugees. The decision was hailed as a success by humanitarian organizations. Yet the scope of the fee waiver was extremely circumscribed from the beginning and its implementation patchy and arbitrary. Very few refugees actually benefited from it (Sanyal, 2018: 71).

For state authorities, the fee waiver process has been a way to distinguish between 'real' refugees and what they see as 'migrant workers.' The fee waiver therefore specifically regarded UNHCR-registered Syrian refugees. It excluded Syrians who were not registered with the UNHCR (either because they entered irregularly or because they entered after 2015 when the UNHCR was no longer allowed to register refugees) as well as UNHCR-registered refugees who renewed their residency through the sponsorship system. This is noteworthy because refugees were in fact often told by the General Security to renew their residency through a sponsor (Atallah and Mahdi, 2017: 25; Janmyr and Mourad, 2018a: 557). Stakeholders explained that ever since 2015 the General Security was quite unwilling to allow a renewal of residency status on the basis of UNHCR registration, even though this was formally possible. This means that in the two years preceding the fee waiver, many people were forced into a category that eventually excluded them from this waiver. As a Lebanese lawyer noted:

> First, they pushed all Syrians to obtain a residency on the basis of a sponsorship, a category that they created in 2015 and that was the sole option for most refugees who wanted to obtain legal status at the time. Then in 2017

they agreed to grant residencies on the basis of the UNHCR registration and to waive the residency fees, but only on condition that the Syrian had not previously obtained a sponsorship residency. This was clearly done with the purpose of reducing as much as possible the number of people who would qualify as refugees.[32]

In addition to limitations pertaining to the scope of the waiver, its implementation has been rife with problems (United Nations Development Program, 2017: 12; Ubels, 2019: 38). There are no organizations actually accompanying refugees in their encounters with the General Security as the General Security does not allow this. But there are a lot of NGOs working on legal protection that support refugees in their attempts to renew or regularize their residency in Lebanon and these organizations have documented widespread arbitrariness in the application of the decree (Ayoub and Mahdi, 2018: 5). Different General Security offices have articulated additional requirements outside the scope of the official decision that vary per region and case, demanding papers and statements not formally requested by the decision. A protection specialist from an international NGO concluded:

> In practice the additional requirements that are typically imposed by General Security offices further decrease the proportion of the refugee population that is eligible in practice for befitting from that fee waiver. And this creates confusion and uncertainty in the refugee community and it also undermines credibility of humanitarian actors. Because whenever the original circulars are issued, we're expected to go out in refugee communities and tell people about the new circulars. But then they never end up actually being implemented the way that they're written.[33]

Such arbitrary and patchy implementation is often explained by the lack of capacity of General Security offices and the enormous strain the refugee presence puts on this organization. The 'Lebanon Partnership Paper' presented after the Brussels II donor conference in April 2018, for instance, recognizes the limited success of the waiver in regularizing refugees' stay, but sees this as the result of limited 'processing capacity' of General Security offices. An interviewee affiliated with the Prime Minister's Office similarly emphasized that problems with the implementation of status renewal and the application of the fee waiver are of an 'administrative and logistical nature' and have 'nothing to do with the policy of the government.'[34]

Yet, as illustrated by the opening quote of this chapter, Lebanese as well as international civil society activists and public administration experts that I spoke with often reminded me of the fact that the burdensome bureaucracy that the General Security apparently does not have the capacity to implement is of their own making. It was installed through decrees that replaced a much more straightforward and easy-to-implement entry and residency regime. Initial information sessions about the fee waiver organized by some General Security offices were canceled through a central-level decision (Ubels, 2019: 38). Moreover, humanitarian professionals stressed, the discretion employed by various General Security offices was enabled by what they saw as the remarkably vague formulation of the circular. Despite extensive experience in this field and in Lebanon, these experts found the wording of the circular so confusing that they wondered how such ambiguity could have gone unnoted. In fact, some of them suggested, it might not have gone unnoted. Since the problematically vague formulation of the decree was often pointed out to relevant General Security officials through informal liaisons but never remedied, they suggested it must have been kept in place for a reason. A protection officer with a legal background working for an international NGO reflected:

> The way that they [General Security circulars regarding the fee waiver] are written is ridiculous; this is not the way you would write a circular that you wanted people to understand. . . . They are written in a sort of confusing fashion. I mean it's almost as if the original circular was meant to have an additional sentence or additional words or clauses in it somewhere and someone's read it and just said 'no' and just sort of like crossed bits out and left the remainder and no one's bothered to check whether anything that remains is actually sort of coherent. . . . What happens is that these things come out, we all read it, we all sort of scratch our heads for a while wondering what exactly that's going to mean and then we try to look at practice in order to understand it.[35]

Noting that limited capacity and resources cannot fully account for the ambiguous nature of the circular and the arbitrary nature of its implementation, humanitarian protection officers and relevant policy consultants pointed to the performative dimensions of these decisions and the political utility of the maneuvering space that ambiguous decrees generate. On the one hand, state officials can stress the official national decision vis-à-vis the donor community that pushed for this in the first place and demonstrate the goodwill required to access further aid.[36]

On the other hand, the actual local practice of partial implementation allows Lebanese authorities to by and large keep in place the reality of mass illegality and the related vulnerability that enables exploitation and control of the refugee population. Experts and practitioners alike expressed their sense that there had never been an intention 'to really make it something big, it's a very limited thing.'[37] Because the fee waiver is vaguely formulated, refugees and those supporting them have a hard time proving eligibility. A protection officer explained that 'since it's not said clearly it's much harder, then, for our lawyers when they accompany refugees: what are they supposed to point to [in the circulars]?'[38] Most of my interlocutors from the humanitarian field were accordingly convinced that

> there is no real commitment to completely removing those obstacles; there was a need to somehow show some good will and do something and it was

kind of constructed in a way that makes it look better on the surface than it practically will be.[39]

In short, then, the ambiguity that permeates the fee waiver that was supposed to attenuate some of the most problematic tenets of the October 2014 policy was arguably largely preventable and served various political purposes. As with the numbers game described earlier, it allowed Lebanese authorities to flexibly cater to various audiences and to by and large keep in place the imposed illegality that enables refugees' demobilization, exploitation, and expulsion. Echoing Fakhoury's (2017: 687) conclusion that the General Security implements a form of 'discretionary governance' through its 'restrictive, tedious and changing' procedures, a Lebanese legal scholar consulted on the matter suggested:

> We can't know, but we can guess. Through my experience in immigration law, I believe the ambiguity is intended because it allows for this arbitrary result and to deprive Syrians of a legal status. The access to legal status will often depend on whether or not a Syrian has the support of someone influential in Lebanon. If you don't have such connections, you will be lost in the bureaucracy and will likely end up without legal status.[40]

According to a representative of the Ministry of Social Affairs, ambiguity creates convenient 'windows of flexibility' (Amnesty International, 2015: 11). These windows, the prior vignette shows, are sometimes skillfully crafted.

The Minister of State for Displaced Affairs: institutionalizing nonperformativity

As illustrated by the previous vignettes, the strategic institutional ambiguity at work in Lebanon's governance of Syrian refugees manifests itself in deliberate non-registration and in conveniently vague decrees. It is also evident in the elusive mandates of the state agencies tasked with governing Syrian refugees in Lebanon. This is particularly so for the Minister of State for Displaced Affairs. This third vignette outlines how disputed terms of reference, competing sectarian-political interests, and lack of resources combined to produce an agency whose responsibilities with regard to refugee governance are constantly reinterpreted depending on the case, audience, and timing. This allows it to function as a strawman. It signals that something is being done about the lack of over-arching policy that has enabled and upheld institutional ambiguity, while what that 'something' actually is remains elusive – and according to many interlocutors was meant to be elusive.

Ministers of State fall directly under the Prime Minister's Office. They do not have the institutional and administrative resources that a normal ministry has and have no executive power. In Lebanon, each Prime Minister can appoint Ministers of State. This practice functions both as a mechanism to delegate institutional capacity to areas where it is needed and to ensure the sectarian and political balance in each cabinet: when all regular ministerial posts are allocated, the

Ministers of State are allotted so that this balance is guaranteed. The government under Prime Minister Saad Hariri that was established in December 2016 had eight Ministers of State, including the newly established position of Minister of State for Displaced Affairs.[41]

The exact mandate of the Minister of State for Displaced Affairs is not clear, a spokesperson of this 'ministry' admitted.[42] Experts working for the Minister explained that it was created to lead the development of an overarching policy that should ensure more consistent and coherent coordination between the line ministries involved in the LCRP and, in essence, update and extend the October 2014 policy paper, the only official government policy presented so far. It was to respond to the increasing critique of donors, humanitarian partners, and Lebanon's civil society on the absence of a sophisticated government policy to deal with Syrian refugees and to their request for a single government interlocutor to engage with on a substantial policy level.

Apart from this official policy purpose, the appointment of a Minister of State for Displaced Affairs also served to establish a political counterweight for the Ministry of Social Affairs. With its position as coordinator of the LCRP, the Ministry of Social Affairs had become the leading ministry with regard to the refugee response since 2014. In the previous cabinet, the Minister of Social Affairs was officially independent, but closely aligned with the Prime Minister's Future Movement. In the new government, however, the Ministry of Social Affairs came under the Lebanese Forces, a Christian party affiliated with the March 14 alliance, but with less direct allegiance to the Prime Minister's Sunni Future Movement. At that point in time, the post of a Minister of State for Displaced Affairs was established and given to a minister directly affiliated with the Future Movement (Uzelac and Meester, 2018: 23).

This appointment was seen as an attempt to avoid conflict among the various political parties and sectarian communities within March 14 and their differing stances on the refugee 'issue.' A previous advisor to various relevant ministries summarized:

> They [the Ministers of Social Affairs and of Displaced Affairs] are from different political parties, but they were allies at the time and then the Prime Minister did not want to upset the head of the other political party, who was his ally, so they decided that . . . let's keep things pending. And in the meantime everything was . . . like everything got a bit lost.[43]

As this citation demonstrates, installing a Minister of State for Displaced Affairs did little to address institutional ambiguity and fragmentation. Its implicit but evident competition with the Ministry of Social Affairs rather produced more deadlock and confusion (Ayoub and Mahdi, 2018: 9). A humanitarian official with a leading position in the coordination about the LCRP noted:

> The Ministry of Social Affairs has been left in charge of the operational coordination of the crisis response. However, they also created this Ministry of Displaced, a State Ministry of Displaced, which we thought at the beginning

of the year would take on . . . possibly, potentially, would take on the coordination. And so did they. And so we met with them several times and presented and whatever. But eventually we said: 'Listen, we can't engage with you unless we have a formal notification from the Prime Minister's Office or, you know, from the sort of highest level to say "the response has shifted from the Ministry of Social Affairs to the State Ministry of Displaced." So how you guys organize that, that's up to you to figure out, but you have to tell us formally.'[44]

Seconding the analysis of a previous advisor to the Minister of State for Displaced Affairs on this matter, she confided:

The Minister of Displaced does not come from the same party as the Minister of Social Affairs. So . . . And then they haven't bothered, or dared, to get into the fight of actually sort of clearly delineating who's doing what. So if you're confused, don't worry, everybody is confused here and there's no . . . there's no real answer to the question [of who is formally in charge of what].

Despite the detrimental effects of this ministerial turf war, some of my interlocutors, especially those from civil society and humanitarian agencies, have hailed the establishment of the Minister of State for Displaced Affairs as a major development, seeing the institution as a constructive partner in their attempts to lobby for more protection for refugees. For them, the Minister of State for Displaced Affairs has the 'will,' but 'is kept small and lacks the resources to do more.'[45] Despite successes in, for instance, the realm of birth registration of refugees, this limited capacity of the Minister of State for Displaced Affairs and its minimal achievements were stressed by most stakeholders. A 'unified policy' to reconsider Lebanon's response to the crisis was allegedly drafted by the Minister of State in 2017, but a Minister of State can merely advise on policy, not actually adopt or implement it. The policy proposal of the Minister of State for Displaced Affairs, moreover, clashed with an opposing policy suggested by the Ministry of Foreign Affairs. No consensus could be reached so neither policy was adopted.

In light of the fact that the Ministry 'has no funds and no power,' many of my interlocutors wondered whether – regardless of the will of its individual staff – the Ministry was ever really meant to make an impact (see also Zaatari, 2016).[46] They noted that for it to be effective, the position of Minister of State for Displaced Affairs should have been filled by a capable Minister, rather than one who was seen as lacking relevant expertise. The Minister of State for Displaced Affairs, furthermore, could have been established as a department under an existing ministry or under the Prime Minister's Office, rather than as a Ministry of State. A leading policy expert involved in the creation of the Minister of State for Displaced Affairs indicated that he had unsuccessfully lobbied for the creation of an 'actual' Ministry for Displaced that would be responsible for governing both the

Palestinian and Syrian refugees in the country.[47] The liminal nature of a Minister of State, which exists by the grace of a specific Prime Minister and might not last longer than the respective electoral term, undermines its credibility.[48] A consultant for the Minister indicated that this was keenly felt by the staff supporting the Minister, which saw the Minister of State as a 'temporary ministry.'[49]

A former advisor to the Ministry of Social Affairs summarized the general impression on the Minister of State for Displaced Affairs I got from interlocutors representing ministries and international agencies, saying that it

> is just for décor, it is just for him [the Minister of State for Displaced Affairs] to be a minister. He really did not . . . he couldn't . . . he was not actually . . . in reality, he was not mandated to do anything on the Syrian refugees. He's just a façade, not more than that.[50]

He added:

> When it comes to institutional prerogatives, it was never the intention of letting him [the Minister of State] do anything. . . . For the outside . . . they established a Minister for Displaced [to show that] they're interested . . . it is on top of the agenda. But actually this is not the case, it is a fake.

The Minister of State for Displaced Affairs thus 'has remained largely inactive' (Mencütek, 2019: 145). The institution has not been able to present or get adopted the comprehensive policy the government allegedly wanted to have. Instead, it has been set up in an unsustainable and under-capacitated format and was apparently squeezed between the Ministry of Social Affairs that did not care to give up any of its de facto policy influence and the Inter-Ministerial Committee that was keen to guard its direct lines with the donor community. The Minister of State for Displaced Affairs, it therefore seems, was created to assuage mounting critiques of Lebanon's lack of policy towards Syrian refugees, rather than to actually address them.

This makes Lebanon's Minister of State for Displaced Affairs the quintessential example of producing ambiguity through formalizing inaction. It is a telling case of institutionalized nonperformativity, which Ahmed (2006: 105) describes as acts 'that work precisely by not bringing about the effects that they name.' Following this logic of nonperformativity, the very utterance of a specific intention, here to finally develop a proper policy to address the Syrian refugee crisis, has not contributed to the realization of that alleged intention, but in fact worked to make it less likely. For many of my interlocutors, the appointment of a Minister of State for Displaced Affairs undermined rather than helped the development of the policy that this Minister was supposed to deliver because it added to the already existing confusion about mandates and multiplicity of institutions. This has only enhanced the institutional ambiguity working to keep refugees down.

Conclusions

Lebanon's overarching response to the Syrian refugee presence in the country evolved from a 'no-policy-policy' to a form of 'formal informality' after the introduction of the October 2014 policy. Informing both of these phases of the response was a set of three fundamental 'nos' that institutionalized ambiguity and amounted to a form of 'national-level evasion of responsibility' (Atallah and Mahdi, 2017: 20). When it comes to status, refugees were withheld formal refugee status and by and large stripped from their official residency status. The no-camp decision meant that in terms of shelter, refugees were left to their own devices. Concerning representation, clear mandates and responsibilities on the Lebanese side were absent, and no counterparts were recognized on Syrian side. The ambiguity this generated importantly contributed to manufacturing the vulnerability that serves to demobilize refugees, exploit them, and 'encourage' them to leave.

This has been the effect not merely of hybrid order and resource deficits but also of concrete political decisions. It points to political unwillingness to produce laws and policies that would set clearer benchmarks for engagement with the 'crisis.' Three vignettes have illustrated the political expediency of maintaining institutional ambiguity. They did so by outlining the utility of non-registration and vague classification and the advantageous 'numbers game' this allows. The vignettes also showed how measures allegedly taken to remedy institutional ambiguity, such as the adoption of a waiver for (some) refugees' residency renewal fees and the installation of a Minister of State for Displaced Affairs, actually contribute to it. This, in many ways, is not a form of failure, but a manifestation of nonperformativity, where measures are taken not so much to actually be implemented but rather to stave off their implementation while keeping critics assuaged.

This chapter has outlined the characteristics, implications, and drivers of the institutional ambiguity that imbues Lebanon's national response to the Syrian refugee 'crisis.' Analyzing the relevant dynamics of Lebanon's national political arena, it explored how informality, liminality, and exceptionality emerged and the political work they do. This is further nuanced and detailed from a more local perspective in the next chapter.

Notes

1 Author's interview with Lebanese human rights lawyer working with refugees – Skype, 16 March 2018.
2 The section on the emergence of institutional ambiguity draws on a joint paper with Jessy Nassar (Nassar and Stel, 2019). This previous analysis was complemented and updated with my own data.
3 Interviews had to be conducted via Skype. They were held in English and then recorded and transcribed. The related citations are verbatim. Many of my interlocutors, especially those associated with the state and the United Nations, did not want to be referred to in their official capacity and will thus be described more generically as 'policy' or 'humanitarian' 'experts' or state 'officials' or 'representatives.'
4 Website consulted on 13 March 2018.

5 This law contains a chapter on political asylum and a related asylum process that states that asylum can be granted by a committee comprising the ministers of Interior, Justice, and Foreign Affairs and the director of General Security (Mencütek, 2019: 138). In practice, asylum has been granted through this mechanism precisely once since 1962 (Stevens, 2017).

6 These regulations were presented in a circular issued by General Security on 31 December 2014 and further detailed in circulars published on 13 January and on 3 and 23 February 2015.

7 The sponsorship system for Syrian refugees was established in an internal memo of the General Security (99/2014). Sponsors have to sign a pledge of responsibility. Such a pledge can take the form of an individual work-related permit, a group sponsorship, or a family sponsorship. It contains a clause of liability for 'any acts committed by the sponsored Syrian,' though the exact form of liability is not explicated (Danish Refugee Council, Norwegian Refugee Council, International Refugee Committee, and Oxfam, 2017: 2). The sponsor also has to obtain a work permit from the Ministry of Labor once legal residency is issued. Since application for work permits is 'complex and costly,' only 1,500 Syrians currently hold work permits in Lebanon (Uzelac and Meester, 2018: 19). Because of the elaborate obligations and the related bureaucracy, sponsors are very difficult to find and/or demand significant 'payback' (Amnesty International, 2015: 14; Janmyr, 2016: 69; Al-Masri and Altabbaa, 2016: 11). The sponsorship system consequently has become extremely exploitative.

8 Author's interview – Skype, 16 March 2018.

9 Author's interview – Skype, 16 March 2018.

10 Author's interview – Skype, 13 April 2018.

11 Author's interview – Skype, 27 March 2018.

12 Borgmann and Slim (2018: 44) dramatically but effectively summarize this sentiment when they note:

> Whether we like it or not, in Lebanon, the word 'camps' represents the mother lode of evils, specifically, the long lasting and definitive period of Palestinian asylum in the country. 'Camps' evoke memories of areas within the state that were not under its control. In short, the word is 'code' for the country's civil war period and the cascade of painful images it still summons. Ultimately, the establishment of 'refugee camps' is an enduring example of collective Lebanese trauma.

13 Author's interview – Skype, 27 March 2018.

14 Author's interview – Skype, 30 January 2018.

15 Not all illegality is forced. Many refugees are wary of registering themselves for fear this information will be shared with the Syrian regime and thus opt for staying under the radar themselves. Considering the dire consequences of lacking legal residency status, however, the large majority of refugees can be assumed to prefer legal status if they would be eligible for it and could afford it.

16 According to them, it 'deliberately created mass legal insecurity and undermined the living conditions of refugees in order to prompt their return.'

17 Author's interview – Skype, 11 December 2017.

18 Author's interview – Skype, 27 March 2018.

19 Author's interview – WhatsApp, 12 January 2018.

20 Author's interview – Skype, 9 February 2018.

21 In addition to this registration stop, the government requested the UNHCR 'to review the cases of all Syrians registered with the Office who had gone to Syria and returned to Lebanon after June 1, 2014' (Mourad, 2017: 258). This led to the inactivation of the UNHCR refugee status of 16,000 Syrians previously registered with the UNHCR.

22 Refugees who arrived after May 2015 were not registered by the UNHCR, but recorded – a less formal categorization that allows refugees to be registered

for internal UNHCR purposes but does not publicly count them as refugees. In June 2016, there were approximately 40,000 such recorded refugees (Janmyr and Mourad, 2018a: 548).

23 Author's interview – Skype, 9 February 2018.
24 Author's interview – WhatsApp, 12 January 2018.
25 Author's interview – Skype, 9 April 2018.
26 Author's interview – Skype, 30 January 2018.
27 Author's interview – WhatsApp, 12 January 2018.
28 Author's interview – Skype, 14 November 2017.
29 Livestream of event at the American University of Beirut – 23 November 2017.
30 Author's interview – Skype, 11 December 2017.
31 Author's interview – Skype, 22 January 2018.
32 Author's interview – Skype, 16 March 2018.
33 Author's interview – Skype, 18 January 2018.
34 Author's interview – Skype, 30 January 2018.
35 Author's interview – Skype, 19 January 2018.
36 This seems corroborated by the fact that the fee waiver was adopted as a result of fierce donor pressure at 'Brussels I' and was flaunted as a major accomplishment by the Lebanese Prime Minister at 'Brussels II' a year later – where no nuance was made to indicate that only a small number of refugees is eligible for the fee waiver and that only a small portion of those eligible have been able to actually benefit so far.
37 Author's interview with Lebanese lawyer working with refugees – Skype, 16 March 2018.
38 Author's interview – Skype, 19 January 2018.
39 Author's interview with a legal assistance specialist for an international humanitarian organization – Skype, 30 November 2017.
40 Author's interview – Skype, 16 March 2018.
41 There was a Ministry for Displaced Affairs (*wizaret al muhajreen*) before the arrival of Syrian refugees. This Ministry was tasked with addressing the issue of Lebanese people internally displaced during the Lebanese Civil War. The new Minister of State for Displaced Affairs (*wizaret al dawle al shu'un al naziheen*) was specifically related to the Syrian refugee presence in the country, but – due to the fact that Lebanon officially does not consider Syrian refugees to be 'refugees' – could not be called a minister of refugee affairs and therefore was given a name that in Arabic denotes a different category of displacement but in English translates as 'displaced' as well.
42 Author's interview – WhatsApp, 12 January 2018.
43 Author's interview – Skype, 27 March 2018.
44 Author's interview – Skype, 5 January 2018.
45 Author's interview – Skype, 12 March 2018.
46 Author's interview with a Lebanese international consultant – Skype, 9 February 2018.
47 Author's interview – Skype, 22 January 2018.
48 The position of Minister of State for Displaced Affairs was retained after the 2018 elections. The new Minister belongs to the opposing political alliance, however. Rather than trying to enhance refugee protection, he has taken a much more assertive stance against the refugee presence in the country, prioritizing repatriation for which he directly liaises with Damascus (gaining him the nickname 'Minister of State for Return Affairs').
49 Author's interview – WhatsApp, 12 January 2018.
50 Author's interview – Skype, 9 April 2018.

References

Ahmed, Sara. 2006. 'The Non-Performativity of Anti-Racism.' *Meridians: Feminism, Race, Transnationalism* 7, no. 1: 104–126.

Akesson, Bree and Kearney Coupland. 2018. 'Seeking Safety, Finding Fear: Syrian Families' Experiences of (Im)Mobility and the Implications for Children and Family Rights.' *Canadian Journal of Children's Rights* 5, no. 1: 6–29.

ALEF-Act for Human Rights. 2018. 'Written Statement at the Support the Future of Syria and the Region Conference.' Unpublished document.

Al-Masri, Muzna. 2015. *Between Local Patronage Relationships and Securitization: The Conflict Context in the Bekaa Region.* Beirut: Lebanon Support & United Nations Development Program.

Al-Masri, Muzna and Marianna Altabbaa. 2016. *Local and Regional Entanglements: The Social Stability Context in Sahel-Akkar.* Beirut: United Nations Development Program.

Amnesty International. 2015. *Pushed to the Edge: Syrian Refugees Face Increased Restrictions in Lebanon.* London: Amnesty International Publications.

Atallah, Sami and Dima Mahdi. 2017. *Law and Politics of "Safe Zones" and Forced Return to Syria: Refugee Politics in Lebanon.* Beirut: Lebanese Center for Policy Studies.

Ayoub, Bachir and Dima Mahdi. 2018. *Making Aid Work in Lebanon.* Oxford: Oxfam International.

Barjas, Elham. 2016. *Restricting Refugees: Measuring Municipal Power in Lebanon.* Beirut: Legal Agenda.

Bidinger, Sarah, Aaron Lang, Danielle Hites, Yoana Kuzmova, Elena Noureddine and Susan M. Akram. 2014. *Protecting Syrian Refugees: Laws, Policies and Global Responsibility Sharing.* Boston: Boston University.

Borgmann, Monika and Lokman Slim. 2018. *Fewer Refugees, More Refugeeism.* Beirut: Umam Documentation and Research and Institute for Auslandsbeziehunger.

Carpi, Estella, Mariam Younes and Marie-Noëlle AbiYaghi. 2016. *Crisis and Control: Formal Hybrid Security in Lebanon.* Beirut: Lebanon Support.

Clarke, Killian. 2017. 'Protest and Informal Leadership in Syrian Refugee Camps.' *POMEPS Studies* 25: 16–21.

Danish Refugee Council, Norwegian Refugee Council, International Refugee Committee and Oxfam. 2017. 'Briefing on Sponsorship of Syrian Refugees in Lebanon.'

Dionigi, Filipo. 2016. *The Syrian Refugee Crisis in Lebanon: State Fragility and Social Resilience.* London: London School of Economics Middle East Centre.

Dorai, Kamel. 2016. 'Palestinian Refugees and the Current Syrian Conflict: From Settled Refugees to Stateless Asylum Seekers?' In *Migration, Mobilities and the Arab Spring: Spaces of Refugee Flight in the Eastern Mediterranean,* edited by Natalia Ribas-Mateos, 158–173. Cheltenham: Edward Elgar Publishing.

El Mufti, Karim. 2014. *Official Response to the Syrian Refugee Crisis in Lebanon, the Disastrous Policy of No-Policy.* Beirut: Civil Society Knowledge Center.

Fakhoury, Tamirace. 2017. 'Governance Strategies and Refugee Response: Lebanon in the Face of Syrian Displacement.' *International Journal of Middle East Studies* 49: 681–700.

Frangieh, Ghida. 2017. *Denying Syrian Refugees Status: Helping or Harming Lebanon?* Beirut: The Legal Agenda.

Frangieh, Ghida and Elham Barjas. 2016. 'Interior Ministry Advisor: Lebanon Refugee Policy Based on Set of "No's".' *Legal Agenda,* 8 November.

Ghaddar, Sima. 2017. *Lebanon Treats Refugees as a Security Problem – And It Doesn't Work.* New York: The Century Foundation.

Ghanem, Nizar. 2016. *Local Governance Under Pressure: Research on Social Stability in T5 Area, North Lebanon.* Arezzo: Oxfam Italia.

Hamdan, Kamal and Lea Bou Khater. 2015. *Strategies of Response to the Syrian Refugee Crisis in Lebanon.* Beirut: Common Space Initiative.

Helou, Hala. 2014. 'Lebanon and Refugees: Between Laws and Reality.' MA thesis, Lebanese American University.

Human Rights Watch. 2016. ' "I Just Wanted to Be Treated like a Person": How Lebanon's Residency Rules Facilitate Abuse of Syrian Refugees. New York: Human Rights Watch.

International Crisis Group. 2015. Lebanon's Self-Defeating Survival Mechanisms. Brussels: International Crisis Group.

Jacobsen, Karen. 2006. 'Editorial Introduction. Refugees and Asylum Seekers in Urban Areas: A Livelihoods Perspective.' Journal of Refugee Studies 19, no. 3: 273–286.

Janmyr, Maja. 2016. 'Precarity in Exile: The Legal Status of Syrian Refugees in Lebanon.' Refugee Survey Quarterly 35: 58–78.

Janmyr, Maja. 2018. 'UNHCR and the Syrian Refugee Response: Negotiating Status and Registration in Lebanon.' The International Journal of Human Rights 22, no. 3: 393–419.

Janmyr, Maja and Lama Mourad. 2018a. 'Modes of Ordering: Labelling, Classification and Categorization in Lebanon's Refugee Response.' Journal of Refugee Studies 31, no. 4: 544–565.

Janmyr, Maja and Lama Mourad. 2018b. 'Millions of Syrians' Lives Depend on Whether They're Designated as "Refugees".' Washington Post – Monkey Cage, 6 March.

Lebanon Support. 2016. 'Formal Informality, Brokering Mechanisms and Illegality: The Impact of the Lebanese State's Policies on Syrian Refugees' Daily Lives.'

Meier, Daniel. 2014. 'The Refugee Issue and the Threat of a Sectarian Confrontation.' Oriente Moderno 94, no. 2: 382–401.

Mencütek, Zeynep. 2019. Refugee Governance, State and Politics in the Middle East. London: Routledge.

Mourad, Lama. 2017. ' "Standoffish" Policy-Making: Inaction and Change in the Lebanese Response to the Syrian Displacement Crisis.' Middle East Law and Governance 9: 249–266.

Mourad, Lama and Laure-Hélène Piron. 2016. Municipal Service Delivery, Stability, Social Cohesion and Legitimacy in Lebanon: An Analytical Literature Review. Beirut: Issam Fares Institute for Public Policy and International Affairs.

Nassar, Jessy. 2014. 'The Syrian Refugee Crisis: A Reification of State Sovereignty in Lebanon?' MSc thesis, University of London.

Nassar, Jessy and Nora Stel. 2019. 'Lebanon's Response to the Syrian Refugee Crisis – Institutional Ambiguity as a Governance Strategy.' Political Geography 70: 44–54.

Norwegian Refugee Council and International Rescue Committee. 2015. Legal Status of Refugees from Syria: Challenges and Consequences of Maintaining Legal Stay in Beirut and Mount Lebanon. Beirut: Norwegian Refugee Council Lebanon and International Rescue Committee Lebanon.

REACH and United Nations High Commissioner for Refugees. 2014. Multi Sector Community Level Assessment of Informal Settlements: Akkar Governorate – Lebanon. Beirut: REACH and United Nations High Commissioner for Refugees.

Saghieh, Nizar. 2015. Manufacturing Vulnerability in Lebanon: Legal Policies and Efficient Tools of Discrimination. Beirut: Legal Agenda.

Sanyal, Romola. 2018. 'Managing Through Ad Hoc Measures: Syrian Refugees and the Politics of Waiting in Lebanon.' Political Geography 66: 67–75.

Shawaf, Nour and Francesca El Asmar. 2017. We're Not There Yet: Voices of Refugees from Syria in Lebanon. Beirut: Oxfam.

Slavova, Ilina. 2017. Justice for Stability: Addressing the Impact of Mass Displacement on Lebanon's Justice System. Beirut: International Alert.

Stevens, Dallal. 2017. 'Access to Justice for Syrian Refugees in Lebanon.' In *States, the Law and Access to Refugee Protection: Fortresses and Fairness*, edited by Maria O'Sullivan and Dallal Stevens, 223–242. Oxford: Hart Publishing.

Thorleifsson, Catherine. 2016. 'The Limits of Hospitality: Coping Strategies Among Displaced Syrians in Lebanon.' *Third World Quarterly* 37, no. 6: 1071–1082.

Ubels, Tessa. 2019. 'Governing Empowerment. How Aid Organisations Negotiate the Empowerment of Refugees in a Context of Hybrid Governance with Donors, Syrian Refugees and the Lebanese State in Beirut Since the Syrian Conflict in 2011.' MA thesis, Utrecht University.

United Nations Development Program. 2017. 'Social Stability Working Group 13 December 2017 Beirut – Presentation.' Unpublished document.

United Nations High Commissioner for Refugees. 2015. *Refugee Response in Lebanon Briefing Documents*. Beirut: United Nations High Commissioner for Refugees.

United Nations High Commissioner for Refugees, United Nations Children's Fund and World Food Program. 2016. 'Vulnerability Assessment of Syrian Refugees in Lebanon.'

United Nations High Commissioner for Refugees, United Nations Children's Fund and World Food Program. 2017. 'Vulnerability Assessment of Syrian Refugees in Lebanon.'

Uzelac, Ana and Jos Meester. 2018. *Is There Protection in the Region? Leveraging Funds and Political Capital in Lebanon's Refugee Crisis*. The Hague: Clingendael Institute.

Yassin, Nasser. 2018. *101 Facts and Figures on the Syrian Refugee Crisis*. Beirut: Issam Fares Institute for Public Policy and International Affairs.

Yassin, Nasser, Tarek Osseiran, Rima Rassi and Marwa Boustani. 2015. *No Place to Stay? Reflections on the Syria Refugee Shelter Policy in Lebanon*. Beirut: United Nations Human Settlements Program & the Issam Fares Institute for Public Policy and International Affairs at the American University of Beirut.

Zaatari, M. 2016. 'Syrians Question Power, Purpose of Minister for Refugees.' *Daily Star*, 20 December.

Chapter 3

Governing Syrian 'informal tented settlements' in Lebanon

Co-opted *shawishes*, elusive permissions, and the specter of eviction

There is no policy here. You deal with it [the refugees] as you think is right.[1]

Lebanon's approach to governing Syrian refugees is, the previous chapter showed, characterized by the absence of a comprehensive, consistent formal policy on the national level, which is often politically convenient. In the wake of this, a wide array of more local informal approaches and guidelines to deal with the presence of refugees has emerged. This chapter explores such sub-national manifestations and implications of the lingering no-policy-policy and the expanding formal informality in Lebanon's response to the Syrian refugee 'crisis.' It thereby enriches and nuances our understanding of how and why informality, liminality, and exceptionalism become institutionally entrenched and what this means for the stakeholders involved. Zooming in on how refugee governance works sheds new light on the ways in which furthering ambiguity can be strategic.

After a brief reflection on the specific research underlying this chapter, I offer a digested analysis of two case-studies that follows the three governance realms prioritized in my conceptual framework, showing how a combination of inaction and ambiguous action reproduces and extends uncertainty for refugees. This illustrates how a national politics of uncertainty is replicated locally – often because of opportunistic negotiation of these nationally imposed governance logics and sometimes despite their contestation. National state authorities either ignore illegal local approaches, denounce them without actually following through with sanctions, or openly criticize them while encouraging them behind closed doors. This does not merely dissolve accountability; it also makes refugees dependent on local 'strongmen' and thereby inherently exploitable.

In the realm of representation, I investigate the rationales and operation of, on the one hand, the regional and local governance actors that are being made responsible for dealing with the presence of Syrian refugees and, on the other hand, the various authorities that have emerged in the Syrian communities living in informal tented settlements. This analysis shows that exploitative institutions are informally encouraged and co-opted by security agencies, but never formally recognized by civil authorities, while more committee-like structures emerging in Syrian settlements are systematically undermined. This crucially premises the paralysis and pacification of refugee communities.

In the domain of status, I engage with the forms of local registration and administration developed by Lebanese state authorities. Municipal engagement with refugees is often reluctant. The local regulation systems that are in place are almost entirely informal, arbitrarily applied, and subject to change, which makes responsibility diffuse – even more so as these systems are increasingly taken over by a complex and shifting assemblage of security agencies.

In terms of space, I demonstrate the ways in which settlement evictions follow from and shape the local governance of refugees. The constant threat of displacement practically as well as psychologically reiterates the liminality and informality imposed on refugees. The arbitrary nature of recurring evictions, furthermore, testifies to the legal as well as political exceptionalism levelled against them. This further contributes to the fundamental unpredictability and insecurity that enables the control, exploitation, and expulsion of Syrian refugees in Lebanon.

Context and cases: studying refugee governance in the Central Bekaa

For the local analysis central to this chapter, I investigated regional and local (settlement-level) refugee governance modalities in the Central Bekaa district, which is part of Lebanon's Bekaa governorate. This governorate hosts most Syrian refugee settlements in the country, both absolutely and relatively (Zapater, 2018). By January 2018, there were 357,395 refugees registered by the United Nations High Commissioner for Refugees (UNHCR) in the Bekaa governorate and 161,202 in the Central Bekaa district.[2] The Bekaa has 540,000 inhabitants and is known for its agricultural richness and sectarian diversity, with major Christian, Armenian, and Shia communities, but also various Sunni and Druze towns and villages. The Central Bekaa is considered the Bekaa's economic hub and is the most diverse district of the province, resulting in a mosaic of political party affiliations and local alliances. Zahle, the main city in the Central Bekaa and home to a predominantly Christian population, particularly boasts a reputation of extreme autonomy and independence vis-à-vis national authorities.

In the Bekaa, relations with Syria have been intense in many ways. Socio-cultural ties are strong, seasonal migration of large numbers of Syrian agricultural workers (and sometimes their families) has been ubiquitous, and cross-border trading and smuggling has always been a major source of income. Throughout the Syrian regime's occupation of Lebanon, its military presence was particularly strong in the Bekaa. This generated resistance and has created a pervasive resentment towards Syria among many in the Bekaa that has also shaped engagement with refugees. This attitude is in many cases only fuelled by sectarian fears (Zahle's Christians feel particularly threatened by the influx of large communities of Sunni Muslims, which they see as destabilizing the demographic balance in the area) and economic concerns (regarding business competition, rent inflation, and undermining of touristic appeal) that prevail throughout the country.

The data for this chapter's analysis was generated during a three-month fieldwork period from February to April 2018 by a research partner based in Zahle.[3] During this period, 35 in-depth, semi-structured interviews were conducted – some in English and some in Arabic (with the help of a translator) – with Syrian refugees and their representatives; humanitarian experts affiliated with local, regional, and international non-governmental organizations (NGOs) and United Nations (UN) agencies; state officials (including representatives at the governorate and district levels, mayors, *mukhtars*, and regional coordinators fielded by national ministries); and Lebanese landlords.[4] In addition, various informal meetings were held with relevant stakeholders, including nine field visits to the two informal settlements serving as case-studies, of which reflexive observational notes were made. Documents were collected and solicited where relevant and possible.[5]

Research consisted of two components. The first sought to explore the regional governance structure in place to govern Syrian refugees by interviewing a variety of state officials and humanitarians. The second research component focused on two case-studies. These explored the local governance dynamics in specific Syrian settlements, investigating both internal dynamics and the relations between refugee representatives and local Lebanese authorities. The vast majority of Syrian refugees in Lebanon lives dispersed in urban settings. I have nevertheless opted to focus on refugee communities living in so-called informal tented settlements in more rural areas because the dynamics of strategic institutional ambiguity can be expected to be particularly relevant – and hence researchable – in these 'sites of experimentation in ad hoc camp management strategies' (Ghaddar, 2017). Informal settlements are thus not directly representative of the broader refugee presence in Lebanon in spatial terms, but the analysis in the previous chapter indicates that the encompassing dynamics of strategic ambiguity that the governance processes in informal settlements render particularly visible do hold across the country.

Informal Syrian refugee settlements are makeshift camps of tents, often made of materials provided by the UNHCR and other humanitarian organizations, that range in size from several tents to hundreds of them. The first settlement studied had around 500 inhabitants living in more than 90 tents and was located in a semi-urban Sunni town that was hosting 80 different Syrian settlements. This settlement was established some two years prior to data generation, when the community that had been living in a settlement not far away was forced to relocate after a dispute with the previous landlord. The second settlement hosted some 400 people and about 70 tents and was set in a rural, tribal Christian area with 45 settlements in total. This settlement did not fall under a specific municipality, but came under the direct responsibility of the governorate. It was established in 2008 to accommodate Syrian agricultural workers in the region. The settlement expanded when relatives and associates of these workers joined them when the situation in Syria worsened, with the most significant influx in 2014.

These two examples can clearly not represent the hundreds of different settlements in the Central Bekaa.[6] Throughout data generation, therefore, dynamics for these two specific cases were always contextualized by asking for broader local and regional governance realities. Case-related findings were extensively triangulated through literature and document analysis reflecting refugee governance more generally to explore to what extent they reflected the situation in the Bekaa at large. Yet, even if findings are relevant to the Bekaa at large, they are not automatically representative for Lebanon at large. Lebanon's various regions are vastly different in terms of sectarian and political affiliations, state presence, and socio-economic realities. They also greatly vary with regard to the number of refugees they are hosting relative to their original population. As Chapter 2 has shown, however, many of the overarching governance logics outlined in this chapter for the Central Bekaa resonate with analyses of refugee governance for Lebanon's other regions.

Preventing representation

Politicization and securitization of Lebanese local governance

The Lebanese governance structure in the Central Bekaa can be conceived of as consisting of several overlapping arenas. First, there is the civil state structure as represented by the various administrative levels of the Ministry of Interior. There is the governor (or *muhafez*) and his office (the *muhafaza*) who direct a district governor for each sub-region (the *qaymaqam*). Then, there are the municipalities (*baladiyat*), each headed by a mayor (or 'head of municipality,' *rais al baladiye*) presiding over a Municipal Council. An additional manifestation of the civil state structure in the Central Bekaa are the agencies headed by the Ministry of Social Affairs, which has offices in each district and manages Social Development Centers in many towns (some 50 in the entire Bekaa).

In its attempt to support the Lebanese state in dealing with the Syrian refugee presence, the UNHCR has reinforced these state structures with several new positions that were created with the aim to better manage the 'crisis,' resulting in a humanitarian governance tier that is partly integrated with the existing state structure. The UNHCR seconded a coordinator, who is under contract of the Minister of Interior, to support the provincial governor. It also fielded a coordinator under the Ministry of Social Affairs. This latter coordinator in particular functioned as the hub in the regional governance network concerned with Syrian refugees, liaising directly with the UNHCR and the Minister of Social Affairs, but also the provincial governor and his coordinator, all municipalities hosting significant refugee populations, and the humanitarian agencies working in the region.

A third set of actors relevant to understand the governance of Syrian refugees in the Bekaa constitutes a complicated assemblage of security agencies. It is extremely challenging to provide a complete and uncontested overview of the mandates and institutional embedding of Lebanese security agencies because these are often not publicly available. Various security agencies with overlapping directives and duplicating practices exist in an attempt to maintain a sectarian balance.

The most relevant security agencies were the Lebanese Armed Forces operating under the Ministry of Defense and its Military Intelligence branch (the *mukhabaraat*), which, in relation to Syrian refugees, is mostly involved in monitoring the informal settlements for 'terrorists.' The General Security (*amn el am*), which falls under the Ministry of Interior, is predominantly concerned with the residency status of refugees and is in charge of detaining people on the basis of illegal entry or residency. The police, or Internal Security Forces, also under the Ministry of Interior, were mostly responsible for maintaining public order, for instance through checkpoints where the identity and legal status of refugees is controlled. The municipal police, functioning directly under the municipality, was regularly involved in monitoring the more daily dynamics of the informal settlements, checking, for instance, the number of tents and inhabitants and liaising with camp representatives. Then there was the elusive State Security (*amn el dawle*), which reports to the Supreme Defense Council and is characterized by its 'rather unclear mandate' (Mazzola, 2019: 7). According to its website, the State Security coordinates with all security agencies, local authorities, and populations to address the issue of displaced people (including matters related to 'statistics' and 'settlements').[7] According to people in the field, the State Security was routinely involved in monitoring informal settlements and their residents (see also Ghaddar, 2017).[8]

There are various initiatives to delineate mandates and develop accountability mechanisms among security agencies (Atallah and Mahdi, 2017: 31). Yet the reality is more like what Wedeen (1999: 147) has called an 'anonymous, panoptic security' field. While security agencies at times cooperate, they do not structurally coordinate and often do not share information (International Alert and Lebanon Support, 2017: 3; Nashabe, 2009; Van Veen, 2015). In the governance of Syrian refugee settlements, this amalgamated security assemblage often takes precedence over the civil state structures in charge of dealing with the refugee presence. This securitization, with its inherently legitimate secrecy, strategic fragmentation and duplication, and self-evident unaccountability, is closely related to institutional ambiguity. It legitimates informality, liminality, and exceptionalism because reference to 'security issues' justifies any kind of measure taken towards refugees and serves to firmly place refugees outside the realm of 'normal politics' (Cassani, 2018: 64).

Considering Lebanon's sectarian consociationalism and the related politicization of the state, it is crucial to restate that the interaction of these three governance structures is decisively shaped by the political affiliations of the relevant agencies and officials. A previous ministerial advisor, for instance, explained that local branches of political parties have given clear directives, both private and public, on how (not) to deal with refugees to municipal officers – directives that become especially influential in light of the absence of consistent and operational-ized guidelines from the Ministry of Interior.[9] Considering Lebanon's sectarian-political diversity, such politicization means fragmentation. Different mayors have different political affiliations, and who they coordinate with and tend to take orders from is determined more by these political relations than by institutional hierarchies. Echoing other accounts, a Lebanese humanitarian working closely with municipal structures explained that the extent to which mayors comply with or ignore regional and national directives

> depends on the mayor's party: if he [the mayor] is with the Prime Minister [i.e. is from the same party as the Prime Minister] he will listen to the Minis-try of Interior, the Ministry of Education, the Ministry of Health, as they are all from the same party. But he is not listening to the others [to those ministers or state officials not affiliated with his party or parties allied with it].[10]

As on the national level, political fragmentation generates deadlock. The various Lebanese authorities involved in the regional governance of the Syrian refugee crisis in the Bekaa operate on different political logics and report via different insti-tutional structures. They do not structurally coordinate and often work in parallel or even against each other. As a foreign humanitarian coordinator working in the Bekaa explained, all sectarian groups and all related parties or political alliances will make sure to have a stake in each major department and issue, which means 'you always need all of them to get anything done.'[11] This, he dryly concluded, is mostly impossible so that often nothing gets done. The national decision-making paralysis regarding the governance of Syrian refugees is thus replicated locally. This absence of de jure local policies, however, should not obscure the de facto governance rationales that are at work on the municipal, district, and provincial levels. Such rationales often reinforce the informal, liminal, and exceptional nature of the Lebanese state's engagement with Syrians. As detailed in the follow-ing, this is potently illustrated by the way in which Lebanese authorities regulate representative institutions among Syrian refugee communities.

Local denunciation and co-optation of Syrian 'representatives'

As Ghaddar (2017) notes, since there are officially no refugee camps in Lebanon there is, again officially, 'no need for a camp management strategy.' In practice, of course, settlements will be governed whether they are officially acknowledged or not. The lack of formal acknowledgement, however, importantly shapes govern-ance realities. Syrian refugees in Lebanon did not develop the strong leadership networks needed to support mobilization that have emerged in, for instance, Jor-dan (Clarke, 2018). The 'absence of consultation on their [refugees'] fears, needs and perceptions on matters of their concern,' Atallah and Mahdi (2017: 18) note, is a key feature of the current Lebanese response to the refugee crisis (see also

Al-Saadi, 2015). This is a direct result of Lebanese authorities' approach towards the organization of refugee communities.

Syrian refugees have been largely abandoned by the Syrian government, whose embassy in Lebanon has not attempted to help or speak for refugees. There have been initiatives towards political mobilization and representation by, for instance, the National Coordination Body for Democracy and Change and the Union of Syrian Democrats, a sub-division of the Syrian National Coalition, but these have been unsuccessful (Kullab, 2014). This is partly because Syrian refugees in Lebanon often lack the will and capacity to organize themselves, not least because of their diverse background and political affiliations. But refugees also describe their tendency to keep a low profile as a form of 'conforming to state policies' (Atallah and Mahdi, 2017: 19). Indeed, Lebanese authorities are 'absolute in [their] opposition' to any form of 'empowering refugees by having dialogue with Syrian representatives' (Al-Saadi, 2015). As Al-Saadi (2015) concludes:

> Any project seeking to facilitate some form of political organization of the Syrian population is immediately nipped in the bud, because viewed from the prism of state security, it endangers political, social, and economic elites who are the main benefactors of the present state of affairs. Without representation from above, compounded by the various rifts within Syrian society itself, and the limitations of the international aid system, the Syrian populace is actively left without a voice, waiting in a limbo state for a change.

The lack of organization and mobilization among Syrian refugees in Lebanon thus at least partly results from Lebanese authorities' concerted efforts to undermine community organization beyond the *shawish*, which they have co-opted (Al-Masri and Altabbaa, 2016; Carpi, Younes and AbiYaghi, 2016; Lebanon Support, 2016). Despite the absence of formally recognized refugee representatives, unofficially there is such a *shawish*, or Syrian superintendent, in almost each settlement. The role of a *shawish* varies from one settlement to another and is a mixture of community representative, broker, and informant. *Shawishes*, various stakeholders reported, hardly coordinate among each other (see also Clarke, 2018: 626). He – although there are several female *shawishes* as well – can thus be considered a local authority inside the settlement and its representative towards external actors but should not be seen as part of a more comprehensive representational structure.

There are reported examples of elected *shawishes* (REACH and UNHCR, 2014: 13). More often *shawishes* are appointed by the landlord based on previous relations between the landlord and the leader of a specific community of Syrian workers or in acknowledgement of existing power relations in Syrian communities of origin. As Ghaddar (2017) importantly stresses, *shawishes* are often both exploited and exploiting. Though there are of course exceptions, *shawishes* are associated with a wide array of abuses and corruption – reportedly hijacking aid distribution and facilitating child labour and sexual exploitation. They benefit from their position economically (often receiving payment for their work from the landlord or extorting refugees) and socially (being under the 'protection' of influential Lebanese).

At the same time, they are at the mercy of Lebanese landlords and security agencies. *Shawishes* almost always work in close coordination with the Lebanese landlord on whose property the settlement they are associated with is established and who also often informally employs refugees. They are, in different ways and to different degrees, dependent on these landlords. This dependence is only exacerbated by the October 2014 policy and its operationalizing decrees which have sought to make landlords (and sponsors) into 'regulatory figures' responsible for monitoring and controlling refugees (Barjas, 2016). An important part of the job description of *shawishes*, furthermore, is 'being the eyes and ears' of the State Security, and to a lesser extent the Military Intelligence, and to report the names, political affiliations, and legal status of the people living in each settlement. In the first case-study settlement, the *shawish* was detained for not pro-actively contacting security services with what they considered to be relevant information to intimidate him into being 'a good eye in the settlement.'[12]

Shawishes are thus co-opted by Lebanese security agencies. They are also propped up by them. While there is no formal recognition of the *shawish*, landlords as well as mayors have reported that security agencies insisted that they appoint a *shawish* in each settlement. One mayor explained that he refused to allow *shawishes* in the settlements in his municipality as he dreaded the exploitation that comes with it, joking that he was 'the only *shawish* in town.'[13] This, however, reportedly got him in a fight with the local representative of the State Security that insisted he installed a Syrian *shawish* in each settlement. In the first settlement studied, the group of refugees that initiated the settlement in 2016 came with an existing *shawish* who was accepted by the landlord. When this *shawish* was deposed after a dispute, there was no *shawish* for half a year, and the landlord collected rent and reported to the municipality. Eventually, the landlord appointed a *shawish*, he said, not because he was in need of one, but because the municipality insisted there should be a Syrian *shawish* present in the settlement. A similar situation apparently occurred in the second settlement we studied. For some time, the associated landlord de facto acted as *shawish*. He only appointed the current *shawish* when the provincial governorate demanded he install a Syrian *shawish*.

Thus, *shawishes* are often imposed on refugee communities. This means that the Lebanese state enables the exploitation that *shawishes* engage in with the backing of and often under pressure of landlords. While *shawishes* are not recognized and often even denounced by Lebanese state authorities, in practice they appear to be strategically used to control Syrian communities. That this constant reinforcing of the informal and exceptional nature of Syrian representative structures reflects a distinct governance pattern becomes even more evident in light of the fact that alternative forms of representation or mobilization among Syrian communities, which may be less easily co-opted and subordinated, are reported to be systematically suppressed.

In many Syrian settlements there are not just *shawishes*, but various sorts of local committees as well. Mostly, such committees have been installed and trained by NGOs. These initiatives usually aim to connect such Syrian committees with local authorities and other relevant Lebanese stakeholders. Yet while committees were sometimes partially successful in their objective to liaise with Lebanese communities and NGOs, relations with local authorities were more problematic to form (Ortmans and Madsen, 2015: 11).[14] Overall, and with notable exceptions, attempts to establish committees as a systematic form of local representation for Syrian refugees living in informal settlements was broadly regarded as a failure by most interlocutors who were involved in such initiatives (see also Cassani, 2018: 53).

Not all aspects of refugee representation can be explained by host country governance. Syrian communities in informal settlements are often said to lack either the educational or cultural familiarity with democratic civil society structures to make committee-like initiatives into a success. Refugees, moreover, have clung to the prospect of going back to Syria as soon as possible, which is not conducive for investing in diaspora representation structures either. The nature of humanitarian involvement for committees is notoriously fragmented and short-term as well. The most important reason for the limited presence and functioning of committees, however, is the fact that Lebanese state authorities have communicated to NGOs that the facilitation of any form of Syrian organization, representation, or mobilization – which they explicitly mentioned included committees – was expressly prohibited for fear that this would suggest the permanent settlement of refugee communities (Ghaddar, 2017).

Reference to Syrian representation, consultation of Syrian communities, or even to the 'empowerment' of refugees, for instance, were anathema to the Lebanon Crisis Response Plan (LCRP), a humanitarian expert involved in drafting the LCRP observed.[15] A protection officer concluded that 'there is a very strong opposition from the Lebanese authorities to anything that can be seen as political, socio-political empowerment of the refugees.'[16] A specialist on legal assistance to refugees recalled humanitarian coordination meetings during which ministerial representatives would 'put PowerPoint presentations on saying: "we don't want committees, we don't want representation, avoid this, avoid that." . . . So the message was very clear.'[17] Local Lebanese state authorities have similar concerns and, as a political analyst active in the refugee response noted, 'many municipalities refuse to have Syrians present in any form of consultation meetings with the argument that they're not representatives of the community and the decision-making is a matter in the hands of the Lebanese.'[18]

While NGOs have not docilely accepted this de facto no-committee policy of the Lebanese state, it has greatly complicated their efforts to enable a more representative alternative to the *shawish*. In the settlements studied, in one case an NGO reported to have established an active committee. No other organizations were aware of the existence of this committee, however, and, on the ground, only one member could be identified. He initially denied he was part of any committee and later indicated he had no tasks but to administer the electricity fees. In the other case, there was no formal committee, but the wife of the *shawish* served as liaison for several NGOs. Thus, what appear to be institutionalized and coherent organizational structures in the discourse of the organizations supporting them, turn out to be elusive and implicit networks in the field.

Instead of the intended committees, which an analyst noted have now become 'imaginary,' many organizations work with individual representatives – so-called 'focal points' or 'outreach volunteers' – that receive minimal training in referrals.[19] These, however, only serve as contacts for the individual NGOs that established them. The more comprehensive ambition to facilitate institutional relations between refugee representatives and local Lebanese authorities has mostly been abandoned under pressure of Lebanese authorities. Instead, NGOs work with the *shawish* when distributing aid or implementing projects, further reinforcing his position.

The fact that there are no actual coherent organizational structures to represent Syrian refugees and that the forms of 'representation' that do emerge are exploitative rather than consultative and serve Lebanese authorities more than Syrian refugees is both cause and consequence of the institutional ambiguity determining Lebanon's engagement with Syrian refugees. It reflects and reinforces informality, because interactions between Lebanese and Syrian stakeholders can never be official. It illustrates and ensures liminality, as representation on the Syrian side and its relation with Lebanese power structures is always temporary and conditional on Lebanese goodwill. And it demonstrates and sustains the exceptionalism Syrian refugees are subjected to, because it makes Lebanese engagement with Syrian refugees arbitrary and opportunistic.

The institutional ambiguity furthered by this particular form of Syrian camp governance is the result of strategic action as much as of contingent inaction. De jure, Lebanese authorities refuse to recognize any form of Syrian representation. De facto, they undermine the creation of relatively representative committees while ambiguously denying yet enabling – even insisting on – exploitative authority in the form of *shawishes*. This has put in place a system of indirect rule that allows authorities to control refugee communities in informal settlement and makes it possible for landlords and their political and economic patrons to benefit from the Syrian presence.

In the settlements studied, landlords systematically threaten refugees who do not pay with eviction. When refugees do pay, they are often forced to pay more than agreed through inflated service bills or 'double payments.' As a Lebanese manager of a local NGO working with refugees in the Bekaa noted: 'Everybody knows if something happens or they fought or break the agreement, the Syrian refugee can't do anything about it.'[20] Such exploitation is facilitated by local authorities. A Lebanese liaison officer with an international refugee organization who was working closely with refugee hosting municipalities in the Bekaa explained:

The major, most of the majors, don't want more refugees, but you know. . . . When the refugee comes to a land to build a tent, the landlord . . . he is from the town. So the major is like: 'I don't want to tell the people in my town "no," because then they don't make money and then they would think I don't want them to make money.'[21]

Other people working in the Bekaa agreed that the Lebanese state is 'using' refugees, as a communication officer of an international refugee organization formulated it.[22] The exploitation enabled through a de facto policy of marginalization following from imposed informality and uncertainty, in the words of a critical international area manager for an international NGO working in the Central Bekaa, allowed 'every rich Lebanese' – referring to 'politicians and landlords and security services' – to get richer.[23]

Obfuscating status

Lebanese authorities in the Central Bekaa thus impose informality, liminality, and exceptionalism on refugees through the parameters they set for Syrians' representational structures. This helps them to prevent the organization and mobilization of refugees. The furthering of institutional ambiguity is also evident in other domains of governance, such as the administrative and regulatory processes that determine refugees' local registration status. This section describes how such processes look, why they take the form they do, and what their consequences are for the people involved. It demonstrates that initiatives to register and order refugees abound, but that these are not officially centrally coordinated and therefore vary per locality and are arbitrary and unstable. This uncertainty makes such measures potent as a disciplinary instrument.

The governance of Syrian refugees in the Central Bekaa as encountered during fieldwork was probably more structured than in most other regions of Lebanon, as interlocutors routinely emphasized. Regional representatives of national ministries that have been seconded by the UNHCR and its representatives in the region have been particularly active in trying to organize the refugee response and coordinate with local authorities and humanitarian organizations. These attempts for regulation, however, have mostly focused on structuring the humanitarian response and keeping in line the wild grow of humanitarian projects and programs and less on the conduct of state agencies.

The governance of refugees by municipalities is crucially premised by the national politics described in the previous chapter. Syrian refugees in Lebanon lack formal refugee status and a vast majority of them does not have legal residency status either. This relegates them to an informal and liminal existence in Lebanon. It also determines the way in which local Lebanese authorities engage with refugees. Municipalities have been confronted with the very real implications of the arrival of large numbers of often destitute people. Due to the initial absence of any national policy or approach, they have played a vanguard role in the de facto response to the arrival of refugees. 'Overburdened, overstretched, and under-resourced' as Lebanese municipalities are, this has been an impressive feat

(Atallah and Mahdi, 2017: 5). Although the central government appears to see municipalities as the main intermediary between them and refugee communities, municipalities have been excluded from any formal policy-making dynamics. Mayors highlighted this lack of guidance, policy, and support from the national level and felt abandoned, 'forgotten,' by what they saw as the failure and indifference of the 'national politicians.'[24] Seconding the mayor cited at the opening of this chapter, another mayor indicated: 'Our government doesn't have a policy towards the refugees, and this is making it very hard for us to put a policy.'[25]

Repressive registration

The local leeway that follows from this experienced abandonment, however, is not total. When it comes to registering refugees, for instance, local dynamics have followed the national development from inaction to ambiguous repressive action described in Chapter 2. Municipalities have increasingly been obliged to engage in some form of registration of refugees. Most refugee settlements emerged in the first few years after the Syrian uprising, when the border between Syria and Lebanon was still open and the 'no-policy-policy' was unchallenged. When the October 2014 policy was issued, local authorities mostly had no clear idea how many camps existed or where and who was residing in them. In the October 2014 policy, however, municipalities were made responsible for the administration of refugees in their territory. Yet no resources were allocated for this and no concrete instructions on how municipalities should actually do this were offered by the Ministry of Interior (Atallah and Mahdi, 2017: 22). The registration practices were thus not centralized and differed per municipality.

All mayors interviewed indicated that they registered refugees, but the ways in which this was done, the type of information that was collected, and the subsequent use of this information varied. Registration entails noting the names of the refugees in their area of jurisdiction as well as their address or the settlement where they live and the related landlord and (where applicable) Lebanese sponsor (Janmyr and Mourad, 2018: 555). In some cases, municipalities have required refugees to pay a monthly fee for renewable identification cards (Barjas, 2016; Stel, 2015a). While most municipalities request refugees (or the landlords and *shawishes* that 'represent' them) to come to the municipality to report new arrivals, other municipalities actively check and monitor such reporting themselves, by sending municipal police or other municipal employees to check with the *shawish*.

In the first case-study settlement, the mayor indicated that he 'monitors ninety percent of them [Syrian refugees]' through the municipal police who register 'all the names, who comes, who leaves.'[26] The area in which the second case-study settlement was located, in contrast, was described as 'the middle of chaos' by an NGO fieldworker active in this settlement.[27] This settlement does not fall under a municipality and is therefore placed directly under the jurisdiction of the governorate. While the governor claimed that he would respond to the requests of Lebanese and Syrians from this area exactly like a municipality would, there did not appear to be any active registration procedure. And according to a humanitarian organization active in this settlement, the governor 'does not even know where it [the settlement in question] is!'[28]

The lack of ministerial oversight of municipal registration of refugees means that the degree and nature and consequences of such registration vary per municipality. In line with the general governance landscape outlined earlier, it also means that municipal registration has been almost completely securitized. Indeed, while there appears to be no central ministerial oversight, the various security agencies seem to have taken up registration in a relatively coordinated campaign. The municipal representatives consulted all indicated that they only started to register refugees in 2016 when they were pressured to do so by various security agencies.

Mayors and municipal council members recounted how security agencies instructed and accompanied municipal police in an effort to map which refugees lived where that lasted several weeks. After that, security agencies expected municipalities to keep updating such records so that the agencies could request this information whenever they wanted (apparently in addition to their own separate surveillance efforts). Indeed, this seems the main reason why municipalities care about and engage in such registration practices at all (Janmyr and Mourad, 2018: 12). Most of the time, apparently, municipalities only update their lists on Syrian refugees when confronted with security agencies' requests for information, in such instances themselves calling on the *shawish* for an update on the current situation. With the exception of particularly powerful and autonomous mayors, municipal authorities do not seem to care about rigorously controlling refugees as much as they care about not getting on the wrong side of security agencies.

Thus, as one interlocutor working for a humanitarian organization noted, 'on a municipal level, people generally know who is who and who is where,' but such local registration is not centralized or shared systematically, particularly when it comes to refugees living in informal settlements. Some mayors indicated that data on refugees was shared with the governorate or the government. A regional state representative indeed insisted that:

> We need to know. They [Lebanese who want to facilitate a refugee settlement on their land] need to tell the municipality, and the municipality has to tell us. If it is possible or not, if there are any problems, how they do it, if there is something; . . . If they arrive . . . all the logistics we need to know. . . . I represent the government with this thing [the refugee response], I am the boss on what happens. They need to tell me. I represent the Ministry: They need to tell me. I am the boss of the area, they need to tell me. All of them, any change, they tell me, everything. If something happened, if there are problems.[29]

This insistence on his authority, however, did not so much reflect a current reality as it indicated frustration with a situation that did not at all correspond to this vision of compliant and information-providing municipalities. Most mayors indicated that they would share information on refugees with other state authorities upon request. Such requests, they subsequently noted, came almost exclusively from security agencies.

Refugee registration practices thus reflect and reify refugees' exceptionalism. As discussed in the previous chapter, the Lebanese government deliberately withholds both refugee status and residency status from refugees. This renders refugees administratively invisible to civil state authorities and creates a protection gap. At the same time, on a municipal level, registration of refugees is commonplace, but highly securitized. Registration is either done exclusively by security agencies or by municipalities who mostly act on their behalf. Refugees, in this way, are made explicitly visible to mostly repressive security agencies. Following the logic of exceptionalism, then, Syrian refugees in the Bekaa are excluded from the civil state's formal purview and included in informal security scrutiny. This form of institutional ambiguity – inaction on the one hand; partial, fragmented, and informal action on the other – contributes to the vulnerability of refugees that makes them controllable, exploitable, and displaceable. Registration in no way amounts to entitlements or protection for refugees, but rather serves to intimidate and undermine them.

The issuing of municipal identity cards for Syrian refugees, for instance, is often motivated as a way to comply with the General Security's request for information. But, as Barjas (2016) convincingly argues, such cards are only provided to refugees holding legal residency, 'leaving the pressing question of why the General Security would need this card, given that they have already collected all the information it contains through the requirements necessary to grant official residency.' Just like the curfews, raids, and evictions described later, registration, for a local observer working for a humanitarian organization, is a way to tell refugees: 'We have an eye on you; don't get comfortable.'[30]

Arbitrary permission

In October 2016 the then-governor of the Bekaa sent a memo to municipalities to 'remind' them that no new tents were to be allowed in the Bekaa. This was a reiteration of circular 21/2014 that followed the October 2014 policy, which formally decided against the set-up of refugee camps (Daily Star, 2016). The translated version of the memo provided by a representative of a humanitarian organization states that:

> Municipalities and Municipal Unions are reminded not to allow the establishment and transfer of Syrian refugee camps within their jurisdictions, and to let us [the governorate] know about any project for setting up a camp or any request in this regard and not to authorize the establishment of a new tent or settlement.

Since – with the exception of some elusive 'humanitarian cases' – officially no refugees could enter Lebanon anymore since 2015 anyway, this was not a shocking announcement. However, as described in the following, evictions of refugee settlements take place regularly. Therefore, an exception was made for tents that had to be relocated after an eviction. In such cases, a specific procedure for obtaining permission was to be followed. This procedure, however, was never standardized, regularized, or clearly communicated to the actors involved. Rather, its logics were contextual and contingent and developed over time. Regional humanitarian experts explained that a landlord, on behalf of the refugee seeking to install a new tent, needs to contact the municipality. Then the municipality applies for permission with the provincial governor, who would consult with the State Security and Military Intelligence. If these found no trouble with the request, the provincial governor would send his approval to the municipality, who would communicate it to the landlord and refugee. In most cases, permission would be verbal. In some cases, written notices or files following various formats were processed and signed by the landlord, the municipality, or the provincial governor.

These regional ordering mechanisms, however, are entirely informal, in that they are not officially documented and are dependent on the agreement and commitment of specific individuals rather than official regulations or mandates. The permission procedure for relocating tents came about in a completely 'unsystematic' way, according to a refugee response coordinator.[31] Personal contacts, he reflected, are 'the key to everything you asked about. I am talking to everyone; it is all our personal contacts – the military, the ISF [Internal Security Forces], my minister, other ministers, we solve our problems through our contacts.'[32] As another key stakeholder in the regional coordination of the refugee response summarized: 'I don't think we have a system, I just know everyone.'[33]

Such informality makes the permission 'system' complicated to navigate for refugees. While it appears relatively logical to humanitarian agencies, for most refugees it is unclear whom they need permission from if they seek to rebuild their tents after being evicted and how to get such permission. Even if they follow the steps outlined by humanitarian agencies, it is tenuous what such permission exactly entails and under which conditions it is extended, so that a sense of perpetual anxiety remains. Despite this situation, refugees have little choice but to try and comply with such de facto regulations. Because when permission – however interpreted – is not sought, interlocutors indicated, there is a fair chance that the 'illegal' tents are indeed demolished by security agencies. This, as a humanitarian coordinator put it, 'is not a law, it is day-to-day reality.'[34] It is a day-to-day reality that leaves refugees at the mercy of landlords and local authorities and, as discussed in the section on the spatial dimensions of governance, works to disperse refugees and facilitate their return to Syria. The unpredictability and obscurity of local registration, reporting, and permission practices make refugees more vulnerable and easier to contain.

'Permissions' are used to call into question rather than validate refugees' presence on the ground. This is well-illustrated by the appointment of a new governor in December 2017. Apparently, in April 2018, this new governor internally announced a plan for a complete overhaul of the aforementioned permission 'system.' Well-informed interlocutors discussed this development as a 'policy' rather than as a mere 'decision' and suggested it was backed up by the Council of Ministers.[35] At the time of research it was unclear whether the plan would actually be implemented, but its very nature is indicative for the way in which institutional ambiguity works. As with the nonperformativity of the Minister of State for Displaced Affairs discussed in Chapter 2, it reveals how even processes that (appear to) attempt to regularize – which may or may not be 'genuine' – end up further fueling uncertainty and how the strategic utilization of ambiguity and its contingent extension are intricately intertwined.

The Bekaa's new governor wanted to see the de facto procedure in place to obtain permission for the establishment of new tents (as an exception to the overall decree that no new tents are allowed in the Bekaa region) changed significantly. The existing protocol had refugees who were evicted in the Bekaa seek permission to relocate elsewhere by having the respective landlord send a request to the governor's office. The governor subsequently consulted the relevant security services and then sent his decision to the municipality in question, a process that could be entirely verbal. The newly suggested procedure, instead, was to be completely in writing, stakeholders stressed. It allegedly stipulated that landlords should approach their municipality and the municipality should file a written request to the regional coordinator for the Ministry of Social Affairs. This coordinator would then need to assess whether the settlement to which the tent is to be added meets the humanitarian standards to host more people and, if this is found to be the case, forward the request to the governor. The governor would then seek to obtain the formal permission of the Ministry of Social Affairs as well as the informal go-ahead of the security agencies, based on which he should make the final decision on the request. This decision, I was told, was to be reported back to the regional Social Affairs coordinator, who communicates it to the municipality that filed the request, who was supposed to inform the relevant landlord, who was expected to brief the refugees in question.

The drive for formalization, regularization, and centralization of the regional refugee response apparent in this plan was in principle warmly welcomed by many stakeholders involved in regional refugee governance. It can be read as an attempt to work against the very institutional ambiguity described earlier. Interlocutors, however, were not only skeptical about the viability of 'following rules in a country without rules' but even more about the genuineness of the initiative.[36] In theory, the plan would improve the situation. In practice, a humanitarian coordinating with state agencies on a daily basis pointed out, it was easy to predict for anyone with experience in the region that it would make matters far worse for refugees.

Some of the people consulted, who worked for either humanitarian organizations or state agencies involved in addressing the refugee presence in the Bekaa, suspected that the plan for the new 'policy' was the result of the new governor's obliviousness of the situation on the ground. Others saw in it a strategic move. They suspected that the governor aimed to be publicly heralded for claiming more leadership for the Lebanese state while counting on the inevitable failure of his over-ambitious plans, which would directly contribute to the government's stated goal to push for refugee return. The eventual failure of the presented plan would, they predicted, generate further chaos and, hence, increase the vulnerability of refugees and accelerate their return. Considering the well-known lack of capacities and resources of the ministries involved at the regional level and the lack of initiatives to remedy this, the new guidelines that allegedly aimed to ensure more regularization and formalization would in reality unsurprisingly amount to passing the buck and stalling, thereby producing a large caseload of unresolved requests and elongating refugees' liminality. A Lebanese humanitarian coordinator observed that while evictions were increasing, permission to relocate tents became almost impossible to obtain due to the new demands. Several critical humanitarian field officers and coordinators, including some seconded to state agencies, thus read the appointment of the new governor as a way to pressure refugees in the area to leave.

It is impossible to determine the 'actual' intentions of the governor for floating this new approach, which are probably multiple and convoluted and circumstantial, but the predictable outcomes of the plan – if it would be implemented – suggest further limbo and marginalization. These expected outcomes also show how, in the context of hybrid order outlined in Chapter 1, individual initiatives towards regularization go against dominant governmentalities and tend to eventually succumb to them – which may or may not be intended. They would help to incentivize refugee return, which has emerged as the key priority of Lebanese engagement with Syrian refugees. This intention to incentivize refugee returns, as the next section shows, is also evident in local authorities' attempts to govern refugee spaces through the implementation of curfews, the prevalence of raids, and the threat of eviction.

Undermining spaces

As noted in the previous chapter, Lebanon has refused the establishment of Syrian refugee camps. This 'no-camp policy' has been the outcome of the inability to make any decision in the early days of the refugee crisis. But refusing to establish official camps for Syrian refugees and forbidding the UN to do so also signalled and ensured the temporary nature, the liminality, of the refugee crisis. Foregoing the establishment of formal camps did not prevent de facto camps from emerging. The uncontrolled spread of informal settlements that occurred under the 'no-camp policy,' Sanyal (2017: 120, 122) suggests, can be seen as having occurred with the 'tacit approval of the state' to combine the 'confinement that is a key feature of camps with the precariousness of informality.'

That Lebanon has sought to retain the apparent temporary nature of the crisis is evident in its stance towards the material and infrastructural aspects of refugee settlement. When it comes to refugee shelter, Achilli, Yassin, and Erdoğan (2018: 27) conclude, 'any kind of built structure was instructed by the government to be temporary.' Utility service provision in Syrian refugee settlements is deliberately kept disconnected. Drinking water, for instance, is provided to settlements through water trucking by private companies sometimes paid for by humanitarian agencies. This is because authorities prohibit the connection of the settlements to local water piping systems or sewage infrastructure, which, they argue, would signal the permanence of the settlements. Analysts affiliated with the UN explained:

> When it comes to electricity and water and so on, as you know, there is no appetite whatsoever to have anything that's even medium-term in terms of infrastructure for refugees. So there is very little connecting places to existing water and electricity infrastructure, etc. So on that front there's very little that's being done and that is not by accident, that is because it's not wanted.[37]

A spokesperson of an international NGO working in the region reflected on her failed lobbying with local authorities and the Ministry of Energy and Water to convince them that the rehabilitation of local service infrastructures and the concomitant connection of Syrian settlements to these structures would be a 'win-win situation.' The unwavering message, she said, was 'if you connect them, they will stay.'[38] This experience came up in many other interviews with humanitarian actors as well, who confirmed this stance as a 'policy' to 'reject local integration' (see also Zapater, 2018).[39]

Curfews and raids

Local authorities go out of their way to avoid such integration not just because of a principled political commitment to ensuring the temporariness of refugee settlements. Lack of national guidance, sectarian concerns, and the pressure that informal settlements put on local communities and infrastructures have made local authorities and communities consider refugees a threat (Ghanem, 2016). One of the most obvious ways in which municipalities have reacted to this perceived threat has been to impose curfews on refugees. Municipal curfews are illegal if they are not sanctioned by the High Military Command, but they have nevertheless been installed throughout the country without such sanctioning (Al-Saadi, 2014). Curfews are declared through either personal or public announcements, using, for instance, banners or local WhatsApp groups. These declare that Syrians (sometimes referred to as 'displaced' or 'foreigners') are not to leave their shelters after a particular time. Their scope is often unclear: sometimes curfews only regard single men or specific age groups or, for instance, refer to refugees with motorized transportation specifically. They are upheld by municipal police or local militias, vigilantes, and 'neighborhood watches,' which are regularly condoned by the police and operate with support of local political parties (Human Rights Watch, 2018: 52; see also Sanyal, 2018: 73). In short, as Al-Saadi (2014) notes, exactly because 'there are no rules or regulations governing the procedure' regarding curfews, their implementation 'is left to the discretion of these forces.'

This means that both refugees and citizens are often not fully aware whether or not curfews are enacted and by whom and what the consequences of violating them actually are (these can range from fines to arrests and molestation) (International Alert and Lebanon Support, 2017: 6). In the settlement that constituted the second case-study that this chapter draws on, for instance, refugees referred to a municipal curfew despite the absence of a municipality in that particular village. A local representative of a humanitarian organization who worked with this community explained that this perceived 'municipal' curfew was in fact an 'unofficial' curfew installed by the local Lebanese community.[40] The owner of the land on which the settlement was built clarified that this curfew only regarded 'unknown' Syrians, saying that each Syrian was free to go wherever whenever as long as she or he was 'known' by 'the locals' and could indicate with which Lebanese landlord (s)he was affiliated.[41] The disciplinary workings of measures such as curfews, then, are not produced simply through the social and spatial restrictions that they entail, as these are often difficult to enforce. Rather, they importantly operate through the uncertainty that surrounds such curfews, which leads to self-policing. Curfew practices thus illustrate how ambiguity is a crucial component of governance and control when authorities lack material and political resources.

This is further illustrated by the occurrence of raids of informal settlements, a second measure to spatially control refugee communities. As described prior, security agencies sometimes rely on municipal registration and monitoring, but they gather their own intelligence as well. As noted earlier, the *shawish* associated with the first case-study settlement explained that security agencies ask their informants for reports on names, legal status, political affiliations, previous 'trouble' with Lebanese or Syrian authorities (ranging from outstanding fines to earlier arrests) of all residents of the settlement and any incidents involving drugs or weapons that might have occurred (see also REACH and UNHCR, 2014: 25).[42] Other *shawishes* consulted similarly insisted that they had no choice but to tell the security agencies what they wanted to know, because they would suffer severe consequences if they were found to withhold information. Withholding information, moreover, is further complicated because surveillance is often unpredictable and violent.

In the first case-study, settlement raids reportedly happened every three to six months by various security agencies. The landlord indicated that once over 40 residents of the settlement were taken by the Military Intelligence and held for a day. In the second settlement, in contrast, after several raids, the landlord pulled his strings with the security agencies and arranged for them to call him to request any information, rather than to come into the settlement unannounced. This reflects other interlocutors' remarks that security agencies tend to disengage from settlements that are under protection of influential local 'bosses.'[43] It further demonstrates the emergence of what Ghaddar (2017) has called 'strong, illegal, and hybrid security networks,' which she defines as 'unnoticed arrangements between formal security agencies and informal security actors backed by powerful landowning families, tribes, and political party bosses' that developed in the absence of a comprehensive refugee policy.

As with curfews, it is not simply the restrictions or violence that raids impose that make them effective disciplinary measures. It is their unpredictability and the unaccountability of the often unspecified actors involved in them that crucially add to the potency of these measures to undermine not just refugees' safety and wellbeing but their ability for concerted collective action. Refugees and humanitarian organizations working with them, tellingly, saw raids not so much as ways for security agencies to obtain information, which, they pointed out, agencies could easily obtain in less violent ways. Instead, they suspected that these practices were part of a campaign to 'let them know they are being watched,' to contain refugees and 'encourage' them to leave.[44]

Evictions

A similar logic underlies the endemic evictions of Syrian refugee settlements that reflect and reproduce the informal, liminal, and exceptional position of Syrian refugees in Lebanon and that demonstrate how such institutional ambiguity works to marginalize and expel. Eviction of refugee settlements is widespread, as carefully documented by Human Rights Watch (2018). In 2014, more than 11,000 people were evicted from informal settlements and other forms of collective shelters (UNHCR, 2015: 6). Since then, numbers have only increased. Eviction is by now the main reason refugees report for leaving a specific locality (UNHCR, United Nations Children's Fund and World Food Program, 2017: 28). In 2017, 43 percent of respondents in a study conducted by Oxfam (2017: 4) had been displaced more than once since their arrival in Lebanon. State agencies – mostly municipalities and security agencies – are involved in the vast majority of these evictions (Human Rights Watch, 2018: 17; UNHCR, United Nations Children's Fund and World Food Program, 2017: 28).

Municipal evictions can best be understood in the context of municipalities' attempts to maintain local order that were discussed earlier. Municipalities, for example, often claim that evictions follow refugees' breaches of housing regulation, for instance when rent contracts are not registered. Such violations are routine among Lebanese citizens as well, however, and these are not targeted in evictions. Violations of labour or visa regulations are also often used as a pretext for evictions despite the fact that, as crucially stressed by Human Rights Watch (2018: 4), these do not constitute a legal basis for eviction under Lebanese law. In practice, then, municipal evictions are often a form of collective punishment for alleged crimes conducted by individual Syrians. This makes almost all municipal evictions illegal.

Municipal evictions are characterized by an absence of uniformity and consistency, varying from municipality to municipality. In some cases, refugees were coerced to sign written eviction orders (which were sometimes pinned to people's doors), Human Rights Watch (2018: 26) chronicles. In other cases, orders were only communicated verbally. The actors implementing evictions are different in different localities as well, often reflecting hybrid arrangements of municipal police, Internal Security Forces, and local 'thugs,' regularly affiliated with specific political parties. At times, those enforcing evictions were extremely aggressive, whereas in other locations they were more civilized.

The process of eviction is equally arbitrary, with vastly different time spans given to refugees to leave and large variations in the severity with which orders were followed up, with extensive violence characterizing some, but not all, eviction cases. When receiving a notice of eviction, 70 percent of Oxfam's (2017: 4) respondents for a study on the implications of eviction were given fewer than 15 days to leave their place of residence, and 20 percent of those were told to leave immediately. Such short notices have contributed to the fact that only one-quarter of the evicted people were able to find a new accommodation right away, turning refugee families to the streets (Oxfam, 2017: 4). Thus, apart from the illegality of their grounds, the process of eviction was consistently illegal as well, lacking any form of proper consultation, information, or compensation.

In addition to evictions ordered by municipalities, Syrian refugee settlements are sometimes evicted through orders of various security agencies. Such evictions are often legitimized with reference to a circular issued by the Military Intelligence that settlements are not allowed in the vicinity of 'security areas,' checkpoints, and major roads and waterways. This circular was referred to routinely by many people in the field, but it could not be obtained formally or provided by them. They, however, noted that the circular is quite vague and applied arbitrarily. What exactly counts as a 'security area,' for instance, is not specified. Which roads and waterways would be 'major' is not either. Because checkpoints are mostly established and relocated ad hoc, moreover, it is quite likely that they are erected near existing settlements rather than settlements being built next to checkpoints. The interpretation of the decision seems to have become increasingly expansive since 2014 as well. Settlements along 'vital supply lines and border areas' are now being included in evictions where these did not appear to be a problem earlier (UNHCR, 2015: 6). The circular thus produces arbitrariness and legitimizes almost any eviction that any security agency deems necessary. It probably also underlies the series of eviction notices that the Lebanese Armed Forces issued in the Bekaa in 2015 and which affected some 9,000 refugees living in settlements close to the border (UNHCR, 2015: 3). Thus, Atallah and Mahdi (2017: 33) conclude, 'legal frameworks are neither useful nor relevant' to assess evictions, which security agencies enforce solely on grounds of non-specified 'security concerns.'

Evictions of refugees by municipalities and security agencies reflect the logics of institutional ambiguity in terms of process as well as outcomes. Eviction processes are unpredictable: Displacement mostly lacks legal grounds, does not follow due process, and instigators and implementers are mostly not clearly identifiable or accountable. The outcome of these processes is uncertainty for refugees and the organizations trying to help them: They do not – and cannot – know how to prevent, challenge, or manage evictions and are left with no guidelines and few alternatives for relocation after eviction. Evictions thus illustrate well the ways in which Lebanon's approach to dealing with Syrian refugees is characterized by informality, liminality, and exceptionalism and how it helps to generate a situation of permanent uncertainty and existential ambiguity for refugees. They contribute to refugees' marginalization, which enables their pacification and exploitation, and they constitute a push factor for refugees' return to Syria.

Evicted refugees are forced to leave behind property and lose already paid rent and deposits. They almost always have to incur debts to finance their relocation, often including bribes for 'permission' to relocate. Evictions severely undermine refugees' income-generating strategies and disrupt education. They undercut their informal protection mechanisms dependent on the local networks they are cut off from by eviction. Evictions, moreover, hamper the operation of NGOs that seek to help refugees. For them, too, investments previously made in evicted settlements are lost. A large amount of staff time and resources that cannot be allocated to the purposes they were initially meant for are needed when NGOs organize relocations (Limoges, 2017).

The perpetual nature of the eviction threat that Syrian refugees living in informal settlements face deepens this marginalization. It produces, as Sanyal (2017: 123) has also noted, 'a sense of emotional insecurity that can limit the activities of people' and undermine their agency. An affected refugee tellingly spoke about his constant 'restlessness' due to fear that 'it will happen again' (Domat, 2017). The fact that evictions are always possible but never predictable also affects humanitarian organizations. An NGO worker explained that one of the reasons why there were relatively few NGOs currently working in the area in which the second case-study settlement was located – which was in the vicinity of Riyak, where one of the largest evictions of Syrian refugee settlements has taken place so far (Stel and Van der Meijden, 2018) – was because there were rumors that further evictions would happen, meaning that investing in the settlements there was a risk for the NGOs in question.

Evictions, enabled by the informal nature of the affected settlements, also correlate with mounting hostility and discrimination against refugees and politicians' increasingly explicit calls for refugees to return to Syria. Human Rights Watch (2018: 2) reports empirical evidence that while written eviction orders merely tell refugees to leave the specific locality, these are often accompanied by verbal orders to 'go back to Syria.' Other organizations, too, have noted how the increasing number of evictions conspicuously corresponds with the 'growing political discourse calling for the return of refugees to Syria' (Oxfam, 2017a: 3; see also Limoges, 2017). In the context of the Bekaa's Syrian refugee settlements, a humanitarian field officer recalled that the *shawish* and landlord who had been in charge of a settlement that had been evicted applied for permission with the governorate to relocate. They were told they would not get the permission to relocate but had to leave the country. If they would consider going back to Syria, they would receive help to do so. Instead of granting permission to relocate, the governorate offered them assistance in safely crossing the border and promised to waive any exit fees or outstanding fines if they did so.[45] This resonates with the comments made by an informed interlocutor who indicated that internal directives inside the governorate on how to deal with the files that request relocation of tents after evictions emphasize the importance of 'letting the number [of Syrian refugees in Lebanon] decrease, letting them go home.'[46] Such directives, he explained, follow from the assumption that not giving permission or delaying permission to reestablish tents after evictions will encourage refugees to return to Syria.

Evictions have thus become a means to enforce 'voluntary' return. NGOs consider evictions as 'closely linked to the new government's strategy to push people to go back to Syria.'[47] Several families have indeed been reported to have left Lebanon as a direct result of their (often repeated) forced evictions (Human Rights Watch, 2018: 4). Thus, while Human Rights Watch (2018: 17) rightfully notes that the increasingly frequent evictions of Syrian refugee settlements are not the result of a 'coherent, national plan,' they do reflect and contribute to the precarity that has emerged in the context of institutional ambiguity.

The national-local 'role play:' encouraging, condoning, denying

Lebanon's response to the Syrian refugee presence in the country has been discussed in two separate chapters, focusing on the national and local levels, respectively. It should be clear, however, that such 'levels' are by no means separate arenas of policy and politics. National and local governance are evidently linked, but because there is no comprehensive official policy to engage with the presence of Syrian refugees in Lebanon, such linkages are either unofficial or limited to specific sectors and projects. National directives never simply dictate local dynamics, but they do influence them. The same goes for the nigh total absence of such directives. The Lebanese government has not provided municipalities with an official overarching policy guideline that instructs local authorities on how to engage in the governance realms of representation, status, and space. As a result, Achilli, Yassin, and Erdoğan (2018: 32) conclude: 'there is no official communication channel that currently exists between the national government and local authorities to respond to the crisis.'

Even in the probably exceptional cases where municipalities explicitly ask national authorities for clarity, they are kept in the dark. A municipal council member from Zgharta-Ehden in North Lebanon interviewed by Legal Agenda, for instance, said his municipality had repeatedly asked the General Security and 'all parties involved with the issue of refugees' to 'define the nature of our authority, and the procedures we can undertake in the matter,' for instance, wondering whether the municipality should arrest refugees without legal residency status (Barjas, 2016). The municipality did not receive any reply.

Supra-local governance actors either ignore or condone local responses to the refugee presence. In fact, local measures are often nationally encouraged while they are publicly denied or disowned at the same time. Interlocutors suggested that national state officials officially do not want to know what is going on locally so that they cannot be held responsible. Unofficially, however, these same officials are often well aware of local realities through information they receive via political party or security agency channels. This paradox of national pretending not to know was characterized as a 'role-play' by a Lebanese human rights analyst. As Sanyal (2017: 117) showed, such role-plays function as a 'system of deregulation [which] is enabling refugee spaces to emerge that are visible, yet unrecognized.'

This informal deregulation functions as a form of outsourcing. The International Crisis Group (2015: 11) found that 'central authorities have partially relinquished their responsibility to maintain law and order, allowing local councils and communities to impose their own abusive, discriminatory measures and even violence against the refugees.' When local authorities ask for national support, a security analyst explained, their superior will often tell them to find a solution without explicating how to do so or providing any form of support to realize this goal. Then, 'he hangs up the phone in his face and the officer has to find his way [and] actually apply it.'[48] In the words of one of the key humanitarian coordinators on the Bekaa level, all successful coordination in the region is the result of the 'green light' he got from Beirut to 'solve problems without reporting back.'[49]

Denying the existence and resisting the formalization of national influence on and knowledge of local refugee governance creates and cements institutional ambiguity. It undermines local as well as national accountability since local state officials know they will not face national sanctions and national state leaders know they will not be held responsible for local transgressions. Simultaneous informal directing and formal distancing of the national state agencies vis-à-vis the local level also furthers insecurity for refugees and aid organizations. This is evident when it comes to representation – national state officials de facto undermine the emergence of refugee committees and then look away when local authorities legitimize repressive alternatives – but also with regard to practices related to registration and regulation as national authorities routinely disregard blatantly illegal local 'security' measures.

National attempts to keep local misbehaviour in check do occur and can be successful. A Lebanese human rights lawyer indicated that any instance of municipalities imposing taxes on refugees was nipped in the bud by the Ministry of Interior. In the first case-study settlement, the mayor indicated that he had once issued a curfew, but he withdrew the decision after the Minister of Interior pointed out the illegality and inhumanity of this measure to him. Upon request of the UNHCR and a regional coordinator supporting the provincial governor, to give yet another example, the then governor reluctantly but effectively ordered a specific mayor in the Bekaa to stop issuing ID cards to refugees (playing on the sentiment that this would enable integration). There have also been other examples of the Ministry of Interior 'cracking down' on such practices, as evident with the arrest of municipal police officers involved in an incident where Syrian men were detained in the central square of a village while policemen confiscated their identification documents.[50]

Mostly, however, local transgressions occur without facing much national constraint. It is often assumed that this is because national authorities do not have the means to keep local authorities in line. Since the national level does not offer municipalities many carrots because municipalities cannot count on much resources from the national level, national authorities often lack credible sticks as well. Many mayors, moreover, in practice have considerable power that goes far beyond their official prerogative and which grants them significant leeway in handling their local affairs, especially when national policy is lacking. Mayors in the Bekaa often have strong tribal ties. They are also regularly successful businessmen and consequently have considerable economic and, therefore, political power so that, as one humanitarian coordinator explained, the ministry will never force them to do something against their will, and therefore the governor will not either.[51] Ministers, he noted, adhere to a policy of 'live and let live' vis-à-vis municipalities. Even more important, in Lebanon's clientelist sectarian system, mayors are important 'vote banks' for the national politicians who decide on ministerial positions (Stel, 2015b). Electoral logics as such often grant them considerable local autonomy.

It might thus very well be that in some cases a minister genuinely fails in attempts to restrain local authorities. What is more likely, however, is that such attempts are rather half-hearted to begin with. 'Failure' to keep local authorities in check is not only the result of limited means but also of limited political will to do so. Mayors are mostly not shy to announce their restrictive policies vis-à-vis refugees publicly, as these can often count on considerable public support. This flagrant nature of local order maintenance means that it is hardly credible for national authorities to maintain that they are not aware of such realities. National looking away can be considered a form of excusing or even encouraging rather than simply ignoring. Municipalities, Barjas (2016) has established, have adopted repressive measures knowing that the Ministry knows about them. Simply put, 'the central government is aware that municipalities are surpassing their legal jurisdiction,' but 'local level policies have been tolerated' (Atallah and Mahdi, 2017: 31).

In fact, despite such formal denouncements of municipal practices, the same practices have been informally encouraged behind the scenes by the same national authorities. Municipal curfews, for instance, are regularly coordinated with the Lebanese Armed Forces (International Alert and Lebanon Support, 2017: 6). Mourad (2017: 263) provides evidence that district-level security cells issued internal statements that recommended curfews. Considering that these security cells should include the district governor as well as representatives from all state security institutions and report directly to the National Security Council, the complicity of national authorities in the local practices they formally denounce as illegal seems evident. In fact, this is where the role-playing alluded to before comes in. As the analyst in question reflected:

> I strongly think that's kind of an interplay between the ministry and the municipalities. It just cannot be that in different areas and in different regions of the country . . . municipalities are forcing restrictions that the ministry doesn't know of. It can't be that municipalities enforce restrictions and the ministry doesn't react or does not take itself to be accountable for those. So that's a role play. The Minister of Interior would deny his knowledge of something. And then a municipality would be holding up big signs for everyone to see that refugees cannot move after six in the evening.[52]

A ministerial advisor similarly considered national attempts to reign in municipalities a form of ritualism, saying that the minister will call a municipality knowing full well that his call will not have any effect, in fact counting on this, just to be able to say that he did what he could. As a result, such illegal local practices are allowed to continue and spread. Atallah and Mahdi (2017: 263) report a 'ripple effect' of municipal curfews, which increased from 25 municipalities at the beginning of 2014 to 45 municipalities at the end of the same year. By 2017, they could be considered the 'status quo.'

These findings concur with Mourad's (2017) conclusion that evictions, curfews, and other local ordering mechanisms should be considered a systemic state practice and not be disregarded as simply a local-level phenomenon. National authorities' publicly 'distancing' themselves from local practices they actually support or allow should be considered an attempt to evade responsibility. When it comes to restrictive local policies such as curfews, municipalities do not so much diverge from national guidelines, but rather are 'a front for the will of the central authorities, [whose official] decisions do not necessarily reflect their true dispositions' (Barjas, 2016).

This interplay between wanting capacity and limited political will facilitates national ignorance – whether real or pretense – of local governance realities, as is further illustrated by the evolution of the Ministry of Interior's 'Security Plan.' As early as September 2013, after meeting with more than 800 municipalities and municipal unions, the Ministry of Interior developed a security plan that was to increase the role of municipalities in ensuring local security (Ghaddar, 2017). Part of this plan was to centralize the data collected on Syrians locally through a system of security cells, whereby regional security cells were supposed to report to a National Security Council (Janmyr and Mourad, 2018: 558). Although according to the website of the Ministry of Interior, the regional security cells are to provide the central cell with periodic statistics based on a unified template,[53] cells in practice meet only when there is a concrete occasion. Even then, apparently, while information was shared, approaches were not actually coordinated, let alone integrated.

National authorities provided neither financial or material support for the security cells nor guidance and oversight, instead refraining 'from pursuing municipal police or guards for actions related to the performance of their duties' (Mencütek, 2019: 173). This essentially provided local security actors with immunity and institutionalized impunity. It encouraged 'the continuation of ad hoc security measures by municipalities' and left 'security at the discretion of elected local governments' (Mourad, 2017: 264). These, as we have seen, have subsequently apparently by and large relegated this to security agencies. At the time of research, surveillance and intelligence collection was apparently back to the 'normal' Lebanese routine of various individual security agencies all running their own operations in an apparently uncoordinated manner. Several people working for humanitarian organizations indicated that security agencies have abandoned the attempt to set up municipal monitoring structures. Instead, there has been a decision, allegedly communicated by the Ministry of Social Affairs during an inter-sectoral working group at the national level, to let go of the October 2014 policy's insistence on municipal registration, which was seen as a failed attempt, and leave registration and monitoring to the security agencies that had de facto already taken over the initiative.

Thus, the security plan that at first sight appeared to put forward cooperation between municipalities and security agencies ended up further cementing the primacy of security agencies over civil state structures. Similarly, while the original plan prioritized centralized data generation, its eventual implementation resulted in further local discretion as its hierarchical elements were left largely unimplemented while its legitimation of local securitization simultaneously took flight. In this context, local processes to register and regulate Syrian refugees by civil state structures do not reflect national planning. Instead, these processes generate informal, volatile, and unequal governance – forms of institutional ambiguity that effectively make refugees 'invisible to the central state, except if they are detained by one of the state security services' (Janmyr and Mourad, 2018: 558).

Policy inaction and ambiguous formulation and implementation of political decisions by national authorities enable and incentivize the measures that local authorities take to govern the ways in which Syrian refugees organize themselves, how they are to register and obtain permissions, and the manner in which their settlements are spatially ordered. The local governance of Syrian refugees in the Bekaa thus entrenches refugees' informality, liminality, and exceptionalism. Refugees' representation is fragmented and undermined. Municipal registration is reluctant and incomplete, and permission to relocate tents unofficial and highly arbitrary. Spatial instruments to maintain order, such as curfews, raids, and evictions, are illegal and inconsistent. That all these dynamics, moreover, happen under the auspices of an elusive and nationally supported security assemblage only extends the resultant uncertainty and insecurity for refugees. Unpredictability, arbitrariness, and unaccountability are not local exceptions. They are systemic in that they are produced by politically convenient national abandonment and serve the government's stated aims of controlling refugees and encouraging their return.

Conclusions

Ambiguity permeated research experiences. That paper realities and the situation 'on the ground' do not neatly coincide is no surprise, but that paper realities often do not even exist and that the situation on the ground is represented so vastly differently by various stakeholders is indicative of an institutional ambiguity that goes beyond the regular challenges of making sense of 'the field.' The most basic concerns regarding the informal Syrian refugee settlements studied proved remarkably difficult to pinpoint or verify. Establishing the actual geographical location of specific settlements based on the contrasting mapping systems of humanitarian organizations routinely led to the 'wrong' settlement, suggesting the complexity of even communicating about specific settlements. Identifying who (claimed to) operate as *shawish* took several visits in some settlements. Determining if and how committees, peer groups, outreach volunteers, or focal points actually functioned in specific settlements was rife with problems even when seemingly straightforward lists of committee members were provided by humanitarian organizations. Ascertaining who was formally in charge of overseeing Syrian settlements on the side of the Lebanese state in the second case-study settlement, where no municipal jurisdiction was in place, revealed a tangle of vague mandates, eschewed responsibilities, and an overall tendency of indifference and abandonment. In short, the very difficulty of establishing 'how things work' points to the complexity, changeability, and multiplicity of local governance.

Much of this institutional ambiguity that pervades local responses to the refugee crisis in Lebanon stems from the absence of national policy. Yet, no policy does not mean no governance. When it comes to shelter, for instance, while Lebanon formerly upholds its 'no-camp' policy, on a sub-national level, state institutions are engaged in an intricate system to regulate encampment, sometimes verbally, but at other times actually signing off on varying formats of permissions for tents. As alluded to throughout the chapter, our interlocutors referred to several notices by state institutions that were announced in the media or through personal meetings with representatives of the relevant organizations, but were not made public in their original written form. This regards, for example, the provincial governor's decision to no longer allow any new tents in the area and the related notification duty of municipalities in this regard; the army's circular about where refugee settlements should not be allowed; the decisions that no permanent structures are allowed, either regarding shelter or concerning services, and that no Syrian representative committees are to be permitted; and the development of a security plan in which national security agencies support municipalities in registration, monitoring, and keeping order.

The Lebanese approach to the refugee presence in the Bekaa is thus definitely ordered in some ways. Such ordering, however, is mostly informal, irregular, securitized, and politicized. What decisions – either in the form of public directives, internal circulars, or verbal notifications – do exist are often vague and interpreted or represented differently by different authorities. This chapter has accordingly demonstrated how the regional and municipal governance of Syrian refugee settlements in the Bekaa are overwhelmingly informal, as they are based on personal initiatives, not institutionalized, and politicized. They are liminal, meaning they are organized in an ad hoc, short-term fashion with the overarching aim to prevent structural solutions that might suggest longer-term settlement, and they are exceptional, largely determined by a securitization process that precludes any form of transparency and accountability. All this is partly inherent in any form of governance, especially when it concerns sensitive issues and takes place in a context of hybrid order. Many local authorities and aid organizations do whatever they can with the sparse means they have to help the Syrian refugees who found themselves stranded in the Bekaa among Lebanese communities that often face socio-economic hardship themselves and have a complicated history with Syria and Syrians.

That does not, however, depreciate that informality, liminality, and exceptionalism serve various interests, locally and nationally. The governance processes and practices central to this chapter are not just informal, liminal, and exceptional themselves, but they also impose such informality, liminality, and exceptionalism on refugees, who are deprived of an official representative, kept in limbo through Kafkaesque registration and permission procedures and constant displacement, and placed outside 'normal' Lebanese society through illegal curfews and raids that are leveled against them with impunity. Such effects may be partly or even largely contingent, but they have strategic components as well. In the end, ambiguity helps to marginalize refugees, which undermines their basis for collective action, allows for their exploitation, and functions as an implicit incentive for premature return. This political convenience of ambiguity becomes evident in the way in which ambiguity is upheld and incentivized in the role-play between national and local authorities.

Notes

1 Interview with a mayor – Central Bekaa, 6 March 2018.
2 Which, as noted in Chapter 2, only captures part of the actual refugee population as many do not have such UNHCR registration.
3 I am incredibly grateful to Anke van der Meijden for conducting the fieldwork underlying this chapter and reviewing the text in previous stages.
4 These meetings were recorded and transcribed where participants agreed, and extensive notes were taken when participants preferred this over recordings. Citations provided are (translations) of verbatim transcriptions unless indicated otherwise. In some instances, the chapter also turns to the national-level interviews described in the previous chapter.
5 This provided several internal governmental directives; more than 30 different examples of 'permissions' for relocating tents; the card of a *shawish* indicating the settlement's location code; and a copy of a rental contract between Syrian refugees and a Lebanese landlord that was brokered by an international NGO.
6 Selected settlements had more than 50 tents and were located in different municipalities, with a varied socio-economic and sectarian background. The settlements that were

eventually selected were chosen after careful consultation with humanitarian field-workers and researchers working in and on the area as well as visits to eight 'short-listed' settlements in the two municipalities chosen.

7 See: www.state-security.gov.lb/.
8 Interestingly, and highlighting its informal role, references to the presence of the State Security were rife among field-level interlocutors, whereas regional coordinators appeared much less aware of the work of this agency.
9 Author's interview – Skype, 9 April 2018.
10 Interview – Zahle, 28 February 2018.
11 Notes from interview – Zahle, 10 April 2018.
12 Interview with former humanitarian field officer – Zahle, 27 February 2018.
13 Interview – Central Bekaa, 6 March 2018.
14 With the exception of South Lebanon, where municipalities were more active in supporting these committees.
15 Author's interview – Skype, 11 December 2017.
16 Author's interview – Skype, 19 December 2017.
17 Author's interview – Skype, 30 November 2017.
18 Author's interview – Skype, 19 December 2017.
19 Author's interview – Skype, 15 January 2018.
20 Interview – Zahle, 14 March 2018.
21 Interview – Zahle, 27 February 2018.
22 Notes from interview – Zahle, 29 March 2018.
23 Notes from interview – Zahle, 4 April 2018.
24 Interview – Central Bekaa, 12 March 2018.
25 Interview – Central Bekaa, 12 March 2018.
26 Interview – Central Bekaa, 16 March 2018.
27 Notes from interview – Zahle, 4 April 2018.
28 Notes from interview – Zahle, 4 April 2018.
29 Interview – Beirut, 16 April 2018.
30 Notes from interview – Zahle, 7 March 2018.
31 Interview – Zahle, 20 March 2018.
32 Interview – Zahle, 20 March 2018.
33 Notes from interview – Zahle, 23 April 2018.
34 Interview – Zahle, 14 March 2018.
35 This could not be verified, but the very assumption seems significant.
36 Notes from interview with humanitarian coordinator – Zahle, 23 April 2018.
37 Author's group interview – Skype, 3 January 2018.
38 Notes from interview – Beirut, 1 March 2018.
39 Notes from interview – Zahle, 29 March 2018.
40 Notes from interview – Zahle, 23 April 2018.
41 Notes from interview – Central Bekaa, 25 April 2018.
42 Notes from interview – Central Bekaa, 15 March 2018.
43 Interview with Lebanese representative of an international NGO – Zahle, 27 February 2018.
44 Notes from interview with local humanitarian officer – Zahle, 23 April 2018.
45 Notes from interview – Zahle, 23 April 2018.
46 Notes from interview – Zahle, 20 April 2018.
47 Rouba Mhaissen, founder and director of the Sawa for Development and Aid group, cited in Limoges (2017).
48 Author's interview – Skype, 19 February 2018.
49 Interview – Zahle, 20 March 2018. Unofficial national support for local practices that are officially denied or criticized is also a form of experimentation, one development analyst suggested: 'In Lebanon the local is used as a way of testing the water

or testing the strength of different political factions.' (Author's interview – Skype, 11 December 2017)
50 Although the heavily publicized arrests of the policemen was followed by their prompt, and silent, release (Mourad, 2017: 265).
51 Notes from interview – Zahle, 10 April 2018.
52 Author's interview – Skype, 17 January 2018.
53 www.interior.gov.lb/AdsDetails.aspx?ida=45.

References

Achilli, Luigi, Nasser Yassin and Murat Erdoğan. 2018. *Neighbouring Host Countries' Policies for Syrian Refugees: The Cases of Jordan, Lebanon, and Turkey*. Barcelona: European Institute of the Mediterranean.
Al-Masri, Munza and Marianna Altabbaa. 2016. *Local and Regional Entanglements: The Social Stability Context in Sahel-Akkar*. Beirut: United Nations Development Program.
Al-Saadi, Yazan. 2014. *Examining Curfews Against Syrians in Lebanon*. Beirut: Civil Society Knowledge Center and Lebanon Support.
Al-Saadi, Yazan. 2015. *Restrictions, Perceptions, and Possibilities of Syrian Refugees' Self-Agency in Lebanon*. Beirut: Civil Society Knowledge Center and Lebanon Support.
Atallah, Sami and Dima Mahdi. 2017. *Law and Politics of "Safe Zones" and Forced Return to Syria: Refugee Politics in Lebanon*. Beirut: Lebanese Center for Policy Studies.
Barjas, Elham. 2016. *Restricting Refugees: Measuring Municipal Power in Lebanon*. Beirut: Legal Agenda.
Carpi, Estella, Mariam Younes and Marie-Noëlle AbiYaghi. 2016. *Crisis and Control: Formal Hybrid Security in Lebanon*. Beirut: Lebanon Support.
Cassani, Jacob. 2018. 'State, Sovereignty, and Sewage: Governance in a Syrian Refugee Camp and Lebanese Village in the Biqa'a Valley.' MA thesis, University College London.
Clarke, Killian. 2018. 'When Do the Dispossessed Protest? Informal Leadership and Mobilization in Syrian Refugee Camps.' *Perspectives on Politics* 16, no. 3: 617–633.
Daily Star. 2016. 'Bekaa Governor: No to Building Syrian Refugee Settlements.' *Daily Star*, 25 October.
Domat, Chloé. 2017. 'Two-Minute Exodus: Syrian Refugees Uprooted for Lebanese "Security".' *Middle East Eye*, 1 May.
Ghaddar, Sima. 2017. *Lebanon Treats Refugees as a Security Problem – And It Doesn't Work*. New York: The Century Foundation.
Ghanem, Nizar. 2016. *Local Governance Under Pressure. Research on Social Stability in T5 Area, North Lebanon*. Arezzo: Oxfam Italia.
Human Rights Watch. 2018. *"Our Homes Are Not for Strangers". Mass Evictions of Syrian Refugees by Lebanese Municipalities*.' New York: Human Rights Watch.
International Alert and Lebanon Support. 2017. *Security that Protects: Informing Policy on Local Security Provision in Lebanese Communities Hosting Syrian Refugees*. Beirut: International Alert and Lebanon Support.
International Crisis Group. 2015. *Lebanon's Self-Defeating Survival Mechanisms*. Brussels: International Crisis Group.
Janmyr, Maja and Lama. Mourad. 2018. 'Modes of Ordering: Labelling, Classification and Categorization in Lebanon's Refugee Response.' *Journal of Refugee Studies* 31, no. 4: 544–565.

Kullab, Samya. 2014. 'League Seeks to Represent Syrian Refugees in North Lebanon.' *Daily Star*, 4 January.

Lebanon Support. 2016. *Syrian Refugees' Livelihoods: The Impact of Progressively Restrained Legislations and Increased Informality on Syrians' Daily Lives*. Beirut: Lebanon Support.

Limoges, Barret. 2017. 'Thousands of Syrians Face Evictions from Lebanon Camps.' *Al Jazeera*, 15 April.

Mazzola, Francisco. 2019. 'Mediating Security – Hybridity and Clientelism in Lebanon's Hybrid Security Sector.' In *Hybrid Governance in the Middle East and Africa: Informal Rule and the Limits of Statehood*, edited by Ruth Hanau Santini, Abel Polese and Rob Kevlihan. London: Routledge.

Mencütek, Zeynep. 2019. *Refugee Governance, State and Politics in the Middle East*. London: Routledge.

Mourad, Lama. 2017. '"Standoffish" Policy-Making: Inaction and Change in the Lebanese Response to the Syrian Displacement Crisis.' *Middle East Law and Governance* 9: 249–266.

Nashabe, Omar. 2009. 'Security Sector Reform in Lebanon: Internal Security Forces and General Security.' The Arab Reform Initiative, unpublished document.

Ortmans, Morgane and Marie Madsen. 2015. *Social Cohesion Programming in a Context of Major Refugee Influx Crisis*. Beirut: Search for Common Ground.

Oxfam. 2017a. *Imagine You Were Evicted*. Oxford: Oxfam International.

Oxfam. 2017b. *Still Looking for Safety: Voices of Refugees from Syria on Solutions for the Present and Future*. Oxford: Oxfam International.

REACH and United Nations High Commissioner for Refugees. 2014. *Multi Sector Community Level Assessment of Informal Settlements. Akkar Governorate – Lebanon*. Beirut: REACH and United Nations High Commissioner for Refugees.

Sanyal, Romola. 2017. 'A No-Camp Policy: Interrogating Informal Settlements in Lebanon.' *Geoforum* 84: 117–125.

Sanyal, Romola. 2018. 'Managing Through Ad Hoc Measures: Syrian Refugees and the Politics of Waiting in Lebanon.' *Political Geography* 66: 67–75.

Stel, Nora. 2015a. 'Mukhtars in the Middle: The Centrality and Utility of Lebanese Mukhtars in Connecting State, Citizens and Refugees.' *Jadaliyya*, 4 December.

Stel, Nora. 2015b. '"The Children of the State?" How Palestinians from the Seven Villages Negotiate Sect, Party and State in Lebanon.' *British Journal of Middle Eastern Studies* 42, no. 4: 538–557.

Stel, Nora and Anke van der Meijden. 2018. *Lebanon's Evictions of Syrian Refugees and the Threat of de facto Refoulement*. Beirut: Lebanese Center for Policy Studies.

United Nations High Commissioner for Refugees. 2015. *Refugee Response in Lebanon Briefing Documents*. Beirut: United Nations High Commissioner for Refugees.

United Nations High Commissioner for Refugees, United Nations Children's Fund and World Food Program. 2017. 'Vulnerability Assessment of Syrian Refugees in Lebanon.'

Van Veen, Erwin. 2015. *Elites, Power, and Security: How the Organization of Security in Lebanon Serves Elite Interests*. The Hague: Clingendael Institute.

Wedeen, Lisa. 1999. *Ambiguities of Domination: Politics, Rhetoric, and Symbols in Contemporary Syria*. Chicago: University of Chicago Press.

Zapater, Josep. 2018. 'The Role of Municipalities in Ensuring Stability.' *Forced Migration Review* 57: 12–15.

Chapter 4

The governance of Palestinian refugees in Lebanon

Permanent temporariness and the state of exception

Summer 2013, long before I have come across academic concepts like institutional ambiguity. Sitting in his make-shift office in Beirut's Mar Elias refugee camp, a Palestinian legal analyst smiles at me in a way that I interpret as being a mixture of sympathy and mocking when I share my frustrations in linking the de facto local governance realities in Palestinian refugee settlements to national policies or laws. He confirms that 'all Lebanese-Palestinian relations are vague,' almost off-handedly adding: 'And it is intended to be vague.' When I ask, puzzled, how such vagueness might be beneficial, he elucidates that his decades of study and activism have led him to believe that the fact that the Lebanese state does not want any formal responsibility 'is the heart of the matter.'[1]

The Syrian and Palestinian refugee crises in Lebanon are very different in both a qualitative and a quantitative sense and so is the country's response to them. But there are also remarkable parallels between the way Lebanon has dealt with the Syrian refugee presence and the way it approached the Palestinian refugee situation. Indeed, Lebanon's engagement with Syrian refugees is determined by nothing so much as the country's Palestinian 'trauma.'

As this chapter will further describe, the Palestinian refugees who fled to Lebanon in 1948 (and after) went through a process of political emancipation and mobilization that, according to the Lebanese narrative, turned them into revolutionaries that operated a state-within-the-state – a situation that eventually helped instigate the infamous Lebanese Civil War. This experience has contributed to the almost automatic securitization of any issue related to refugees. Faced with a new influx of refugees in the wake of the Syrian War, Lebanon's priority has been to avert such a protracted and politicized refugee presence this time around.

The 'set of nos' that defined Lebanon's response to the Syrian 'crisis' was explicitly meant to avoid replicating the problems associated with the Palestinian 'issue,' which loomed like a 'scarecrow' over the Syrian situation (Yassin et al., 2015: 46). Refusing to recognize Syrians seeking refuge in Lebanon as refugees was meant to prevent a protracted presence like that of the Palestinian refugees in the country. *Tawteen*, the fear of naturalization and its demographic consequences that has been explicitly acknowledged in the Lebanese constitution, originated from Lebanon's experience with Palestinian refugees. Lebanese political actors now explicitly link it to Syrian refugees (Janmyr, 2017: 4536; see also Atallah and Mahdi, 2017: 16). Forbidding official camps for Syrians was meant to avoid the emergence of 'security islands' from which Lebanese sovereignty could be threatened, as had happened with the Palestinian camps throughout the 1970s. And undermining Syrian refugees' political and organizational mobilization was an attempt to evade the rise of an organization like the Palestine Liberation Organization (PLO) that might challenge the Lebanese status quo and the socio-economic interests of the related political elites. In the words of an international development analyst working with Syrian refugees in Lebanon: 'There are quite explicit efforts on the part of the Lebanese government to avoid any structures of political representation from developing because of what they see as the lessons learned from the Palestinian presence.'[2]

Considering these explicit efforts that Lebanese authorities made to avoid what Carpi (2017: 127) has called the 'Palestinization' of the Syrian situation, one would assume that their response to the Syrian refugee 'crisis' would be diametrically opposed to the governance of Palestinian refugees. This is only partially the case, however. The current Lebanese response to the mass arrival of Syrian refugees is indeed in many ways almost the opposite of the country's initial engagement with the Palestinian refugees and their representatives. However, it closely resembles Lebanon's post–Civil War approach to governing the Palestinian refugees. After the Civil War, Lebanon systematically marginalized and politically demobilized Palestinian refugees in an attempt to prevent them from regaining their former political potency and military might. Such marginalization was effectuated through outright repression, but also through institutional ambiguity.

Although Palestinians have the refugee status that Lebanon now denies Syrians, the precarious legal status of Syrian refugees is a replication of the deliberate legal protection gaps that Palestinian refugees face.[3] There is a panoply of Palestinian political parties with which Lebanese authorities liaise. Yet, as with Syrian refugees, their settlement-level leaders are systematically disregarded and formally unrecognized by Lebanese state agencies. And although the no-camp policy regarding Syrian refugees at first sight seems to be the opposite of the camp-oriented governance of Palestinian refugees, this disregards the fact that the majority of Palestinian refugees in Lebanon does not live in formal camps either. The Syrian refugees' 'informal tented settlements' and the hybrid governance and ambiguous sovereignty arrangements that define them in fact resemble the unofficial settlements in which over one-third of Lebanon's Palestinians live.

The informality, liminality, and exceptionalism that are shaping the fate of Lebanon's Syrian refugees, in short, have similarly governed the lives of Palestinian refugees in Lebanon over the last three decades. Lebanon's experience with Palestinian refugees led Lebanese to perceive Syrian refugees as primarily a threat. But the same post–Civil War Palestinian experience provided many of the governance modalities that are used to deal with this new 'threat.' The similarities in the governance regimes that Syrians and Palestinians face are evident in the ways in which Palestinians teach Syrians how to deal with Lebanon's institutional ambiguity, with which they have such extensive experience. As Parkinson (2014) documents, Palestinian refugees 'have come to serve as an informal social database' for Syrian refugees in terms of coping with the Lebanese institutional environment. Their accumulated experience in Lebanon, she notes, has taught Palestinian refugees how to navigate the 'maze' of opaque bureaucracies and informal rules that defines displacement in Lebanon (Parkinson, 2014).

The parallels between Syrian and Palestinian refugee governance in Lebanon are not just evident for refugees. They are further illustrated by ministerial advisers who have argued for the establishment of a generic department or ministry of refugee affairs that would be responsible for addressing both refugee populations. Because, as a public policy expert consulting for a relevant ministry noted: 'Even if there is some divergence in how we can deal with these crises, [there are] of course a lot of similarities in the governance.'[4] Highlighting this commonality, representatives of the Minister of State for Displaced Affairs that is tasked with addressing the Syrian refugee presence have informally approached people working for the Lebanese-Palestinian Dialogue Committee (LPDC) to ask for advice on issues relating to registration and political dialogue.[5]

The strategic furthering of institutional ambiguity that characterizes the Lebanese engagement with Syrian refugees in many ways thus finds its precedent in Lebanon's handling of Palestinian refugees. Lebanese authorities subject Syrian refugees to a state of exception, Cassani (2018: 65) shows, because the Palestinian experience has conditioned them to see the presence of refugees as an almost inevitable challenge to Lebanese sovereignty. The critical inaction that defined Lebanon's initial response to the Syrian refugee influx, Mourad (2017: 266) similarly argues, mirrors the state's 'standoffishness' towards Palestinian refugees.

This premise, that Lebanon's governance of Syrian refugees is crucially determined by the country's experience with Palestinian refugees, is the starting point for this chapter. While the fateful connection between these two refugee experiences is routinely asserted by scholars, a conceptual analysis of the ways in which Lebanon's Palestinian refugee situation institutionally prefigures the country's response to the Syrian predicament is unique to this book. The chapter traces the emergence and strategic reproduction of institutional ambiguity over the seven decades that Palestinian refugees have lived in Lebanon. This exercise sheds new light on the current forms of refugee governance that Lebanon employs to deal with Syrians. Taking on board Syrian refugees' experiences also enables me to revisit our understanding of the politics and policies that Lebanon has leveled against Palestinian refugees and offers new insights into the different ways in which Lebanese repression and marginalization of Palestinian refugees operates.

It has been well-established that Palestinian refugees in Lebanon face 'chronic uncertainty' (Afifi et al., 2019; see also Sayigh, 1995). It has been similarly agreed upon that Lebanon has leveled severe repression against Palestinians living in the country. This chapter links these two key characteristics of the governance of

Palestinian refugees in Lebanon, demonstrating that uncertainty is not merely an outcome of repression, but an instrument of it.

The data on which this chapter draws were collected during fieldwork in 2012, 2013, and 2014 and regard specific local case-studies as well as a more generic national contextualization of these cases that had the objective to explore the formal as well as informal governance interactions between Lebanese and Palestinian authorities. The body of data entails more than 270 semi-structured, in-depth interviews and informal meetings, five focus groups, extensive field observations, and various documents. Where the next chapter predominantly builds on the case-study data, this chapter is based primarily on a review of documents and academic and 'grey' literature as well as conversations and interviews with Lebanese and Palestinian political authorities, scholars, and activists. These interviews were conducted in English or in Arabic, in which case I was assisted by a local research partner who helped with translation.[6]

The chapter first offers a brief narration of the historical presence of Palestinians in Lebanon. The next section lays down how institutional ambiguity has been a constant throughout these different historical phases. It demonstrates the ways in which informality, liminality, and exceptionalism run through Lebanese elites' approaches to governing Palestinian refugees in terms of space, status, and representation. This, the subsequent section shows, has contributed to the emergence of what is presented as 'benign strangulation' of refugees: making refugees' lives unliveable under the pretense that this will increase their chance to return. As with Syrian refugees, institutional ambiguity and the marginalization it helps produce serve intertwined political and socio-economic interests and are therefore often maintained or reproduced. Two related vignettes that explore the apparent breakthroughs that have recently been made by the LPDC show how informality, liminality, and exceptionalism have been challenged but are also protected by the behaviour of politicians and state officials – signaling both the contentious and the persistent nature of institutional ambiguity.

Context and history

In 1948 approximately 700,000 people were forcefully displaced from Mandatory Palestine during the *Nakba* ('catastrophe' in Arabic), a campaign of ethnic cleansing committed by Zionist armed groups (such as Haganah, Irgun, and Stern) in the process of the establishment of the state of Israel. Approximately 100,000 of them sought refuge in Lebanon. There are currently around 200,000 Palestinian refugees residing in the country.

Lebanon's approach to and relation with these refugees has known several phases. Not anticipating the eventually protracted nature of the Palestinians' stay in the country, Lebanon initially warmly welcomed Palestinians. This first decade of 'adaptation and hope' saw Palestinians as victimized brethren and, not unimportantly, a much-needed cheap labour force during a boom in the Lebanese economy (Suleiman, 2006). Freedom of expression and organization for the refugees was overall ensured. In 1950, the Central Committee for Refugee Affairs was established to deal with the administrative implications of hosting such a large refugee population. Despite political, social, material, and administrative support, however, it was clear from the outset that the Lebanese saw the Palestinian presence as temporary. Lebanon emphasized the Palestinian's right to return to their homes in the land that was by then declared Israel, a right that was recognized by the United Nations (UN's) General Assembly's Resolution 194. Responsibility for the refugees was placed in the hands of the newly developed UN agency for Palestine refugees, the United Nations Relief and Works Agency for Palestine Refugees in the Near East (UNRWA). Those refugees who could not provide for themselves were sheltered in 16 camps that were run by UNRWA.[7]

This relatively benign phase, however, ended with the increasingly independent organization of the Palestinians' struggle for self-determination and the liberation of Palestine, which was epitomized by the establishment of the PLO in 1964 and its progressive autonomy vis-à-vis Arab states. In the wake of this growing Palestinian political emancipation and military activity, Lebanese-Palestinian relations entered what became known as the 'phase of the Deuxième Bureau,' after the army intelligence agency that implemented an ever-more restrictive regime on Palestinian communities in coordination with the police and UNRWA-appointed leaders. The Lebanese government under General Fouad Chehab started to crack down on Palestinian organization and subjected the settlements to strict control. The standoff between the Lebanese state and the increasingly powerful PLO eventually resulted in the 'intifada of the camps,' an uprising against this increasing oppression. This, in turn, led to what Ramadan and Fregonese (2017: 8) describe as 'a fundamental rearrangement of sovereignty and of the relation of exception between the camp and the state.' This rearrangement was reflected in the 1969 Cairo Agreement that initiated the Palestinians' 'golden era' in Lebanon, which lasted until the Israeli army expulsed the PLO from Lebanon in 1982.

The Cairo Agreement was brokered in secret by Egyptian President Gamal Abdel Nasser and signed by the leader of the PLO, Yasser Arafat, and the commander of the Lebanese army, Emile Boustani. It formalized the parameters of the Palestinian armed activity in Lebanon by supporting the PLO's resistance against Israel; acknowledged the right to residency, employment, and movement of all Palestinians in Lebanon; and allowed for the formation of local governance committees as well as the presence of weapons within the camps. As such, the agreement postulated the relation between the Lebanese state and the PLO, now the primary representative of the Palestinian people, as an equal one. It has therefore often been seen as undermining state sovereignty. Despite such concerns, in 1973, the Cairo Agreement was reinforced and updated through the 'Melkart Protocol.' In 1976, at an Arab Summit meeting, the Lebanese President formally validated the agreement once more.

Under these arrangements, the 1970s saw the PLO's institutional heyday in Lebanon, now nostalgically referred to by Palestinians as the 'days of the revolution' (Stel, 2017). The PLO initially organized its resistance against Israel's occupation of Palestine from Jordan, but was ousted from the country in 'Black September' 1970. It then relocated to Lebanon which, from 1970 until 1982, served as 'the political and military centre of gravity of the Palestinian movement,' providing a logistical base for military and civilian activities (Brynen, 1989: 48 in Stel, 2017: 353). Palestinian political and military organization in Lebanon and the related bureaucracy and taxation systems were extensive. The PLO's military forces encompassed the Palestine Liberation Army, counting over 10,000 fighters, and various militias (Rubenberg, 1983: 55). The PLO's National Council, the Central Council, and the Executive Committee provided a legislative and executive infrastructure. The Palestine National Fund managed the financial component of the PLO's governance operations, and the Revolutionary Council maintained order among the organization's different factions. The PLO created a range of trade unions and social institutions. Through its Department of Mass Organizations, it encompassed ten national unions. These representative institutions were closely related to an elaborate structure of welfare organizations that included hospitals, clinics, factories, cultural bureaus, art galleries, orphanages, schools, and a research centre that published various media outlets.

Throughout this institutional and political zenith of the PLO, however, the Palestinian liberation struggle became ever more entangled with the Lebanese internal conflicts that eventually culminated in the Lebanese Civil War (1975–1990). The dilemma of whether the PLO should be allowed to launch its resistance against Israel from Lebanese soil, with all the ensuing retaliations that would entail, was one of the instigators of the war. Many Lebanese hold the PLO and its struggle against Israel responsible for the breakdown of the Lebanese state throughout the war. The 'Palestinian Revolution' that the PLO represented was initially welcomed with enthusiasm by many Lebanese. Its pan-Arab, socialist, and secular ideology combined with militant resistance against Israeli occupation appealed to Lebanese from different classes and sects. A decade later, however, little was left of this solidarity. This was the result of both an effective Israeli divide-and-rule strategy – retaliation for Palestinian attacks launched from South Lebanon was systematically directed at Lebanese civilian targets so as to alienate the population from the PLO – as well as increasing misconduct by Palestinian militias (Beydoun, 1992: 36; Brynen, 1989: 54; Siklawi, 2010: 602). Due to the weakness of the Lebanese state, the professionally institutionalized Palestinian public authority was perceived as fundamentally undermining its sovereignty. The PLO, and eventually the broader Palestinian community in Lebanon, was considered a 'fifth column,' a 'cuckoo' or 'Trojan horse' that 'superseded' the state and held Lebanon 'hostage' (Hirst, 2010: 91; Knudsen, 2010: 102, Sayigh, 1997a: 675, 49, 551).

In 1982, the PLO was expelled from Lebanon by Israel. Officially, operation 'Peace for Galilee' had the objective to end Palestinian attacks on Israel from Lebanon, but underlying that was the unstated yet evident aim to dismantle the PLO's governance project in Lebanon (Brynen, 1989: 60; Rubenberg, 1983: 54). The vast majority of the PLO's armed forces as well as a large segment of its political leadership were forced to leave Lebanon and relocated to Tunisia. The expulsion of the PLO leadership from Lebanon and the subsequent Sabra and Shatila massacres – when, under the auspices of the Israeli army, Lebanese Christian right-wing militias killed thousands of Palestinian civilians – heralded a new period for Lebanon's Palestinians. The PLO's institutions collapsed. During the 1985–1988 'War of the Camps,' Palestinian settlements were assaulted by the Amal militia in a widely supported campaign to prevent the resurfacing of any form of armed Palestinian organization in Lebanon. In 1987 the Cairo Agreement was unilaterally abrogated.

The Lebanese Civil War ended with the 1989 Ta'if Agreement that made official the country's commitment to avoid any form of integration or settlement of non-nationals, a hardly veiled reference to the Palestinian community. In fact, as elaborated on later, the issue of *tawteen* has been one of the few pieces of common ground that the various sectarian-political communities in Lebanon have been able to reach since the war: Palestinians would no longer be a political factor of influence in the 'new Lebanon' (Hanafi, 2008: 16). Under the flag of preventing integration, or steps towards it, Palestinians in post-war Lebanon have been disenfranchised politically as well as socio-economically. This was to punish them for their role during the war but also to prevent them from interfering in future intra-Lebanese conflict. Palestinian refugees are not simply withheld citizenship, which would suffice to prevent their feared integration, but are legally discriminated against in the labour market and cannot own real estate.

This initial post-war phase under the so-called *Pax Syriana*, the de facto occupation and political control of Lebanon by Syria that lasted until 2005, was characterized by what Suleiman (2006: 21) has called 'deliberate neglect.' Mirroring its general management of the Lebanese political arena, the Syrian regime implemented a policy of institutional and political multiplicity towards Palestinian refugees, gradually bringing the Palestinians in Beirut and the north of the country under their influence through proxy factions in the Palestinian settlements. As Rougier (2007: 11) documented, the Syrian intelligence services controlling Lebanon systematically encouraged inter-Palestinian rifts and blocked 'any possibility of direct negotiation between the Lebanese government and the local representatives' of Palestinian communities.

In the early 1990s, political dialogue between Lebanese and Palestinian representatives was cautiously resumed, but policies remained extremely restrictive. With the end of the Syrian dominance in Lebanon in 2005, increasing Lebanese-Palestinian engagement has been noted. A formal Lebanese-Palestinian dialogue committee was established in 2005 to further both intra-Lebanese consensus on how to deal with the Palestinian issue and Lebanese-Palestinian dialogue on how to structure the resurfacing institutional relations. In 2006, the PLO reopened its representative office in Beirut that had been closed since 1982. In 2011, the Palestinian Authority opened an Embassy in Lebanon.

Yet, as the next section shows, the national governance of the 'Palestinian issue' in Lebanon remains crucially affected by the country's sectarian logic and the role of the Palestinians in its conflicted history. Thus, Long and Hanafi (2010: 678) conclude, the 'deep-seated prejudice that many Lebanese hold for Palestinians, which is in favour of keeping the Palestinians socially, politically and economically marginalized' remains (see also Sfeir, 2010). Institutional ambiguity, this chapter will demonstrate, helps produce this marginalization.

The roots of institutional ambiguity: balancing the taboo of integration and the impossibility of return

Informality, liminality, and exceptionalism are manifest in the Lebanese governance of Palestinian spaces, status, and representatives. This section outlines how the institutional ambiguity that this amounts to is rooted in the fundamental and existential paradox of Palestinian life in Lebanon: Palestinian refugees cannot return, yet are not allowed to settle.

According to the official Lebanese discourse, integration of Palestinian refugees is to be avoided because it would undermine the Palestinians' right to return. Many Lebanese see the protracted Palestinian presence as the result of an international wish to have Lebanon function as a de facto substitute homeland for Palestinians so that Israel would not have to worry about the refugees' return. In addition, the fear that settlement would eventually result in naturalization and thereby upset the carefully maintained illusion[8] of sectarian balance and the related status quo is a crucial driver to uphold the marginalization and segregation of refugees in the country. Considering the existential implications of demographics for the division of political power in Lebanon's peculiar consociational system, the possibility of nationalizing Palestinian refugees has always been seen as an existential threat that would decisively upturn the country's precarious confessional parity – even more so after the PLO, according to many Lebanese, had played the role of a 'Sunni army' during the Lebanese Civil War.

The result is a widely recognized 'permanent temporariness' (El Ali, 2011: 18; Doraï and Puig, 2008; Hanafi, 2008: 9). This refers to the Lebanese tendency to never acknowledge the protracted and long-term nature of the Palestinians' existence in Lebanon, but rather to keep all engagements – legal, political, institutional – effectively short-term and under probation. This form of 'existential impasse,' as Allan (2014: 174) defined it, has at times served as an excuse not to make any laws or policies at all (for instance, as explored in more detail later, when it comes to recognizing Palestinian representatives or regulating Palestinian refugee camps and other forms of shelter). As documented by Klaus (2000: 42), Lebanon's governance of Palestinian refugees is effectively 'prevented by a complete absence of any clearly defined programmatic state guidelines for dealing with the refugees.' Those decisions that were formally stated revolve around avoiding any measure that might reek of integration. As a result, Palestinian refugees, as Allan (2014: 10) describes, 'hover in an ill-defined space, out of place and between states, as Lebanon denies their naturalization and Israel rejects their return.'

The pivotal work by Hanafi (2008, 2010, 2011, 2014) acutely demonstrates the practical impossibility of 'permanent temporariness.' The governance of and within Palestinian communities in Lebanon is dictated by a 'state of exception' that instates crisis as the status quo and reproduces instability and vulnerability. The governance of Lebanon's Palestinian refugees, Hanafi (2008: 10) argues, reproduces a situation in which 'nothing is legally defined [and] everything is suspended but upheld without written documents concerning this suspension.' This generates a legal and often institutional void that can be filled in an ad hoc and arbitrary way when it comes to the spatial, representational, and administrative aspects of governing Lebanon's Palestinians.

Lebanon's Palestinian refugee settlements and the 'art of inclusive exclusion'

Nothing embodies permanent temporariness like the semi-formal and informal spatial arrangements in which Lebanon's Palestinian refugees are made to live. As further described in the next chapter, they are the material manifestation of liminality, signifying the alleged temporary nature of the Palestinian presence, and are governed through extreme exceptionalism. In their influential analysis of life in Lebanon's Palestinian refugee camps, Hanafi and Long (2010: 135) declared an 'endemic crisis of governance' in and of Palestinian settlements which, they found, are characterized by 'rampant factionalism, clientelism, sectarian strife, oppressive Lebanese security and surveillance, and a lack of central administrative and juridical Palestinian authority.' A decade later, not much has changed. In contrast to the situation in other regional host countries, generations after their expulsion from Mandatory Palestine, the large majority of Palestinians in Lebanon lives in one of several varieties of refugee settlements.

There are currently 12 official UN-administered camps for Palestinian refugees in Lebanon. In addition to these formal settlements, there are two types of informal settlements. 'Adjacent areas' are basically illegal extensions of the formal camps (Hilal, 2010). The close to 50 'gatherings' are autonomous unofficial settlements that are not connected to the UN camps.[9] According to the most recent census of Palestinians living in refugee settlements in Lebanon, 45 percent of them reside in the official camps and 55 percent live in adjacent areas and gatherings. There are important differences between formal and informal settlements (Stel, 2017), but both are de facto excluded from Lebanese governance responsibilities (most importantly the provision of services and security) while included in the state's punitive and disciplinary reach. The uncertain legal status following this 'art of inclusive exclusions' (Hanafi, 2010: 29) results in endemic housing and tenure insecurity for refugees, who are not allowed to maintain or extend their dwellings and, as illustrated in more detail in the next chapter, face an ever-present threat of eviction.[10]

With the 1969 Cairo Agreement, Palestinian camps in Lebanon have been formally excluded from the normal legal order. This suspension is kept in place even though officially the Cairo Agreement is no longer in force. Considering this, the Lebanese government could, and perhaps legally should, treat the camps as being under its sovereignty again, but it has chosen not to. Yet while it has put on hold its own responsibility for these places indefinitely, it has not officially recognized any other actor as responsible for the camps. Instead, as Ramadan and Fregonese (2017: 10) conclude, 'The camps are simply treated as extraterritorial spaces – outside the state's sphere of control and responsibility, present absences.'

The state's de facto abandonment of sovereignty and the resultant outsourcing of governance is thus never made official. This means that it can always be denied or withdrawn. The Palestinian informal settlements are not officially put under the auspices of either the UN or the PLO, even if they are in practice 'left' to them. Regarding the formal camps, the Cairo Agreement was officially abrogated to claim back the possibility to intervene in the camps, yet unofficially continues to be referred to as a reason not to interfere. In governing through such, as Oesch (2015: 2) has called it, 'constitutive ambivalence,' Lebanese authorities can have their cake and eat it too; they can use the same agreement as a legitimation of their action (referring to the de jure abrogated status of the agreement) or inaction (referring to its de facto potent legacy). This manipulation generates unpredictability, inconsistency, and instability for the residents of these settlements and for those actors that try to provide welfare or regulate security there.

The status of Lebanon's Palestinian refugees: legal limbo and protection gaps

The spatial ambiguity evident in the informal and liminal nature of Lebanon's Palestinian refugee settlements and their governance through exceptionalism reflects the broader uncertainty related to their 'status ambiguity' (Sayigh, 1988; see also Al-Natour, 1997). The institutional environment that Palestinians in Lebanon face, consequently, is routinely characterized in terms of 'arbitrariness,' 'disorder,' 'chaos,' and 'unruliness' (Hanafi, 2010: 17, 29).

As established before, Lebanon does not adhere to international refugee law. Other international covenants potentially relevant to the Palestinian case, such as the 1948 UN Universal Declaration of Human Rights, the 1954 Convention Regarding Stateless Persons, the 1966 International Covenant for Civil and Political Rights, and the 1996 International Covenant on Economic, Social, and Cultural Rights, are not acknowledged by Lebanon either. Yet the 'legal limbo' that Palestinian refugees face is not exclusively Lebanon's doing (Al-Natour, 1997; Knudsen, 2007). Rather than facilitating their actual return, the 1948 UN's General Assembly Resolution 194 that puts forwards the Palestinian refugees' right to return to the homes they were expelled from has served to withhold from them the legal protection extended to all other refugees in the world. In anticipation of an ever-more-implausible return, Palestinian refugees merely receive 'assistance' from UNRWA.

In creating UNRWA, Arab states, Lebanon among them, excluded the Palestinians from the broader UNHCR mandate and the associated Convention Relating to the Status of Refugees with the specific objective to maintain their unique status. This deliberate exceptionalism was meant to keep pressure on Israel and to protect neighboring countries from shouldering costs for hosting refugees. UNRWA, however, has suffered from ambiguous and seemingly contradictory objectives, as well as wanting resources, since its inception. It lacks the explicit mandate to provide legal and political protection that the UNHCR operates under. This means that, unlike other refugees, Palestinian refugees do not receive legal protection that can help them claim their rights. In many ways, humanitarian assistance has been presented as a substitute for rights (Weighill, 1997: 294).

Considering Lebanon's retreat from international law in this domain, regional arrangements would increase in significance for the Palestinian community in the country. However, the 1965 Casablanca Protocol, which called on Arab countries to grant Palestinian refugees the rights of work, travel, and residency, was signed by Lebanon with such far-reaching reservations that it could practically disregard the protocol's main objectives. This was even more blatant after the protocol was further watered down in September 1991 as a response to the Palestinian support for Saddam Hussein during the First Gulf War. The protocol was amended with a 'highly ambiguous formulation' to relegate the issue of refugee rights a national rather than a collective Arab responsibility (Frontiers-Ruwad, 2005), creating a situation in which, as Hanafi and Long (2010: 144) point out, these rights 'could be revoked with little ceremony and without justification.' In political agreements such as the Oslo Accords, Palestinian refugees are dealt 'with intentional ambiguity' as well, which consigns the refugee issue to the discretion of host states (Al-Natour, 1997: 360).

In Lebanon, however, the state never took up this responsibility to legally regulate the refugee presence. There is no specific legislation in Lebanon that addresses Palestinians' unique situation as stateless refugees. Palestinian refugees in Lebanon, as a result, 'fall through the cracks:' They are not governed through relevant laws, but mostly through 'informally adopted regulations that in some cases were never formally published,' which allows for tremendous discretion (Frontiers-Ruwad, 2005: 9). This is even more pronounced considering the fact that there has never been a comprehensive agreement that regulates the institutional relation between the Lebanese state and UNRWA. Thus, responsibility for the refugees is largely transferred to the UN's surrogate state, without any accommodating framework to define that responsibility, establish its scope, and ground it in existing international or national law (Kagan, 2011; Ramadan and Fregonese, 2017).

Unlike Syrian refugees, Palestinian refugees are recognized by the Lebanese state as refugees, but because there is no relevant national or regional refugee law and Lebanon does not subscribe to international refugee law, it is not altogether clear what that recognition means. In practice, Palestinians in Lebanon are treated as foreigners. To avoid *tawteen*, moreover, in a particularly blatant

streak of exceptionalism, they are designated as a special category of foreigners. Ordinance No. 319 (issued by the Ministry of Interior in 1962) regulates the
situation of foreigners in Lebanon and classifies Palestinian refugees in a special
category of

> Foreigners who do not carry documentation from their countries of origin,
> and reside in Lebanon on the basis of resident cards issued by the Directorate
> of Public Security, or identity cards issued by the General Directorate of the
> Department of Affairs of the Palestinian Refugees in Lebanon. (see Suleiman,
> 2006: 14)

In short, Palestinians in Lebanon enjoy neither the rights of citizens nor those of
refugees or 'normal' foreigners. This has produced a 'protection gap' (Knudsen,
2009). Palestinians' legal exclusion is a direct result of inaction by Lebanese governments regarding the creation or ratification of relevant national, regional, and
international laws. It has been used to legitimize the suspension of regularization,
recognition, or formalization. Over the years, subsequent Lebanese governments
have used legal ambiguity to make the refugee file subservient to their domestic
power struggles and patronage dynamics. This is particularly evident with regard
to the question of Palestinian representation.

Dividing and ruling Palestinian representatives

Historically, various Lebanese state institutions have been tasked with admin-
istering the Palestinian refugee presence. In 1950, under Decree No. 11657, the
Lebanese President created a Central Committee for Refugee Affairs to administer Palestinian refugees. In 1959, a new Department of Affairs of Palestinian
Refugees was established through Presidential Decree No. 42. Its tasks were
defined in the accompanying Decree No. 927, 'the first bits of Lebanese legislation' to provide an institutional framework for the Palestinian presence in Lebanon (Suleiman, 2006: 12).[11] Many of the provisions in the Department of Affairs
of Palestinian Refugees' framework, however, 'lack clear definitions and criteria' (Frontiers-Ruwad, 2005: 68). The decree left undefined who could register
as a refugee in Lebanon. More fundamentally, it remains 'unclear whether the
1959 Decree recognizes that the refugees have rights that the Ministry of Interior should facilitate, or whether it gives the ministry unrestricted authority' over
them (Frontiers-Ruwad, 2005: 68). Beyond these ambiguous administrative tasks,
the Department of Affairs of Palestinian Refugees has a quite unambiguous surveillance function. An additional decree (No. 2867) establishes regional 'liaison
officers' for the department that were supposed to monitor 'refugees' political
activities and report on political and social unrest that may be caused by them.'[12]
Thus, the Lebanese state has developed an elaborate system of control and surveillance to deal with the Palestinian refugee population. Lebanon's governing
authorities have access to elaborate intelligence and informant networks. These

agencies, however, do not in any way officially engage with Palestinian political authorities, a task that is instead undertaken by Lebanese political parties. As shown in Chapter 5, these all have their own relationships with Palestinian parties.

Both the surveillance by Lebanese state institutions and the political relations between Lebanese and Palestinian parties are fundamentally securitized. Ever since the PLO's militarization – and despite its subsequent demilitarization – Palestinians in Lebanon are considered an existential threat to Lebanon's political status quo. Security concerns form the dominant prism through which Lebanese authorities perceive anything related to Palestinian refugees, and this has legitimized much of the extra-legality and exceptionalism discussed previously. Such securitization also means that all Palestinian political organization is inherently considered a threat to the Lebanese state. This, in turn, forecloses the possibility of actual Palestinian self-governance – something Lebanese authorities have claimed they want for Palestinians, but have simultaneously made impossible through their dealings with them.

The question of who can speak for and act on behalf of Palestinian refugees becomes inherently complicated in such a context. This question is already contested due to several factors, most importantly the undefined institutional status of the Palestinian state and the internal political divisions among Palestinians. These complexities are not of Lebanon's making. Yet, consecutive Lebanese governments have gone out of their way to aggravate such existing ambiguities and intra-Palestinian divisions through an implicit divide-and-rule-strategy so as to maintain the absence of a unified Palestinian authority in Lebanon. A Lebanese consultant on refugee affairs to the Prime Minister's Office was of the opinion that in this regard there is a 'tendency to keep it informal, because this is good for everyone, it's convenient.'[13] This is evident in dealings with the Palestinian Embassy, the PLO, individual political parties, and, as will be the focus in the next chapter, local Palestinian authorities.

The government of Lebanon regularly engages with the Embassy of the Palestinian Authority and often appears to treat it as the de facto spokesperson for Palestinian refugees in Lebanon. This does not amount to formal recognition or engagement with Lebanon's Palestinian authorities, however, because officially the embassy represents the Palestinian citizens under the Palestinian Authority in Gaza and the West Bank, but not the Palestinian refugees in Lebanon, who are not citizens of this Palestinian state. Far more encompassing than the Palestinian Authority and its Embassy, the PLO has traditionally fulfilled the role of the official political representative of all Palestinians worldwide. It has long functioned as the dominant 'institutional embodiment' of the dispersed Palestinian community (Sayigh, 1997b: 20). In Lebanon it has historically embraced this role both diplomatically, in its dealings with the Lebanese government, and institutionally, by operating its state in exile in Lebanon in the long 1970s. These institutional relations between the PLO and the Lebanese state were widespread and culminated in the Cairo Agreement. They were, however, shattered with the PLO's expulsion from Lebanon. By the end of the Lebanese Civil War in 1990, the PLO had started to gradually rebuild some of its institutional structures and political presence in Lebanon, but it never recaptured the power position it held in the 1970s.

The PLO, moreover, has always been an internally divided organization that hosts various, often opposing, factions. A significant number of important Palestinian political parties now operates outside the framework of the PLO. In addition, there is an ever-growing fatigue among Palestinians with the democratic and performative deficits of the PLO. The PLO can thus no longer be taken as the unilateral or undisputed representative of Palestinians in Lebanon. This has been especially true since the signing of the Oslo Accords in 1993, after which the PLO has increasingly focused its political activities and resources on the West Bank and Gaza Strip at the expense of the refugees in the diaspora. The envisioned rebuilding of the PLO on an inclusive, transnational foundation that was attempted repeatedly since the 1990s has so far failed.

This leaves the Lebanese state free to deal with the individual Palestinian political parties – of which Fatah, the Popular Front for the Liberation of Palestine, and the Democratic Front for the Liberation of Palestine are the leading ones within the PLO and Hamas and Islamic Jihad are most important within the Alliance (*Tahaluf*)[14] that is now the PLO's main rival. At various occasions, Lebanese politicians and officials meet with representatives of the leading Palestinian parties to discuss the issues of the day. Since 2005, these dispersed and ad hoc dialogue sessions with various Palestinian structures (the Palestinian Authority, the PLO, and individual parties) have become institutionalized in the LPDC. The LPDC, operating under the office of the presidency of the Council of Ministers, has the stated aim to improve 'the relations between the Lebanese government and all Palestinian parties,' but, as I discuss later, so far this has predominantly been a diplomatic endeavour with few structural or tangible results (Knudsen, 2011: 102).

Although the LPDC officially recognizes the parties related to the PLO and *Tahaluf* as political counterparts, these parties do not operate on the basis of popular membership, and their leaders are in no way elected or mandated by the refugees they purport to represent. Rather, many of them are self-appointed political elites clinging to their power positions. As discussed in the next chapter, local initiatives to develop more genuine representative structures have been undermined by both Lebanese and Palestinian authorities. Palestinian political parties, moreover, even while officially organized under two broad coalitions (the PLO and *Tahaluf*), operate autonomously, also in the context of the LPDC. A previous LPDC spokesperson lamented that: 'They never act as one. I told them at the beginning that if they wanted to be effective in the dialogue with the Lebanese, they would have to shrink their number; choose six representatives and rotate. They refused.'[15]

Added to this political fragmentation are the continuous institutional tensions stemming from the rivalry between the Embassy and the PLO leadership that were described earlier. All of this means that the question of Palestinian representation in Lebanon is rife with pertinent but unanswered questions. It is entirely unclear, as Suleiman (2017: 31–32) chronicles, whether there is a distinct embodiment of the PLO in Lebanon in addition to the Embassy in Lebanon which represents the Palestinian Authority in Ramallah or whether the Embassy has taken over the representative functions of the PLO in Lebanon; what the official role of the PLO (and its main institution, the Department of Refugee Affairs) in Lebanon is; and how we should see the status of the unilateral dealings of various Lebanese state institutions and political and religious officials with Palestinian parties. The only thing that is clear is that since the stillborn Higher Political Committee for the Palestinians in Lebanon, which was formed after the signing of the Cairo Agreement and was supposed to be a referential authority for the Palestinians' relationship with the Lebanese state, there has been no single Palestinian representation in Lebanon in an institutional sense, and there is no unified political leadership.

Lebanon's political elites and the state institutions at their disposal have not single-handedly created this fragmentation and delegitimation of Palestinian authority in their country, but they have certainly helped to produce and maintain it. After the Lebanese Civil War, a general amnesty allowed Lebanese warlords to transform their military authority into political power. Palestinians, however, were excluded from the amnesty law, allowing Lebanese authorities (and, until 2005, their Syrian overlords) to decimate the ranks of the Palestinian leadership, jailing or exiling any Palestinian leader who withstood them.

An equally divisive approach was apparent in post-Syria Lebanon. In 2005, the PLO sent an envoy to Lebanon to manage the effects of the Syrian withdrawal on Lebanon's Palestinian refugees. In his capacity as 'PLO ambassador,' this delegate simultaneously represented the PLO and the Palestinian Authority and was tasked by them to 'bridge the divide between Palestinian and Lebanese institutions' (Hanafi and Long, 2010: 143). Yet, analysts soon concluded, his authority to do so was so circumscribed by discriminatory Lebanese laws towards Palestinians that he was unable to implement his mission. He was met by the Lebanese state with, on the one hand, a significant curtailing of his resources and authority and, on the other hand, the expectation of 'him to exercise absolute control over the Palestinians in Lebanon, to keep the refugees quiet, subdued' (Hanafi and Long, 2010: 144). These contradicting expectations essentially set him up for failure.

In addition to fragmenting the political representation of Palestinians in the country, Lebanon's ruling elites have forced non-political forms of Palestinian representation underground by prohibiting the establishment of associations by non-Lebanese. This has crippled Palestinian non-governmental organizations (NGOs) and civil society organizations in Lebanon that might offer substitutes for direct political representation in the form of social organization.[16] Various Lebanese parties, in fact, clung to this stance in the consultation sessions organized by the LPDC that eventually led to the LPDC's Vision Document that is discussed later. A facilitator of these sessions noted that 'enabling Palestinian NGOs to operate' was 'the key thing that they were rejecting' to be included in the eventual document.[17]

Lebanese governments, themselves divided, have often contributed to rather than assuaged Palestinian strife and division. This culminated in the Civil War, but has continued in many ways in the post-war era under Syrian tutelage and after the Syrian withdrawal from Lebanon, with Lebanese politicians and officials demanding Palestinian self-governance but withholding local Palestinian governance recognition and thereby undermining it at the same time. Lebanon's hybrid political order and the behaviour of the Lebanese 'twilight' parties operating in it have exacerbated institutional ambiguity in terms of refugees' organizational and representational structures. Lebanese political elites have co-created and maintained the vagueness about representational responsibilities that shape decisions on how to organize the life of Palestinian refugees in Lebanon.

Benign strangulation[18]

The governance of the spaces where Palestinians in Lebanon live, their legal status, and the mandates of those actors claiming or aiming to represent them are all fundamentally defined by informality, liminality, and exceptionalism. This institutional ambiguity has very real consequences for Palestinian refugees.

The most recent survey on the socio-economic situation of Palestinian refugees in Lebanon paints a bleak picture (Chaaban et al., 2016). Palestinian refugees in Lebanon face higher poverty rates than Palestinians in all other UNRWA areas of operation, including Gaza: in 2015, 65 percent of them lived in poverty and 62.2 percent of refugees faced food insecurity. Despite relatively high educational enrollment rates, in 2015, the unemployment rate among Lebanon's Palestinian refugees was 23.2 percent. Due to labour market restrictions, even those Palestinians who are employed in Lebanon have low-paid, low-skilled jobs characterized by harsh, insecure, and exploitative working conditions, with half of them living in poverty despite being employed. The health of Lebanon's Palestinians is precarious, with over 81.3 percent of them reporting at least one family member suffering from chronic illness and the vast majority having at least one household member who was acutely ill. Palestinian dwellings in Lebanon are often in a bad condition. Leakages, dampness, pollution by waste, poor ventilation, and precarious electricity constructions are the rule rather than the exception.

This situation certainly cannot be solely blamed on Lebanon. The international community that allows UNRWA's budget to shrink progressively each year and the Palestinian Authority and the PLO that increasingly disregard the Palestinians in the diaspora both contribute to this political and economic marginalization. But the situation of Palestinian refugees being more dire in Lebanon than anywhere else is also the result of evident inaction and ambiguity on the side of Lebanese authorities.

In Lebanon, Palestinian refugees' socio-economic rights are systematically circumscribed. At first instance, such discrimination may appear to have little to do with institutional ambiguity. Restrictive policies are, after all, there. And they may be repressive, but they are unambiguously so. But such unambiguous repression is enabled by ambiguous legislation. 'Intentional delays' in the introduction of comprehensive policies (Mencütek, 2019: 137) and the deliberate absence of a tailored legal framework, Al-Natour (1997: 360) documents, has made Palestinian refugees particularly vulnerable to marginalization in Lebanon.[19] Due to the legal limbo and the absence of laws that accommodate Palestinians' statelessness that were outlined earlier, what 'rights' Palestinians are allocated in terms of residence, property, and labour can be withdrawn at any time.[20] This, as Knudsen (2007: 12) contends, makes them privileges rather than rights, whose actual implementation is extremely arbitrary.

Palestinians' 'right' to work in Lebanon reveals much of this dynamic. Since Palestinians are stateless foreigners in Lebanon, their labour rights have since 1962 been regulated by Decree No. 17561 that revolves around three core principles: the logic of national preference; the need to obtain a work permit; and the doctrine of national reciprocity. With reference to the idea of 'national preference,' the decree provides a list, to be updated annually, with jobs restricted to Lebanese nationals. This creates room for extending and amending the categories of labour that are off limits to refugees as respective governments see fit. Since 1964, Palestinians are excluded from joining syndicates, which is a prerequisite for professional work, relegating them to do menial labour or work on the black market. For those jobs that are open to Palestinians, they have to get a work permit, making them unattractive in the competition with other foreigners who do not need such a permit. In 2016, less than 3.3 percent of Lebanon's Palestinian refugees had the kind of official employment contract by a public notary that is required to apply for a work permit in the first place (Chaaban et al., 2016: 7). In 2010, the amendment of the Labour Law waived the fee for working permits for Palestinians in various job categories (excluding, however, the so-called liberal professions). But regardless of the related fee, the allocation of permits is conditional and, Suleiman (2006: 16) points out, thereby dependent on 'the personal attitude and goodwill of the minister himself.' In practice, work permits are hardly ever provided to Palestinians. In 2012, the number of Palestinians with work permits was less than 2 percent (Helou, 2014: 85). Recent research suggests that of the 210,000 work permits granted to foreigners since 2010, only several hundred went to Palestinians.[21]

The issue of property rights for Palestinians in Lebanon similarly shows how restrictive and fickle legislation and arbitrary implementation work to marginalize refugees and enable their exploitation. Until 2001, Palestinians in Lebanon could own land and real estate. To do so, they had to register the ownership with both a notary and the relevant government agency. Because they did not understand the relevant legal frameworks or were not willing or able to pay the high taxes involved, however, Palestinians often failed to register their property with the state cadaster. To resolve this, in 2000, Palestinian civil society organizations petitioned to be allowed the same tax rate as Lebanese, rather than the higher tax rate leveled against foreigners.[22]

Instead of being granted their request, however, the government negated their right to purchase land and real estate altogether. The law specifically targeted Palestinians, stating:

> All forms of real estate rights are forbidden to any person who is not hold-ing a nationality of a recognized state, or any person in general – should the ownership be nonconforming to the provisions of the Constitution in terms of rejecting permanent settlement.[23]

This meant that Palestinians could no longer buy land or real estate. Moreover, if they were in the process of buying property through installments or could not provide cadastral registration in addition to the ownership papers provided by the notary, they lost the right to property they already owned. Palestinians with-out such cadastral registration, a renowned Palestinian lawyer working on this issue explained, became entirely dependent on the goodwill of the Lebanese per-son from which they originally bought the land as these could – and often did – reclaim the land they previously sold if the transaction had not been registered in the cadaster.[24]

Legislation on Palestinians' social rights in practice thus generates dispropor-tionate discretionary power. In Lebanon, the legislature and judiciary are 'tools in the legal discrimination against refugees'; discrimination that operates in the form of repression through discretion (Knudsen, 2009: 69). This concerns state officials in charge of deciding on work permits and Lebanese landowners, who are often part of the economic elite that constitutes Lebanon's ruling class, dealing with Palestinian property. The need to constantly underscore the liminality of the Pal-estinian presence in Lebanon, the legal and institutional exceptionalism that this need produces, and the informal arrangements that then determine the interpreta-tion and implementation of these exceptional decisions characterize Lebanon's dealing with Palestinian refugees.

This institutionalized ambiguity helps to produce socio-economic marginaliza-tion, a form of vulnerability that, as with Syrian refugees, can be considered man-ufactured because it is the evident result of specific political actions and inactions in the realms of status, space, and representation. Legal limbo has enabled the imposition of labour and ownership restrictions on refugees that have contributed to their poverty and made them vulnerable to exploitation. Refugees' encampment came with bans on shelter rehabilitation and extension and has made refugees dependent on an ever-more-depleted UNRWA and unaccountable Palestinian par-ties. Divided political representation has undermined refugees' agency to structur-ally challenge these conditions. Thus, while Lebanese and Palestinians appear to entirely agree on what they want (for Palestinians to return to Palestine) and do not want (for Palestinians to stay in Lebanon indefinitely), the improbability of realizing this shared desire has resulted in marginalization of the Palestinian com-munity in Lebanon.

Such vulnerability is not merely largely avoidable and thereby partially manu-factured. It is, remarkably, construed as being in the best interest of Palestinians themselves. Their continuing misery supposedly keeps the pressure on the inter-national community to make Israel honor the Palestinian refugees' right to return and is meant to lend credence to the Palestinians' claim that their presence in exile is temporary and their will to return unwavering. This logic, that improve-ment of socio-economic parameters would undermine Palestinians' willingness to return and Israel's willingness to let them, holds little empirical or analytical value considering that Israel is adamant in its stance that there is no possibility for the Palestinians to return, regardless of either their misery or their prosperity, and the international community's acquiescence to this stance. But it has great political value in the Lebanese context, where such 'benign' strangulation – which purports that any form of civil or socio-economic rights for Palestinians inevi-tably leads to political rights and permanent settlement and hence threatens the sectarian status quo – helps to reconcile support for the Palestinian cause on the one hand and preservation of the fiction of sectarian balance on the other (Peteet, 2005: 174). It allows Lebanon to be 'with Palestine, but against the Palestinians' (Raffonelli, 2004).

A politics of uncertainty

So far, the chapter has established that institutional ambiguity is prevalent in Leb-anon's governance of Palestinian refugees and that, together with outright repres-sion, it results in extreme socio-economic and political marginalization. This section will demonstrate that such institutional ambiguity closely resonates with the political interests of Lebanese authorities and follows from their sometimes strategic inaction and ambiguous action.

As with Syrian refugees, much of the institutional ambiguity described pre-viously stems from Lebanon's hybrid political order. This regards the extreme political polarization across Lebanon's sects and political alliances regarding the 'Palestinian issue.' It also concerns the severe lack of governance capacities that have Lebanese authorities struggling to provide a fraction of security, welfare, and representation that they would want to offer even to citizens. Yet more explicitly than with the Syrian refugee 'crisis,' institutional ambiguity in the case of Leba-non's Palestinians also has a significant ideological component. Producing long-term informality, liminality, and exceptionalism is a way for the Lebanese state to reinstate its conviction that the international community should be responsible for taking care of the Palestinians and, however perverse, to signal its commitment to the Palestinians' right of return. But institutional ambiguity is strategic not merely in an ideological or geopolitical manner, but also in a more opportunistic sense. Informality, liminality, and exceptionalism produce effects that are in line with the stated interests of Lebanon's governing elites: as further evidenced in Chapter 6, they help prevent the (re-)mobilization of refugees, enable economic and political exploitation, and 'encourage' refugees to leave.

Institutional ambiguity is neither complete nor uncontested. The political actions that create or keep in place informality, liminality, and exceptionalism are often specifically apparent when existing forms of institutional ambiguity are challenged. It is in these instances that the strategic elements of ambiguous action and inaction become particularly visible. As noted in Chapter 1, there is no such thing as *the* Lebanese state or *the* Lebanese authorities. Political division and competition are omnipresent. This is also evident in the vignettes presented in this section. These illustrate how some actors seek to partially remedy institutional ambiguity, whereas others seek to maintain it. Challenges to informal, liminal, and exceptional forms of governance often partially or completely fail, due to institutional complications as well as resistance. The vignettes explored here certainly do not suggest that all attempts to formalize and regularize are strategically undermined or set up to fail. Often, they are genuine and at least partially successful. But the vignettes do reveal the efforts made to keep ambiguity in place, which offers a unique window on the incentives that (re-)produce institutional ambiguity.

The two vignettes analyze, first, the creation of the LPDC and, second, its census of Lebanon's Palestinian population. They show how this unprecedented institutionalization and formalization of Lebanese-Palestinian relations in the country has brought real change, but also faced curtailed mandates, resources, and follow-up that were, according to officials and analysts involved in the process, the result of political sabotage. Similarly, the LPDC's revolutionary attempt to address the absence of formal state statistics regarding Palestinians in the country was co-opted to the extent that this census provided further ammunition for the ongoing 'numbers game' rather than once and for all concluding this game as it allegedly set out to do.

Contested formalization: crippling the Lebanese-Palestinian Dialogue Committee and preventing the High Commission for Palestinian Affairs

Lebanon's institutional parameters for governing Palestinians were long limited to administration and surveillance by the Department of Affairs of the Palestinian Refugees and a set of restrictions on labour, education, property ownership, and social security. These were in line with the shared conviction of Lebanon's ruling elite that any engagement with the Palestinian refugees should have the sole purpose to underscore the temporariness of their presence. The 'policy,' in a way, was to limit formal political decision-making in this realm to restrictions only. The informal arrangements that subsequently emerged to deal with refugee spaces and representatives in practice were not to be recognized or coordinated upon officially. This deliberate inaction in many policy realms has led to a discrepancy between de jure and de facto realities that steeped the lives of Palestinian refugees in informality, liminality, and exceptionalism. As the then spokesperson of the LPDC concluded without much ado in 2014: 'There is no official or clear state policy concerning the Palestinians.'[25]

But over the last decade, there have been significant changes in Lebanon's engagement with Palestinian refugees. These developments have been heralded as a potential paradigm shift in the way the Lebanese state and the political factions running it approach the Palestinian 'question.' Cautious suggestions are increasingly being made about 'rapprochement' (Knudsen, 2009: 66), 'normalization' (Doraï, 2011: 71), and a possible 'new era' (Suleiman, 2006: 23) of Lebanese-Palestinian relations that would be characterized by a tendency towards 'a more conciliatory relationship between Palestinian refugees and the Lebanese state and the latter's interest in a partial regularization of Palestinian refugee presence' (Czajka, 2012: 239).

The institutional environment for refugee governance started to change after the Nahr al-Bared crisis. In 2007, the Lebanese army destroyed large parts of the Nahr al-Bared camp in North Lebanon to eliminate militants hiding the camp. The camp's reconstruction process subsequently encompassed a controversial new model for camp governance that was implicitly launched as a blueprint for other camps as well. Knudsen and Hanafi (2011: 7) therefore describe this calamity as a starting point for redefining the 'political relations between refugees, their political representatives and the state.' The Nahr al-Bared crisis, moreover, boosted the LPDC's relevance and mandate and provided the impetus for the installation of a Palestinian embassy in Lebanon in 2011.[26] In short, it generated an unprecedented awareness of the need for Lebanese-Palestinian coordination on governance in Palestinian camps.

Under the stewardship of an increasingly emboldened LPDC, the Lebanese Working Group on Palestinian Refugee Affairs has, over the last few years, engaged in an extensive consultation process that resulted in a document titled 'A Unified Lebanese Vision for the Palestinian Refugees Affairs in Lebanon.' This Vision claims to have the objective to 'provide the Lebanese State and its institutions with stable national guidelines regarding refugees and their cause' and 'recommends the Lebanese government to launch the development of an integrated and consistent national policy on Palestinian refugees in Lebanon' (LPDC, 2016: 2, 16).[27] In doing so, the working group, and thereby presumably the entire Lebanese political elite it officially represented, explicitly recognized the previous 'strategy of neglect' and 'absence of a coherent government policy' (Suleiman, 2017: 14). Indeed, the LPDC was created to be 'filling a void in the Lebanese government dealing with the issue of refugees' (LPDC, 2013: 8) – and was to function as the delineated agency to propose much-needed policies.

To remedy policy inconsistency and instability, the Unified Vision document suggests that rather than seeking to accrue sovereignty through securitization and segregation as in the past, it should be guaranteed through extensive interaction with Palestinian representatives on all levels. In essence this means lifting the current exceptionalism. It, for instance, suggests to 'facilitate interaction between the refugees, public service administrations, and surrounding municipalities' and to unify 'the Lebanese and Palestinian administrative authorities and organizing their collaboration based on sound principles' (LPDC, 2016: 10–11). Indeed, with the LPDC there now is, for the first time in history, a formal interaction channel between Lebanese and Palestinian authorities in the country. This is revolutionary in itself. And in addition to its mere existence, the LPDC can boast some remarkable achievements such as the May 2008 decision to issue special identity cards to undocumented Palestinians and, first and foremost, its Unified Vision.

Yet, so far, the LPDC itself recognizes, these formal diplomatic breakthroughs have not seen any executive or practical implications. The LPDC's various studies and important recommendations on previous taboo topics such as the right to work, right to study, right to association, and living conditions in Palestinian settlements have not (yet) been translated into action. The 2017 Unified Vision calls for a 'Lebanese public policy regarding the issues of Palestinian refugees' and the *establishment* of 'an official framework for the Lebanese State to address Palestinian issues and ensuring the appropriate relevant structures,' but it does not function as such a policy or framework in and of itself.

This might, of course, still happen. The developments discussed are, after all, very recent. Limited capacities and resources, the paralysis associated with hybrid order, and the urgency of more pressing political developments – foremost among them the Syrian refugee situation – hamper further policy development and implementation. However, people involved in the LPDC's endeavours as well as analysts closely observing the process also suggest that the bulk of the LPDC's new vision will never be implemented because the officials that mandated the LPDC never meant it to be implemented.

As one observer notes, 'the slow and disruptive pace' of Lebanese procedures, even those few that are agreed upon, 'characterises the situation of Palestinian refuge in Lebanon' (Saleh, 2019; see also Yan, 2017). Apparently banking on their twilight nature, Lebanon's political parties can count on their ability to obstruct ratification and implementation even of those initiatives they have officially embraced. They know that 'crystallising procedures into laws and the unequivocal drafting of legislations is very important to prevent the use of ambiguity or loopholes' on which they depend and thus work to avert such crystallization (Saleh, 2019). In advising me on my research, one consultant who has been involved in the initiation and early days of the LPDC emphasized that I would need to look beyond what people say and scrutinize their actual behaviour, urging me to 'read between the lines and try and see the benefits of maintaining the status quo.'[28]

Taking this to heart and bearing in mind the history of Lebanon's tendency towards institutional ambiguity when it comes to the Palestinians, the current developments can be read as a form of nonperformativity. As with the Minister of State for Displaced Affairs that was put in charge of the Syrian refugee file without being granted sufficient mandate and resources, discussed in Chapter 2, the LPDC and its new approach might signal a process of stalling actual change by proclaiming paper change. This is not to say that all implementation challenges are indications of strategic ambiguity. It is to explore the extent to which implementation challenges (also) follow from deliberate 'footdragging.'

The limited institutional follow-up of the LPDC's studies, recommendations, and vision, Lebanese policy analysts explained, are importantly related to the LPDC's mandate. The limited executive powers of the LPDC are a continuing frustration of its technical team. These limited powers, however, are likely to be no coincidence. They appear to reflect a deliberate outcome of political elites' lack of political will to change the governance of Palestinian refugees and their concomitant need for a toothless tiger. Attempts by the LPDC to enhance its implementation capacity have been in vain. In 2013, the previous LPDC president drafted a 'future vision' for the LPDC. To have an actual impact, this document states, the LPDC would require further institutionalization and a new structure and mandate. The document stresses the necessity to establish a 'government institution that would fulfill the executive functions necessary to deal with the Palestinian refugee issue in Lebanon in all its dimensions' (LPDC, 2013: 9).

After exploring various options – such as turning the LPDC into a ministry or refashioning it as a General Directorate or a Minister of State – through broad consultation with relevant officials and experts, the then president of the LPDC concluded it would be most efficient to turn the committee into a High Commission. The High Commission would have the 'purpose to set up frameworks for managing the state's relationship with the refugees' and 'design mechanisms to implement the decisions taken' with the aim to 'better organize this file and start developing future plans for its management' – frameworks, mechanisms, and organization that were apparently inexistent at the time of writing (LPDC, 2013: 4). Indeed, a fully developed draft law for the creation of this High Commission of Palestinian Affairs that outlines its mandate and organizational structure – to 'be referred to Parliament through a decree that is issued by the Council of Ministers' – was proposed by the LPDC in 2013 (LPDC, 2013: 9). The structure of this High Commission of Palestinian Refugee Affairs is laid down in detail in the document in question. It would have a planning and an executive department made up of ministers 'with a specific mandate defined by legislation' (LPDC, 2013: 9). Its article 1 proposed that the High Commission would enjoy an 'independent legal framework as well as financial and administrative autonomy' and would supervise 'all the issues related to the Palestinian refugees in Lebanon' (LPDC, 2013: 10).

This essential institutional reorganization, however, was never followed through, and the president of the LPDC who had proposed it resigned. Thus, while the dependence, vulnerability, and limited authority of the LPDC have been recognized explicitly and practical solutions for these shortcomings have been identified, they have not been addressed. This, a former representative of the LPDC suggested, allows Lebanese governments its cherished 'position of denial,' hiding behind good intentions without following these through or having others see them through.[29] In 2014, leading facilitators of the LPDC noted that the fact that the LPDC falls directly under the Prime Minister's office means that it cannot function independently and is deliberately limited to an advisory function.[30] This view was seconded by a member of the LPDC's technical team, who observed that 'what we're doing is not leading to major changes, not even in the long term,'[31] and later concluded: 'We don't have a lot of authority to do things right now.'[32]

The LPDC thus explicitly recognizes the informality, liminality, and exceptionalism that Palestinian refugees in Lebanon face and works to remedy some of this ambiguity. These attempts are partly successful. They are also extremely contested. This is evident in the limited mandate of the LPDC and its lack of executive power and the fact that these are recognized as problematic but not adjusted. Inaction – not solving the recognized institutional deficiencies of the LPDC – thereby results in ambiguous action, with ambitious policy recommendations on the one hand, but lagging policy decisions and implementations on the other. For refugees and those seeking to represent and help them, this makes it even more unclear what they may count on and hope for.

This dynamic is well-illustrated by what is often presented as the LPDC's most significant achievement: The execution of a census of the inhabitants of the country's formal and informal refugee settlements. Heralded as an effort to once and for all settle the contested issue of the number of Palestinian refugees in the country and to provide a starting point for evidence-based policy-making regarding the Palestinian refugee issue, the outcome of the census was disputed to the extent that it amplified rather than solved existing demographic and statistical uncertainties.

The LPDC's groundbreaking census: disputed surveying and the existential numbers game

Refugees are often ambivalent about registration. It is a way to validate their existence, explicate their presence, draw attention to their plight, access rights, and claim entitlements. But it also carries risks. Syrian refugees are wary of any form of registration in light of the dictatorial state surveillance they have been subjected to in their home country. With strategic processes of (partisan) mapping, counting, and documenting lying at the heart of Israel's project of colonial dispossession, Palestinian refugees are apprehensive about registration as well. Registration is highly contentious for states too, specifically so in Lebanon.

Just like the number of Syrian refugees in the country is continuously contested yet simultaneously kept vague, the question of how many Palestinians Lebanon actually hosts is 'obviously at the heart of the Palestinian refugee problem' (Suleiman, 2006: 6). In Lebanon's sectarian political arena, demographics are sensitive. Because the great majority of Palestinian refugees in Lebanon that has not been naturalized is of a Sunni Muslim denomination,[33] their mere presence is assumed to undermine the brittle sectarian equilibrium of the country – even if this is a presence without formal rights or political power. The downplaying or exacerbating of the number of Palestinians living in Lebanon therefore has acute political implications.

As with the figure of Syrian refugees, the number of Palestinian refugees in Lebanon is disputed. This confusion is the result of different categorizations of refugees, with most refugees being registered with UNRWA and the Lebanese state, but some with only one of the two and some with neither one. Both the state's and UNRWA's registration, moreover, have their complications. As Frontiers-Ruwad (2005: 69) notes, there is an 'ambiguity surrounding the registration of Palestinian refugees in Lebanese law,' with the definition of who constitutes a Palestinian refugee being disputed and some refugees, most notably those who arrived after 1948, facing obstacles to state registration. UNRWA registration is similarly inaccurate. As is the case with the UNHCR, UNRWA faces many 'registration gaps,' which are often the result of attempts to 'accommodate government demands and restrictions' (Frontiers-Ruwad, 2005: 11).

Then there is the discrepancy between those people registered in Lebanon and those actually residing in the country (with the latter number being significantly lower than the former). In addition, numbers vary based on whether they include only those Palestinians living in the formal and informal refugee camps or all Palestinians in the country. Thus, while there are 469,331 Palestinians registered with UNRWA in Lebanon, studies suggested that the number of Palestinians living in the country would not exceed 270,000 people (UNRWA, 2019). Until recently it was often routinely stated that Palestinian refugees made up approximately 10 percent of the Lebanese population, some 400,000 people (Khalidi and Riskedahl, 2010: 1).

The LPDC has acknowledged 'the absence of official, comprehensive and accurate data' on the Palestinian presence in the country, which it saw as a key factor that 'limits the ability of the Government of Lebanon to base sound policies affecting the living conditions of the Palestinian refugees on solid grounds.'[34] To remedy this situation, in 2017 it conducted the first Lebanese census of Palestinian refugees in Lebanon. The LPDC census established that the number of Palestinian refugees living in Lebanon's camps and gatherings is 174,422. Even if this excludes some 10 percent of self-settled Palestinian refugees in Lebanon who do not live in either the camps or the gatherings,[35] the actual number of Palestinians in Lebanon would be far less than the number previously customarily cited.

While the LPDC presented this new number as the first reliable statistic in this realm and a historical breakthrough, the outcomes of the census are widely questioned. The most important concern, a senior Palestinian scholar working with the LPDC explained, was that the census only included those Palestinians living in Palestinian camps and gatherings and that the number of Palestinians living outside of these spaces is much larger than the 10 percent estimated by the LPDC.[36] In addition, the census only captured the people residing there at the moment, excluding those Palestinians who are temporarily abroad for various reasons. A significant number of refugees, moreover, was seen to have evaded the survey, as Halkort (2019: 322) alludes to, refusing to participate and even actively obstructing it.

As a Lebanese civil society expert involved in the LPDC dialogue process summarized the general sentiment:

> They came up with a number that. . ., let me say . . . it confused everyone in the country . . . yeah, it confused everyone. And if you ask the people they

will say 'no, no, no, this is not correct, this number.' No one, no one, you know, can believe that this is the right number of Palestinian refugees in Lebanon.[37]

This means that whether or not the new number produced by the 2017 census is correct or not, the perception that it is not actually known how many Palestinian refugees there are in Lebanon remains. As a senior Lebanese journalist concluded: 'The numbers are important but what is more important is their exploitation.'[38] The remaining ambiguity, whether real or perceived, is convenient to Lebanese politicians as it aligns well with the Janus-faced nature of Lebanon's approach to the Palestinian community residing in the country. From the perspective of keeping alive the Palestinians' right to return and the related responsibility of the international community, it is important to stress the significance of the 'problem' and hence to have as high as possible a number of (registered) refugees. On the other hand, bearing in mind the undesirability of settlement and the Lebanese population's resentment of the Palestinian presence in Lebanon since the Civil War, for domestic purposes a low number of 'actually residing refugees' is more expedient. To be able to simultaneously downplay and magnify the Palestinian presence depending on the issue at stake and the audience to be addressed, the absence of an undisputed number remains opportune.[39] As an LPDC analyst involved in the census lamented, 'nobody wants to look at empirical data.'[40] The 'laziness to correctly understand' the various figures available that one expert on Palestinian refugees in Lebanon identified among Lebanese politicians is, he concluded, 'convenient.'[41]

But the fact that vague numbers serve interests does not have to mean they are produced or maintained deliberately. The absence of reliable statistics importantly results from limited capacity. As the LPDC notes on its website, 'the Lebanese Public Institutions mandated with the registry of the Palestinian refugees heavily suffer from outdated operational systems and limited human resources.'[42] In fact, if there ever was a credible claim that ambiguous statistics were at least partly the result of a lack of political will to produce unambiguous ones, the recent census, which, after all, was carried out by a Lebanese state agency, should do away with this idea. The celebration of empirical evidence and hard data as the foundation for policy that the census exemplified was publicly embraced by the government. The Prime Minister, in his speech at the event that was organized to present the census outcomes, stated that the data 'leave no room for ambiguity' and contribute to the formulation of projects and plans.[43]

This public celebration of the census and its implications by the powers that be, however, seems to have been premature, or perhaps even hypocritical. Experts representing the LPDC and involved in the census process emphasized that the census never aimed or claimed to establish the total number of Palestinians in the country and focused merely on those living in the camps and gatherings. It was thus never mandated to answer the question of how many Palestinian refugees Lebanon counts. This limited mandate, according to a senior official involved in the census project, was not coincidental. In fact, he reflected, the census was never taken seriously at all by the advisory and steering committees that were overseeing it and that included representatives from all relevant ministries. He said: 'I imagine that there were a lot of people who expected that this exercise would fall in the middle or would not have the impact it had.'[44] This would suggest that the very officials who agreed on the census silently counted on its failure. An LPDC analyst cynically and only half-jokingly concluded:

> I do believe it may be the last census ever in Lebanon. . . . I think there is a lot of lessons learned from this that politicians will draw. And most probably they will avoid such . . . being cornered at a certain point.[45]

Interlocutors seemed adamant that despite the valid and reliable method underlying the census, it would not actually upturn the dominant Lebanese tendency to keep alive a multitude of contested statistics instead of a single consensus number (see also Yan, 2017). I was reminded time and again that such statistical contestation was central to Lebanese politics, as the last national census in Lebanon was held in 1932, and would remain defining for both Palestinian and Lebanese refugee populations. The stakes of 'manipulation,' a Lebanese public policy expert working on refugee issues concluded, were just too high.[46] Speaking on the implications of the 2017 LPDC census, the director of Lebanon's leading research institute on public policy predicted that regardless of the scientific rigor of the census and despite its ambition to put an end to such schemes,[47] 'the number of Palestinian refugees in Lebanon continues to be a contentious issue wielded to advance political agendas' (Yan, 2018).

Reflecting on the backlash the LPDC has faced during and after the census, an analyst who was involved concluded that, apparently, 'there are entire structures that also are counting on this misinformation about the Palestinians.'[48] In presenting the census' key findings, the president of the LPDC (2018: 3) noted that 'the numbers of refugees estimated by different agencies were used to drive inaccurate and sometimes falsely [sic] understandings of the Palestinian refugees' population presence in the country.' The political interests underlying such manipulation mean that rather than being accepted as the final and undisputable number, the LPDC count will inevitably become yet another option from the varied menu of available numbers of Palestinian refugees in Lebanon.

Conclusions

These vignettes about the creation and increasing significance of the LPDC and the impact of its census illustrate several key aspects of the functioning of institutional ambiguity in governing Lebanon's Palestinians. First, through the LPDC's promotion of future policy consistency and comprehension, Lebanese state officials have, for the first time, explicitly recognized the previous absence of policy. The objectives of the LPDC confirmed Lebanon's long-standing de facto no-policy-policy vis-à-vis not just Syrians but also Palestinians. Second, the

LPDC's mandate and activities suggest that genuine initiatives to remedy institutional ambiguity can easily be co-opted by forms of nonperformativity, whereby they are publicly embraced but privately undermined by preventing actual implementation. As the LPDC's census shows, third, in situations of hybrid order with powerful precedents of institutional ambiguity, there is a major risk that attempts to remedy confusion end up adding to it. None of this diminishes the relevance or possibility of genuine change to lift maleficent forms of informality, liminality, and exceptionalism. But it does document the tenacity of institutional ambiguity. Withholding any executive power from the LPDC despite the existence of draft laws to remedy this agreed-upon deficiency and maintaining controversies around numbers despite having solicited a survey to allegedly remedy such contention keep in place the institutional ambiguity through which Lebanon's Palestinian refugees are governed and that facilitates their control, exploitation, and expulsion.

This chapter, then, has chronicled how the institutional ambiguity that determines Lebanon's response to the Syrian refugee presence as described in Chapters 2 and 3 is not merely rooted in its hybrid political order, but also finds its precedent in the country's post–Civil War engagement with Palestinian refugees. The relentless emphasis on Palestinians' return, fueled by geopolitical as well as internal Lebanese political considerations, put Palestinian refugees under the curse of permanent temporariness. This obsession with institutionally upholding liminality manifests itself in forms of hybrid encampment, legal limbo, and informalized political interaction that produce exceptionalism, excluding Palestinian refugees from state responsibilities and including them in state surveillance and control mechanisms. The socio-economic marginalization that this institutional ambiguity produces further undermines refugees' ability to contest the chronic uncertainty that they face. Ambiguity helps create vulnerability and vulnerability furthers ambiguity.

The next chapter will further delve into exactly how informality, liminality, and exceptionalism operate in the governance of refugee spaces, status, and representation. Exploring these dynamics in the context of specific refugee settlements, Chapter 5 interrogates both the mechanisms and the effects of institutional ambiguity as a form of governance. It thereby further studies what it actually means that 'state-level vacillation and confusion' is a common factor in the Lebanese management of Palestinian affairs (Borgmann and Slim, 2018: 32).

Notes

1 Author's interview – Beirut, 6 June 2013.
2 Author's interview with development specialist – Skype, 11 December 2017.
3 Reflecting on the legal marginalization of Syrian refugees, a humanitarian representative mused, 'Lebanese authorities have treated the Palestinians in exactly the same way' (Author's group interview – Skype, 3 January 2018).
4 Author's interview – Skype, 22 January 2018.
5 Author's interview – Skype, 10 January 2018.
6 They were not recorded due to the sensitive nature of the 'Palestinian issue' in Lebanon; the citations provided are based on extensive notes.

Some of the interviews that underlie the vignettes in the last section of the chapter were conducted more recently (in 2017 and 2018) via Skype. These interviews were recorded and transcribed, and citations are verbatim.

7 Three of which were destroyed during the Lebanese Civil War. Another camp was evacuated.

8 Sectarian balance is an illusion because recent estimates indicate that the 1932 census on which the current confessional allocation of state positions depends is blatantly outdated and no longer reflects the actual demographic situation in the country (Mencütek, 2019: 131).

9 In my analysis, I will speak of settlements as an overarching category to refer to all of these types of encampment. To refer to the UNRWA-run camps, I will use 'camps' or 'formal camps.' The term 'gatherings' is used to refer to the settlements not formally recognized by the Lebanese state.

10 Those in formal camps less than those in informal settlements, but the specter of displacement is present in both types of settings, as explicated by the nearly complete destruction of the Nahr el-Bared camp in 2017.

11 These tasks included coordination with UNRWA; handling applications for identification and residency cards and travel documents in coordination with the General Security; managing personal documentation (birth, residence, marriage, divorce, death); dealing with family reunification requests; and handling the lease arrangements of the formal camps (Suleiman, 2006: 12). The department also has the discretionary power to accept or refuse any foreign aid for Palestinians in the country (Mencütek, 2019: 140).

12 In 1960, a Higher Authority of Palestinian Affairs was established (via Presidential Decree No. 3909). It was supposed to operate under the supervision of the Ministry of Foreign Affairs. This Higher Authority was never actually activated, but it clearly testifies to the political and security priorities that drive the Lebanese state's engagement with Palestinian refugees (Suleiman, 2006: 13). It included a wide array of security authorities (the Director General of the Ministry of National Defense, officers of 'Deuxieme Bureau,' the General Director of the Department of Affairs of Palestinian Refugees, the Chief of the Israel Boycott office in the Ministry of National Economy and Tourism, and the Chief of the Palestine Division in the Ministry of Foreign and Repatriate Affairs) and was to have the following tasks: 'Gathering all information pertaining to political, military, economic, and other aspects of the Palestinian cause; studying all aspects of the Palestine Question, monitoring its developments and drafting solutions in response to it; and confronting the Zionist propaganda abroad' (unpublished document cited by Suleiman, 2006: 13).

13 Author's interview – Beirut, 11 March 2011. An analyst related to the Lebanese-Palestinian dialogue sessions reflected on my long but fruitless search for documentation on previous political interactions between Lebanese and Palestinian authorities in the country with the offhand remark that I would not find such documents because, simply, 'they're not there' (Author's interview – Beirut, 11 March 2011). All engagement of Lebanese governments with Palestinian representatives has been informal, her colleague noted: 'No reports or archives or minutes' (Author's interview – Beirut, 28 May 2013).

14 *Tahaluf al-Qiwa al-Falastiniyya* (Alliance of Palestinian Forces, or *Tahaluf*/Alliance in short).

15 Author's interview – Beirut, 22 July 2013.

16 Palestinians in Lebanon do not have the right to establish associations. Technically speaking there are therefore no 'Palestinian' NGOs. Many organizations are, however, established and ran by Palestinians but under the formal name of a Lebanese penholder. I refer to these as 'Palestinian.'

17 Author's interview – Skype, 10 January 2018.

18 I came across this term years ago in a newspaper article which I was unable to find
     again when writing the book. I am thankful to the person who came up with this
     notion that so aptly captures the perverse paradox of discrimination of Palestinians in
     Lebanon.
19 In 1991, an attempt to formalize the rights of Palestinian refugees in Lebanon was
     stillborn when the Ministerial Committee appointed to 'formulate an understanding on
     rights, duties and forms of mutual relations' was suspended without having achieved
     any results (Al-Natour, 1997: 361).
20 For more details, please refer to Akram (2002), El Natour (2012), Suleiman (2006),
     and Ugland (2003).
21 Author's interview with a Palestinian scholar associated with the LPDC – Skype, 18
     January 2018.
22 Author's interview with Palestinian lawyer – Beirut, 21 March 2013.
23 Law 296/2001 issued on April 3, 2001, containing an amendment to the law imple-
     mented as per decree no. 11614 issued on January 4, 1969 (www.lpdc.gov.lb/
     property-ownership/the-palestinian-refugee-and-the-property-ownership/56/en).
24 Author's interview with Palestinian lawyer – Beirut, 28 June 2014.
25 Author's interview – Beirut, 17 September 2014.
26 These improved relations with the Palestinian Authority have helped some Palestinians
     in Lebanon: In July 2006, passports issued by the Palestinian Authority were recog-
     nized by Lebanon, and in November 2011, further status documents were as well.
     Overall, however, it has not really benefited Palestinian refugees in Lebanon as they
     do not fall under the authority of the Palestinian Authority, which is limited to Palestine
     proper, but defer to the PLO – which has been further marginalized at the expense of
     the Palestinian Authority.
27 The document is signed by all of Lebanon's major political parties, which is a feat in
     its own right. It puts forward a unique consensus on narrowly defining settlement (or
     tawteen) as

>   granting Palestinian refugees in Lebanon the Lebanese nationality collectively, to
>   all or some, outside the legal context by virtue of a political decision imposed in
>   the context of a regional or international settlement and contrary to the Constitu-
>   tion, whether done all at once or gradually.
>   (LPDC unified vision, 2016: 7)

     This definition importantly departs from the previous, deliberately broad, understand-
     ing of resettlement or integration as implicated in any form of improving the social,
     economic, or legal conditions of Palestinian refugees that had stood at the root of so
     much of the Palestinians' marginalization in Lebanon (LPDC, 2016: 2).
28 Author's informal meeting – Beirut, 11 March 2011.
29 Author's interview – Beirut, 22 July 2013.
30 Author's interview – Beirut, 17 September 2014.
31 Author's informal meeting – Beirut, 26 March 2013.
32 Author's interview – Beirut, 17 September 2014.
33 Most of the minority of Christian Palestinians that fled to Lebanon had an urban, middle-
     class background and were eventually granted citizenship (Stel, 2015).
34 www.lpdc.gov.lb/strategic-planning/8/en
35 As explained in personal email correspondence with an LPDC expert.
36 The sum of individuals attending UNRWA's schools and vocational centres, obtaining
     health care, and receiving food assistance, for instance, amounts to 259,000 refugees
     in Lebanon (Yan, 2018). This would mean that on top of the 174,422 Palestinians
     counted in the LDPC census, there are approximately an additional 84,000 people
     using UNRWA services.

37 Author's interview – Skype, 9 February 2018.
38 www.memri.org/reports/after-census-finds-174422-palestinian-refugees-lebanon-some-lebanese-fear-they-will-be
39 Importantly, statistical ambiguity serves the Palestinian political leadership as well. A lower number of refugees can be cited in the Lebanese arena to indicate that refugees are not a significant threat to Lebanon and that lifting some of the country's marginal-izing measures should therefore be considered. A higher number of refugees is impor-tant in the Palestinian political arena, when Lebanon's Palestinian leadership seeks to remind the Palestinian Authority that the Palestinian diaspora is of significant size and should not be disregarded politically or 'sold out' in a peace deal between the Palestin-ian Authority and Israel.
40 Author's interview – Skype, 10 January 2018.
41 Jalal al Husseini, cited in Yan (2018).
42 www.lpdc.gov.lb/capacity-building/9/en
43 www.memri.org/reports/after-census-finds-174422-palestinian-refugees-lebanon-some-lebanese-fear-they-will-be
44 Author's interview – Skype, 10 January 2018.
45 Author's interview – Skype, 10 January 2018.
46 Author's interview – Skype, 22 January 2018.
47 In the introduction to the LPDC report presenting the census's key findings, the LPDC's president states:

> The census, in the making and afterwards, has caused controversy and skepti-cism around its objectives and timing. Some consider it a step towards settlement (*tawte'en*) of Palestinian refugees, while others were concerned by the political implications that may result from it. Though we understand the backgrounds of such concerns, the lack of trust as well as the negative historical backdrop, we still believe that this fact-based approach is the optimum approach that can lead to public policy reform. Creating the climate for developing public policies based on reliable data and facts in parallel to the consensual political processes, on even the most sensitive files, is today, an absolute necessity.
>
> (LPDC, 2018: 4)

48 Author's interview – Skype, 10 January 2018.

References

Afifi, Tamara D., Walid A. Afifi, Michelle Acevedo Callejas, Ariana Shahnazi, Amanda White and Najib Nimah. 2019. 'The Functionality of Communal Coping in Chronic Uncertainty Environments: The Context of Palestinian Refugees in Lebanon.' *Health Communication* 34, no. 13: 1585–1596.

Akram, Susan. 2002. 'Palestinian Refugees and Their Legal Status: Rights, Politics and Implications for a Just Solution.' *Journal of Palestine Studies* 31, no. 3: 36–51.

Allan, Diana. 2014. *Refugees of the Revolution: Experiences of Palestinian Exile*. Stanford: Stanford University Press.

Al-Natour, Souheil. 1997. 'The Legal Status of Palestinians in Lebanon.' *Journal of Refugee Studies* 10, no. 3: 360–377.

Atallah, Sami and Dima Mahdi. 2017. *Law and Politics of "Safe Zones" and Forced Return to Syria: Refugee Politics in Lebanon*. Beirut: Lebanese Center for Policy Studies.

Beydoun, Ahmad. 1992. 'The South Lebanon Border Zone: A Local Perspective.' *Journal of Palestine Studies* 21, no. 3: 35–53.

Borgmann, Monika and Lokman Slim. 2018. *Fewer Refugees, More Refugeeism*. Beirut: Umam Documentation and Research and Institute for Auslandsbeziehunger.

Brynen, Rex. 1989. 'PLO Policy in Lebanon: Legacies and Lessons.' *Journal of Palestine Studies* 18, no. 2: 48–70.

Carpi, Estella. 2017. 'Rethinking Lebanese Welfare in Ageing Emergencies.' In *Lebanon Facing the Arab Uprisings*, edited by Rosita Di Peri and Daniel Meier, 115–133. London: Palgrave Macmillan.

Cassani, Jacob. 2018. 'State, Sovereignty, and Sewage: Governance in a Syrian Refugee Camp and Lebanese Village in the Biqa'a Valley.' MA thesis, University College London.

Chaaban, Jad, Nisreen Salti, Hala Ghattas, Alexandra Irani, Tala Ismail and Lara Batlouni. 2016. *Survey on the Socioeconomic Status of Palestine Refugees in Lebanon 2015*. Beirut: American University of Beirut and United Nations Relief and Works Agency for Palestine Refugees in the Near East.

Czajka, Agnes. 2012. 'Discursive Constructions of Palestinian Refugees in Lebanon.' *Comparative Studies of South Asia, Africa and the Middle East* 32, no. 1: 238–254.

Doraï, Kamel. 2011. 'Palestinian Refugee Camps in Lebanon. Migration, Mobility and the Urbanization Process.' In *Palestinian Refugees. Identity, Space and Place in the Levant*, edited by A. Knudsen and S. Hanafi, 67–80. New York: Routledge.

Doraï, Kamel and Nicolas Puig. 2008. 'Introduction: Palestiniens en/hors Camps. Formes Sociales, Pratiques des Interstices.' *REVUE Asylon(s)* 5: 1–8.

El Ali, Mahmoud. 2011. *EinHilweh Camp and Saida Municipality: Towards a Positive Interaction in Place and Space*. Beirut: Common Space Initiative, unpublished report.

El Natour, Suhail. 2012. *Real Estate Ownership for Palestinian Refugees in Lebanon: The Legal Amendments (5/4/2001) and Impacts on Actual Reality*. Beirut: The Campaign for Real Estate Property Ownership for the Palestinian Refugees in Lebanon.

Frontiers-Ruwad. 2005. *Falling Through the Cracks. Legal and Practical Gaps in Palestinian Refugee Status*. Beirut: Frontiers-Ruwad.

Halkort, Monika. 2019. 'Decolonizing Data Relations: On the Moral Economy of Data Sharing in Palestinian Refugee Camps.' *Canadian Journal of Communication* 44: 317–329.

Hanafi, Sari. 2008. 'Palestinian Refugee Camps in Lebanon: Laboratories of State-in-the-Making, Discipline and Islamist Radicalism.' Unpublished document.

Hanafi, Sari. 2010. *Governing Palestinian Refugee Camps in the Arab East: Governmentalities in Search of Legitimacy*. Beirut: Issam Fares Institute for Public Policy and International Affairs.

Hanafi, Sari. 2011. 'Governing the Palestinian Refugee Camps in Lebanon and Syria.' In *Palestinian Refugees: Identity, Space and Place in the Levant*, edited by Are Knudsen and Sari Hanafi, 29–49. New York: Routledge.

Hanafi, Sari. 2014. 'Forced Migration in the Middle East and North Africa.' In *The Oxford Handbook of Refugee and Forced Migration Studies*, edited by Elena Fiddian-Qasmiyeh, Gil Loescher, Katy Long and Nando Sigona, 583–598. Oxford: Oxford University Press.

Hanafi, Sari and Taylor Long. 2010. 'Governance, Governmentalities, and the State of Exception in the Palestinian Refugee Camps of Lebanon.' *Journal of Refugee Studies* 23, no. 2: 134–159.

Helou, Hala. 2014. 'Lebanon and Refugees: Between Laws and Reality.' MA thesis, Lebanese American University.

Hilal, Nancy. 2010. *Investigating Grey Areas: Access to Basic Urban Services in the Adjacent Areas of Palestinian Refugee Camps in Lebanon*. Beirut: United Nations Development Programme.

Hirst, David. 2010. *Beware of Small States: Lebanon, Battleground of the Middle East*. London: Faber and Faber.

Janmyr, Maja. 2017. 'No Country of Asylum: "Legitimizing" Lebanon's Rejection of the 1951 Refugee Convention.' *International Journal of Refugee Law* 29, no. 3: 438–465.

Kagan, Michael. 2011. *"We Live in a Country of UNHCR": The UN Surrogate State and Refugee Policy in the Middle East*. Geneva: United Nations High Commissioner for Refugees Policy Development and Evaluation Service.

Khalidi, Muhammad Ali and Diane Riskedahl. 2010. 'The Lived Reality of Palestinian Refugees in Lebanon.' In *Manifestations of Identity: The Lived Reality of Palestinian Refugees in Lebanon*, edited by Muhammad Ali Khalidi, 1–12. Beirut: Institute for Palestine Studies and Institut Francais du Proche-Orient.

Klaus, Dorothee. 2000. 'Palestinians in Lebanon Between Integration and Segregation: Contextualisation of a Conflict.' PhD thesis, Ruhr-Universität.

Knudsen, Are. 2007. *The Law, the Loss and the Lives of Palestinian Refugees in Lebanon*. Bergen: Christian Michelsen Institute.

Knudsen, Are. 2009. 'Widening the Protection Gap: The "Politics of Citizenship" for Palestinian Refugees in Lebanon, 1948–2008.' *Journal of Refugee Studies* 22, no. 1: 51–73.

Knudsen, Are. 2010. '(In)Security in a Space of Exception: The Destruction of the Nahr el-Bared Refugee Camp.' In *Security and Development*, edited by John-Andrew McNeish and Jon Harald Sande Lie, 99–112. New York and Oxford: Berghahn.

Knudsen, Are. 2011. 'Nahr al-Bared: The Political Fallout of a Refugee Disaster.' In *Palestinian Refugees. Identity, Space and Place in the Levant*, edited by Are Knudsen and Sari Hanafi, 97–110. New York: Routledge.

Knudsen, Are and Sari Hanafi, eds. 2011. *Palestinian Refugees: Identity, Space and Place in the Levant*. New York: Routledge.

Lebanese-Palestinian Dialogue Committee. 2013. *From Dialogue to Vision: Towards a Unified National Policy for Palestinian Refugees in Lebanon and a Future Vision for LPDC*. Beirut: Lebanese Republic, Presidency of the Council of Ministers.

Lebanese-Palestinian Dialogue Committee. 2016. *A Unified Lebanese Vision for Palestinian Refugee Affairs in Lebanon*. Beirut: Lebanese Working Group on Palestinian Refugee Affairs.

Lebanese-Palestinian Dialogue Committee. 2018. *Population and Housing Census in Palestinian Camps and Gatherings in Lebanon 2017: Key Findings Report*. Beirut: Lebanese Republic, Presidency of the Council of Ministers.

Long, Taylor and Sari Hanafi. 2010. 'Human (In)Security: Palestinian Perceptions of Security in and Around the Refugee Camps in Lebanon.' *Conflict, Security and Development* 10, no. 5: 673–692.

Mencütek, Zeynep. 2019. *Refugee Governance, State and Politics in the Middle East*. London: Routledge.

Mourad, Lama. 2017. '"Standoffish" Policy-Making: Inaction and Change in the Lebanese Response to the Syrian Displacement Crisis.' *Middle East Law and Governance* 9: 249–266.

Oesch, Lucas. 2015. 'The Ambiguous Encampment of the World.' *Jadaliyya*, 11 December.

Parkinson, Sarah E. 2014. 'Refugee 101: Palestinians in Lebanon Show Refugees from Syria the Ropes.' *Middle East Report Online*, 3 April.

Peteet, Julie. 2005. *Landscapes of Hope and Despair: Place and Identity in Palestinian Refugee Camps*. Philadelphia: University of Pennsylvania Press.

Raffonelli, Lisa. 2004. 'With Palestine, Against the Palestinians: The Warehousing of Palestinian Refugees in Lebanon.' *World Refugee Survey* 66–73.

Ramadan, Adam and Sara Fregonese. 2017. 'Hybrid Sovereignty and the State of Exception in the Palestinian Refugee Camps in Lebanon.' *Annals of the American Association of Geographers* 107, no. 4: 949–963.

Rougier, Bernard. 2007. *Everyday Jihad: The Rise of Militant Islam Among Palestinians in Lebanon.* Cambridge: Harvard University Press.

Rubenberg, Cheryl A.1983. 'The Civilian Infrastructure of the Palestine Liberation Organization: An Analysis of the PLO in Lebanon Until June 1982.' *Journal of Palestine Studies* 12, no. 3: 54–78.

Saleh, Mohsen. 2019. 'A Reading in the Lebanese Vision of Dealing with Palestinian Refugees.' *Middle East Monitor*, 6 February.

Sayigh, Rosemary. 1988. 'Palestinians in Lebanon: Status Ambiguity, Insecurity, and Flux.' *Race & Class* 30, no. 1: 13–32.

Sayigh, Rosemary. 1995. 'Palestinians in Lebanon: Harsh Present, Uncertain Future.' *Journal of Palestine Studies* 25, no. 1: 37–53.

Sayigh, Yezid. 1997a. *Armed Struggle and the Search for State: The Palestinian National Movement, 1949–1993.* Oxford: Oxford University Press.

Sayigh, Yezid. 1997b. 'Armed Struggle and State Formation.' *Journal of Palestine Studies* 26, no. 4: 17–32.

Sfeir, Jihane. 2010. 'Palestinians in Lebanon: The Birth of the "Enemy Within".' In *Manifestations of Identity: The Lived Reality of Palestinian Refugees in Lebanon*, edited by Muhammad Ali Khalidi, 13–34. Beirut: Institute for Palestine Studies.

Siklawi, Rami. 2010. 'The Dynamics of Palestinian Political Endurance in Lebanon.' *Middle East Journal* 64, no. 4: 597–611.

Stel, Nora. 2015. ' "The Children of the State?" How Palestinians from the Seven Villages Negotiate Sect, Party and State in Lebanon.' *British Journal of Middle Eastern Studies* 42, no. 4: 538–557.

Stel, Nora. 2017. 'Mediated Stateness as a Continuum: Exploring the Changing Governance Relations Between the PLO and the Lebanese State.' *Civil Wars* 19, no. 3: 348–376.

Suleiman, Jaber. 2006. *Marginalised Community: The Case of Palestinian Refugees in Lebanon.* Brighton: University of Sussex.

Suleiman, Jaber. 2017. *Lebanese-Palestinian Relations: A Political, Human Rights and Security Perspective.* Beirut: Common Space Initiative.

Ugland, Ole Fr., ed. 2003. *Difficult Past, Uncertain Future: Living Conditions Among Palestinian Refugees in Camps and Gatherings in Lebanon.* Oslo: Norwegian People's Aid and Partners.

United Nations Relief and Works Agency for Palestine Refugees in the Near East. 2019. 'Protection in Lebanon.' UNRWA website. www.unrwa.org/activity/protection-lebanon.

Weighill, Marie-Louise. 1997. 'Palestinians in Lebanon: The Politics of Assistance.' *Journal of Refugee Studies* 10, no. 3: 294–313.

Yan, Victoria. 2017. 'Change Unlikely in Light of Palestinian Census Results.' *Daily Star*, 30 December.

Yan, Victoria. 2018. 'Why UNRWA's Refugee Count Is so High.' *Daily Star*, 6 January.

Yassin, Nasser, Tarek Osseiran, Rima Rassi and Marwa Boustani. 2015. *No Place to Stay? Reflections on the Syria Refugee Shelter Policy in Lebanon.* Beirut: United Nations Human Settlements Program & the Issam Fares Institute for Public Policy and International Affairs at the American University of Beirut.

Chapter 5

Governing Lebanon's Palestinian 'gatherings'

Forsaken settlements, disowned committees, and looming displacement

Spring 2013. A Lebanese major in South Lebanon tells me about his commitment to building a 'state of institutions' in Lebanon, where rules and regulations instead of connections and capital govern public administration. I ask him about the Palestinian gathering under his jurisdiction. He emphasizes the illegal nature of the settlement, suggesting the Palestinians should have just bought the land they built on. When I remind him Palestinians are legally prohibited from doing so, he shrugs this off as not his responsibility and reiterates his dedication to following the law.

Roughly one year later. I am in another municipal office less than ten kilometers down the road. About the refugees in his area, the mayor here matter-of-factly concludes that 'you have to do some things illegally' if they are to have their basic needs met. He is happy to help them where he can, he assures me, but doing so 'in an illegal way, without writing.' Giving voice to my thoughts, he concludes that the quality of life in the gatherings to a large extent 'depends on the mayor.'[1]

The previous chapter demonstrated that Palestinian refugees in Lebanon face a chronic uncertainty that contributes to their systematic marginalization. This uncertainty can be traced back to the legal limbo and the spatial discrimination they are subjected to and the fragmentation of their representative organizations. Such institutional ambiguity is legitimized with reference to the desirability of permanent temporariness that would facilitate the Palestinians' right to return and prevent their dreaded 'implantation' into Lebanon's sectarian society. While institutional ambiguity is at times successfully contested, it remains entrenched. This chapter moves from a focus on national decision-making – or the lack of it – to the local manifestations and implications of inaction and ambiguous action. It explores the political functions of informality, liminality, and exceptionalism by analyzing governance in and of two unofficial Palestinian refugee settlements in Lebanon.

To this aim, I first introduce the specifics of the research context and cases and the data that underlies my analysis. The subsequent section brings to the fore the legal and administrative complexities of the status of Palestinian 'gatherings' and the consequences this has for residents' welfare. Building on this, the chapter proceeds with an investigation of the ways in which authority and responsibility are structured in Palestinian refugee settlements. This section highlights how Lebanese local state agencies undermine the authority of the Palestinian governance structures in these settlements by the de facto legitimation but simultaneous de jure disowning of Palestinian local governance committees that operate in the gatherings. The ramifications of such uncertainty in terms of status and representation are further examined in the consecutive section that presents three vignettes that focus on the spatial governance of the settlements. It looks into the contested building practices in these settlements and investigates the relentless threats of eviction that the Palestinian refugees who live there face. Highlighting the arbitrary governance that occurs in situations where the status of refugee communities and their rights and the position of those representing them is ambiguous, these vignettes reveal the disciplinary power of institutionalized uncertainty and its political and socio-economic expediency.

Context and cases: studying refugee governance in South Lebanon

The two settlements that provide the empirical heart of this chapter are located in South Lebanon. This region hosts five of the twelve camps run by the United Nations Relief and Works Agency for Palestine Refugees in the Near East (UNRWA) and more than half of the country's informal settlements (Chabaan, 2014). The area of South Lebanon in which these case-studies are located has been inhabited primarily by Shia and Christian communities. Despite the trade and fishery around the once wealthy coastal town of Tyre, the region's recent history has been one of marginalization. Disregarded by the political elites in Beirut that for long did not include significant Shia representation, the area was economically discriminated against by the Lebanese state. South Lebanon was also hard hit by the Lebanese Civil War, facing the retaliation of Israel against the Palestinian guerillas that operated from the border area and undergoing the devastating effects of the Israeli invasion of Lebanon in 1982 and the subsequent occupation by Israel of the region's southernmost areas until 2000. In 2006, Israel targeted South Lebanon in the war it waged against Hezbollah.

The history of South Lebanon is thus closely intertwined with that of the Palestinians. It was characterized by extensive mutual trade and social ties forged by inter-marriage and cultural proximity. Musa Sadr's Shia political emancipation movement of the 1970s closely aligned with the liberation struggle waged by the Palestine Liberation Organization (PLO) both politically and organizationally. The polarizing effect of the Civil War, however, complicated Lebanese-Palestinian relations in the South. The impression that Lebanese villages were sacrificed for the Palestinian cause and the increasing power and arrogance of the Palestinian revolutionaries undercut sympathy and support for Palestinians. This was only amplified by the renewed premium that the Civil War put on sectarian sensitivities, which further complicated the relations between the mostly Shia Lebanese and the predominantly Sunni Palestinians in South Lebanon. These tensions culminated in the War of the Camps during which the Amal militia besieged Palestinian settlements in Beirut and the South. In the post-war era and with the rise of Hezbollah, championed as a vanguard in resisting Israel, relations have normalized. Historical traumas, however, have never been resolved. The region's ambivalence towards the Palestinians – veering between socio-cultural closeness and sectarian strain – thus remains.[2]

The two Palestinian settlements that this chapter focuses on are among the largest in the country. The first of the two gatherings is located predominantly on public land owned by the neighboring municipality. This settlement now counts more than 4,000 inhabitants, including a large population of refugees, Syrian as well as Palestinian, from Syria. It is located right next to a Lebanese village. The second gathering hosts some 5,000 refugees, including refugees from Syria. Around 20 percent of the land on which the gathering is built is public land and the rest is owned privately by various Lebanese citizens. This settlement does not border directly on a Lebanese village and has less intensive relations with the municipality on whose land it is located.

These settlements were created in the early 1950s by Bedouin tribes, mostly from the Akka and Safad regions of North Palestine, that found the official UNRWA camps unsuitable places to accommodate their cattle and preferred to settle near the orchards where they had found work (Stel, 2016a). The gatherings' main source of income now is through agricultural work, but residents are also highly dependent on remittances from Europe. Both gatherings have an UNRWA health clinic that is open a few days a week, in one case complemented by a first aid service run by a non-governmental organization (NGO). They also have an UNRWA primary school and a kindergarten run by the PLO's General Union of Palestinian Women. Each gathering has a youth centre and a soccer court. Electricity is provided by national electricity provider *Électricité du Liban*. Water is obtained through a well dug by the PLO and operated by the respective Popular Committees (which are introduced in more detail later in this chapter). Waste is collected by a local NGO.

The data underlying the analysis in this chapter are based on 12 months of fieldwork in 2012, 2013, and 2014, eight months of which were spent living in the gatherings in question. They consist of more than 270 semi-structured, in-depth interviews[3] and informal expert meetings with Lebanese as well as Palestinian communal and political leaders, state representatives, residents, NGO staff, and analysts targeted via purposive and snowball sampling. I also conducted five focus groups. Where possible, I collected and analyzed documents as well. A significant part of the data, finally, regarded field observations. These were not limited to the two gatherings constituting my case-study, but also encompassed field visits to eight of Lebanon's 12 Palestinian refugee camps and visits to almost all of South Lebanon's Palestinian gatherings. In both cases, data were generated with the help of a local research partner from the respective gathering. Insights from these two specific settlements are inevitably particular, but they have been systematically contextualized through a broader regional analysis and literature review. They can thus serve to elucidate the broader governance logics outlined in Chapter 3 that operate throughout the country and across formal as well as informal settlements.

Producing and ordering 'gray spaces': the status of the gatherings

Chapter 4 conceptualized Palestinian refugee settlements in Lebanon as the materialization of informality, liminality, and exceptionalism. The camps are a foundation of the notion of permanent temporariness. Their provisional and transitory living environment potently symbolizes the assumed transient nature of Palestinians' stay. At the same time, the camps loom large in the Lebanese public's imagination as 'states-within-the-state,' 'security islands,' or 'zones of outlaw' and are central in the depiction of the Palestinian refugee presence as a sovereignty threat. Following such securitized discourses, Palestinian camps and their inhabitants are simultaneously included in Lebanese state governance, when it comes to security, and excluded from it, when it comes to service provision – a duality that is legitimized with reference to the officially abrogated yet practically observed Cairo Agreement. Such ambiguous responsibility allows Lebanese state agencies – and Palestinian authorities, for that matter – to claim and deny authority as they see fit.

Thus, as Hanafi and Long (2010: 147) have concluded, rather than contending for power over the camps, as happened in the years before the Cairo Agreement, or agreeing on sharing power, Lebanese and Palestinian authorities have together endorsed 'the suspension of all sovereign authority over the camp and, in its place, the implementation of other "temporary" or "emergency" powers.' These temporary informal arrangements, however, 'often exist in mutual contradiction, and rather than order the camp, they leave it in a state of void, of chaos and anomie' (Hanafi and Long, 2010: 147). But despite such evident institutional ambiguity, these 12 official camps have at least some sort of status. Their existence has been recognized by the Lebanese state, and the land they are built on is formally leased by UNRWA.

Yet less than half of the Palestinian refugees in Lebanon currently live in these UNRWA camps. The majority of Lebanon's Palestinians, an estimated 90,862 people, lives in some 40-plus informal settlements, so-called gatherings (*tajamu'aat* in Arabic) (Lebanese Palestinian Dialogue Committee (LPDC), 2018). The Danish Refugee Council (2005: 4–5), one of the first organizations to work in the gatherings, defines a gathering as a settlement that:

1. Has a population of Palestinian refugees. . . . 2. Has no official UNRWA camp status or any other legal authority identified with responsibility for camp management. 3. Is expected to have clearly defined humanitarian and protection needs, or have a minimum of 25 households. 4. Has a population with a sense of being a distinct group living in a geographically identifiable area.

In many ways the gatherings face a similar regime of institutionalized temporariness and exceptionalism as the camps, but for the gatherings, ambiguity goes even further. These informal settlements are not acknowledged as Palestinian spaces by the Lebanese state,[4] and they are illegally built on Lebanese land, which prevents UNRWA from extending its mandate there in many ways. As with Syrian 'informal tented settlements,' no agreement or decision to regulate them, not even one to designate them to the non-state authority of the PLO or UNRWA, exists for the gatherings.

The gatherings were never part of the Cairo Agreement and are thus not included in its lingering influence. For residents of the informal settlements, this means that 'the gatherings are under the Lebanese authorities, not under the Palestinian authorities; this is the difference with camps.'[5] Yet this is not fully recognized by the Lebanese state. In fact, the gatherings even more pertinently illustrate the way in which the Lebanese state simultaneously includes Palestinian spaces in their control and excludes them from their responsibility than the UNRWA camps do: state agencies, including security institutions, can and do enter the gatherings, but civil authorities mostly do not make themselves responsible for them. Lebanese municipalities by and large do not consider the gatherings their responsibility, even when they are located on municipal land, as residents are neither citizens nor taxpayers. UNRWA's territorial mandate is largely limited to the official camps as well. While residents of the gatherings make use of UNRWA schools and clinics, UNRWA does not provide utility services such as electricity, waste management, and infrastructure maintenance to them as it does in the camps.

In addition to this partial disregard by the Lebanese state and UNRWA, the gatherings are also to some extent abandoned by NGOs and Palestinian authorities. Because of the gatherings' relatively smaller population, NGOs are less active in the gatherings, where their projects will serve fewer beneficiaries than in the infamous camps that are well-known by donors. Their impact is more precarious in the gatherings, moreover, due to the uncertain tenancy status of these spaces. Palestinian political parties, finally, tend to concentrate their projects and presence in the camps, and they have the largest constituency, most significant power (due to their armed status there), and biggest symbolic resonance there. Someone working for an NGO active in the gatherings concluded: 'The gatherings are not worth fighting over for the Palestinian factions.'[6]

Regularizing crisis

In the gatherings, the Palestinians' ambiguous legal status and their lack of citizenship and socio-economic rights coalesces with the undefined status of the settlements they live in. The result is amplified uncertainty and poverty. Socio-economic marginalization in the gatherings is rampant. Two-thirds of the residents of the gatherings live below the poverty line (Chabaan, 2014: 59). While poverty is not more extreme in the gatherings than it is in the camps, in the gatherings it is exacerbated by uncertain access to services. According to national Lebanese law, people living in 'informal settlements' have no right to public services. Law 7279, which was issued in 1961, states that 'it is forbidden to connect property owners or residents of a lot with a phone, service or electricity if s/he does not provide a residency permit' (Yassin, Stel and Rassi, 2016: 8). While suspended in 1967, this provision was reinstated in 1971 through a new Lebanese building code.

Residents of Palestinian gatherings are excluded from public services, which are minimal in Lebanon to begin with, and from part of the UNRWA mandate. They also face impediments to private solutions due to the illegal nature of their residence in the gatherings. Thus, to access services they resort to complex and diverse strategies. With regard to electricity, for instance, in many gatherings there is an informal grid inside the settlement that illegally taps electricity from the public network. Such collective illegal hooking is supervised by the committees operating in the gatherings. This arrangement depends on informal taxation as well as efforts of Palestinian authorities to mobilize funding for maintenance through their political networks. The water infrastructure in the gatherings is built and maintained without the approval of Lebanese local water authorities or the relevant ministry. It functions under the auspices of the PLO, which relies on informal and voluntary taxation as well as support from NGOs to raise the necessary funds to operate the local wells. The gatherings are mostly not connected to the Lebanese water network nor to the public sewage system.

Access to services, consequently, is irregular. It depends on personal relations between Palestinian and Lebanese authorities and the latter's occasional goodwill towards the former. A waste management crisis in the gatherings in the summer of 2013 shows this well (Stel and Van der Molen, 2015). For a long time, a local NGO collected solid waste from Palestinian gatherings and discarded it on municipal waste dump sites. When the capacity of these sites was saturated, a new recycling factory was opened by the Union of Municipalities, but this recycling plant had a limited capacity as well. It was therefore decided that it would only treat waste collected by municipal operators. Upon protest by UNRWA, waste collected by UNRWA from the formal Palestinian camps was accepted as well. Garbage from the Palestinian gatherings, serviced by neither the municipalities nor UNRWA, however, could not be disposed of in the new facility.

Only after extensive lobbying by UNRWA was the situation resolved, but the 'solution' here, an UNRWA employee anonymously explained, is unstable and precarious. In convincing the Municipal Union's waste recycling factory to accept waste collected in the Palestinian gatherings, UNRWA had to operate extremely carefully:

> The factory is a municipal constellation. The whole situation is very sensitive. . . . Because some agreements aren't exactly official, but rather depend on personal relations. The municipalities involved might be concerned this arrangement gets public. We fought really hard for this deal and I don't want to endanger it. We talked a lot with the mayors and the municipalities. A lot of *wasta*[7] went into this.

Thus, as my interlocutors noted, because the official legal and institutional arrangements were not changed, this resolution would only hold until the next crisis. Indeed, the continuity of 'crisis' and the omnipresence of 'chaos' in the daily life in the gatherings were a constant in the accounts of people living in the gatherings (Stel and Van der Molen, 2015). In discussing these problems with waste collection, for instance, a communal representative from one of the gatherings replied: 'It lasted long, but because we're used to crises, maybe it didn't feel so long.'[8]

The distinction between 'crises' and 'normal times' is misleading when it comes to the governance of Palestinian refugees in Lebanon. A key character- istic of the Palestinian life in Lebanon, as Chapter 4 laid down, is that there are no regular processes. There are certain informal modus operandi that hold over longer periods of time, and the governance dynamics in the gatherings accord- ingly reflect chains of ad hoc crisis management. Describing life in the gatherings, a participant in a focus group stated:

> We live in a situation of chaos. No one is ruling on the ground, each one has its own laws that he applies according to his benefits. No one cares for the people; they are living; they are suffering; this is not important for them [Lebanese and Palestinian authorities]. You are in Lebanon and you must know this – we're in the jungle, not in a state. . . . We have no court, we have no law, we have no state, we're discriminated, we're animals to them; we resemble everything but people to them.[9]

Preventing formalization, reiterating liminality

Service provision arrangements in the gatherings, as the Common Space Ini- tiative (2011) noted, remain personal and occasional, 'lacking the institutional framework that ensures its continuity and sustainability.' Written documentation about the provision and regulation of services is non-existent for the gatherings. This is due to strong traditions of oral communication in much of the govern- ance institutions involved, including state agencies, but is clearly increased by the lack of a formal status for the gatherings. As a Palestinian analyst explained: 'Written things imply commitments; not to write something down is to escape responsibility. If someone is just paying lip service, it is preferable if it isn't documented.'[10]

Marginalization and deprivation are thus directly related to the informal nature of the gatherings, the non-status of which continues to be upheld. Most of the gatherings have been there since the early days of the Palestinian refugee presence in Lebanon, yet their status has never been resolved. The possibility of formalizing the gatherings was a recurrent theme in my interviews, especially in light of the eviction threats discussed later. Some inhabitants from the gatherings or people working there suggested that the gatherings could be allocated formal camp status. This, however, was without exception followed by stressing the absolute taboo in

Lebanon to recognize new camps. While at least three formal camps have been destroyed or closed since the 1950s, it is anathema for the Lebanese state to allow for new camps to be recognized. With reference to the annihilation of the Nahr el-Bared camp and the perpetual delays in its reconstruction, many of the people I spoke with suggested that the Lebanese state was out to minimize the number of formal camps, not allow for new ones. As one UNRWA representative in South Lebanon agitatedly noted: 'Do you think the Lebanese would accept to go from 12 to 24 camps?![11] They [the people who suggest camp status for the gatherings would be possible] are crazy!'[12]

In fact, the gatherings' uncertain status seems to serve to underscore Lebanon's institutionalization of permanent temporariness, as discussed in Chapter 4. The very term 'gathering' projects a transience that does not reflect reality. The word 'gathering' suggests a 'simplistic, even atomistic and haphazard assembly of people' that is illusory (Knudsen, 2018: 9). Like the camps, the gatherings constitute clearly bounded and relatively stable spatial, social, and political communities. Yet due to such associations with fleetingness and insignificance, many residents of the gatherings, I was told by my interlocutors, 'prefer to call gatherings camps because this makes them sound more important; "gathering" has associations with randomness, with "a group of people gathered together," whereas the word "camp" signifies joint relations.'[13] The temporariness that the notion of 'gathering' suggests, however, is perfectly in line with the anti-*tawteen* discourse of Lebanese authorities discussed in the previous chapter.

Lack of formal status for the gatherings and the absence of formal service delivery arrangements allow authorities to ignore the gatherings. A former spokesperson of the Lebanese-Palestinian Dialogue Committee (LPDC) confided in me that he 'knew everything about the Palestinian cause, as I have always been a supporter of Palestine, but very little about Palestinian-Lebanese relations on the ground.'[14] Even formalization of service delivery practices in the gatherings – a far cry from actual formalization of the status of gatherings as such – was a taboo for Lebanese authorities. While they routinely deal with the gatherings, they have neither the resources nor the political will to take actual responsibility. And, in the current informal set-up, they do not have to.

Thus, the informal status of the gatherings allows for what Allan (2014: 104) has called 'malign neglect.' This resonates closely with Yiftachel's (2009) work on 'gray spacing,' with which he refers to the production of spatially confined informalities and the indefinite positioning of populations between legality and illegality as a method of control. Such spaces that are neither integrated nor eliminated, as also shown by the prior account of the status of the gatherings, serve variegated purposes. This functionality ensures that such uncertainty is kept in place. The largely informal status of the gatherings has pragmatic considerations, allowing various governance actors to shirk responsibility, as well as political ones, in that it allows for upholding the illusion of temporariness. It is thereby a core foundation of institutional ambiguity that governs the life of Palestinian refugees in Lebanon.

Representation and the Palestinian 'Popular Committees:' withholding recognition, dictating responsibility

It is not just the status of Palestinian settlements itself that is ambiguous. The same goes for the status of representative organizations in these settlements. Chapter 4 outlined that Lebanese authorities recognize the Palestinian Authority and the Palestinian Liberation Organization (PLO) as well as individual Palestinian political parties (both those inside and outside the PLO). Due to the complexities of the transnationally fragmented and politically polarized Palestinian polity, there is no clear-cut representative for the Palestinian community in Lebanon. This situation is convenient with an eye to the Lebanese post–Civil War objective of marginalizing Palestinian refugees and, therefore, is exacerbated by Lebanese divide-and-rule tactics. Governance in the gatherings extends this logic: the organizational bodies that claim to represent specific Palestinian settlement communities have no formal status. But while they are not officially recognized as counterparts by Lebanese authorities, these same Lebanese state agencies routinely deal with them. This simultaneous de facto validation and de jure disownment undermines the capacity and legitimacy of Palestinian committees and prevents coordinated political grassroots organization of Palestinian communities.

Drawing on the previously introduced case-studies, this section presents how local governance in and of Palestinian settlements operates under these conditions, and it explains how official denial and unofficial engagement serves Lebanese and Palestinian authorities. Lebanese state agencies can keep the upper hand in any encounter with Palestinian communities through dependent and therefore dependable local Palestinian counterparts. The Lebanese political parties that run state agencies reinforce their power as indispensable brokers between officially illegal committees and state agencies formally precluded to deal with them. This arrangement allows Palestinian political authorities to maintain their own resented leadership positions, as the current status of the committees enables Palestinian political parties to capture local structures and ignore calls for more accountability.

Whose popularity, whose committees?

Lebanon's camps and gatherings are governed by a hybrid, dynamic arrangement of various state and non-state actors. As Hanafi (2011: 32) describes, rather than being controlled by a single sovereign, since the expulsion and subsequent marginalization of the PLO Lebanon's Palestinian settlements are governed by 'a multi-layered tapestry' of 'groups, individuals and factions' that compete for power. This 'web of complex power structures' includes local governance committees, related security committees, networks of notables, political factions, religious structures, NGOs, and UNRWA representatives (Hanafi, 2008: 10). While all of these fulfil crucial functions in arrangements for services, security, justice, and consultation, my argument here will focus on the role of the committees in the settlements, as these are – in one way or another – recognized by most other actors as the closest thing to an overarching public representative body for these localities.

In the 1960s, the PLO installed so-called Popular Committees as civil bodies to provide services, security, and political representation in the camps. They were described in article two of the Cairo Agreement as 'local governance committees' (Suleiman, 2017: 27). The Popular Committees, in a nutshell, are the PLO's instrument to organize local governance, including coordination with Lebanese authorities. In 70 percent of the settlements, Popular Committees are the main coordinating body within the community (Ugland, 2003: 185, see also Danish Refugee Council, 2005: 155; Ramadan and Fregonese, 2017: 11). They are often referred to as municipality-like bodies in the sense that they oversee service provision and the related informal taxation, operate as a land registry, serve as intermediaries in judicial matters and social conflict, and have a related security committee that polices the settlements.

The Palestinian Popular Committees in Lebanon fall under the Lebanese office of the PLO's Department of Refugee Affairs that oversees a Central Follow-Up Committee on the national level, five regional Popular Committee offices, and a Popular Committee in each settlement (Stel, 2016b). The statutes for the Popular Committees outline detailed procedures for the creation and operation of the committees and its monthly magazine aims to convey the image of a structured organization that is governed through a formal hierarchy, meets on a regular basis, and whose functioning is formally documented. All of this, however, is a far cry from reality. Although the statutes prescribe elections, these almost never take place, and allocation of the different positions in each committee rather reflects the current power balance among the various Palestinian parties within the PLO (and the current dominance of Fatah).[15] This also means that while the Popular Committees are officially civil bodies, they are heavily politicized and are perceived by Palestinians as party structures rather than public, communal bodies.

Committee members are appointed by the political leadership based on party loyalty rather than skills or popular support. And while they should officially step down after several years, this hardly ever happens. While committees should have 13 members – one for each PLO faction – with demarcated and specialized positions, in practice it is often just the president of the committee and the secretary that have an active role. Overall then, Popular Committees face a severe crisis of capacity and legitimacy. They lack the capabilities and resources to govern as their official mandate dictates and have very little support from the communities they claim to represent, who widely lament their corruption.

The wane of the Palestinian Committees started with the expulsion of the PLO from Lebanon. After 1982, PLO-related institutions were almost entirely dismantled by the Syrian-Lebanese military intelligence apparatus. Alternative, pro-Syrian committees were established, but these suffered from wanting legitimacy and resources. After the withdrawal of Syria from Lebanon in 2005, these alternative committees have continued to exist, becoming more closely tied to the institutional structures of the anti-PLO Islamist Palestinian parties joined under the alliance led by Hamas. Inside the settlements, these 'Family Committees' duplicate much of the work and mandate of the Popular Committees, and there is fierce competition between them, but Family Committees overall take less of a representative position to actors external to the settlements, mostly deferring to the PLO's Popular Committees in this regard.

Although facing many problems and deficits, the Popular Committees are thus present in each Palestinian settlement and have a long institutional history and broad social reach. In the last decade, moreover, there have been extensive attempts – varying in their degree of success – to professionalize the committees. The most recent initiative regards a series of consultative meetings in August 2017 in which, according to the legal scholar and activist who initiated it, all relevant factions and representatives agreed to work towards 'uniting, rehabilitating and activating the Popular Committees' (Suleiman, 2017: 26). In theory, then, Popular Committees are a logical focal point for governance in the gatherings, especially when it comes to the relations with Lebanese state agencies.

They are part of a clear institutional structure that is not undisputed but comes closest to what the Palestinians have in terms of a representative authority. Their mandate gives them a suitable framework to operate as municipality-like structures and provides instructions for linking this Palestinian local representation to the structures of the Lebanese state. Indeed, in many ways, Palestinian Popular Committees style themselves as such and in some regards prioritize their role as interlocutor for the Lebanese state over their position as representative of Palestinian communities (Stel, 2016b). The importance of coordination with the Lebanese state for these Palestinian committees is also evident in the vision of the Central Follow-Up Committee for the Popular Committees in Lebanon that commands its regional offices to 'work towards the activation and improvement of the relations with the neighbourhood, especially with the municipalities in the cities and the surrounding Lebanese villages.'[16] Popular Committees in some instances institutionally mirror Lebanese state authorities in terms of structure and operation. In 2010, for instance, the PLO's Department for Refugee Affairs has amended the previous statutes of the Popular Committees. This was partly done to align the organizational hierarchy of the Popular Committees with the administrative echelons of the Lebanese state to thereby enable closer coordination.

Yet this will to coordinate does not seem to be reciprocated on the Lebanese side – at least not formally. In day-to-day governance, the Popular Committees feature as the main reference point for Lebanese authorities if and when they engage with Palestinian communities. Local Lebanese state agencies – such as provincial and district governors, municipalities, and *mukhtars* – in many instances cannot avoid dealing with the informal Palestinian settlements within their areas. Residents of the Palestinian gatherings generally saw service provision and socio-political life in the gatherings as crucially dependent on relations with Lebanese authorities. As one Popular Committee member rhetorically asked me: 'How would you solve issues if you don't sit together?'[17]

As Suleiman (2017: 27) concludes after decades of studying this issue, many municipalities have long-term engagements with both camps and gatherings with regard to matters of waste collection, maintenance of electricity supply equipment, and permits to repair and build houses. This is also illustrated by the vignettes in this chapter's next section. Municipalities, *mukhtars*, and utility companies routinely work with Popular Committees (Stel, 2015a). A regional manager of *Électicité du Liban*, for instance, explained:

> There is a Popular Committee present in all gatherings. . . . There is coordination between us. . . . It's true the Lebanese state doesn't consider it as official, but if there are problems in the gathering as a whole, the Popular Committee is responsible. We cooperate with them as a reality on the ground, but not official. . . . And for us it's better if the Popular Committee comes to apply than if twenty people all come by themselves.[18]

A state representative in a village in the vicinity of a Palestinian gathering said it was 'natural' for him to work with the Popular Committee there since, he explained, 'it's just me and the Popular Committee who do the local governance here.'[19] Even representatives of the LPDC, whose policy vision does not so much as mention the Popular Committees (see LPDC, 2013), matter-of-factly explained that on 'construction, infrastructure, electricity, water, sewage . . . we call them directly.'[20]

But despite routine engagement with Popular Committees by a wide range of local Lebanese state agencies, they are not officially recognized by the Lebanese state as relevant official representatives. This is evident in a lack of documented acknowledgement and is reinstated regularly on the ground. The non-status of the Popular Committees became acutely obvious, for instance, in the aftermath of the Nahr el-Bared crisis, when the new model for camp governance presented at the Vienna conference completely disregarded any existing governance structures and authorities in the camp. In fact, as the director of a leading Palestinian NGO in Lebanon explained, Nahr el-Bared's Popular Committees were sidelined by the Lebanese state by means of a circular from the Ministry of Interior that stated the Lebanese state would not work with 'illegal bodies' in the areas surrounding the camp and which included the Popular Committees operating there as an example of such illegal bodies.[21] The lack of formal status of the Popular Committees was also a constant in my interviews with Lebanese authorities in South Lebanon, where one mayor referred to the Popular Committee in a neighboring gathering as a 'delegation of tribal spokesmen.'[22]

Locally, then, there is no formal representative of Palestinian communities. On a national level, the LPDC does meet with PLO representatives who fulfil functions in the national tier of the Popular Committee structure. But even then Popular Committees, referred to by the LPDC (2012) as 'quasi local authorities,' are not acknowledged as formal partners, a legal officer working for the LDPC confirmed.[23] In the words of an LPDC representative:

> Apart from the embassy, the government also recognized the PLO and Hamas. Hamas because Hamas now has a government in Gaza. And it recognizes all Palestinian factions as entities. But the PLO is the representative, Abu Mazen [Palestinian President Mahmoud Abbas]. And not just the PLO now, we're talking about Palestine, about the PA [the Palestinian National Authority in Palestine]. If there're dealings, they're between the PLO and the government of Lebanon. The government of Lebanon doesn't care about the Popular Committees; it doesn't have to recognize them, they're not important for the government of Lebanon.[24]

This means that the local bodies that, despite their immense limitations in terms of capacity and legitimacy, have the most potential to directly represent the Palestinian communities in Lebanon are sidelined by the Lebanese state – even if in their own local practical engagements with these committees Lebanese authorities seem to corroborate the committees' relevance. This makes the delegitimation that follows from lack of formal status and recognition, in Hanafi's (2011: 36) words, 'purposeful.'

When discussing Lebanese authorities' balancing act – dealing with and making use of the committees while withholding any form of official status from them – with one of the main facilitators of the dialogue sessions organized by the LPDC, she reflected:

> At this moment, I don't think it's wise to push for a law that recognizes the Popular Committees or anything. Because on a political level this isn't going anywhere. For some, if not most, if not all Lebanese parties, this is really a big red line; anything that has to do with a legal status for the Popular Committees is.[25]

But she then added: 'But they expressed a national consensus to look at the Popular Committees as a representative of the camp and of camp services.' In her answer to my question as to what exactly was the difference between formal recognition of the Popular Committees as representatives and 'looking at the Popular Committees as a representative,' the creation of institutional ambiguity becomes apparent. She explained:

> The question is how to move from total ad hocness to some sort of administrative status that would recognize them, but without giving them a legal status. . . . This would be something in between; formalizing their way of work, this is a grey area, so to say. We have to look into this grey area.

Not giving the Popular Committees official status is tied up with historical sensitivities. Many Lebanese parties are haunted by the legacy of the Cairo Agreement.

The local 'self-governance' legitimized under the Cairo Agreement, for them, pre-ceded and enabled the PLO's eventual state-within-the-state, going far beyond the parameters defined in the agreement that stipulated, according to Suleiman (2017: 27), that such self-governance should happen 'in cooperation with the local Leba-nese authorities and within the framework of Lebanese sovereignty.' The echoes of such self-governance that would be implicit in recognizing Palestinian Popular Committees make Lebanese politicians uncomfortable to say the least.

Local non-recognition is thus legitimated by and simultaneously extends the divide-and-rule approach that the Lebanese state takes vis-à-vis Palestinian rep-resentatives nationally. As Knudsen (2009: 67) carefully documents, because the Popular Committees are affiliated with the PLO and the PLO no longer represents the entirety of the Palestinian political spectrum, the Lebanese state refuses to acknowledge it as a formal representative, fearing this would sideline *Tahaluf* and the related Family Committees. It is allegedly unwilling to take sides in what it considers to be an internal Palestinian issue. But while this political and institu-tional divide between the PLO and the *Tahaluf*, between the Popular Committees and the Family Committees, is lamented by Lebanese authorities, it is facilitated by the Lebanese political parties that staff these state authorities, who, accord-ing to Borgmann and Slim (2018: 30), 'manage Palestinian infighting to impose their will on the camps.' Moreover, since the Popular Committees are affiliated with the PLO's Department of Refugee Affairs, which *is* formally recognized by the Lebanese state as the representative of the Palestinian people, withholding this recognition from their local organizational tier appears inconsistent since the desire to avoid partiality in the PLO-*Tahaluf* strife apparently does not impede the PLO's recognition nationally.

Propping up the middlemen

But why would this de jure recognition matter at all if the reality on the ground is characterized by extensive de facto engagement of the state with Popular Com-mittees anyway? It matters because non-recognition of the Popular Committees – especially in combination with the vague status of refugee settlements – has acute consequences (Stel, 2017). The absence of formal recognition is certainly not the only impediment for the Popular Committees to carry out their official responsi-bilities, but it is a major one. It makes engagement with the Lebanese authorities, and by extension the entire governance situation in the gatherings, informal. It renders governance irregular, because Popular Committees cannot count on their relations with local authorities and because Popular Committees do not have the mandate or right to speak for and act on behalf of their communities, but rather have to be granted, allowed, this position on a case-by-case basis. And it results in indirect forms of rule, because the unofficial nature of the Popular Committees makes them dependent on a wide array of political brokers and middlemen that, in Suleiman's (2017: 24) words, 'control the channels of municipal support for the Popular Committees.'

Ultimately, as long as Popular Committees lack an official status, it is always up to the discretion of the Lebanese state to either deal with them as the representative of the Palestinian community and hold them responsible for it when this suits them or disown them as such and treat them as a 'a delegation of tribal spokesmen' when this is more convenient. This does not mean that there are no local Lebanese state representatives who work constructively with the Popular Committees, but – as the opening vignette to this chapter illustrates – it does mean that such engagement is always conditional and temporary, always depending on the mercy and personal goodwill of the Lebanese authority in question, making governance unpredictable. When I asked him about the many Lebanese officials that do occasionally help Palestinian authorities, an interlocutor associated with the Palestinian Embassy in Lebanon reflected: 'This is about "I woke up in a good mood today and I'm going to help you." It happens from time to time. But we need a system; we need things done properly, not depending on moods.'[26]

Non-recognition does not merely have national political expediency. It also works as a practical local governance strategy. State authorities in South Lebanon have little means to govern, but they do need to control. The crippled nature of the Popular Committees that stems from their non-recognition helps local Lebanese authorities – themselves struggling with vast capacity deficits and legitimacy problems – to maintain the upper hand in their engagements with Palestinian communities. This is relevant specifically in light of the violent history of the Palestinian political presence in South Lebanon.

It helps Lebanese local governance actors to have the committees work for them rather than for the Palestinian people they theoretically represent. When discussing the relations between local Lebanese authorities and Palestinian Popular Committees, a Palestinian analyst bluntly concluded: 'The Popular Committees are not in power. They are delegalized and unrecognized. [But] . . . they are sometimes used by the security apparatus to get them to hand people over.'[27] The informal status of the committees makes their relations with Lebanese state agencies conditional upon, for instance, their policing of their communities for the Lebanese state. As Hanafi (2010: 28) concludes, the co-option of the Popular Committees by the Lebanese state, which is enabled by its delegitimation of these same committees, ensures that Palestinian settlements are 'perfectly under the control of the Lebanese state.' Delegitimized and under-capacitated Popular Committees are an element of indirect rule. In its attempt to control refugee spaces without taking direct responsibility for them, Lebanese state authorities need a client authority, a role that the Popular Committees now regularly fulfil. Martin (2011: 160) has previously noted that the Lebanese government has a history of exercising control over Palestinian settlements 'through the PLO.' Indeed, a local PLO official went so far as to claim that 'we help the Lebanese government to control.'[28]

The lack of formal status of the committees is also arguably convenient for Lebanese political parties. Because state authorities are limited in some ways in their engagement with the committees exactly because of the committees' lack of legal status, interactions between Popular Committees and state agencies are often mediated by Lebanese politicians. In the gatherings I studied, this mediated form of governance was the result of the fact that the Popular Committees ultimately needed something – such as permission for construction, coordination on infrastructural services, or authorization of events – from the municipality (Stel, 2015a). But since they did not have the formal authority to demand or request this from state agencies directly, they often had to turn to brokers. These brokers included NGOs and UNRWA, but most importantly consisted of Lebanese and Palestinian politicians.

As described in Chapter 1, Lebanon's political parties operate a vast institutional network outside the framework of the formal state. This makes them particularly well-suited to function as a broker between the Palestinian communities and their representatives on the one hand and the official institutions of the Lebanese state on the other. Residents from one of the gatherings I studied explained that the Popular Committee alerts the local PLO/Fatah representative if it needs anything from the state. This person would then either contact the relevant Lebanese political representative in Tyre or pass the request on to his superiors in Beirut, who would then liaise with their relative Lebanese counterparts. The Lebanese politician would subsequently contact his 'people within the state institutions,' whether ministers, mayors, or employees, to get the job done (Stel, 2015a: 81). A representative of the national Union of Popular Committees explained to me: 'We cannot talk with state employees directly. Our direct relations are with the political leaders who can affect these employees.'[29] NGOs similarly found that 'political parties remain more important than municipalities. Palestinian bodies will lobby with political parties that will then pressure the relevant functionary in the municipality.'[30] Even the LPDC follows this logic. According to a former spokesperson, it always goes 'through the political parties: . . . You have to see who is supporting this municipality, Amal or Hezbollah, and go to them.'[31]

In fact, the two dominant parties in South Lebanon have liaison committees or officers to strengthen their ties with Palestinian groups (Stel, 2015a). A representative of Hezbollah found that his party operated as 'the channel between the Palestinians and the state.'[32] A person introduced as a 'liaison' with the Palestinians in South Lebanon for Amal similarly explained how his party employs its 'presence in the government' to facilitate communication between Palestinian parties and state institutions.[33] This logic of political mediation was compellingly explained to me by a leading figure within the Popular Committee hierarchy in the Tyre region:

> The Lebanese structure is different. If I talk to the district governor, he frankly says he's not the suitable person to talk to. We all know where to go. If we need an electricity transmitter and we have a problem with the manager of the company in Sidon, we search for a manager affiliated with either Bahia or Osama [the leaders of the two major competing Lebanese parties in Sidon] who can pressure him and we go directly to this person and convince him to

give the transformer. Here [in Tyre], we have to know if the manager in question is from Amal or Hezbollah and then we can go to talk to the leadership directly. If we go the long way, the official way, you don't get anything like you do when you take the shortest way. The question is: Who can influence this person? Before we talk. . ., we have to ask this question. This is the structure of the country.[34]

The same Lebanese political parties that are represented in the national government that is unable and unwilling to recognize the Palestinian Popular Committees that local state agencies deal with on a daily basis, play a crucial role in mediating between the committees and state agencies locally. This brokerage confirms their political relevance in Lebanon's hybrid political order, which works through the informal lubricant constituted by these parties that are simultaneously part of and separate from the state system. Were the Popular Committees to be regularized and recognized, Lebanon's political parties would lose much of their informal political power in the local governance of Palestinian communities – and, with that, grip on an 'issue' or 'file' that is historically, politically, and militarily salient to them.[35]

The absence of formal status does not exclusively serve Lebanese political actors. Palestinian political leaders are implicated in the current governance arrangements as well. On the one hand, Palestinian authorities are keenly aware of the importance of formal acknowledgement of the Lebanese state for their local structures. In the Mar Elias meeting of August 2017, the adopted recommendation explicitly calls upon the Lebanese state 'to recognize the committees as a service and municipal authority in the Palestinian camps and gatherings' (Suleiman, 2017: 26). On the other hand, the Palestinian political parties that have basically captured the Popular Committees and run them without most of the consultation and accountability measures that the committees should formally respect arguably benefit from the informal status of the committees as well.

By now, any power the Popular Committees may have depends on the goodwill of Lebanese authorities more than on the support of Palestinian refugees. Lebanon's Palestinians broadly feel that their leaders care more about 'political relations' with Lebanese than about the 'lives of ordinary Palestinian refugees' (Ramadan, 2008: 673). Recognition from the Lebanese state might come with strings attached, such as the demand to actually implement the committees' statutes, whereas now the Palestinian communities that the Popular Committees claim to represent have few means to hold the committees accountable. Formal status, then, risks severely undermining the current modus operandi of the widely unpopular Palestinian 'factions' that is characterized by repression and impunity.

Thus, as an LPDC analyst concluded, in Palestinian settlements 'the reality on the ground, the current situation, is a consequence of mutual interests.'[36] This resonates with other evidence of 'the tacit complicity between institutional stakeholders on the Palestinian political scene and the Lebanese government in maintaining the status quo' (Allan, 2014: 203). Popular Committees are propped up and undermined at the same time and encouraged in a deliberately informal guise that makes their operation unstable and liminal and their interaction with the Lebanese state exceptional and conditional. This aligns with the unpopular and unaccountable power positions of Lebanese as well as Palestinian political parties.

Life in suspended spaces: ever-imminent destruction and eviction

Informality, liminality, and exceptionalism are institutionalized through the non-status of Palestinian refugee settlements and Palestinian refugee representatives. The implications of this institutional ambiguity for the governance of Lebanon's Palestinian refugees are, as documented previously, evident across the board, impacting access to services and justice, prospects for collective action, and the accountability of Palestinian leadership. This section zooms in on one of the most existential aspects of life in the gatherings to explore how the different effects of institutional ambiguity intersect. By looking at the legal, temporal, and material precarity of the houses that make up Palestinian gatherings, it shows the spatial implications of institutional ambiguity. The section presents three vignettes that revolve around the spatial domain of governance: one concerning a short and demarcated period of unprecedented building and renovation activity and two regarding pending eviction threats.[37]

The issue of building and housing in Palestinian communities and spaces is extremely sensitive because it is so closely related to the notion of permanence. As Ramadan and Fregonese (2017: 5) conclude, the Lebanese state has 'consistently sought to maintain the transience of the Palestinian presence through intense restrictions on construction . . . and on property rights.' This is, for instance, why Lebanese authorities fret over apparently inconsequential issues like roofing material: New buildings are more likely to be condoned if they have a zinc roof than if they have a cement one, because the latter would enable eventual vertical expansion and would make destruction harder. It also explains the widespread reluctance of Lebanese authorities to allow gatherings to connect to physical infrastructure such as sewage networks or water provision, as these – just as with Syrian informal settlements – are seen to acknowledge or encourage the normalization of the refugees' presence.

Since 2001, Palestinians are legally prohibited from owning land or real estate, because, according to Lebanese authorities, allowing Palestinian refugees to own a home encourages them to envision their future in Lebanon rather than in a prospective Palestinian state. The 2001 law has had relatively little consequences for refugees living in formal camps, as these have their own internal renting and ownership dynamics within the closed-off perimeters of the UNRWA-leased land. It has, however, severely impacted all Palestinians outside the recognized refugee camps, who generally do not hold official titles for the land they are living on. Unsurprisingly, consequently, residents of the 'gray spaces' that the gatherings represent identify housing, land, and tenure issues as their most pressing problem (Chabaan, 2014: 35).[38] Unpublished documentation provided to me by a representative of the Popular Committee structure in the Tyre region went as far as to identify the risk of eviction as a definitional feature of a gathering.[39]

Legally speaking, Palestinians living in the gatherings do so illicitly. This means they cannot fulfil the criteria to obtain the necessary permissions to build, extend, or rehabilitate houses. Initially, this was hardly problematic. Most families living in the two gatherings studied built their houses in the 1950s. At that time, construction was not an issue if the landowner consented. In the 1960s, residents described their building activities in a way that resembles Bayat's (1997) 'quiet encroachment.' Throughout the Lebanese Civil War, under the tutelage of the PLO, this encroachment became considerably less quiet and took place virtually unchecked (Stel, 2015b). Only with the post-war reinstallation of the municipalities from the mid-1990s onward did local authorities start to exercise control over construction.

In the gatherings, then, building new houses and even repairing existing ones is prohibited. With the help of an informant network, the police closely monitor building activity and, in principle, destroy nascent construction. As a result of these restrictions, shelter in the gatherings is currently of poor quality, lacking proper water and sanitary services. Other infrastructure and services are affected, too. To do basic reparations on electricity lines, for example, specific permits from Lebanese authorities are required (Yassin, Stel and Rassi, 2016). Obtaining these permits is often impossible, because they can only be requested by a person holding legal title to the land. Yet during my stay in the gatherings, it was obvious that construction and renovation was continuously taking place. This gap between official regulations and reality followed from the residents' creative strategies to enhance their living situations. In many cases, people built in secret, often under cover of night, and hoped the police would not discover their building activity until it constituted a 'fact on the ground' (Stel, 2015b). Then they would try to prevent the police from destroying their house either through bribes or *wasta* with authorities able to pressure the police to, as they described it, 'look the other way.'[40]

More often, though, residents would ask the municipality for permission to build, which in many cases would be given. This permission, however, was widely described as 'humanitarian' or 'illegal,' meaning it was in principle conditional and temporary and could always be withdrawn without notice or explanation.[41] This is partly because municipalities cannot in fact give permission to build on privately owned land, which constitutes large parts of the gatherings. Even on public land, moreover, permission is a two-step procedure that entails not merely municipal consent but also approval from the Association of Engineers (which would be given only to the landowner). Municipal 'permission' here thus entails the exchange of money for a verbal promise that the police will not show up.[42] In the words of one resident:

> We get an illegal permission; it's a permission just to keep the police away. For a legal permission you have to be the owner and bring papers from the

police and from different departments. The kind of permission we get is just to cover the eyes of the police.[43]

Thus, despite legal obstacles, financial costs, and social anxiety, residents of the gatherings have found a way to tend to their houses. The municipality plays a crucial gatekeeper role in this situation: without it, residents are at the mercy of the police and the landowners. Describing the realization of a soccer field in one of the gatherings, a resident explained:

> The mayor agreed with us. He said he couldn't give us a paper as it wasn't his land, but he said 'go ahead' even if he couldn't do so officially. And neither the state nor the police came. When we were finished, the police came and we told them to go see the mayor.[44]

The conduct of the municipality is to some extent informed by compassion. The municipality's incentive to go against official state laws in 'covering' residents of the gatherings, however, also lies in the political ties between Palestinian parties and the dominant political party in the municipality in question. A senior Palestinian political cadre living in one of the gatherings commented that regional Members of Parliament encourage the municipality to condone the Palestinians' construction. The municipality is clearly also driven by economic incentives. As Beer (2011: 7) construes:

> The willingness of the municipality and the police to intervene to prevent construction, rehabilitation, and extension of property should be viewed as an effort, primarily, to protect an income source rather than an attempt to fully uphold Lebanese HLP [housing, land, and property] law.

The institutional ambiguity and the arbitrary power that this ambiguity allots to local state agencies are evident in the 'normal' housing dynamics in the gatherings, as described earlier, but they were even more obvious during a development that residents of the gatherings have come to call the 'building revolution.'

The win-win of looking the other way: constructing a window of opportunity

The 'illegal permissions' and the 'looking the other way' described in the prior section allow for basic renovations, but throughout my stay in the gatherings, I also saw a host of entirely new homes. These, it turned out, mostly originated from 2011, when many households in the gatherings in the South added rooms, or even entire floors, to their houses (Stel, 2014). Here, I will relay the specific dynamics of this 'building revolution' in one specific gathering, exploring how these dynamics were shaped by institutional ambiguity.

Through rumours, media reports, and their own observations, people in the gathering knew that Lebanese people in their region were building without permissions. Following this observation, residents of the gathering took their chances and started construction work on their own houses. After a few weeks, the police installed a blockade of checkpoints around the settlement to prevent the entering of construction materials. Despite the region-wide precedents, the municipality on whose land this gathering was built repeatedly reinstated the illegality of construction. Municipal representatives emphasized this in meetings with representatives of the gatherings that took place at the municipality as well as during visits to the gathering. In the beginning of the building episode and towards the end of it, the municipal police entered the gathering several times to demolish nascent construction.

But where one state authority, the municipality, was vehemently opposed to the building, another local state authority, the *mukhtar* of a neighbouring Lebanese village, was more sympathetic of Palestinian construction activities. Arrangements to facilitate construction were entirely informal and largely secretive. The bribing of policemen manning the checkpoints to smuggle in building materials happened through a double-blind system wherein Palestinians from the gathering had a contact who met with a representative of the policemen at the checkpoints:

> The bribes reached the checkpoints indirectly, through two or three people who are close to the police. We cannot go to the policemen directly to pay them. These two or three people are relatives of the policemen and they have secret relations between them. The policemen can't take from the people directly; they were afraid someone might take pictures and send them to their leadership. . . . These three or two persons they deal with us directly, but they pay a secret person who has the relations with the policemen and we didn't talk with that person. The policemen don't deal with these three or two; they deal only with the one.[45]

Other important 'facilitators' were the Lebanese political parties holding sway in the region. Political leaders and their local representatives condoned the building, creating an implicit obstacle for local state representatives to directly go against the building. Someone working for a Palestinian NGO in the region explained:

> During this period, some two months during summer, each party supported their own followers to do whatever they wanted without repercussions in order to pressure their political adversaries. It was an internal Lebanese political problem. They message was 'do what you want and no one will prevent this.' Under the table each party let their followers know to go ahead. And then in some instances the police would come to stop them, but someone would intervene to tell the police to look the other way.[46]

The building revolution was ultimately a manifestation of a political showdown between Lebanon's two political blocks at the time, March 8 and March 14. A national politician confirmed this:

> This happened between two governments, after the fall of the government two and a half years ago. There was a great political conflict between the Lebanese political forces. And in such periods, the security forces are weak, because they can't fight one and not the other. And during election times there is an understanding between all political leaders to let people build, this is a kind of facilitation for people. The political leaders can affect the police and the army and make them squeeze their eyes.[47]

In the gathering in question, the implicit support that political figures gave to the building activity was widely considered the main enabling factor for construction. The absence of national state control and the overt discrepancy between national political leaders and local state authorities provided people with a unique opportunity. In light of this, a local state representative described the construction spree, which was not permitted but not hindered either, as the way the 'system works' or even the 'state's will.'[48]

These events acutely illustrate the ways in which institutional ambiguity functions in the gatherings. They were of course welcomed by residents as a great opportunity, but this should not obscure the structural conditions of the gatherings that dictate that such unpredictable and conditional 'opportunities' are the only option that people have to realize some form of decent housing. The informality of the gatherings' institutional status and the Popular Committees' representative position runs throughout the episode. The Popular Committees were relegated to a marginal position. People in the gathering emphasized that they operated on an individual basis and that no one represented them or arranged building permissions. They said no one would want to take the collective responsibility for such an overtly illegal project. The Popular Committee, I was told, 'couldn't interfere, they don't have the authority.'[49] According to one contractor facilitating the building in the gatherings, the Popular Committee did not play a significant role in the building, because 'the police don't respect the Popular Committee.'[50] Instead of operating collectively under Palestinian leadership, the gathering's residents were made dependent on indirect relations with Lebanese state and political authorities for what was paradoxically called 'illegal permission.'

Residents as well as their representatives were overall at the mercy of Lebanese political parties and their inclination to 'look the other way.' Rather than receiving official or unequivocal permission, their actions were illegal but condoned. For the residents of the gatherings, tending to their housing needs was an exceptional and implicit favour, never a right. The construction episode was a trial-and-error process, testing the water to see how far they could go. Opposing state agencies were seen to play a role that was ritualistic: announcing building restrictions but ignoring transgressions; installing checkpoints but allowing these to be circumvented. But, Palestinians from the gatherings were keen to stress, these rituals always carried the potential to be implemented 'for real.'

Eviction as a continually adjourned but never abating threat

If exceptional opportunities to build are the carrots that Lebanese authorities can extend to those living in 'gray spaces,' evictions are the concomitant stick. Together, they demonstrate how institutional ambiguity dictates the fickle possibilities and impossibilities of living in the gatherings.

In one of the gatherings I studied, one specific area has long been threatened with eviction. This part of the settlement is located on municipal land that is supposed to be used for the construction of a national highway (Stel, 2016a). The precise number of houses affected is disputed, but the engineer in charge of the construction project estimated that some 50 houses would be destroyed. These belonged to both Palestinian families from the gathering and Lebanese residents of a neighbouring village. The first stages of the project started in the mid-1990s, and residents have been aware of the eviction threats ever since. Some ten years later, they heard that the land on which they built their houses would be expropriated in the highway construction process. A court case was opened, during which the municipality was informed about the procedure. However, follow-up hearings were required to sort out compensation issues. Partly because of these delays, the affected residents hoped or expected that the highway plan would be altered or cancelled and their houses might be spared, but in 2007 residents reported engineers who came to mark houses. A few years later, construction started with more houses added to the eviction list. The subsequent arrival of engineering teams made it clear that the construction of the highway was imminent.

The Council for Development and Reconstruction, a national inter-ministerial body with the aim to efficiently implement construction projects, was in charge of the highway construction. It hired a consulting company to manage the actual construction and contracted various construction companies to implement the building. After the government published a decree in which it announced the highway's final route and the affected land plots, an expropriation file was sent to a legal committee headed by a judge. As the municipality is the landowner in question, its lawyer was the main interlocutor for this legal committee. The legal committee, a lawyer of the Council for Development and Reconstruction explained to me, was aware of the fact that there are people living illegally on the municipal land, but could not take these people into consideration because of the gatherings' lack of legal status. Thus, the committee relied on the municipality – as the legal landowner – to help them deal with the residents of the land. Both the Council for Development and Reconstruction and the legal committee assumed that the municipality would represent and inform the residents, facilitate their exit and relocation, and arrange compensation on their behalf.[51] The municipality, however, refused to do so. A municipal officer explained: 'When they built, these families didn't take permission and now they want us to bear responsibility.'[52]

The affected households could not count on the Popular Committee either, which would not or could not intervene on their behalf against the municipality. Instead, residents eventually established what they called a 'highway committee,' which consisted of communal leaders from the affected neighbourhoods in both the Palestinian gathering and the Lebanese village. This committee, however, had trouble representing the residents vis-à-vis the Council for Development and Reconstruction, which did not consider them an official party in the procedure, and the municipality, which was not interested in liaising with the residents in the first place. Interactions between the Council for Development and Reconstruction and the highway committee, tellingly, were all coincidental and occasional and depended on the impromptu presence of engineers sent by the Council. As the relevant Council for Development and Reconstruction project manager observed:

> They didn't get any letter or anything. We see them in the field when we pass by. We asked the municipality what they were doing there and he [the representative of the municipality] told us that they live there illegally. There is no communication with them, not official and not unofficial. We saw them and we know there is a problem, but legally there is no relation between us and them.[53]

The 'highway committee' then sought support from political parties. Lebanese members of the highway committee tried to arrange meetings with Lebanese Members of Parliament. Palestinian members contacted representatives of Palestinian political parties, in the hope that these would subsequently address their Lebanese counterparts, who might then take up the matter with their ministers or the Council for Development and Reconstruction. When asked whether his organization talked to the Council or the court, someone working for an NGO that sought to help the affected people explained:

> No. We made a plan, but we didn't reach this step. Because when we met with [the representatives of the relevant political parties], all said it would stop and there was no need any more to meet the CDR [Council for Development and Reconstruction] and the engineers. And they get their orders from the politicians anyway. . . . There are no legal solutions; it's about political interference here and there. . . . It's about relations here and there.[54]

Lebanese political parties confirmed this reading. A spokesperson for a Lebanese party said: 'Via our Members of Parliament and ministers we make communication with the Council for Development and Reconstruction.'[55]

It appeared to genuinely frustrate some of the people working for the Council for Development and Reconstruction and the municipality that they could not fit the Palestinian residents within their legal and formal system and were therefore forced to 'leave them to the politicians,' as a municipal spokesperson put it.[56] Yet, there appears to have been little effort from their side to adjust these legal and formal systems. This ambivalence, the coexistence of legal impossibility and political possibility, was repeatedly invoked. The legal representative in charge of the case said: 'We're looking for a practical solution, not a legal one. Because legally, they don't have any rights. But they're here and we have to deal with the reality.'[57] A political representative in the region similarly noted: 'When we do it according to the law, the situation will be bad for them. So we have to find a solution with the state to give them a better alternative.'[58] The 'solution' that the various political interventions managed to broker was delay and postponement. For a long time, the eviction was not implemented, even as the highway neared the gathering. Eventually, however, all people were forced to leave, with only some of them getting minimal compensation.

Many of the dynamics that shaped this eviction were also evident in the threats of displacement facing the other gathering. Here, the danger of eviction did not come from a public infrastructure project, but from private landowners reclaiming their property (Stel, 2016a). In this gathering, only approximately 20 percent of the land is public (municipal) land, and the rest is held by various Lebanese private owners. In the 1950s, most of these landowners gave the Palestinians who worked on their land as field laborers permission to live there. Their heirs, facing ever-expanding construction by Palestinian residents and encouraged by rising property prices, however, no longer feel bound by the promises their (grand) fathers made (Stel, 2016a: 174). In the absence of legal title to land, Palestinian refugees can face criminal prosecution for use and occupation of land. This issue affects almost all gatherings. In the gathering in question, at least four different lawsuits are currently pending. Here, I will focus on the largest and most pertinent case.

In the late 1990s, the residents of approximately 50 houses in a specific neighborhood of the gathering were accused of illegally residing and building on private land and summoned to court. The prosecutors demanded that the residents leave their property, pay for the immediate removal of the illegal structures, and compensate them for the use of the land since the 1970s. After almost a decade of recurrent court sessions, the judge ruled in favour of the landowner in 2006. In 2010, the residents' appeal was rejected as well. One year later, the residents received a warrant from the police that informed them they had five days to leave. The people I spoke with, however, lacking any alternative residence, refused to leave. Nor did the police come to physically evict them. An impasse commenced. The landowner finally had her eviction warrant, but it somehow would not be executed. Thus, for now the situation is, as residents said, 'frozen.'[59]

But how can such a legally indisputable case be put 'in the fridge'?[60] For the affected inhabitants, the answer was straightforward: politics! (Stel, 2016a) As in the other case, interference of political parties was essential to deal with the eviction threat. Indeed, the failure to implement the court decision appears to be the effect of high-profile political intervention. Residents here were represented by a communal authority figure, whose house was also on the land threatened with eviction. Together with several other communal leaders affected by the court case, including the then head of the Popular Committee, he formed a committee to deal with the eviction threat. This committee raised the issue with what they called the 'political leadership,' mostly meaning the PLO. The PLO leadership, in turn, together with the Palestinian embassy, discussed the matter with those Lebanese politicians and officials with the power to prevent implementation of the court order.

Concerned with the political sensitivity of displacing Palestinians, these Lebanese leaders agreed with the Palestinian political leadership that it would not be acceptable to 'have people say that in the South they destroy Palestinian houses.'[61] Thus, with an eye to Lebanon's volatile political situation, the police charged with implementing the eviction order was instructed to refrain from doing so for the sake of preserving the calm in the region. This, however, does not settle the issue. The 'solution' is widely felt to be temporary. A resident explained that the court case might be halted, but it was not concluded and might be reopened at any time. A communal leader added: 'They stopped it; it was postponed. But we didn't solve anything; it's just suspended.'[62]

Residents threatened with eviction are very much aware that they are at the mercy of what they call 'the political situation.' They keenly understand that the court's ruling has not been reconsidered and the eviction order has not been retracted (Stel, 2016a: 181). They perceive the current non-implementation of the eviction as explicitly conditional and temporary, noting that political decisions can be withdrawn at any time. Reflecting on the volatile relationship between the PLO and Lebanese political parties, a Popular Committee member worried:

> Politics controls everything here. Now he [the main political authority in South Lebanon] helps us and our relationship with him is very good. But if there is a change in the situation or his opinion, this stops. Before, they were killing us![63]

Others voiced similar sentiments. A communal leader had no illusions when he explained to me that:

> Now, the landowner can't do much because the situation with the Palestinians would be too sensitive. But in the future there may be a change in the political situation in Lebanon, in the sectarian relations. And maybe then the landowner will refer to certain people to kick them out. The political situation in Lebanon isn't stable, you know; it varies.[64]

Building ambiguity into the gatherings

These vignettes about the negotiated nature of Palestinian living spaces and shelters show how ambiguity is produced by the clash between formal procedures and informal realities, by the carefully protected 'temporariness' of the gatherings, and by the legal and representational exceptionalism that marks these spaces.

State agencies insist on following official regulations that excluded or were inapplicable to the Palestinians gatherings – and were meant to be so, because the same state, albeit embodied by different agencies, generated and maintained this legal-institutional exclusion in the first place. Residents of the gatherings are first excluded from formal residential status and then punished for this imposed illegality. The Council for Development and Reconstruction, for instance, insists that it can only deal with the residents based on legal papers of ownership and defends the state's right to expropriate land for development projects with reference to the law. Palestinians, however, are keenly aware that they have little to expect from 'the law', and when authorities refer to the law they consider this particularly unfair and extremely ironic. The same ambivalence extends to the issue of representation. Palestinian refugees are withheld a formal local representative by the very political parties that then locally interfere on their behalf. Paradoxically, in eviction cases, Lebanese political parties position themselves as representatives of the Palestinians against the government. This ignores the fact that their own representation in the government means that they could have prevented much of the tenure problems that Palestinian refugees face from arising in the first place or could solve these issues more structurally.

This institutionalized informality, liminality, and exceptionalism undermines agency and options for collective action. In the form of a continually suspended but never lifted threat of displacement, liminality and informality become instruments of discipline. Crucially, Palestinian refugees themselves become implicated in these disciplining structures. Because what the vignettes illustrate too is the ways in which Palestinian residents inevitably reinforce the very informality, irregularity, and politicization that produced their problems in the first place (Stel, 2017). As the first vignette illustrated, they do this by grasping the few opportunities they do have to build, making them further indebted to local politicians and rendering them more vulnerable to accusations of deliberate squatting. But they also do this through the coping mechanisms they devise to deal with eviction threats. As the last two vignettes showed, people living in gatherings seek solace in politicized facts on the ground that ultimately risk further undermining their claims for legal status and formal representation in the long run.

The informal status of their living situation and representational structures crucially affect the access to information and hence the agency of the residents of the gatherings and their representatives. Not being informed about the process and not having a right to information that directly affects them produces passivity and seems to give people few alternatives to stalling. In the gatherings, institutional ambiguity functions in a two-step fashion. First, it complicates construction and exposes residents to eviction. Second, it determines the coping mechanisms available to residents to then deal with these predicaments. In the absence of formal entitlements related to citizenship or land ownership, rights that are deliberately withheld from them, inhabitants of the gatherings are forced to rely on informal and politicized strategies geared towards foot-dragging instead of actual problem-solving.

Conclusions

Palestinians in Lebanon continue to face the most uncertain fate of all Palestinian refugees (Suleiman, 2006: 28). In Lebanon, their exile is, in Khalili's (2005) words, a 'landscape of uncertainty.' Yet while the day-to-day implications of the socio-economic strangulation and legal discrimination that Palestinians in Lebanon face have been documented exhaustively, the drivers, dynamics, and consequences of uncertainty have not been explicitly studied. This chapter has therefore explored how informality, liminality, and exceptionalism emerge and function in the governance of Palestinian refugee settlements in Lebanon.

The informal administrative status of Palestinian gatherings – and, albeit in a different way, the formal camps as well – is meant to underwrite the liminality of the Palestinian presence in the country and produces exceptionalism in that it allows Lebanese and Palestinian authorities to address or disregard certain issues in an arbitrary fashion. In practice, it allows for abandonment of the refugee communities living there by Lebanese, Palestinian, and international organizations. Representation of the Palestinians living in South Lebanon's gatherings is determined by exceptionalism. The lack of formal recognition of Popular Committees enables Lebanese authorities to include them in their unofficial governance arrangements – and use them as instruments to maintain order – while excluding them from official governance.

The spatial governance of the gatherings reveals the disciplinary effect of institutionalized informality, liminality, and exceptionalism particularly well. The status and representation of refugees remains unofficial, temporary, and simultaneously deniable and enforceable. Palestinian refugees and the organizations that claim or aim to represent or help them consequently depend on the goodwill of Lebanese authorities to look away, interpret favourably, or condone. This regards Lebanese state agencies, but also, crucially, the Lebanese political authorities that both control these state agencies and operate in parallel to them.

As the next chapter will think through more systematically, institutional ambiguity works as a governance strategy through the logic of potenza: the creation of a situation in which everything is simultaneously prohibited and allowed, renounced yet encouraged, deniable and enforceable. Crucially, strategic institutional ambiguity is not about straightforward discrimination, which is a form of 'inclusion through exclusion,' but rather about the unpredictability of what is included and what is excluded in the governance practices of specific authorities. Ambiguity is located in the arbitrary alternation and seeming simultaneity of inclusion and exclusion (Oesch, 2017: 110). The vignettes on construction and eviction illustrate that the gatherings are governed, that solutions can be reached. Houses are renovated despite the official ban on construction and evictions are 'frozen' or postponed despite clear court orders. But such 'solutions' are always temporary and conditional. They can, and are, withdrawn when this suits the Lebanese authorities that have brokered them.

The ad hoc and politicized nature of such 'deals' – whether it comes to halting evictions, operating informal service networks, or the ability of local committees to speak for these communities – thus essentially reinforces the parameters of the institutional ambiguity that caused residents' precarity and uncertainty in the first place. This demonstrates that institutional ambiguity is an expression as well as an instrument of power. Chapter 6 further conceptualizes how this power is wielded and whom it serves.

Notes

1 Author's interview – 14 July 2014.
2 For more specifics on the history of the Palestinian presence in South Lebanon, please refer to Beydoun (1992), Brynen (1990), Doraï (2006), Puig (2013), Ramadan (2008), Sayigh (1997a, 1997b), and Stel (2015c, 2017).
3 Most of the interviews referred to in this chapter were conducted in Arabic, which was made possible through the support with translation provided by my research partners. The other interviews were done in English. Considering the sensitivity of doing research in a context rife with surveillance by foreign intelligence agencies and Lebanese and Palestinian security agencies, these interviews were not recorded. The citations provided are based on extensive notes. For more reflections on data generation and analysis, please refer to Stel (2017).
4 They are included in, for instance, the census discussed in Chapter 4 and other studies, but without clear status as either Lebanese villages or Palestinian camps.
5 Author's interview with a communal leader in one of the gatherings – South Lebanon, 21 May 2013.
6 Author's interview – Beirut, 13 September 2012.
7 The Arabic word for socio-political capital or 'connections' that allow one to 'get things done.'
8 Author's interview – 19 July 2013.
9 Author's focus group – South Lebanon, 14 June 2013.
10 Author's interview – Sidon, 8 June 2013.
11 The number of 24 seems random, referring to a duplication of the number of camps. It would refer to recognizing just some of the larger gatherings, not all gatherings.
12 Author's interview – Tyre, 21 August 2014.
13 Author's interview – Sidon, 25 July 2013.
14 Author's interview – Beirut, 22 July 2013.
15 There have been some exceptions where Popular Committees have been elected. Examples from Shatila have been well-documented by Khalili (2005) and Kortam (2011).
16 Unpublished document produced by the Central Follow-Up Committee for Popular Committees in Lebanon in 2013, which was provided to me in hard copy by a representative of the Central Follow-Up Committee on 29 September 2014. The document consists of various sub-documents and was translated from Arabic by my research partner.
17 Author's interview – Tyre, 13 June 2013.
18 Author's interview – South Lebanon, 15 October 2014.
19 Author's interview – South Lebanon, 3 April 2013.

20 Author's interview – Beirut, 22 July 2013.
21 Author's interview – Sidon, 13 July 2012.
22 Author's interview – South Lebanon, 10 June 2013.
23 Author's interview – Beirut, 20 June 2013.
24 Author's interview – Beirut, 22 July 2013.
25 Author's interview – Beirut, 26 June 2014.
26 Author's interview – Beirut, 22 September 2014.
27 Author's interview – Sidon, 12 July 2012
28 Author's interview – Tyre, Rashidiye camp, 14 May 2013.
29 Author's interview – Tyre, Bourj el-Shemali camp, 25 July 2013.
30 Author's interview with NGO representative – Beirut, 13 September 2012.
31 Author's interview – Beirut, 22 July 2013.
32 Author's interview – Beirut, 26 June 2013.
33 Author's interview – South Lebanon, 29 June 2013.
34 Author's interview – Tyre, Bourj al-Shemali camp, 25 July 2013.
35 Some Lebanese parties are interested in gaining votes from the small minority of naturalized Palestinians (Stel, 2015c). They also care about the support of Palestinian armed groups in Lebanon's ever-anticipated war (Bou Akar, 2019; Khalili, 2007; Knudsen, 2011). Overall, positioning themselves as a crucial element in any engagement between Palestinians and the Lebanese state is a way of showcasing control over 'their' region of south Lebanon and reinstating their central position in Lebanese governance.
36 Author's interview – Beirut, 9 June 2014.
37 These vignettes are also featured in previous papers (Stel, 2014, 2015b, 2016a). For more information on housing in the gatherings, please refer to Beer (2011), Chabaan (2014), Hilal (2010), Knudsen (2018), Rasul (2013), Saghieh and Saghieh (2008), and Williams (2011).
38 Then why would people live in the gatherings in the first place? As I explained in Stel (2016a), the simple answer is that for most of them, there is no realistic alternative. They cannot buy a house, even if they somehow had the money for it, because Palestinians are not allowed to own and register real estate. Their exclusion from some 70 job categories also makes it extremely difficult for them to rent an apartment considering Lebanon's relatively high rents. Relocating to an official refugee camp is mostly out of the question, too. Formal Palestinian camps are notoriously overcrowded and cannot possibly absorb more people since they are not allowed to extend their geographical boundaries set in the 1950s.
39 It states:

> Definition of a gathering: A geographic area that is not demarcated and not officially recognized by the Lebanese state and UNRWA because the refugees live on the land owned by the Lebanese state or private owners illegally. The people who live there always face the insecurity of being displaced.
> (translated from Arabic by my research partner)

40 Author's interview with Popular Committee member – South Lebanon, 4 June 2014.
41 Author's interviews with PLO official (South Lebanon, 9 October 2014) and Palestinian analyst (South Lebanon, 20 June 2014) and focus group (South Lebanon, 30 September 2014).
42 Interlocutors living in the gatherings indicated they paid an amount ranging from US$500 to US$5,000 depending on their request and connections. Rasul (2013: 54) found bribes varying between US$1,000 and US$2,000, and Beer (2011: 35) between US$100 and US$1,000.

43 Author's interview – South Lebanon, 13 September 2014.
44 Author's interview – South Lebanon, 11 July 2014.
45 Participant of author's focus group – South Lebanon, 28 July 2013.
46 Author's interview – Tyre, 22 March 2013.
47 Author's interview – Beirut, 26 June 2013.
48 Author's interview – South Lebanon, 29 April 2013.
49 Participant of author's focus group – South Lebanon, 28 July 2013.
50 Author's interview – South Lebanon, 20 May 2013.
51 Author's interviews with a representative of the consultancy company (Beirut, 20 June 2013) and a lawyer of the Council for Development and Reconstruction (Beirut, 3 July 2013).
52 Author's interview – South Lebanon, 1 July 2013.
53 Author's interview – Beirut, 3 July 2013.
54 Author's interview – Beirut, 21 June 2013.
55 Author's interview – South Lebanon, 29 June 2013.
56 Author's interview – South Lebanon, 11 April 2013.
57 Author's interview – Baabda, 17 July 2013.
58 Author's interview – South Lebanon, 27 July 2013.
59 Author's interviews with Popular Committee members (South Lebanon, 4 June and 24 July 2014), a Lebanese Member of Parliament (Tyre, 24 October 2014), an NGO employee (South Lebanon, 7 July 2014), and residents of the gatherings (South Lebanon, 3 July and 13 September 2014).
60 Author's interview with UNRWA representative – Tyre, 21 August 2014.
61 Author's interview with a communal authority – South Lebanon, 11 April 2013.
62 Author's interview – South Lebanon, 16 July 2014.
63 Author's interview – South Lebanon, 2 September 2014. He refers to the War of the Camps.
64 Author's interview – South Lebanon, 11 July 2014.

References

Allan, Diana. 2014. *Refugees of the Revolution: Experiences of Palestinian Exile*. Stanford: Stanford University Press.

Bayat, Asef. 1997. 'Un-Civil Society: The Politics of the "Informal People".' *Third World Quarterly* 18, no. 1: 53–72.

Beer, Robert. 2011. *Housing, Land and Property Practices in the Palestinian Gatherings in Lebanon*. Beirut: Norwegian Refugee Council, unpublished document.

Beydoun, Ahmad. 1992. 'The South Lebanon Border Zone: A Local Perspective.' *Journal of Palestine Studies* 21, no. 3: 35–53.

Borgmann, Monika and Lokman Slim. 2018. *Fewer Refugees, More Refugeeism*. Beirut: Umam Documentation and Research and Institute for Auslandsbeziehunger.

Bou Akar, Hiba. 2019. *For the War Yet to Come: Planning Beirut's Frontiers*. Stanford: Stanford University Press.

Brynen, Rex. 1989. 'PLO Policy in Lebanon: Legacies and Lessons.' *Journal of Palestine Studies* 18, no. 2: 48–70.

Brynen, Rex. 1990. *Sanctuary and Survival: The PLO in Lebanon*. Boulder: Westview Press.

Chabaan, Jad. 2014. *Profiling Deprivation. An Analysis of the Rapid Needs Assessment in Palestinian Gatherings Host Communities in Lebanon*. Beirut: United Nations Human Settlements Program and United Nations Development Program.

Common Space Initiative. 2011. 'Action Research and Facilitation of Lebanese-Palestinian Local Relations and Interactive Frameworks: Local Relations in the Nahr el Bared Camp and Surrounding Municipalities. Findings and Recommendations Report April 2011.' Unpublished document.

Danish Refugee Council. 2005. *Needs Assessment of Palestinian Refugees in Gatherings in Lebanon*. Beirut: Danish Refugee Council.

Doraï, Kamel. 2006. 'Aux Marges de la Ville, les Camps des Refugies Palestiniens a Tyr.' *Outre-Terre. Revue Française de Géopolitique* 13: 373–389.

Hanafi, Sari. 2008. 'Palestinian Refugee Camps in Lebanon: Laboratories of State-in-the-Making, Discipline and Islamist Radicalism.' Unpublished document.

Hanafi, Sari. 2011. 'Governing the Palestinian Refugee Camps in Lebanon and Syria.' In *Palestinian Refugees: Identity, Space and Place in the Levant*, edited by Are Knudsen and Sari Hanafi, 29–49. New York: Routledge.

Hanafi, Sari and Taylor Long. 2010. 'Governance, Governmentalities, and the State of Exception in the Palestinian Refugee Camps of Lebanon.' *Journal of Refugee Studies* 23, no. 2: 134–159.

Hilal, Nancy. 2010. *Investigating Grey Areas: Access to Basic Urban Services in the Adjacent Areas of Palestinian Refugee Camps in Lebanon*. Beirut: United Nations Development Programme.

Khalili, Laleh. 2005. 'A Landscape of Uncertainty: Palestinians in Lebanon.' *Middle East Report* 236: 34–39.

Khalili, Laleh. 2007. ' "Standing with My Brother": Hizbullah, Palestinians, and the Limits of Solidarity.' *Comparative Studies in Society and History* 49, no. 2: 276–303.

Knudsen, Are. 2009. 'Widening the Protection Gap: The "Politics of Citizenship" for Palestinian Refugees in Lebanon, 1948–2008.' *Journal of Refugee Studies* 22, no. 1: 51–73.

Knudsen, Are. 2011. 'Nahr al-Bared: The Political Fallout of a Refugee Disaster.' In *Palestinian Refugees. Identity, Space and Place in the Levant*, edited by Are Knudsen and Sari Hanafi, 97–110. New York: Routledge.

Knudsen, Are. 2018. 'The Great Escape? Converging Refugee Crises in Tyre, Lebanon.' *Refugee Survey Quarterly* 37, no. 1: 96–115.

Kortam, Manal. 2011. 'Politics, Patronage and Popular Committees in the Shatila Refugee Camp, Lebanon.' In *Palestinian Refugees: Identity, Space and Place in the Levant*, edited by Are Knudsen and Sari Hanafi, 193–204. New York: Routledge.

Lebanese-Palestinian Dialogue Committee. 2012. *Access to Basic Urban Services in the Adjacent Areas of Palestinian Refugee Camps in Lebanon: Consultations with National and Local Stakeholders. Synthesis Report*. Beirut: Lebanese-Palestinian Dialogue Committee.

Lebanese-Palestinian Dialogue Committee. 2013. *From Dialogue to Vision: Towards a Unified National Policy for Palestinian Refugees in Lebanon and a Future Vision for LPDC*. Beirut: Lebanese Republic, Presidency of the Council of Ministers.

Lebanese-Palestinian Dialogue Committee. 2018. *Population and Housing Census in Palestinian Camps and Gatherings in Lebanon 2017: Key Findings Report*. Beirut: Lebanese Republic, Presidency of the Council of Ministers.

Martin, Diana. 2011. 'The "Where" of Sovereign Power and Exception. Palestinian Life and Refugee Camps in Lebanon.' PhD thesis, Durham University.

Oesch, Lucas. 2017. 'The Refugee Camp as a Space of Multiple Ambiguities and Subjectivities.' *Political Geography* 60: 110–120.

Puig, Nicolas. 2013. 'Lost in Transition: Ordeals of Passage of Palestinian Refugees in Lebanon.' *Mediterranean Politics* 18, no. 3: 394–410.

Ramadan, Adam. 2008. 'The Guests' Guests: Palestinian Refugees, Lebanese Civilians, and the War of 2006.' *Antipode* 40, no. 4: 658–677.

Ramadan, Adam and Sara Fregonese. 2017. 'Hybrid Sovereignty and the State of Exception in the Palestinian Refugee Camps in Lebanon.' *Annals of the American Association of Geographers* 107, no. 4: 949–963.

Rasul, Majida. 2013. *No Place Like Home: An Assessment of the Housing, Land, and Property Rights of Palestinian Refugee Women in Camps and Gatherings in Lebanon.* Beirut: Norwegian Refugee Council.

Saghieh, Nizar and Rana Saghieh. 2008. *Legal Assessment of Housing, Land and Property Ownership, Rights and Property Law Related to Palestinian Refugees in Lebanon.* Beirut: Norwegian Refugee Council.

Sayigh, Yezid. 1997a. *Armed Struggle and the Search for State: The Palestinian National Movement, 1949–1993.* Oxford: Oxford University Press.

Sayigh, Yezid. 1997b. 'Armed Struggle and State Formation.' *Journal of Palestine Studies* 26, no. 4: 17–32.

Stel, Nora. 2014. *Governance Between Isolation and Integration: A Study on the Interaction Between Lebanese State Institutions and Palestinian Authorities in Shabriha Gathering, South Lebanon.* Beirut: Issam Fares Institute for Public Policy and International Affairs.

Stel, Nora. 2015a. 'Lebanese-Palestinian Governance Interaction in the Palestinian Gathering of Shabriha, South Lebanon – A Tentative Extension of the "Mediated State" from Africa to the Mediterranean.' *Mediterranean Politics* 20, no. 1: 76–96.

Stel, Nora. 2015b. *Facilitating Facts on the Ground: The "Politics of Uncertainty" and the Governance of Housing, Land, and Tenure in the Palestinian Gathering of Qasmiye, South Lebanon.* New Haven and Gothenburg: Yale University and Gothenburg University.

Stel, Nora. 2015c. ' "The Children of the State?" How Palestinians from the Seven Villages Negotiate Sect, Party and State in Lebanon.' *British Journal of Middle Eastern Studies* 42, no. 4: 538–557.

Stel, Nora. 2016a. 'The Agnotology of Eviction in South Lebanon's Palestinian Gatherings: How Institutional Ambiguity and Deliberate Ignorance Shape Sensitive Spaces.' *Antipode* 48, no. 5: 1400–1419.

Stel, Nora. 2016b. 'Languages of Stateness in South Lebanon's Palestinian Gatherings: The PLO's Popular Committees as Twilight Institutions.' *Development and Change* 47, no. 3: 446–471.

Stel, Nora. 2017. 'Governing the Gatherings: The Interaction of Lebanese State Institutions and Palestinian Authorities in the Hybrid Political Order of South Lebanon's Informal Palestinian Settlements.' PhD dissertation, Utrecht University.

Stel, Nora and Irna van der Molen. 2015. 'Environmental Vulnerability as a Legacy of Violent Conflict: A Case Study of the 2012 Waste Crisis in the Palestinian Gathering of Shabriha, South Lebanon.' *Conflict, Security and Development* 15, no. 4: 387–414.

Suleiman, Jaber. 2006. *Marginalised Community: The Case of Palestinian Refugees in Lebanon.* Brighton: University of Sussex.

Suleiman, Jaber. 2017. *Lebanese-Palestinian Relations: A Political, Human Rights and Security Perspective.* Beirut: Common Space Initiative.

Ugland, Ole Fr., ed. 2003. *Difficult Past, Uncertain Future: Living Conditions Among Palestinian Refugees in Camps and Gatherings in Lebanon.* Oslo: Norwegian People's Aid and Partners.

Williams, Rhodri C. 2011. *From Shelter to Housing: Security of Tenure and Integration in Protracted Displacement Settings*. Oslo: Norwegian Refugee Council.

Yassin, Nasser, Nora Stel and Rima Rassi. 2016. 'Organized Chaos: Informal Institution Building Among Palestinian Refugees in the Maashouk Gathering in South Lebanon.' *Journal of Refugee Studies* 29, no. 3: 341–362.

Yiftachel, Oren. 2009. 'Critical Theory and "Gray Space": Mobilization and the Colonized.' *City* 13, no. 2–3: 240–256.

Chapter 6

Knowledge and power revisited

The politics of uncertainty as maintaining, feigning, and imposing 'ignorance'

> The margin for maneuver is everywhere, ok? Be sure. We are trying to maneuver everything and to manipulate everything.[1]

Palestinians in Lebanon have over the last three decades experienced a steady development 'from autonomy to ambiguity' (Ramadan and Fregonese, 2017: 10). The country's Syrian refugees face a 'fickle and ambiguous' institutional environment that traps them in a 'bureaucratic maze' (Al-Masri and Altabbaa, 2016: 11).

This situation is routinely explained with reference to the unprecedented nature of these 'crises,' Lebanon's still precarious recovery from a range of devastating wars, its ailing economy, wanting international support, and the fragile nature of Lebanon's political system that generates paralysis and polarization – in short, by a lack of capacity to 'properly' deal with refugee 'crises.' But such structural and contextual explanations, crucial though they are, do not convey the functionality and resilience of institutional ambiguity in its entirety. They largely obscure the behaviour and decisions of authorities governing in hybrid orders. To get at these strategic dimensions of institutional ambiguity, I introduced the idea of a politics of uncertainty. Through a combination of inaction and ambiguous action, governance actors can reproduce institutional ambiguity for various purposes. Revisiting the cases presented in the empirical chapters, this chapter brings together the explanatory power of the hybrid political order, central to Chapter 1, and the politics of uncertainty, developed in the book's Introduction, by considering their interplay from the perspective of ignorance studies.

Governance through uncertainty is a form of epistemic politics (Aradau, 2014). It assumes that power can derive from controlling and withholding knowledge. Tracing agency in this process means establishing who knows and does not know or could (not) have known what at particular instances. This is the domain of ignorance studies, an emerging school of thought concerned with the political functionality of not-knowing. Ignorance studies proposes that if political power revolves around information, it will be crucially shaped through cultivating, simulating, and inflicting not-knowing. The politics of uncertainty operates through authorities' imposing uncertainty or 'not-knowing' on others – refugees and their representatives, civil society organizations and humanitarian 'partners,' and other state agencies – but also through authorities' maintaining and feigning their own lack of knowledge. This dissection of the relevant 'knowledge economies' (Van der Haar, Heijmans and Hilhorst, 2013) that constitute Lebanon's refugee governance sheds light on how political authorities not only navigate but also actively utilize structural forms of institutional ambiguity.

The chapter has three main sections. It starts out with an introduction on ignorance studies, showing that it provides further insight into the operation and the rationalities of institutional ambiguity. The subsequent two sections respectively explore the 'how' and 'why' of institutional ambiguity. The chapter's second section reveals how considering inaction and ambiguous action as ways to maintain, feign, and impose ignorance indicates the agency at work in the politics of uncertainty while doing justice to its structural dimensions. The third section delves into the interests underpinning institutional ambiguity. It demonstrates that these are not limited to amassing the generic political capital inherent in creating leeway, but also encompass more specific objectives that revolve around controlling, expelling, and exploiting refugees. The concluding section reflects on the relations between capacity and political will in understanding how institutional ambiguity emerges and functions.

Ignorance studies

The field of ignorance studies is concerned with what social and political actors do not know, claim not to know, and aspire not to know (Gross and McGoey, 2015; McGoey, 2019; Proctor and Schiebinger, 2008; Smithson, 2015). By thinking through governance actors' behaviour as potential ways to feign or maintain their own ignorance and impose ignorance on others, this perspective helps to construe institutional ambiguity as a governmentality, rather than as only or predominantly a convenient contingency. The Foucauldian idea of governmentality sees power as working through implicitly invasive and internalized regulation. Authority is then fundamentally mediated through knowledge. Ignorance studies crucially complements this reading of governance through its focus on the subversion, denial, and evasion of knowledge. It explores what Aradau (2017: 331) has called the socio-political 'assemblages generative of non-knowledge.'

'Splattered across disciplines' and taking inspiration from critical feminist and postcolonial studies, ignorance studies shows how the instrumentalization and institutionalization of not-knowing, in the form of silences, gaps, uncertainties, and ambiguities, affects all governance (Smithson, 2015: 385).[2] Ignorance, here, is decoupled from popular normative connotations and simply refers to 'not-knowing' – which can be 'real' or 'pretence,' absolute or partial. Ignorance studies has a specific interest in the forms of not-knowing that follow from practices through which knowledge 'is obscured, silenced or deflected' (Aradau, 2014: 76).

The study of such 'agnogenesis,' the process of generating or maintaining ignorance, has been specifically pursued by scholars working in the realm of agnotology (Christensen, 2008). Agnotology is concerned with 'strategic' (Bailey, 2007; Mallard and McGoey, 2018; McGoey, 2007, 2012; Pénet and Mallard, 2014) or 'wilful' (Tuana, 2006) ignorance. It aims to 'explore how ignorance is produced or maintained in diverse settings, through mechanisms such as deliberate or inadvertent neglect, secrecy, and suppression, document destruction, unquestioned tradition, and myriad forms of inherent (or avoidable) culturopolitical selectivity' (Proctor and Schiebinger, 2008: vii). Resonating with a critical anthropology of ignorance, it focuses on 'the production and the productivity' of not-knowing (Mair, Kelly and High, 2012: 16).

Smithson's (2008: 209) social theory of ignorance is based on three core premises: that ignorance is pervasive; that it is socially constructed; and that it can be advantageous. Agnotology, then, proposes an explicitly political reading of not-knowing (Code, 2014: 48; Slater, 2012: 951). Ignorance is 'not just a natural consequence of the ever-shifting boundary between the known and the unknown but a political consequence of decisions concerning how to approach (or neglect) what could be and should be done' (Proctor, 1995: 13). It is in this attempt to locate power in governance modalities that ignorance studies and my central concepts of institutional ambiguity, hybrid political order, and a politics of uncertainty come together. By construing the not-knowing that is feigned and imposed through institutional ambiguity as a 'constructive, agentive space' (Chua, 2015: 253), ignorance studies helps to locate the interests and motivations behind forms of governance and power characterized by uncertainty. Not-knowing is 'made, maintained, and manipulated' (Proctor, 2008: 8; see also Alcoff, 2007: 39). The premise of agnotology, then, is that, like knowledge, not-knowing can be a 'tool of governance and usurpation' (McGoey, 2012: 10).

Institutional ambiguity is not the same as ignorance, but it is a way to simultaneously profess and dictate ignorance; a form of 'agnotological power' (Davies, Isakjee and Dhesi, 2017) that allows for shirking formal responsibility while accumulating informal control and enabling the disciplining, exploitation, and expulsion of certain societal groups. By approaching the two components of the politics of uncertainty – inaction and ambiguous action – from an ignorance studies perspective, they can be understood as strategically claiming and imposing 'unknowledge' (McGoey, 2019). Authorities feign and maintain their own not-knowing by hiding behind informal, temporary, and exceptional measures in the realm of status, shelter, and representation – for instance, through practices of non-recording, cultivating limited capacities, generating diffuse mandates and hierarchies, and by actively 'looking away.'

These same measures impose ignorance on the people that authorities seek to govern by excluding them from legal frameworks and subjecting them to vague policies and directives, incomplete and arbitrary implementation, and unstable representation structures. This has crucial implications for the knowledge economies in which people operate, which become 'fundamentally structured by uncertainty' (Whyte, 2011), and ensures that official as well as tacit and experiential information available to people is 'minimal, contradictory or erroneous' (Griffiths, 2013: 268).

Feigning and maintaining ignorance

So how does 'governing by ignoring' work in Lebanon? (Dedieu, Jouzel and Prête, 2015: 297) The first component of the politics of uncertainty regards the strategic ignorance of state agencies; the tendency to, in order to protect interests, resist rather than pursue knowledge (McGoey, 2019: 28). This concerns both feigned or professed ignorance, where agencies are aware of specific issues but deny it, as well as maintained ignorance, where actors keep in place their not-knowing (Luhmann, 1998; McGoey, 2007; Spelman, 2007). These overlap. Mostly, governance actors know a bit about something and choose not to know more, as such knowledge would be inconvenient. Or, similarly protecting their 'ignorance alibis,' they do know more but find it advantageous not to admit as much (McGoey, 2019: 56, 315).

This speaks to the assembled nature of state systems. As Eule et al. (2018: 237) show for the European migration regime, there is often a 'tacit ignorance' among policy-makers in the sense that 'the "head" prefers not to know what the "hands" are doing.' Lebanese authorities involved in the governance of refugees indeed in many instances maintain not-knowing, by 'looking away' or 'squeezing their eyes,' so as not having to deal with particular issues. This also regards the limited information-production of the Lebanese state. As noted by Hamdan and Bou Khater (2015: 10), Lebanese government institutions hardly engage in or commission public knowledge-production in the realm of refugee governance. This once more demonstrates that power does not just work through legibility, but also through the strategic avoidance of datafication or its purposefully ambiguous nature.

There are many civil society organizations, think tanks, journalists, and non-governmental organizations (NGOs) involved in studying refugees. They produce a wealth of information that is actively brought to the attention of state representatives. Interviewees associated with such organizations recounted how they routinely brief state agencies and officials and provide them with tailored policy recommendations, a claim that is backed up by the bounty of relevant reports. There are, moreover, various donor initiatives to map and share information across regions, sectors, and levels that further undermine the idea that state agencies cannot know what is going on, even if they lack the capacity to generate such information themselves.

Yet, Lebanese state agencies often disregard or discard such information. As Halkort (2019: 321) notes, in Lebanon refugee data is 'a highly unpredictable and ambivalent force, something knowingly unknowable.' Local exploitation of refugees is part of a system that, Ghaddar (2017) claims, 'is reinforced by State Security actors, ignored by the ministry of interior and local municipalities, convenient for landowners, and problematic for aid organizations and refugees.' The presence and functioning of governance institutions inside Syrian settlements is often ignored and/or denied by mayors even though other actors structurally brief them on these institutions. Such professed ignorance is replicated higher up in the state hierarchy. The main advisor on refugee issues of the Minister of Interior claims the ministry is not aware of the governing structures in informal refugee settlements (Ghaddar, 2017). This is unlikely since these structures are public knowledge among humanitarians and are discussed during the monthly meetings of the Central Security Council, which are presided over by the Minister of Interior himself.

Throughout my research on Palestinian gatherings, local Lebanese state representatives were often ignorant – or pretended to be ignorant – about the gatherings, reproducing the image of Lebanon's Palestinian spaces as 'impenetrable and closed, unknowable, foreign' (Ramadan, 2009: 157). Officials, for instance, said they were not aware of a Palestinian gathering in the village that constituted one of my cases. This while representatives of this gathering routinely engaged with politicians represented in the municipal council and civil servants. Such absence of knowledge is often actively protected. One mayor told me: 'Don't tell me how things are arranged [in the gathering]; I don't want to know!'[3] Another mayor similarly advised me to 'not get into this; to dig on the surface.'[4]

Governance actors do not merely level such professed ignorance at researchers. As one protection officer working for an international NGO recounted:

> I remember one of the representatives of the interior ministry telling me 'yeah, we don't know what they [refugees] are doing, I mean, we don't know about this whole *shawish* thing.' I'm sure he's lying to me. . . . Pretending that 'I don't know what's going on in another agency that doesn't have to fall under my jurisdiction' is a kind of way of saying 'I don't want to answer your question.' So 'I don't know' is like a better answer than 'let me explain to you the problem on the side of the government.'[5]

Maintained and feigned ignorance regards individual considerations, but also takes collective forms. These are connected by 'ignorance pathways' through which individual, 'micro-ignorance' and societal, 'macro-ignorance' reinforce and legitimate each other (McGoey, 2019: 168). This, for instance, regards the performative nature of the constantly reinforced temporariness of refugees' stay, while state representatives privately acknowledge that return is highly unlikely. It is similarly evident when refugees are systematically not registered or not granted a legally defined status so that authorities do not have a comprehensive overview of the scope and nature of the refugee population. The 'numbers games' discussed in earlier chapters show how the Lebanese state instructs the United Nations (UN) to stop registering refugees to then claim it does not know the number of refugees, which allows it to subsequently politically utilize this ignorance to 'play' various audiences. This helps to appreciate how the maintenance of not-knowing becomes inherent to bureaucratic structures, with governance actors reproducing this state of not-knowing by not asking questions or not wanting to hear answers (Borrelli, 2018).

Not-knowing, a Lebanese lawyer working with refugees reflected, is closely related to passivity: 'Because you can do what you want with the ambiguity. When it's clear, you are committing yourself.'[6] Janmyr points out that Lebanese authorities legitimize their refusal to ratify the 1951 Refugee Convention by saying that they are 'uncertain' about the commitments such ratification would entail. She shows, however, that they need not be, and are not actually, uncertain about the obligations involved, as experts have repeatedly clearly outlined these to them. Authorities' apparent uncertainty about the Convention is a form of 'politically expedient' not-knowing (Janmyr, 2017: 449). It is 'a strategic misconception' that allows them to abstain from ratification to protect the leeway they currently enjoy without having to bear the consequences of outright rejecting the Convention's principles (Janmyr, 2017: 453).

Institutional ambiguity allows states to abandon unwanted populations (Agier, 2008, 2011). This is no different in Lebanon. The vagueness of the mandates of various state agencies is indicative of this approach. Throughout fieldwork, it was often remarkably complicated to establish who was responsible for which aspects of refugee governance, for instance where it concerned obtaining permits for installing tents in Syrian settlements, the responsibility for which was allocated to a vast array of different actors by different interlocutors. The result, the UNHCR noted in his speech during a donor conference on 'Supporting the Future of Syria and the Region,' is a form of 'blurred' responsibility that inhibits accountability.[7] Professed not-knowing, whether real and maintained or whether feigned, then legitimates, even necessitates, inaction. If one does not know about something, after all, how can one be expected to deal with it?

Imposing ignorance

If given the choice, people often prefer to act on the basis of ignorance rather than knowledge (Gigerenzer and Garcia-Retamero, 2017 in McGoey, 2019: 39). What my politics of uncertainty demands attention for, however, are those instances where people's ignorance is not a choice. Institutional ambiguity is part of a politics of uncertainty when it allows political elites to govern refugees by imposing ignorance on them and those supporting them. The opacity and apparent randomness of decisions, and thereby their unpredictability, undermines stakeholders' agency, as they will find it almost impossible to plan or strategize for the infinite range of scenarios opened up under extreme uncertainty (Eule et al., 2018: 121). The production of ignorance, Slater (2016: 23) shows, carves out 'economic and political paths' for exploitation that are particularly difficult to map and hence to counter. As Griffiths (2013: 279) demonstrates, governments can exert 'extreme control over people . . . through systemic uncertainty and disorder, through which individuals are made powerless, hopeless.' Tapscott (2017) similarly shows that when populations cannot find a predictable pattern or regularity in the behaviour of state agencies, they cannot establish shared expectations for state behaviour, which hampers collective action. The paralyzing quality of uncertainty works by undermining the organizational capacity of those suffering under it and by diffusing targets for contention through the blurred responsibilities it produces (Rodgers, 2019).

The book's empirical chapters showed that the destabilization of expectations and imposition of uncertainty through institutionalizing informality, liminality, and exceptionalism is not merely a contingency of capacity deficits, but also reflects political will. With regard to the Syrian refugee crisis, Atallah and Mahdi (2017: 8, emphasis added) unequivocally state that 'as the crisis has entered its seventh year, the Lebanese state does not *intend* to formalize a national response toward the humanitarian crisis unless it is focused on the repatriation of Syrian refugees to Syria.' Fakhoury (2017: 688, emphasis added) considers the institutional ambiguity central to my analysis a deliberate choice as well:

> Lebanon's incoherent policy frame over the issue of Syrian displacement has established itself over the years as the *desired* state of affairs. Behind its facade of incongruity, it reveals a *deliberate choice* to avoid the adoption of a well-articulated refugee regime. This has led to a widening gap between international actors' plea for an improved legal framework and the Lebanese state's *preferences*.

In the Palestinian case the lack of formal status of the gatherings and the absence of de jure recognition of refugees' local governance actors, which produce institutional ambiguity, are political choices too. In theory, nothing stops the Lebanese government from recognizing the gatherings as formal camps and granting Popular Committees the status of refugee representatives. Institutional ambiguity may then not have been the direct objective of these political decisions, which were primarily related to the geopolitical sensitivities of the Palestinian 'issue,' but cannot be relegated to a side effect either.

Imposing ignorance can work through not acting (formally) at all. Not engaging is often 'the simplest manner' of dealing with a difficult issue and a good way to 'buy time' (Mathews, 2008: 490). This is intuitively evident in refugee governance, where the default approach is often to wish refugee realities away (Agier, 2008: 40). This was apparent in the 'no-policy-policy' initially levelled against Syrian refugees. Laws and policies are then simply not developed or adopted: it is not accidental that Lebanon has no refugee law.

Ambiguity does not stem only from inaction, but also from proliferous action: a multitude of constantly shifting and inconsistent regulations and their arbitrary implementation (Parkinson, 2014). Those policies that are adopted are implemented in an incomplete and inconsistent fashion that amounts to ambiguous action. Both the absence of policies and the arbitrary implementation of policies creates political maneuvering space. Ambiguous action entails the generation of confusion around legal categories, resulting in an avoidable situation of mass illegality for Syrian refugees. It concerns numbers and statistics, when there is a tacit political agreement towards non-recording. It relates to shelter, producing ambiguous refugee spaces that fall outside state responsibility but under state control, and it has to do with mandates and responsibilities, with emerging refugee representation structures simultaneously being co-opted and disowned.

Uncertainty is not the same as not-knowing. Rather, it can be regarded as a category of ignorance that amounts to doubt, 'not knowing for sure.' 'Potenza' is central in imposing uncertainty (Minca, 2005 in Martin, 2011: 195). Following a Gramscian take on 'laissez faire as a disciplinary strategy,' potenza locates power in capacity, rather than the exercise of that capacity; in the discretionary 'potentiality to-act or not-to-act, to-control or not-to-control' (Lukes, 2005: 12; Davies, 2012: 2692). It refers to epistemic regimes in which 'events are always emergent and potential' (Aradau, 2014: 77). Potenza denotes a situation where the institutional environment is so ambiguous, so open to multiple interpretations, that governance implementation is almost entirely dependent on the discretionary power of the authority at hand, which can opt for repression or abandonment or compassion, seemingly at will. The project manager of a European NGO working with Syrian refugees described potenza as follows:

> I like to define this country [Lebanon] as a country with like ten thousand problems, but in theory there are a hundred thousand solutions. . . . In theory everything is possible. . . . In terms of law enforcement it's so blurred, that just depends on the municipalities or the police units etc. In some areas they just don't stop them [refugees]. In some areas they raid houses or homes or informal settlements and they arrest people and bring them to another town.[8]

This idea of potenza resonates with the sentiment that 'everything is possible in Lebanon.'[9] This importantly relates to the rule of law. Refugees are actively encouraged or expected to behave against the law. Yet while refugees are often 'forced to commit . . . the slew of transgressions' they are accused of, state-produced and condoned transgression can nevertheless always be held against them (Cullen Dunn and Cons, 2014: 101).

Life in informal refugee settlements shows this well. Palestinian gatherings and Syrian informal tented settlements are condoned but never formally permitted, always allowing for evictions and arrests. The same logic applies to the illegal residency status of the great majority of Syrian refugees in Lebanon, which is routinely overlooked but never formally pardoned. Illegal stay in the country is a criminal offense under Lebanese law. Yet, such illegality is created and accepted by the state. Lack of legal status has repercussions for refugees' mobility and access to services (Atallah and Mahdi, 2017: 25; Janmyr, 2016: 72), but, at the time of fieldwork, it did not lead to actual deportation. Yet the threat of deportation perpetually hovers over Syrian refugees. Refugees, those organizations seeking to help them, and expert observers insist that imposed illegality should be seen as opening up possibilities for the Lebanese state. Following De Genova (2002,

2016), refugees were not (yet) deported, but rather made deportable. As one Syrian refugee (illegally) working for an internationally registered NGO in Lebanon explained:

> Until now nothing happened with those who don't have residency. . . . But, also, we don't know, because also they write in the passport that you have to leave within one month. And if the Lebanese government suddenly decided to practice this law maybe most of the Syrians . . . they will kick out most of the Syrians to go back to Syria or force them to leave Lebanon. . . . If the Lebanese government decided to implement this law, yes, 70% of the Syrians will have to leave Lebanon.[10]

Potenza, in a nutshell, illustrates how institutional ambiguity produces the discretion to, with equal legitimacy, act or not act. This enables a constant threat that importantly produces pliancy and enables control.

Reproducing ignorance

Incomplete and unstable knowledge economies follow from inaction and ambiguous action, which produce informality, liminality and exceptionalism, so as to amount to a distinct governmentality: a politics of uncertainty. The main aim of this book has been to show how various agencies that constitute the Lebanese state feign and maintain ignorance and thereby force it on others. The ways in which those 'others' respond to this, however, are often an integral part of the governmentality at stake. In the following section, I briefly outline the role of crucial 'non-state' stakeholders in the reproduction of the politics of uncertainty.

Refugees: coping with and replicating ambiguity

One response to institutional ambiguity is to push for the 'hardening' of institutions, which increases predictability (Yassin, Stel and Rassi, 2016). Refugees in Lebanon, however, often have no official representative, few socio-economic assets, and little political clout. Producing regularization, consequently, is mostly not within their ability. Situational adjustment, the exploitation of the 'soft' status of institutions, then becomes the default response to institutional ambiguity (Cleaver, 2002: 15). Rather than resisting ambiguity, refugees cope with it to the best of their abilities. But in doing so they often replicate the politics of uncertainty imposed on them (Stel, 2015, 2016).

Marginalized groups are well-known for exploiting 'inconsistency, contradiction, conflict, [and] ambiguity' (Razzaz, 1994: 11). Residents of Palestinian informal settlements use indirect, informal, and politicized social networks and relations to access services, ensure shelter, and negotiate security. To avoid evictions they actively utilize the liminality of their protracted refugeeness and their exceptionality within the Lebanese polity. They generate deliberate disinformation, employ stalling tactics, and invoke ignorance about their predicament. Syrian refugees' accounts, too, are rife with the notion that their lives are deliberately made impossible through informality, liminality, and exceptionalism. And they push back against this reality. Cassani (2018) shows how Syrians resist imposed refugee identities by refusing to be held collectively responsible by Lebanese authorities. Institutional invisibility, remaining under the radar through non-registration, has been a routine coping mechanism for them too. Refugee communities in Lebanon have to some extent mastered the 'art of not being governed' (Scott, 2009; Stel, 2015).

Ignorance can be constructive and strategic for refugees as well as for authorities (Bailey, 2007; Mair, Kelly and High, 2012; Brun, 2015; Scheel, 2019; Scott, 1985, 1990). In line with this, over the last decades the field of refugee studies has made a productive move from seeing refugees predominantly as victims and recipients towards considering them active political agents (Fiddian-Qasmiyeh et al., 2014; Griffiths, 2013; Harrell-Bond, 1986; Richter-Devroe, 2013). Refugees' alternative knowledges, or 'counter-apodemics,' and coping mechanisms, however, often invoke and reinforce the very institutional ambiguity that marginalizes them (Walters, 2015; see also Ansems de Vries, 2016). The 'ignorance' of refugee communities is itself ambiguous. It is both imposed on refugees as well as strategically coveted as a protection mechanism against the arbitrariness they face. Ambiguity is a response to power and a way of exercising power.

The steadfastness and defiance of refugees and their sometimes creative appropriation of ambiguity is remarkable. But while the informality, liminality, and exceptionalism that refugees are forced to embrace might serve as short-term survival mechanisms, they further entrench the governmentality that victimizes refugees in the long run. Ultimately, 'some people are better positioned to exploit their own and other peoples' ignorance' (McGoey, 2019: 47) and these are usually not 'those living at the bottom of the class structure' (Slater, 2012: 951). Without succumbing to the view of refugees as victims only, then, refugees' part in the production and enactment of a politics of uncertainty should be seen as a coping mechanism, rather than resistance. As a Palestinian youth leader sarcastically surmised: 'We're normalizing the abnormal. I think this is what one calls a negative coping mechanism.'[11]

Refugee 'representatives:' indirect rule between impotency and complicity

The actors who claim to represent refugees play a crucial role in these negative coping mechanisms. Syrian *shawishes* and Palestinian Popular Committee members are themselves refugees and residents of informal settlements. Their strategies reflect the broader coping mechanisms of refugees. Yet these 'representatives' also have their own interests that are often aligned with those of Lebanese (local) elites and thereby the current status quo of ambiguity and uncertainty.

Refugee representatives operate as an informal link between refugee populations and Lebanese state representatives and political elites. As such they are an essential component of the politics of uncertainty. Their role is a form of indirect rule. *Shawishes* and Popular Committee members hold their positions of relative power by the grace of Lebanese authorities. The authority of *shawishes* is seen as 'given to them by State Security' (Ghaddar, 2017). The same goes for Palestinian refugee authorities, who are instrumentalized by security agencies to gather intelligence and monitor wanted persons (Hanafi and Long, 2010). According to a leader in the regional popular committee structure, Popular Committees were '*created* to officially work with the government.'[12]

This is not merely boasting, wishful thinking, or attempted legitimization from the side of refugee representatives. State institutions routinely deal with *shawishes* and Popular Committees and make them de facto responsible for controlling refugees. They do so without ever formally acknowledging these representatives or allowing them to develop sufficient capacity to do the things they are held responsible for. Such indirect rule reflects and entrenches institutional ambiguity through state actors' unpredictable giving and withdrawing assent to actors on the ground (Lamontagne, 2018: 9).

The work of Ramadan and Fregonese (2017) on the hybrid governance of Palestinian refugee communities in Lebanon reveals how such ambiguous indirect rule is a crucial component of imposing uncertainty on refugees. They note that Lebanese elites govern refugee populations through 'hybrid arrangement between the Lebanese authorities and Palestinian (non-)authorities,' which implicates Palestinian authorities in the informality, liminality, and exceptionalism that refugees struggle with (Ramadan and Fregonese, 2017: 11). Ensuring the informal nature of their 'partners in crime' is a crucial way for Lebanese political authorities to maintain the upper hand in such dynamics.

To keep their relative power positions, refugee 'representatives' thus depend on Lebanese authorities more than on their 'constituencies.' They accrue a vested interest in the politics of uncertainty that have put them in place. Their informal and politicized engagements with Lebanese political elites and the related state agencies inevitably further entrench institutional ambiguity. In the Palestinian gatherings, according to an analyst involved in Lebanese-Palestinian dialogue sessions, 'the reality on the ground, the current situation, is a consequence of mutual interests.'[13] A Palestinian lawyer summarized a widely prevalent impression among refugees when he concluded that 'after sixty-six years of refuge, I know the problems won't be solved, because they don't *want* them to be solved' – the 'they' referring to Palestinian as much as Lebanese 'leaders.'[14]

Humanitarian organizations: frustration, resignation, reproduction

The funding conditionalities of the international donors for which humanitarian organizations work reflect the interest to keep refugees in 'the region' and away from Europe. This clearly enables Lebanon's current institutional ambiguity. The meta-logics of the humanitarian regime itself are fundamentally shaped by 'adhocracy,' the paralyzing arbitrariness and unpredictability that follows from the fragmented and short-term perspectives ingrained in humanitarianism (Cullen Dunn, 2012: 2; see also Ferguson, 1994; Agier, 2008: 70). International development logics are infused with what Hilhorst (2016) has called 'ignorancy,' the expression of a wilful naivety in the face of evident political economies and the stubborn insistence on technocratic approaches. Humanitarianism thus produces ambiguities of its own, through for example the non-transfer of knowledge among humanitarians or by keeping eligibility criteria vague to avoid beneficiaries' anticipating on them (Atme, 2019).

The fragmented nature of the response to the Syrian refugee crisis in Lebanon does not just follow from the project-based and funding-dependent nature of the humanitarian regime, however. It also results from the restrictions imposed on humanitarian organizations by the Lebanese state, whose obsession with temporariness entrenches humanitarianism to the detriment of development (Ubels, 2019). The ban on supporting grassroots refugee organizations severely limits the counterparts with which organizations can work. The imposed illegality and the related arbitrary arrests of Syrian refugees, to give another example, make NGOs hesitant to refer refugees seeking to legalize their stay to the General Security. A Lebanese lawyer working in refugee protection noted that the changeability of the regulations around refugees' entry and stay was undermining her work to such an extent that she tended to avoid related cases altogether.[15] This suggests that institutional ambiguity discourages organizations committed to refugee protection from doing their job.

Instead, a major focus for such organizations becomes their provision of 'information services' to help explain the complexities of the Lebanese refugee regime to refugees. This, one interlocutor representing an international refugee organization explained, constitutes a major demand of refugees, who

> always say 'lack of information! lack of information is the biggest obstacle,' so sometimes they would have some basic information, sometimes they would have conflicting information, sometimes they've heard something but they're not confident that they know exactly what to do now.[16]

She explained this crucially drains resources:

> You have forty-two General Security offices across the country and each of them has a slightly different practice. So for us a lot of our time and energy goes into mapping those local practices and making sure that our teams and our lawyers know exactly what works how in which location.

Despite these efforts, however, information services are compromised because these organizations often do not fully understand the highly volatile and ambiguous policies in place either (Ubels, 2019: 53). Refugees nevertheless hold them responsible for the information they provide, leaving protection officers to bear the brunt of state-imposed ambiguity.

This particularly affects the UN. Occasional efforts to 'take back control' notwithstanding, Lebanese political elites have conveniently outsourced the care for refugees to UN agencies without clarifying their exact legal standing (Norman, 2019). This has prevented the UN from pressing the government for policy reform or more commitment to international refugee law (Janmyr, 2017). The very documents that at first glance confirm the Lebanese state's commitment to donor demands are often characterized by what Uzelac and Meester (2018: 52) identify as a 'lack of explicit discussion of Lebanon's obligations towards refugees' that stems from a 'shared understanding that the ambiguity was essential for maintaining any form of political acceptance' on the side of Lebanon's political elites. Humanitarian interlocutors were keenly aware that many of the government's regularization attempts – such as the 2017 residency fee waiver for Syrian refugees and decisions to make available more work permits and avoid statelessness through facilitating birth registration – were little more than lip service that would be undone through paralyzed and arbitrary implementation. They were very frustrated about this issue, but also resigned to working around and adapting to these facts on the ground.

In a context of institutional ambiguity, denial and looking away might become the best way for humanitarian organizations to 'do no harm.' An NGO working with Palestinian residents of a gathering threatened with eviction constitutes a telling example. When I asked if they could explain to me what was going on, legal experts working for this organization told me that they were careful not to harm refugees' 'coping mechanisms that are based on discretion and not making noise.'[17] They added: 'we could have all the information that you're asking for, but we don't want to have it – for their sake.' NGOs supporting Syrian refugees report similar concerns. When asked if they aim to rectify incomplete or faulty government statistics with their own, possibly more accurate, information, a field officer of an international NGO responded that her organization does not want to 'raise red flags' by coming up with numbers, which always risks having 'implications' for refugees.[18] Humanitarian organizations thereby reluctantly but inevitably become implicated in the ambiguity they lament.

Local Lebanese authorities: 'stove piping' and 'role-playing'

There is a vast gap between the aloof stalling, denial, and non-engagement in national policy-making and local level dealings with the actual refugee presence on the ground under such institutional ambiguity. But local authorities nevertheless often replicate informality, liminality, and exceptionalism, either as a last-resort coping mechanism or as a more strategic governance device in keeping with their national superiors.

Local authorities are left hanging by national state representatives. They do not have the resources to properly deal with the challenges they face. More importantly for my central thesis, however, they often fundamentally lack the information and instructions to handle the refugee presence well. Municipalities do not know what is expected of them in terms of, for instance, shelter management, registration and residency practices, and maintaining order. They hardly receive guidance on these issues and what direction is offered is conflicting – with different ministries giving different orders, political parties internally contradicting public governmental decisions, and civil and security agencies insisting on different priorities. Administrative procedures and regulations are communicated in a piecemeal fashion, subject to constant changes, and not monitored. The local interpretation of vague directives and circulars is crucially determined by diverging contextual policy legacies, which further fragments policy.

This illustrates the intricate links between professed and maintained ignorance and imposed ignorance. It shows, as also recognized by the literature on 'street-level bureaucracy' (Lipsky, 1980), how ignorance is built into bureaucratic systems. State institutions become 'unreadable' not just to the outside but even to many of their own officials (Lindberg and Borrelli, 2019; Borrelli, 2018; Das and Poole, 2004; Eule et al., 2018; Gupta, 2012). This is so not merely because of their inevitable complexity, but also because it is politically convenient. It is partly genuine and partly, as detailed in Chapter 3, a role-play in which national state agencies enact denial of local realities and local authorities profess ignorance of national realities.

The perils of potenza loom large for local authorities: If they are not sure about how their decisions will be evaluated by their local peers and national superiors – and how can they know if no proper course of action is outlined? – then openly making any unambiguous decision on even seemingly minor local issues is a risk that can have serious political consequences. This fear of making decisions manifests itself in what Hanafi (2010: 34) has called 'stove piping:' wiring everything back to higher echelons of power, where issues often get stalled. Thus, if authorities lack the *wasta* that will protect them from the unpredictable consequences of operating under ambiguity, inaction is clearly the wisest course of action.

The behaviour of local state representatives under a regime of institutional ambiguity imposed by national authorities is thus paradoxical. On the one hand, local authorities sometimes resist the policy vacuum in which they operate. The feeling of being abandoned by the very state system they are officially part of themselves was a recurring theme in the narratives of local authorities. On the other hand, many mayors, through their tight personal and political connections to national elites, are complicit in the inconsistencies created or complacent in the face of institutional ambiguity, embracing the combined lack of resources and guidance as an excuse not to act. In either case, local authorities' responses to institutional ambiguity end up contributing to it and extending confusion, fragmentation, instability, and arbitrariness.

The utility of ambiguity

Through detailing the dynamics of protected and pretended not-knowing on the one hand and imposed not-knowing on the other, I explored how the institutional ambiguity that follows from inaction and ambiguous action works as a governmentality. This, however, leaves the question of why Lebanese authorities would want to pursue such a governmentality. I argue that this goes beyond the generic convenience of institutional ambiguity as an instrument to avoid responsibility and liability and maximize leeway. In governing Lebanon's refugees, institutional ambiguity serves more specific purposes.

Lebanon today has a refugee trauma. Its experience with the historically politicized and militarized Palestinian refugee presence in combination with its extreme demographic sensitivities means that the general public as well as political elites fear nothing as much as a politically mobilized refugee community. As a result, and despite Lebanon's polarized political landscape, when it comes to refugees the country's political parties have the same stated objective to prevent integration. Controlling refugees is a shared priority. Lebanon's political authorities agree on the importance of discouraging refugees to come to Lebanon and encouraging those that are there to return or move on. In addition to these stated aims of control and expulsion, Lebanon's governing elites share an unstated interest in the exploitation of refugees. Most of them directly or indirectly benefit from the 'refugee economy' (Anderson, 2014; Cranston, Schapendonk and Spaan, 2018; Dyke, 2015 in Mencütek, 2019: 154; Franck, 2018) that revolves around cheap labour, increased demand for services and goods, black markets for all kinds of documentation, and peaking donor funding. Institutional ambiguity facilitates all three objectives.

These overarching interests that institutional ambiguity serves are mostly those of the people that I described in Chapter 1 as the country's ruling elite. Through Lebanon's political parties, which act as twilight institutions that work inside and beyond the state system, these elites determine national (no-)policy-making dynamics. Institutional ambiguity, however, also crucially emerges through the more diffuse operations of bureaucratic actors that operationalize and implement these decisions. These are not always directly managed by national political elites, but they are not separated from them either. Lebanon's sectarian patronage system ensures close ties among various levels and domains of governance and dissolves any imagined differentiation between politics and public administration. More generic benefits of ambiguity that operate on bureaucratic levels – maximizing leeway and minimizing responsibilities – accrue to more strategic benefits politically – enabling the control, exploitation, and expulsion of refugees.

Control

Following the generic logic outlined in the book's Introduction, this chapter so far has described how institutional ambiguity helps authorities to discipline refugees through existential unpredictability and confusion. Since the experience with the Palestine Liberation Organization, there is hardly anything Lebanese elites fear more than mobilized refugee collectives. Institutional ambiguity helps prevent such mobilization. Informality, liminality, and exceptionalism create potenza for authorities. This paralyzes refugees and undermines their agency and capacity to organize, plan, and act collectively. Control is also furthered through the overall marginalization of refugees. People focused on survival and figuring out how to navigate the unpredictable institutional landscape of their host country will be less concerned with political organization.

Expel

While nominally adhering to the internationally sacred principle of *non-refoulement*, Lebanese politicians and officials appear to be doing everything in their power to 'encourage' refugees to leave the country. Institutional ambiguity serves as a crucial instrument towards this end.

Expulsion through the strangulation that is enabled by institutional ambiguity has been a key feature of the Palestinian experience in Lebanon (Sayigh, 2001). Although Palestinians are officially recognized as refugees by the Lebanese state and have been in Lebanon for generations, they have been subjected to various strategies of encouraged departure (Serhan, 2019: 246; Stevens, 2017). Palestinians registered in Lebanon but working abroad face arbitrary but severe restrictions on their (re-)entry to Lebanon (Suleiman, 2006: 15). An estimated 100,000 Palestinians have left the country over the last decades (Tiltnes, 2005 in Suleiman, 2006: 6), fleeing Israeli invasions and Lebanese conflict, but also social exclusion and protracted uncertainty (Hanafi, 2008; Knudsen, 2009, 2018). Support for Palestinians' 'right of return,' Khalili (2005: 35) concludes, 'is less about principle than about eviction of Palestinians from Lebanon.' The legal limbo, spatial exceptionalism, and non-recognition of local governance structures that constitutes the ambiguous reality of Lebanon's Palestinians' status, shelter, and representation is a root cause for the lack of perspective that is meant to 'push' Palestinians to leave the country (Yan, 2017).

That working towards return is by now the only consistent element in the Lebanese approach towards Syrian refugees is undisputed. The October 2014 policy calls for encouraging refugees to leave Lebanon 'by all possible means' (UNHCR, 2015: 4). This was put into practice by subsequent measures of the General Security to, according to Frangieh (2014), turn 'refugees into outlaws bereft of legal protection in order to drive them out of Lebanon.' Since then, the discourse of all political parties is increasingly infused with the call for refugees to return home now that the war in Syria is considered over. After the General Security's May 2019 decision to deport Syrian refugees who irregularly entered Lebanon after 24 April 2019, thousands of refugees have been forcibly returned, often instantaneously, without due process.

In addition to these deportations, the General Security claims that its registration centres have voluntarily returned 170,000 Syrians (Fakhoury and Ozkul,

2019: 27). The Minister of State for Displaced Affairs openly liaises with Damascus to enable such returns. This 'voluntary' return, however, is at least partly a result of the uncertainty generated by the institutional ambiguity refugees face. An associate of a Lebanese human rights organization explained that some years ago already Syrian refugees she worked with indicated that they considered going back to the 'evil they know' in Syria. They told her: 'however horrible it is and however much I disagree with the situation, at least I know how it works and what I can expect.'[19]

This reading is backed up by Amnesty International (2015: 26), which concludes that the 'onerous requirements introduced by Lebanon appear to be part of a deliberate policy to deny refuge to people fleeing Syria and to reduce the number of refugees in Lebanon by making life there next to impossible.' Ghanem (2016: 55), too, understands the 'selectivity and nebulousness' that characterize the application of the categories for entry established by the October 2014 policy as a tactical approach to force refugees out of the country through creating a 'hostile environment' (Sanyal, 2018: 73). Enab Baladi (2017) reports how the General Security confiscates passports and gives them back only after people sign a compulsory deportation paper, which it sees as indicative of 'a policy of unjustified and systematic disregard in order to make immigrants leave.'

'Encouraged' return is not only closely linked with imposed informality, but also with inflicted liminality. NGOs report that the seeming arbitrariness of the evictions of informal settlements creates anxiety and confusion among refugees. Chapter 3 demonstrated that evictions often serve to expel Syrian refugees not just from specific refugee localities, but from the country altogether. Lebanon's Foreign Minister argued that 'the demolition drive would prevent refugees from permanently settling in Lebanon' (Chehayeb, 2019 in Ubels, 2019: 40). This liminality-return nexus reflects a self-fulfilling prophecy. At first, assumptions that conflict would be short-lived and refugee crises would be resolved soon lessen the urgency of comprehensive responses. Later, this absence of policy becomes symbolic 'proof' of refugees' enduring temporariness. The more clearly refugee crises become protracted, the more explicit the attempts to signal their illusory temporariness.

Exploit

The informality, liminality, and exceptionalism that determine how Lebanon has approached the status, shelter, and representation of refugee communities contributed to manufactured vulnerability, the avoidable precarity of refugees. Such vulnerability allows widespread exploitation. When navigating Lebanon's ambiguous institutional landscape, Syrian refugees are largely at the mercy of Lebanese landlords, sponsors, notaries, and (local) state authorities to obtain documentation. The 'no-camp-policy' has made refugees vulnerable to raids and evictions and exploitation by landowners and *shawishes*, who, for instance, face no restriction on setting rent prices. Sponsors also hold tremendous power over refugees, who are caught in a relation that Janmyr (2016: 76) describes as analogous to 'master and slave.' Such dynamics have become even more entrenched by the increasing implication of landlords and sponsors in the surveillance of refugees (Al-Masri and Altabbaa, 2016; Ghaddar, 2017).

As a result, and notwithstanding genuine hospitality and support from Lebanese individuals and associations, exploitation in terms of residency and labour is omnipresent and human rights violations are widespread. Extortion and abuse, also by security services and municipal police who 'rob refugees' through implementing costly registration systems, are routine (Barjas, 2016). This also affects humanitarian aid, which in the wake of the refugee crisis has become a significant source of revenue for the Lebanese state and thus, following sectarian clientelism, for the country's political elite (Meier, 2014; Saghieh, 2015; Uzelac and Meester, 2018). Lebanese middlemen are reported to highjack development projects, take shares of the assistance distributed to refugees to sell such aid for an inflated price, and take commission fees on services they provide to refugees and NGOs (Nassar and Stel, 2019).

This economy of refugee exploitation that various Lebanese middlemen benefit from is not only an issue of individual abuse. Local strongmen benefiting from exploiting refugees are structurally linked to national politicians and state officials. The refugee economy has become part of existing systems of political clientelism and socio-economic patronage. Refugee eviction cases, for instance, are often part of political feuds between powerful families vying for economic and political power. Businessmen informally employing refugees are usually connected to municipal power blocks, which in turn are backed by a political party or operate under the auspices of security services that 'sell' sponsorships to refugees (Atme, 2019: 91). Mayors turn a blind eye to illegal refugee markets hosted by local Lebanese entrepreneurs, look away from security agencies extorting refugee populations, or allow local landlords to host refugee settlements while abstaining from establishing a maximum rent. For this, they will likely get political or electoral support, considering that security agencies are closely allied with political parties and businessmen and landowners are often affiliated with strong families that command large voting blocks.[20] In many cases, mayors are themselves influential businessmen with interests in the refugee economy.

The protracted Palestinian case further illustrates how exploitation goes beyond individual landlords, sponsors, or authorities and is systematically related to the country's political system. Lebanese businessmen economically benefit from the consequences of institutional ambiguity. Because Palestinians can only work informally in most sectors, employers can determine work conditions almost unilaterally. Since Palestinians do not have the right to establish associations, furthermore, the Lebanese that officially head Palestinian NGOs and companies have unchecked power over these organizations. Similarly, ever since Palestinians are no longer allowed to own real estate, the Lebanese frontmen they are forced to use to 'own' property have unprecedented possibilities to extort them or 'legally' steal their property (El Natour, 2012).

It is, however, not only the private Lebanese middlemen who (do not) allow Palestinians to work, organize, and own property that reveal the systematic nature of the exploitation allowed by institutional ambiguity. This is also apparent in the political mediation that enables such practices. Both nationally and locally, Lebanese authorities claim crucial gatekeeper functions in the adjustment strategies of the Palestinians aiming to navigate institutional ambiguity. Residents of Palestinian gatherings are dependent on Popular Committees that they find overwhelmingly illegitimate and incapable. Yet they cannot bypass them because these committees broker the ties with Lebanese political parties that in turn determine access to the state representatives that dictate whether or not an eviction order is implemented, whether or not an electricity transformer is installed, or whether or not garbage is collected.

Repressive Palestinian governance institutions are in this way propped up by the political logic of Lebanon's hybrid order. Lebanese parties aptly positioned themselves between Palestinian actors caught in illegality and a state at least nominally bound by the law. As such, it is fair to assume, as Sheikh-Hassan and Hanafi (2010: 27, 42) do, that political parties' behavior within and beyond the state system will be inclined to protect institutional ambiguity so as to maintain this niche. Ultimately, after all, it is political parties that make – or prevent, or unmake – government policy.

Controlling knowledge, managing ignorance

Institutional ambiguity serves important stated and unstated interests of Lebanon's governing elite, but that does not mean it is strategically produced. In fact, the default explanation for the emergence of institutional ambiguity of many authorities and most analysts would be the country's limited governance capacities. My point is not that there are no resource-related drivers of institutional ambiguity, but that those cannot be meaningfully separated from its strategic drivers. Capacity does not 'in and of itself' determine states' engagement with refugees (Norman, 2017: 31). State inaction or ambiguity, Mourad (2017: 250) reminds us, reflects state appetites, and not just state capacities, to govern.

Capacity and political will, ultimately, are crucially interlinked. One can have the will not to have more capacity. State officials, for instance, on the one hand refer to local capacity problems to explain instances of inconsistency, while on the other hand they obstruct the decentralization that would remedy this problem. The absence of central state registration of Syrian refugees, to give another example, is routinely considered a result of lack of resources. But the current reality in which registration and monitoring is both fragmented and duplicated by a wide array of state institutions in the end logically demands much more state capacity than equipping and training one designated institution. Building state capacity to deal with refugees has been a cornerstone of the Lebanese Crisis Response Plan, moreover. As Uzelac and Meester (2018) demonstrate, however, this investment has had very limited effects so far. Many of my interlocutors accordingly concluded that state agencies often hide behind capacity problems.

But if capacity and will are entangled, how to identify the strategic dimensions of institutional ambiguity? As Wedeen (1999: 6) has compellingly demonstrated in her seminal work on 'ambiguities of domination,' it may be 'impossible to get into policymakers' heads and come away with exact knowledge of why they do what they do.' Political decision-makers are unlikely to see their own approach as promoting institutional ambiguity and, even if they do, would have little incentive to admit as much. The 'bugbear' with strategic ignorance, after all, is that it is '*most* successful when it is *least* detectable' (McGoey, 2019: 229). Simplistic ideas of singularly masterminded chaos are evidently unhelpful: There is 'no shadowy puppeteer working the strings' (Whyte, 2011: 19). But seeing institutional ambiguity as a 'strategy without strategists' is equally unsatisfying conceptually as well as politically (Wedeen, 1999: 153). I have shown that institutional ambiguity, like any other institutional arrangement, 'is not a matter of inertia or self-sustaining equilibria,' but the product of political decision-making (Schedler, 2013: 28).

Institutional ambiguity is a structural aspect of Lebanon's political order that is reproduced by specific governance decisions and practices. Crucially, in line with structuration theory, while Lebanon's specific hybrid order may put a premium on the reproduction of ambiguity, it does not preclude its contestation. Actors are importantly 'situated' and their agency is 'bounded,' but they *are* purposive (Jabri, 1996 in Demmers, 2017: 114). This is especially so for Lebanon's oligopolistic political elites. Power, in the end, is relative agency – the comparative capacity to change structures. That Lebanon's generic ambiguity is overwhelmingly kept in place in the realm of refugee governance thus suggests that this reproduction, overall, is in line with the interests of those with the power to initiate or prevent change.

In Lebanon, institutional ambiguity is a default logic. It would take active defiance to counterbalance it, and its reproduction will often be passive. Much of the inaction and ambiguous action that entrench institutional ambiguity evolve along the lines of status quo interests served by 'muddling through,' and in this way become cemented institutionally (Lindblom, 1959; see also Mencütek, 2019: 135). Mostly, ambiguity is not actively created as much as its existence is embraced, made use of, and thereby extended. But although the behaviour that keeps uncertainty in place will often be unintentional, state authorities 'also actively take part in the production of misunderstandings and fogginess' (Eule et al., 2018: 128). As my empirical chapters have shown, there are instances in which the production of informality, liminality, and/or exceptionalism can be linked to a specific political subject and a particular decision-making process. At crucial governance junctures, authorities opt to keep things undecided and vague, maximizing their options, which include disciplining, exploiting, and expelling refugees.

This chapter has brought the different drivers of institutional ambiguity together. It outlined how capacity and will and contingency and strategy co-constitute each other to produce and entrench institutional ambiguity. My agnotological reading of Lebanon's refugee governance thereby offers an innovative inroad into the dialectic between agency and structure in the process of governing refugees by showing how Lebanese authorities 'govern ambiguity' and are 'governing through ambiguity' at the same time (Best, 2008; see also Pinker and Harvey, 2015). Coping with or navigating institutional ambiguity and reproducing it are often two sides of the same coin, which is exactly why institutional ambiguity is so persistent. Ultimately, what makes institutional ambiguity strategic is its recurrent and systematic nature and the fact that it serves interests. Even if the often discrete individual actions of state authorities lack an explicitly coordinated shared logic, taken together they produce a form of institutional ambiguity that operates as a governmentality.

This conclusion demands a reflection on the famous dictum that knowledge is power. Approaching the many empirical paradoxes, inconsistencies, and surprises in my case-studies of Lebanon's governance of Palestinian and Syrian refugees from an ignorance studies perspective reveals that there is considerable power in being or pretending to be ignorant and in undermining others' access to clear and complete information and knowledge. This power overwhelmingly works for Lebanon's ruling regime and against refugees. Thus, while the wisdom conveyed through 'Hanlon's razor' alerts us to not attribute to malice what can adequately be explained by ignorance, there might be instances in which 'ignorance' is part of 'malice.'

Notes

1 Author's interview with a former advisor to the Minister of State for Displaced Affairs – Skype, 22 January 2018.
2 See Ashcroft, Griffiths and Tiffin (1995), Ayoob (2002), Hill (2005), Mbembe (2001), Mills (1997), Said (1978), and Sullivan and Tuana (2007) on ignorance in postcolonial thinking and Haraway (1988), Harding (1987), Hesse-Biber and Leavy (2007), Kronsell (2006), McLeod (2015), and Pinder and Harlos (2001) on ambiguity in feminist scholarship.
3 Author's interview – South Lebanon, 11 April 2013.
4 Author's interview – South Lebanon, 15 July 2014.
5 Author's interview – Skype, 15 January 2018.
6 Author's interview – Skype, 16 March 2018.
7 Author's field notes – Brussels, 24 April 2018.
8 Author's interview – Skype, 19 December 2017.
9 Author's interview with a former advisor to the Minister of Social Affairs – Skype, 9 April 2018.
10 Author's interview – Skype, 22 January 2018. This perspective that imposed illegality was state-produced to prime for eventual deportation was seconded by local authorities. A previous mayor from the Bekaa commented:

> Send them back? It is easy when the decision will be taken. We will make checkpoints. No paper? You leave! It is easy. When the decision will be taken and you have no papers you will be deported. It is not that hard to put them out. It is a political decision.
>
> (Interview – 26 March 2018)

This is now validated by the increasing deportations enabled by a decision to deport people who have irregularly entered Lebanon after 24 April 2019 – also of 'irregular entries' before that date.
11 Author's interview – Tyre, 6 July 2014.
12 Author's interview – 7 May 2013, emphasis added.
13 Author's interview – Beirut, June 9 2014.
14 Author's interview – Mar Elias camp, Beirut, 28 June 2014.
15 Author's interview – Skype, 27 March 2018.
16 Author's interview – Skype, 30 November 2017.
17 Author's interview – Tyre, 14 August 2014.
18 Notes from interview – Zahle, 7 March 2018.
19 Author's interview – Skype, 14 November 2017. Refugees may not know the evil back home as well as they think they do. Research among refugees who have returned to Syria reveals that most returnees regret this decision, which they feel they made based on misleading information about the situation in Syria (Syrian Association for Citizens' Dignity, 2019: 14).
20 Does the exploitation of refugees clash with the stated interest in refugee return? My interlocutors explained that the politicians and officials calling for refugees to leave the country know full well that mass return is unlikely. They can thus safely support this position publicly, tapping into the popular support for it, while simultaneously protecting their interests in the presence of refugees and the exploitation this allows.

References

Agier, Michel. 2008. *On the Margins of the World: The Refugee Experience Today*. Cambridge: Polity Press.
Agier, Michel. 2011. *Managing the Undesirables: Refugee Camps and Humanitarian Government*. Cambridge: Polity Press.
Alcoff, Linda Martín. 2007. 'Epistemologies of Ignorance. Three Types.' In *Race and Epistemologies of Ignorance*, edited by Shannon Sullivan and Nancy Tuana, 39–58. Albany: State University of New York Press.
Al-Masri, Muzna and Marianna Altabbaa. 2016. *Local and Regional Entanglements: The Social Stability Context in Sahel-Akkar*. Beirut: United Nations Development Program.
Amnesty International. 2015. *Pushed to the Edge: Syrian Refugees Face Increased Restrictions in Lebanon*. London: Amnesty International Publications.
Anderson, Ruben. 2014. *Illegality, Inc. Clandestine Migration and the Business of Bordering Europe*. Oakland: University of California Press.
Ansems de Vries, Leonie. 2016. 'Politics of (In)visibility: Governance-Resistance and the Constitution of Refugee Subjectivities in Malaysia.' *Review of International Studies* 42, no. 5: 876–894.
Aradau, Claudia. 2014. 'The Promise of Security: Resilience, Surprise and Epistemic Politics.' *Resilience* 2, no. 2: 73–87.
Aradau, Claudia. 2017. 'Assembling (Non-)Knowledge: Security, Law and Surveillance in a Digital World.' *International Political Sociology* 11: 327–342.
Ashcroft, Bill, Gareth Griffiths and Helen Tiffin. 1995. *The Post-Colonial Studies Reader*. London: Routledge.
Atallah, Sami and Dima Mahdi. 2017. *Law and Politics of "Safe Zones" and Forced Return to Syria: Refugee Politics in Lebanon*. Beirut: Lebanese Center for Policy Studies.
Atme, Cybele. 2019. 'Finnovation: The Case of Financializing Humanitarian Interventions in Lebanon.' MSc thesis, University of Amsterdam.

Ayoob, Mohammed. 2002. 'Inequality and Theorizing in International Relations: The Case for Subaltern Realism.' *International Studies Review* 4, no. 3: 27–48.

Bailey, Alison. 2007. 'Strategic Ignorance.' In *Race and Epistemologies of Ignorance*, edited by Shannon Sullivan and Nancy Tuana, 77–94. Albany: State University of New York Press.

Barjas, Elham. 2016. *Restricting Refugees: Measuring Municipal Power in Lebanon*. Beirut: Legal Agenda.

Best, Jacqueline. 2008. 'Ambiguity, Uncertainty and Risk: Rethinking Indeterminacy.' *International Political Sociology* 2, no. 4: 355–374.

Borrelli, Lisa Marie. 2018. 'Using Ignorance as an (Un)conscious Bureaucratic Strategy: Street-Level Practices and Structural Influences in the Field of Migration Enforcement.' *Qualitative Studies* 5, no. 2: 95–109.

Brun, Catharine. 2015. 'Active Waiting and Changing Hopes: Toward a Time Perspective on Protracted Displacement.' *Social Analysis* 59, no. 1: 19–37.

Cassani, Jacob. 2018. 'State, Sovereignty, and Sewage: Governance in a Syrian Refugee Camp and Lebanese Village in the Biqa'a Valley.' MA thesis, University College London.

Chehayeb, Kareem. 2019. 'Lebanon Troops Demolish Syrian Refugee Homes as Deadline Expires.' *Al Jazeera*, 1 July.

Christensen, Jon. 2008. 'Smoking Out Objectivity: Journalistic Gears in the Agnogenesis Machine.' In *Agnotology: The Making & Unmaking of Ignorance*, edited by Robert N. Proctor and Londa Schiebinger, 266–282. Stanford: Stanford University Press.

Chua, Liana. 2015. 'Anthropological Perspectives on Ritual and Religious Ignorance.' In *Routledge International Handbook of Ignorance Studies*, edited by Matthias Gross and Linsey McGoey, 247–255. London and New York: Routledge.

Cleaver, Francis. 2002. 'Reinventing Institutions: Bricolage and the Social Embeddedness of Natural Resource Management.' *European Journal of Development Research* 14, no. 2: 13–30.

Code, Lorraine. 2014. 'Ignorance, Injustice and the Politics of Knowledge.' *Australian Feminist Studies* 29, no. 80: 148–160.

Cranston, Sophie, Joris Schapendonk and Ernst Spaan. 2018. 'New Directions in Exploring the Migration Industries: Introduction to Special Issue.' *Journal of Ethnic and Migration Studies* 44, no. 4: 543–557.

Cullen Dunn, Elizabeth. 2012. 'The Chaos of Humanitarianism: Adhocracy in the Republic of Georgia.' *Humanity* 3, no. 1: 1–23.

Cullen Dunn, Elizabeth and Jason Cons. 2014. 'Aleatory Sovereignty and the Rule of Sensitive Spaces.' *Antipode* 46, no. 1: 92–109.

Das, Veena and Deborah Poole, eds. 2004. *Anthropology in the Margins of the State*. Oxford: James Curry.

Davies, Jonathan S. 2012. 'Network Governance Theory: A Gramscian Critique.' *Environment and Planning A: Economy and Space* 44, no. 11: 2687–2704.

Davies, Thom, Arshad Isakjee and Surindar Dhesi. 2017. 'Violent Inaction: The Necropolitical Experience of Refugees in Europe.' *Antipode* 49, no. 5: 1263–1284.

De Genova, Nicholas P. 2002. 'Migrant "Illegality" and Deportability in Everyday Life.' *Annual Review of Anthropology* 31: 419–447.

De Genova, Nicholas P. 2016. *Detention, Deportation, and Waiting: Toward a Theory of Migrant Detainability*. Geneva: Global Detention Project.

Dedieu, François, Jean-Noëll Jouzel and Giovanni Prête. 2015. 'The Production and the Function of the Under-Reporting of Farm-Workers' Pesticide Poisoning in French and Californian Regulations.' In *Routledge International Handbook of Ignorance Studies*, edited by Matthias Gross and Linsey McGoey, 297–307. London and New York: Routledge.

Demmers, Jolle. 2017. *Theories of Violent Conflict: An Introduction*. London: Routledge.

Dyke, Joe. 2015. 'Stranded Syrians at Serious Risk of Losing Refugee Status in Lebanon.' *IRIN News*, 16 March.

El Natour, Suhail. 2012. *Real Estate Ownership for Palestinian Refugees in Lebanon: The Legal Amendments (5/4/2001) and Impacts on Actual Reality*. Beirut: The Campaign for Real Estate Property Ownership for the Palestinian Refugees in Lebanon.

Enab Baladi. 2017. 'Discouraging Refugees from Staying – How Lebanon Is Forcing Syrian Refugees to Leave.' *Enab Baladi*, 18 April.

Eule, Tobias G., Lisa Marie Borrelli, Annika Lindberg and Anna Wyss. 2018. *Migrants Before the Law: Contested Migration Control in Europe*. Cham: Palgrave Macmillan.

Fakhoury, Tamirace. 2017. 'Governance Strategies and Refugee Response: Lebanon in the Face of Syrian Displacement.' *International Journal of Middle East Studies* 49: 681–700.

Fakhoury, Tamirace and Derya Ozkul. 2019. 'Syrian Refugees Return from Lebanon.' *Forced Migration Review* 62: 26–28.

Ferguson, James. 1994. *The Anti-Politics Machine: Depoliticization and Bureaucratic Power in Lesotho*. London: University of Minnesota Press.

Fiddian-Qasmiyeh, Elena, Gil Loescher, Katy Long and Nando Sigona, eds. 2014. *The Oxford Handbook of Refugee and Forced Migration Studies*. Oxford: Oxford University Press.

Franck, Anja. 2018. 'The Lesvos Refugee Crisis as Disaster Capitalism.' *Peace Review* 30, no. 2: 199–205.

Frangieh, Ghida. 2014. 'Forced Departure: How Lebanon Evades the International Principle of Non-Refoulement.' *The Legal Agenda*, 29 December.

Ghaddar, Sima. 2017. *Lebanon Treats Refugees as a Security Problem – And It Doesn't Work*. New York: The Century Foundation.

Ghanem, Nizar. 2016. *Local Governance Under Pressure. Research on Social Stability in T5 Area, North Lebanon*. Arezzo: Oxfam Italia.

Gigerenzer, Gerd and Rocio Garcia-Retamero. 2017. 'Cassandra's Regret: The Psychology of Not Wanting to Know.' *Psychological Review* 124, no. 2: 179–196.

Griffiths, Melanie. 2013. 'Living with Uncertainty: Indefinite Immigration Detention.' *Journal of Legal Anthropology* 1, no. 3: 263–286.

Gross, Matthias and Linsey McGoey, eds. 2015. *Routledge International Handbook of Ignorance Studies*. London and New York: Routledge.

Gupta, Akhil. 2012. *Red Tape: Bureaucracy, Structural Violence, and Poverty in India*. Durham: Duke University Press.

Halkort, Monika. 2019. 'Decolonizing Data Relations: On the Moral Economy of Data Sharing in Palestinian Refugee Camps.' *Canadian Journal of Communication* 44: 317–329.

Hamdan, Kamal and Lea Bou Khater. 2015. *Strategies of Response to the Syrian Refugee Crisis in Lebanon*. Beirut: Common Space Initiative.

Hanafi, Sari. 2008. 'Palestinian Refugee Camps in Lebanon: Laboratories of State-in-the-Making, Discipline and Islamist Radicalism.' Unpublished document.

Hanafi, Sari. 2010. *Governing Palestinian Refugee Camps in the Arab East: Governmentalities in Search of Legitimacy*. Beirut: American University of Beirut, the Issam Fares Institute for Public Policy and International Affairs.

Hanafi, Sari and Taylor Long. 2010. 'Governance, Governmentalities, and the State of Exception in the Palestinian Refugee Camps of Lebanon.' *Journal of Refugee Studies* 23, no. 2: 134–159.

Haraway, Donna. 1988. 'Situated Knowledges: The Science Question in Feminism and the Privilige of Partial Knowledge.' *Feminist Studies* 14, no. 3: 575–599.

Harding, Sandra, ed. 1987. *Feminism and Methodology*. Bloomington: Indiana University Press.

Harrell-Bond, Barbara. 1986. *Imposing Aid. Emergency Assistance to Refugees*. Oxford: Oxford University Press.

Hesse-Biber, Sharlene Nagy and Patricia Lina Leavy. 2007. *Feminist Research Practices: A Primer*. London: Sage Publications.

Hilhorst, Dorothea. 2016. 'Aid-Society Relations in Humanitarian Crises and Crisis Recovery.' Inaugural lecture, Erasmus University Rotterdam.

Hill, Jonathan. 2005. 'Beyond the Other? A Postcolonial Critique of the Failed State Thesis.' *African Identities* 3, no. 2: 139–154.

Jabri, Vivienne. 1996. *Discourses on Violence: Conflict Analysis Reconsidered*. Manchester: Manchester University Press.

Janmyr, Maja. 2016. 'Precarity in Exile: The Legal Status of Syrian Refugees in Lebanon.' *Refugee Survey Quarterly* 35: 58–78.

Janmyr, Maja. 2017. 'No Country of Asylum: "Legitimizing" Lebanon's Rejection of the 1951 Refugee Convention.' *International Journal of Refugee Law* 29, no. 3: 438–465.

Khalili, Laleh. 2005. 'A Landscape of Uncertainty: Palestinians in Lebanon.' *Middle East Report* 236: 34–39.

Knudsen, Are. 2009. 'Widening the Protection Gap: The "Politics of Citizenship" for Palestinian Refugees in Lebanon, 1948–2008.' *Journal of Refugee Studies* 22, no. 1: 51–73.

Knudsen, Are. 2018. 'The Great Escape? Converging Refugee Crises in Tyre, Lebanon.' *Refugee Survey Quarterly* 37, no. 1: 96–115.

Kronsell, Annica. 2006. 'Methods for Studying Silences: Gender Analysis in Institutions of Hegemonic Masculinity.' In *Feminist Methodologies for International Relations*, edited by Brooke A. Ackerly, Maria Stern and Jacqui True, 108–128. Cambridge: Cambridge University Press.

Lamontagne, Robert. 2018. 'Making the Most of Disorder: Governance and Development in Melanesia.' Paper presented at the Development Studies Association annual conference *Global Inequalities*, Manchester, 27–29 June.

Lindberg, Annika and Lisa Marie Borrelli. 2019. 'Let the Right One In? On European Migration Authorities' Resistance to Research.' *Social Anthropology* 27, no. 1: 17–32.

Lindblom, Charles E. 1959. 'The Science of "Muddling Through".' *Public Administration Review* 19, no. 2: 79–88.

Lipsky, Michael. 1980. *Street-Level Bureaucracy: Dilemmas of the Individual in Public Services*. New York: Russell Sage Foundation.

Luhmann, Niklas. 1998. 'The Ecology of Ignorance.' In *Observations on Modernity*, edited by Niklas Luhmann, 75–114. Stanford: Stanford University Press.

Lukes, Steven. 2005. *Power: A Radical View*. New York: Palgrave Macmillan.

Mair, Jonathan, Ann Kelly and Casey High. 2012. 'Introduction: Making Ignorance an Ethnographic Object.' In *The Anthropology of Ignorance: An Ethnographic Approach*, edited by Casey High, Ann Kelly and Jonathan Mair, 1–32. New York: Palgrave Macmillan.

Mallard, Grégoire and Linsey McGoey. 2018. 'Constructed Ignorance and Global Governance: An Ecumenical Approach to Epistemologies of Power.' *The British Journal of Sociology* 69, no. 4: 884–909.

Martin, Diana. 2011. 'The "Where" of Sovereign Power and Exception. Palestinian Life and Refugee Camps in Lebanon.' PhD thesis, Durham University.

Mathews, Andrew. 2008. 'State Making, Knowledge and Ignorance: Translation and Concealment in Mexican Forestry Institutions.' *American Anthropologist* 110, no. 4: 484–494.

Mbembe, Achille. 2001. *On the Postcolony.* Berkeley: University of California Press.

McGoey, Linsey. 2007. 'On the Will to Ignorance in Bureaucracy.' *Economy and Society* 36, no. 2: 212–235.

McGoey, Linsey. 2012. 'Strategic Unknowns: Towards a Sociology of Ignorance.' *Economy and Society* 41, no. 1: 1–16.

McGoey, Linsey. 2019. *The Unknowers: How Strategic Ignorance Rules the World.* London: Zed Books.

McLeod, Laura. 2015. 'A Feminist Approach to Hybridity.' *Journal of Intervention and Statebuilding* 9, no. 1: 48–69.

Meier, Daniel. 2014. 'The Refugee Issue and the Threat of a Sectarian Confrontation.' *Oriente Moderno* 94, no. 2: 382–401.

Mencütek, Zeynep. 2019. *Refugee Governance, State and Politics in the Middle East.* London: Routledge.

Mills, Charles. 1997. *The Racial Contract.* Ithaca: Cornell University Press.

Minca, Claudio. 2005. 'The Return of the Camp.' *Progress in Human Geography* 29, no. 4: 405–412.

Mourad, Lama. 2017. '"Standoffish" Policy-Making: Inaction and Change in the Lebanese Response to the Syrian Displacement Crisis.' *Middle East Law and Governance* 9: 249–266.

Nassar, Jessy and Nora Stel. 2019. 'Lebanon's Response to the Syrian Refugee Crisis – Institutional Ambiguity as a Governance Strategy.' *Political Geography* 70: 44–54.

Norman, Kelsey P. 2017. 'Ambivalence as Policy: Consequences for Refugees in Egypt.' *Égypte/Monde Arabe* 1, no. 15: 27–45.

Norman, Kelsey P. 2019. 'Inclusion, Exclusion or Indifference? Redefining Migrant and Refugee Host State Engagement Options in Mediterranean "Transit" Countries.' *Journal of Ethnic and Migration Studies* 45, no. 1: 42–60.

Parkinson, Sarah E. 2014. 'Refugee 101: Palestinians in Lebanon Show Refugees from Syria the Ropes.' *Middle East Report Online*, 3 April.

Pénet, Pierre and Grégoire Mallard. 2014. 'From Risk Models to Loan Contracts: Austerity as the Continuation of Calculation by Other Means.' *Journal of Critical Globalisation Studies* 7: 4–47.

Pinder, Craig C. and Karen Harlos. 2001. 'Employee Silence: Quiescence and Acquiescence as Responses to Perceived Injustices.' *Research in Personnel and Human Resource Management* 20: 331–369.

Pinker, Annabel and Penny Harvey. 2015. 'Negotiating Uncertainty: Neo-Liberal Statecraft in Contemporary Peru.' *Social Analysis* 59, no. 4: 15–31.

Proctor, Robert. 1995. *Cancer Wars: How Politics Shapes What We Know and Don't Know About Cancer.* New York: Basic Books.

Proctor, Robert. 2008. 'Agnotology. A Missing Term to Describe the Cultural Production of Ignorance (and Its Study).' In *Agnotology: The Making and Unmaking of Ignorance*, edited by Robert Proctor and Londa Schiebinger, 1–33. Stanford: Stanford University Press.

Proctor, Robert and Londa Schiebinger, eds. 2008. *Agnotology: The Making and Unmaking of Ignorance*. Stanford: Stanford University Press.

Ramadan, Adam. 2009. 'Destroying Nahr el-Bared: Sovereignty and Urbicide in the Space of Exception.' *Political Geography* 28: 153–163.

Ramadan, Adam and Sara Fregonese. 2017. 'Hybrid Sovereignty and the State of Exception in the Palestinian Refugee Camps in Lebanon.' *Annals of the American Association of Geographers* 107, no. 4: 949–963.

Razzaz, Omar. 1994. 'Contestation and Mutual Adjustment: The Process of Controlling Land in Yajouz, Jordan.' *Law and Society Review* 28, no. 1: 7–40.

Richter-Devroe, Sophie. 2013. '"Like Something Sacred": Palestinian Refugees' Narratives on the Right of Return.' *Refugee Survey Quarterly* 32, no. 2: 92–115.

Rodgers, Dennis. 2019. 'Gang Rule(s): Toward a Political Economy of Violence in Gangland Nicaragua.' Paper presented at the workshop Democracy and Disorder: Political Unpredictability, Illiberal Governance and Prospects for Democratic Voice, Geneva, 2–4 May.

Saghieh, Nizar. 2015. 'Manufacturing Vulnerability in Lebanon: Legal Policies and Efficient Tools of Discrimination.' *Legal Agenda*, 19 March.

Said, Edward W. 1978. *Orientalism*. New York: Random House Inc.

Sayigh, Rosemary. 2001. 'Palestinian Refugees in Lebanon: Implantation, Transfer or Return?' *Middle East Policy* 8, no. 1: 94–105.

Schedler, Andreas. 2013. *The Politics of Uncertainty: Sustaining and Subverting Electoral Authoritarianism*. Oxford: Oxford University Press.

Scheel, Stephan. 2019. *Autonomy of Migration? Appropriating Mobility Within Biometric Border Regimes*. New York: Routledge.

Scott, James. 1985. *Weapons of the Weak: Everyday Forms of Peasant Resistance*. New Haven and London: Yale University Press.

Scott, James. 1990. *Domination and the Arts of Resistance: Hidden Transcripts*. New Haven and London: Yale University Press.

Scott, James. 2009. *The Art of Not Being Governed: An Anarchist History of Upland South Asia*. New Haven: Yale University Press.

Serhan, Waleed. 2019. 'Consociational Lebanon and the Palestinian Threat of Sameness.' *Journal of Immigrant and Refugee Studies* 17, no. 2: 240–259.

Sheikh Hassan, Ismael and Sari Hanafi. 2010. '(In)Security and Reconstruction in Post-Conflict Nahr al-Barid Refugee Camp.' *Journal of Palestine Studies* 40, no. 1: 27–48.

Slater, Tom. 2012. 'The Myth of "Broken Britain": Welfare Reform and the Production of Ignorance.' *Antipode* 46, no. 4: 948–969.

Slater, Tom. 2016. 'Revanchism, Stigma, and the Production of Ignorance: Housing Struggles in Austerity Britain.' *Risking Capitalism: Research in Political Economy* 31: 23–48.

Smithson, Michael. 2008. 'Agnotology: Social Theories of Ignorance.' In *Agnotology: The Making and Unmaking of Ignorance*, edited by Robert Proctor and Londa Schiebinger, 209–229. Stanford: Stanford University Press.

Smithson, Michael. 2015. 'Ignorance Studies: Interdisciplinary, Multidisciplinary, and Transdisciplinary.' In *Routledge International Handbook of Ignorance Studies*, edited by Matthias Gross and Linsey McGoey, 385–399. London and New York: Routledge.

Spelman, Elizabeth V. 2007. 'Managing Ignorance.' In *Race and Epistemologies of Ignorance*, edited by Shannon Sullivan and Nancy Tuana, 119–131. Albany: State University of New York Press.

Stel, Nora. 2015. 'Facilitating Facts on the Ground: The "Politics of Uncertainty" and the Governance of Housing, Land, and Tenure in the Palestinian Gathering of Qasmiye, South Lebanon.' Governance and Local Development Program working paper no. 5, Yale University.

Stel, Nora. 2016. 'The Agnotology of Eviction in South Lebanon's Palestinian Gatherings: How Institutional Ambiguity and Deliberate Ignorance Shape Sensitive Spaces.' *Antipode* 48, no. 5: 1400–1419.

Stevens, Dallal. 2017. 'Access to Justice for Syrian Refugees in Lebanon.' In *States, the Law and Access to Refugee Protection: Fortresses and Fairness*, edited by Maria O'Sullivan and Dallal Stevens, 223–242. Oxford: Hart Publishing.

Suleiman, Jaber. 2006. *Marginalised Community: The Case of Palestinian Refugees in Lebanon*. Brighton: University of Sussex.

Sullivan, Shannon and Nancy Tuana. 2007. *Race and Epistemologies of Ignorance*. Albany: State University of New York Press.

Syrian Association for Citizens' Dignity. 2019. 'Between Hammer and Anvil: Motives and Experiences of Syrians Forced to Return to Assad-Held Areas.' Syrian Association for Citizens' Dignity.

Tapscott, Rebecca. 2017. 'Local Security and the (Un)Making of Public Authority in Gulu, Northern Uganda.' *African Affairs* 116, no. 462: 39–59.

Tiltnes, Age A. 2005. *Falling Behind: A Brief on the Living Condition of Palestinian Refugees in Lebanon*. Oslo: FAFO.

Tuana, Nancy. 2006. 'The Speculum of Ignorance: The Women's Health Movement and Epistemologies of Ignorance.' *Hypatia* 21, no. 3: 1–19.

Ubels, Tessa. 2019. 'Governing Empowerment. How Aid Organisations Negotiate the Empowerment of Refugees in a Context of Hybrid Governance with Donors, Syrian Refugees and the Lebanese State in Beirut since the Syrian Conflict in 2011.' MA thesis, Utrecht University.

United Nations High Commissioner for Refugees. 2015. *Syrian Refugees in Lebanon. Government Policy and Protection Concerns*. Beirut: United Nations High Commissioner for Refugees.

Uzelac, Ana and Jos Meester. 2018. *Is There Protection in the Region? Leveraging Funds and Political Capital in Lebanon's Refugee Crisis*. The Hague: Clingendael Institute.

Van der Haar, Gemma, Annelies Heijmans and Dorothea Hilhorst. 2013. 'Interactive Research and the Construction of Knowledge in Conflict-Affected Settings.' *Disasters* 37, no. 1: 20–35.

Walters, William. 2015. 'Reflections on Migration and Governmentality.' *Movements: Journal für Kritische Migrations- und Grenzregimeforschung* 1, no. 1: 1–30.

Wedeen, Lisa. 1999. *Ambiguities of Domination: Politics, Rhetoric, and Symbols in Contemporary Syria*. Chicago: University of Chicago Press.

Whyte, Zachary. 2011. 'Enter the Myopticon: Uncertain Surveillance in the Danish Asylum System.' *Anthropology Today* 2, no. 3: 18–21.

Yan, Victoria. 2017. 'Change Unlikely in Light of Palestinian Census Results.' *Daily Star*, 30 December.

Yassin, Nasser, Nora Stel and Rima Rassi. 2016. 'Organized Chaos: Informal Institution Building Among Palestinian Refugees in the Maashouk Gathering in South Lebanon.' *Journal of Refugee Studies* 29, no. 3: 341–362.

Reflections and contributions
Critically studying refugeeness, governance, and strategic ambiguity in Lebanon and beyond

> I think again that in one way or another [uncertainty] is something that's used across our region by governments to control whether it is associations or whether it is to control migrants or whether it is people. Like, to put you in a place where, like, you don't really know; it's neither black nor white, you don't know, it's a grey area where they . . . whereby they can come at one point and say 'ah, you're not registered, get out of the country.' So it can play in different ways. Being in a way in an illegal situation or under an illegal entry would in the power balance shift against you.[1]

This concluding chapter has three main objectives. It starts out with explicating the book's empirical contributions and exploring how the insights produced for refugee governance in Lebanon and the role of strategic ambiguity in it resonate more broadly. It then proceeds to outline the conceptual contributions of the book, reflecting on the implications of my core argument for debates in the fields of refugee studies, policy and governance studies, and ignorance studies. My analysis, on the one hand, brings the idea of institutionalized ambiguity as a governmentality to the field of refugee studies to help explain the systemic uncertainty that refugees often face. On the other hand, it develops thinking on strategic institutional ambiguity through the empirical insights yielded by the extreme case of refugees. In putting into conversation relevant schools of thought from refugee studies, governance and policy studies, and ignorance studies, the book analytically links the epistemic, operational, and political dimensions of institutional ambiguity.

The core thesis of this book is that the endemic informality, liminality, and exceptionalism that characterize Lebanese refugee governance have crucial strategic dimensions. Institutional ambiguity is not merely the consequence of the inevitable crisis modality of large-scale refugee arrivals or the reflection of inherent leeway built into any form of political decision-making and policy implementation. Nor is it simply the result of capacity or resource deficits characteristic of 'fragile' states. Rather, institutional ambiguity is the result of the interplay between the systemic features of hybrid order and the strategic operation of political authorities within such hybridity. Inaction and arbitrary action in terms of policy-making as well as implementation define Lebanon's engagement with refugees. This behaviour reproduces but also enhances existing unpredictability and uncertainty. Such utilization and extension of institutional ambiguity at times amounts to a politics of uncertainty that serves to bolster positions of power vis-à-vis political competitors, as well as to discipline, exploit, and expel specific populations.

In explicating the contributions that this argument makes, two crucial disclaimers that have featured throughout the book merit reiteration: Institutional ambiguity is not total and it is not always detrimental. First, institutional ambiguity is neither omnipresent, nor complete. Not-knowing is routinely strategically upheld, professed, or imposed, but this is never uncontested. I have sought to identify the manifestations and workings of institutional ambiguity and tease out their strategic dimensions, but this does not mean that any action and decision of authorities dealing with refugees will produce or reflect informality, liminality, and exceptionalism. There are ample examples of state officials, local authorities, and refugee representatives who work to defy and counter the vagueness and unpredictability that shape refugee life in Lebanon. As we have seen with the Palestinian case, recent developments promise a more explicit acknowledgement, regulation, and engagement with Palestinians living in Lebanon. For Syrians, too, the importance of the watershed moments in 2014 and 2015, when the government shifted from denial to repression and thereby left no-policy-policy behind, should not be downplayed.

I have focused on the policy realms of status, shelter, and representation specifically, where ambiguity has been particularly prone and which thus serve as helpful cases to explore the work that uncertainty does as a governmentality. In other sectors, such as service provision and the labour market, regularization by the relevant national line ministries has been less opaque, at least with regard to Syrian refugees. The distribution of institutional ambiguity can vary across sectors, populations, and regions. Indeed, it is exactly the fact that ambiguity is not omnipresent that denotes its strategic nature. That the Lebanese government now extensively organizes and plans the so-desired return of Syrian refugees, for instance, highlights that previous inactivity in different governance realms has been a matter of choice as much as capacity. There is sufficient ability to restrict, but not enough resources to protect.

Institutional ambiguity is thus always partial. And it need not be problematic. 'Unknowing' has emancipatory potential (McGoey, 2019). Institutional ambiguity is also simply indispensable from an opportunistic point of view. Any form of governance and policy-making requires a dose of ambiguity to operate beyond theory and ideology, regardless of the issue or setting. When it comes to refugee governance, ambivalent policies can, for instance, help integrate refugees (Norman, 2019). Although this is arguably not the case in Lebanon, the fact that Lebanon alone for a long time hosted more Syrian refugees than the entire European Union, many have argued, was only possible because of the ambiguity that was enabled by the absence of 'parameters governing migration and refugee policy' (Hourani and Sensenig-Dabbous, n.d.).

My own cases also show that ambiguity may sometimes be the best possible option under restrictive circumstances. Reflecting on the prospective regularization of provincial refugee governance in the Syrian case, a humanitarian professional lamented the overturning of the previous, more informal, system, which 'had its flaws,' but at least was faster.[2] Non-implementation, too, was at times heralded as something positive. A lawyer working for a Lebanese human rights organization noted that in the face of restrictive policies, 'it is a good thing not to practice the official policy.'[3] The stance of local authorities looking away in the face of refugee 'transgressions' such as electricity hooking was similarly considered a form of ambiguity that was sympathetic rather than repressive. But while institutional ambiguity in principle also allows for constructive or subversive forms of (self-)governance, this, as detailed in Chapter 6, is not how it plays out overall when it comes to refugee governance in Lebanon. The appropriation of ignorance that underlies the politics of uncertainty is overwhelmingly a privilege of the powerful.

Empirical contributions: Lebanon and its refugees

This book has been one of the first to offer an analysis of Lebanon's response to the Syrian refugee crisis that is comprehensive in that it regards multiple fundamental domains of governance and considers both policy and practice on a national as well as a local level. It has gone beyond description and offered a specific reading of Lebanon's response to the arrival of Syrian refugees through the lens of strategic ambiguity. Bringing Lebanon's historical experiences with Palestinian refugees into the analysis of the more recent Syrian refugee crisis and exploring the parallels between these cases in terms of the constitutive role of institutional ambiguity, moreover, reveals how the Lebanese engagement with Syrians may be determined by the attempt to avoid another Palestinian conundrum, but in many ways nevertheless replicates it. These new analytical vantage points show that many of the apparent contradictions in Lebanon's response to the Syrian refugee presence – simultaneous paralysis and repression, denial and securitization, benefiting and suffering from – are often mutually constitutive.

Lebanon's protracted Palestinian refugee presence has logically been scrutinized longer and more extensively than the more recent presence of Syrian refugees. What my analysis adds to this plethora of existing studies of Palestinians in Lebanon is an encompassing perspective that brings together historical accounts and contemporary case-studies. As with the Syrian case, the innovative vantage point of a politics of uncertainty sheds new light on some of the central paradoxes in previous work on Lebanon's Palestinians. The insights facilitated by the notion of strategic institutional ambiguity can help understand how Palestinian refugees in Lebanon have been tightly controlled and largely abandoned at the same time, politically integrated into Lebanon's sectarian oligopolistic logics on the one hand while institutionally excluded on the other. Juxtaposing the Palestinian case with the more recent dealings with Syrian refugees, furthermore, reminds us that no-policy-policies and formal informalities do not just historically emerge but are actively produced. This foregrounds the strategic dimensions of the protracted status quo that Lebanon's Palestinian refugees face.

My analysis does not just help us to better understand Lebanon's engagement with refugees. In many ways, Lebanese authorities' engagement with refugees is an extreme version of the manner in which they consolidate power over their Lebanese constituencies (Al-Masri, Altabaa and Abla, 2016: 5; International Alert and Lebanon Support, 2017: 5). A refugee expert who has worked for several Lebanese ministries linked what she called a politics of evasion to the specificities of Lebanon's political order that is characterized by veto-power:

> Anything that is problematic and that might not get a consensus gets evaded, any kind of topic. So if this is something there is no agreement on among the political parties, instead of dealing with it, we just live in denial and we evade it, put it on the side. So it's this policy of evasion throughout, where you just start accumulating all these problems on the side because you don't want to deal with them. And when you don't want to deal with your problems, you're just leaving them to sort themselves out. If some of these decisions were against, like . . . the conviction or the opinion of some political party in the Council of Ministers, then these kinds of decisions would get vetoed because our Council of Ministers has the veto power. So anyone . . . all the decisions need to come out with consensus. And if that's not the case, it's always easier to get consensus on not doing anything.[4]

There are more parallels. Deliberate ambiguity regarding, or the flagrant absence of, numbers and statistics is a common Lebanese feature, too. It is not just refugees who are not registered in Lebanon, which has carefully avoided any national census since 1932 and is renowned for its lack of governmental statistics. One analyst pointedly noted that: 'I think there is a certain history here in terms of not counting things very clearly.'[5] Similarly, Lebanese policy that has nothing to do with refugees is hardly clear-cut in its formulation, communication, and implementation either. It routinely exhibits a 'high degree of vagueness,' which prevents relevant stakeholders from holding state agencies accountable (Atallah, Dagher and Mahmalat, 2019: 1). The forms of indirect rule that Lebanese authorities impose on refugee communities and their representatives reflect the mediated forms of stateness that characterize the country at large. The use of informal brokers that are co-opted as security agents reflects the tactics that Lebanon's sectarian bosses use to 'police their political enclaves' (Ghaddar, 2017). Through studying Lebanon's ambiguous governance of refugees, this book thus breaks new ground in understanding Lebanese governance in general. Specifically, it offers food for thought regarding two dominant debates on the contemporary Lebanese state.

This first regards the never-abating discussion on state fragility and state absence referred to in Chapter 1. Using refugee governance as an entry point towards revealing the centrality of strategic ambiguity in the operations of Lebanese state agencies, my book construes the Lebanese state as not so much weak, fragmented, or failed, but rather as mediated and hybrid. Lebanon's refugee governance offers an inroad into the 'multifarious landscape of fractured and hybrid sovereignties' (Ramadan and Fregonese, 2017: 2). Exploring hybrid order as the systemic reflection of a constantly reproduced politics of uncertainty allows for a constructive rather than pathological understanding of its 'quasischizophrenic' concurrent weakness and menace (Kosmatopoulos, 2011; Obeid, 2010).

Borgmann and Slim (2018: 10) have provocatively pointed out that when the informality, liminality, and exceptionalism that shape the Lebanese approach to refugees are explained away as a contingency of asylum-specific capacity deficits, crucial questions remain unanswered. Taking stock of the country's ambivalent policy towards refugees, they wonder: 'Is the absence of Lebanese public policy and widespread contentment with both the litany of rhetorical statements and the oppressive silence on this important topic the most genuine example of targeted Lebanese policy?' (Borgmann and Slim, 2018: 10–11). This book has demonstrated that – with the usual collection of nuances and disclaimers – the answer would be 'yes.'

The second key debate about the nature of the post–Civil War Lebanese state that the book speaks to is that of consensus versus polarization. Lebanon's consociational system puts a premium on elite consensus as sectarian-political leaders depend on each other as much as on their constituencies to maintain their power positions. But the extreme polarization between different political alliances in terms of geopolitical positioning, most strikingly so with regard to the Syrian tutelage over Lebanon until 2005 and the Syrian War since 2011, has been a defining feature of modern Lebanon. The governance of refugees – although it displays significant variation across Lebanon's regions and the respective local political-sectarian regimes – overall underscores that the basic elite consensus that is at the heart of the country's formal consociational system and informal oligopolistic logic remains an essential foundation of post–Civil War Lebanon. It confirms Mazzola's (2019: 14) reading of Lebanon's hybrid order as an 'intentional product of institutional engineering' to facilitate sectarian clientelism.

As crucially validated by the events of the 2019 'October Revolution,' no matter how antagonistic they may be with regard to regional politics, domestically Lebanon's elites share crucial stakes in the status quo. These stakes include the minimization and pacification of refugee populations. According to Lebanese advisors and consultants that have worked inside various ministries, this common interest in the status quo extends beyond refugee governance. Institutional ambiguity allows Lebanon's elites to agree to disagree politically without having to resolve such disagreements through actual policies and to protect their mutually dependent power positions accordingly.

Beyond these empirical contributions to discussions centred on Lebanon, my case-studies offer conceptual insights in terms of our understanding of forced displacement, of power and authority, and of knowledge and ignorance. The next

section accordingly engages with critical scholarly debates in the respective fields
of refugee studies, governance and policy studies, and ignorance studies.

Conceptual contributions: implications for studying strategic institutional ambiguity

Refugee studies

Lebanon featured as the central case in this book for a reason, But that the idea
of a politics of uncertainty isespecially relevant there, does not mean it is only
relevant there. Although the Lebanese state is particularly fragmented in terms of
policy-making, Mencütek (2019: 244, 2, 252) notes that institutionally ambiguous refugee governance emerged not just in Lebanon, but in Turkey and Jordan
as well, particularly around the demarcation of mandates, but also with regard to
registration practices (see also Fakhoury, 2017: 694; Norman, 2019). In Turkey,
Ilcan, Rygiel, and Baban (2018) demonstrate, precarity is produced through ambiguity in registration status (see also Memişoğlu and Ilgit, 2017; Öner and Genç,
2015). In Jordan, ambiguity is the defining feature of refugee spaces (Achilli and
Oesch, 2016; Oesch, 2017). Inconsistent and volatile policies (Schmidt, 2019) and
the political utilization of discrepant refugee figures (Lenner, 2019) are indicative
of wider institutional ambiguity in Jordan as well. These parallels mean that by
further conceptualizing the political productivity of ambiguity, the book enhances
our understanding of refugee governance in the Middle East, a region usually
underappreciated in migration studies (Mencütek, 2019: 5).

The reach of the argument that strategic institutional ambiguity can be a key
feature of refugee governance does not stop with the Middle East. It can be
extended to European governance. In fact, the idea of a politics of uncertainty
could help undercut one of the most problematic assumptions in the refugee studies field, namely that 'regional' refugee governance in the Global South is fundamentally different from 'third country' refugee governance in the Global North
(Chimni, 1998; see also Sanyal, 2018: 70). This dominant idea that, as Nawyn
(2016: 164 in Mencütek, 2019: 31) suggests, 'migration in the Global South constitutes something that is consistently and starkly distinct from what we see in the
Global North' may be true on many accounts, but there are also crucial similarities
in the migration regimes of regional host countries and Europe. The centrality of
strategic ambiguity is one of those (Stel, 2018).

A full exploration of the parallels between regional and European refugee governance in terms of governing through uncertainty is beyond the scope of the
current book. However, as illustrated in the references to literature based on European case-studies throughout my analysis, there is ample evidence that strategic
inaction and ambiguity and the feigning, maintaining, and imposing of ignorance
are a central aspect of the European migration regime (Ansems de Vries and
Guild, 2019; Oomen et al., 2019; Borrelli, 2018; De Genova, 2017; Eule et al.,
2018; Scheel, 2019; Scheel and Ustek-Spilda, 2019; Schuster, 2011; Slominski

and Trauner, 2018; Tekin, 2019; Vianelli, 2017) – with striking examples available from, for instance, the Balkans (Minca, Šantić and Umek, 2019), Denmark (Suárez-Krabbe and Lindberg, 2019; Whyte, 2011), France (Davies, Isakjee and Dhesi, 2017; Hagan, 2018, 2020), Malta (Lemaire, 2014, 2019), Sweden (Qvist, 2017), the Netherlands (Kalir, 2017), the United Kingdom (Canning, 2018; Darling, 2017a, 2017b; Hughes, 2019), and Greece (Franck, 2019; Rozakou, 2017), Italy (Caprioglio, Ferri and Gennari, 2018; Heyer, 2019; Pinelli, 2018; Tuckett, 2019), and the broader Mediterranean hotspot system.

Investigating these similarities in terms of ambiguity is important because it helps us to better understand the entirety of modern governmentalities of forced migration, but also because it crucially interrogates the moral exceptionalism often bestowed on the assumed rational and rule of law–based approach of Western states. The conceptual vocabulary used to explore refugee governance 'in the region' can shine a new, more critical light on refugee governance closer to home. As the first account to explicitly and comprehensively theorize strategic institutional ambiguity as a central governmentality in state approaches to refugees, the book has sought to open up an analytical arena to juxtapose accounts of refugee governance from what so far have usually been considered essentially different contexts.

Beyond putting into conversation the often geographically siloed accounts of refugee governance through reflecting on the commonality of institutional ambiguity, my argument resonates with various elemental debates in the refugee studies field. The first of these regards ambiguity specifically, more precisely the fact that the focus of refugee scholars is still predominantly on the destabilizing effect of displacement. This book lends further credibility to the emerging work that poses that host state policy is at least as important in creating and upholding the institutional ambiguity that refugees experience. My book has traced the political 'production of doubt' and placed it squarely at the centre of refugee governance (Aradau, 2017: 330). Bringing insights from scholars working on hybrid order and strategic ignorance to refugee studies, it suggests handles to not just acknowledge uncertainty as a governmentality, but to actually study it as such. This underpins critical refugee studies' mission to go beyond the traditional focus on the humanitarian conditions of displaced people and put their political conditions centre stage (Chimni, 1998; Hanafi, 2008). If the foundational mission of refugee studies is to make experiences of forced displacement, the 'placeless spaces' and 'chaotic socio-political states' of people 'left waiting,' understandable, then the idea of a politics of uncertainty is my contribution towards furthering such understanding (Agier, 2008: vii).

A second core theme of refugee studies that this book links to concerns the interplay between protracted and recent refugee 'crises' and related questions of policy legacies and institutional learning (Lenner, 2016). I analyzed the world's most drawn-out refugee experience in tandem with a more recently created refugee situation. This uniquely illustrates how states' attempts to prevent the replication of previous episodes of refugee governance often generate different forms of ambiguity but at the same time reinstate its centrality. Lebanon's Palestinian and Syrian refugees importantly differ in terms of status (Palestinians are recognized as refugees, Syrians are not), shelter (Palestinians mostly live in formal and informal camps, Syrians are largely 'self-settled'), and representation (Palestinians have established political institutions, Syrians are precluded from any such political organization). But both communities face legal, spatial, temporal, and political ambiguities that determine much of their lives in Lebanon and that render them controllable, exploitable, and expellable. Authorities' institutional learning and institutional entrapment thus go hand-in-hand. The crucial tenet of strategic institutional ambiguity to keep refugee presences informal, temporary, and exceptional shows how refugeeness can be almost indefinitely reproduced as a result of not merely enduring displacement but also enduring uncertainty.

My conceptualization of strategic institutional ambiguity as a governmentality also takes the scholarship on the constituent parts of refugee governance that I have focused on – status, shelter, and representation – further. It does so by conceptually linking them, demonstrating that precarious legal status, informal encampment, and impediments to political mobilization do not come alone but tend to be part of a more intricately related governmentality. This makes their marginalizing power more profound and the need to determine the political economies behind them more pressing. The absence of legal frameworks for asylum is not a given but a choice of ruling elites. Formal camps are not 'machines of ordering,' but in reality are as 'ambiguous, undetermined, and unfulfilled' as informal settlements or self-settlement modalities (Diken and Laustsen, 2005: 17 in Katz, 2016: 146; Agier, 2008: 65). Lack of refugee organization, 'voice,' or 'ownership' is the result of refugees' personal considerations and the ad-hocish committee obsession of many humanitarian actors, but it also stems from authorities' fragmentation, co-optation, and divide-and-rule tactics that keep in place informality, liminality, and exceptionalism.

These conclusions help account for why, despite far-reaching socio-economic inclusion, institutional exclusion of refugees can remain firmly in place. They also demand a reconsideration of the (un)voluntary nature of refugee returns. While the prevention of refoulement has been the cornerstone of international refugee law, critical scholars have long since shown how deportation (Kalir, 2014, 2019), deportability (De Genova, 2002), and enforced mobility (Tazzioli, 2017) in practice often result in de facto refoulement or even a 'deadly refoulement industry' (Stierl, 2019). As my cases have shown, uncertainty can be such a profoundly undermining and unsettling state that precludes wellbeing to such an extent that the voluntary nature of returns that occur as the result of a politics of uncertainty should be considered with extreme skepticism.

Governance and policy studies

My central argument draws on emerging insights in critical refugee studies and builds on empirical cases of refugee governance. The insights that this analysis yields, however, are not limited to the governance of refugees. On the one hand, scholars assume that the way refugees are treated can tell us something about broader dynamics of state power because refugees are construed as the antithesis of citizens, the exception that sheds light on the rule. This particularly regards questions of order and disorder since refugees are routinely considered a threat to the 'national order of things' (Malkki, 1995). On the other hand, it is often argued that the governance of refugees can elucidate governance at large not because it reveals the opposite of the ways in which political authorities govern citizens but because it exposes extreme versions of such 'normal' governance.

It is evident that refugees are discursively produced as the ultimate 'other.' This has been amply demonstrated for Palestinians (Czajka, 2012; Hanafi, 2008; Peteet, 2005; Serhan, 2019) as well as Syrians (Atallah and Mahdi, 2017; Ghaddar, 2017) in Lebanon. These political realities notwithstanding, analytically this book validates the second perspective. Refugee governance can be read as an extreme case of governance at large and offers a unique window on, or 'weathervane' for, power dynamics more broadly (Bakewell, 2014: 135; Bully, 2014: 76; Edwards and Van Waas, 2014: 290; Eule et al., 2018: 56; Gibney, 2014: 54; Oesch, 2015: 3; Stepputat and Nyberg Sørensen, 2014: 88; Biehl, 2015: 68).

Some aspects of the politics of uncertainty leveled against refugees are specific to their situation as displaced people. Subjecting them to institutional ambiguity might be easier to legitimate because of their limited political capital as non-citizens. Refugees face even more informality (due to lack of citizenship and residency status), more extreme liminality (due to temporary stay), and more exceptionalism (due to distinct and often patchy legal frameworks). But the ways in which institutional ambiguity is utilized in governing refugees reveals logics of rule that are equally pertinent to understand the governance of citizens. This is the case because while those being governed might differ, those doing the governing do not. The governance repertoires developed to control one population affect the strategies of governance adopted to deal with other populations.

In this sense, refugees reflect a broader category of those considered 'undesirable' by political elites, ranging from the poor to the foreign (Agier, 2008: viii; Bayat, 1997: 55–56; Malkki, 1995: 495; Sanyal, 2014: 559). As recognized in Chomsky's (2012) notion of the 'precariat,' a class deemed expendable and kept perpetually on the edge of subsistence by dominant economic and political elites, for many rulers undesirables include citizens as well. In contexts where the civil and political rights that set citizens apart from refugees are notoriously provisional in reality, the very distinction between these different populations might be questioned. In political orders, whether authoritarian or democratic, where those in charge regard citizens – or certain groups of citizens – as an obstacle to rather than a legitimation for their power, the strategic use of institutional ambiguity will be a relevant modality of governance.

Then what exactly does the institutional engagement with refugees tell us about the organization of public goods and collective representation and the workings of power at large? Synthesizing refugee studies and ignorance studies, this book suggests it says two fundamental things. First, that policies and practices of rule do not emerge or prevail only despite of or in opposition to ambiguity, but function through it. Institutional ambiguity is not an anomaly; it is constitutive of governance. Informality, liminality, and exceptionalism do not just happen, but are made to happen – sometimes unconsciously and indirectly, sometimes quite deliberately. The complication and disturbance of knowledge economies occasionally stems from concrete inactions and arbitrary actions that can and should be identified, explored, and, where possible, attributed. Doing so has implications for how we might conceive of power. Further sophisticating potential applications of Foucauldian governmentality, the idea of strategic institutional ambiguity allows for a reconsideration of what we regard as reasons, techniques, and subjects of government. It further substantiates the potential rationality of illegibility; construes inaction and ambiguity as a possible mechanism of governance; and allows for the consideration of strategically produced 'ambiguous subjects' (Atme, 2019: 107). Power is the capacity to set agendas for what is not known and to exploit the uncertainty that follows from this capacity (McGoey, 2019: 40).

Second, the twin notions of institutional ambiguity and the politics of uncertainty allow us to take our analysis of the strategic nature of ambiguity further than the general claim that it serves governing actors to accumulate power. That policy paradoxes follow from inter- and intra-organizational conflicts and tensions is usually well-recognized. What my analysis shows, however, is that in some cases the political utilization of uncertainty is not just an instrument in inter-elite competition for power and resources, but can also function as a more concerted governmentality to undermine and fragment the organization of specific 'problematic' groups. It thereby reveals logics of rule that tie together elites who are often perceived as predominantly antagonistic.

These points particularly resonate with academic debates on state hybridity. The hybrid nature of specific state systems, shaped by colonial legacies and neocolonial geopolitics, is in policy circles often still considered a form of fragility or failure. Yet hybridity can only be understood when looking into the productive aspects of chaos, disorder, and uncertainty. The 'renewed sociology of governance' that hybrid settings demand requires a recognition of the strategic as well as the contingent components of institutional ambiguity (Raeymaekers, Menkhaus and Vlassenroot, 2008: 9). As I further detail in the next section, the occurrence of institutional ambiguity need not signal a 'breakdown in rationality,' but points towards different, more complex, rationalities (McGoey, 2007: 228, 2019; see also Hull, 2012: 25). The fluidity of the boundaries between categories that political scientists prefer to project as binaries – the legal and the illegal, the public and the private, state weakness and strength – serves political purposes (Migdal, 2001; Tapscott, 2017).

This conclusion revitalizes key insights produced by the anthropology of the state, specifically on how stateness might be generated in hybrid orders. My findings add empirical substance to work that shows that ideas of stateness are produced through the inaction or absence of state systems (Eule et al., 2018: 230;

Lund, 2006; Nielsen, 2007: 695). Ambiguity or illegibility can define the state not as a failing but as a potent assemblage of actors (Das and Poole, 2004). State authority is not just conjured through performances and claims of expert knowledge and official legibility (Boswell, 2009). The uncertainty that follows from the unpredictability and arbitrariness facilitated by institutional ambiguity is a powerful 'state effect' as well (Mitchell, 1990: 94).

As acknowledged in my conceptual framework and evident throughout my empirical analysis, the linkages between the practices of particular state representatives and the strategies of state agencies, or even 'the state' as such, are inherently complicated, even more so in hybrid political orders where the state idea and the state system are only loosely aligned, but particular knowledge patterns or styles can be associated with governance by particular organizations (Freeman and Sturdy, 2014 in Sedlacko and Dahlvik, 2017). This is no different for patterns or styles of not-knowing. As my case-studies showed, this might be demonstrated by juxtaposing the experiences and practices of state representatives at different bureaucratic levels and investigating their 'role-play' of denying or ignoring information that is evidently exchanged between them (see also Eule et al., 2018; Kalir and Rozakou, 2016: 9). Studying the production, protection, and amplification of institutional ambiguity helps account for the persistence of mediated and negotiated forms of stateness that encompass strategic forms of indirect rule (Blundo, 2006; Hagmann and Péclard, 2010; Menkhaus, 2006; Stel, 2015, 2016, 2017).

The 'real' governance that takes place in defiance of Weberian ideal types is, unsurprisingly, most often captured in studies that focus on non-Western settings (Blundo and Le Meur, 2009; Gupta, 1995; Olivier de Sardan, 2008). The insights produced by these studies, however, are also relevant to the Western countries whose aspirations these classical political science concepts reflect. Like scholars of migration, scholars of governance, policy, and politics would do well to shed the assumptions that logics of rule and modalities of governing are inherently or inevitably different in the South and the North. Synthesizing insights on strategic uncertainty from refugee, governance, and ignorance studies reveals the universality of institutional ambiguity and its political utilization. It shows that institutional ambiguity is more prevalent in some places at some times for some people and that its strategic uses are highly contextual, but it also discards the idea that governance through uncertainty is a phenomenon that is typical for or limited to 'weak' or hybrid states. The 'troubling relationship between (mis)information and state power' is evident everywhere (Slater, 2012: 948).

This book reiterates the relevance of studying the state even, or especially, when it is deemed absent and despite the humanitarianization of refugee governance (see also Ilcan, Rygiel and Baban, 2018). But producing unpredictability and arbitrariness through institutionalizing informality, liminality, and exceptionalism as a way to 'sabotage accountability,' 'disable voice' and control, and discipline rivalling authorities and constituencies is a crucial feature of 'strong' authoritarian states as well (Glasius, 2018). As considered in detail in the Introduction, practices like deliberate non-recording are omnipresent in liberal democracies too, suggesting that state control anywhere operates through ambiguity as well as specification (Hull, 2012: 248). The diffuse and polycentric assemblages and opaque regimes that emerge in contexts of New Public Management initiatives and neoliberal outsourcing are rife with strategic forms of ambiguity that might be different from those that prevail in hybrid orders, but can be very similar as well (Best, 2012; Guazzone and Pioppi, 2012; McGoey, 2019).

Strategic inaction and ambiguity may then well go hand in hand with bureaucratic illusions of legibility, expertise, and capacity (Griffiths, 2013: 279; Kalir and Van Schendel, 2017; Norman, 2005: 196). To define 'modernity' by its efforts to eliminate ambivalence is to buy into these illusions (Bauman, 1993; Scott, 1985, 2009; Chabal and Daloz, 1999). Those interested in the different guises that power can take should look beyond rituals of order. Although politics of uncertainty may be most palpable with regard to refugee populations in hybrid political orders, it is fruitful for scholars of political authority, governance, and public administration everywhere to infuse their analyses with the consideration that sometimes 'uncertainty rather than certainty is the norm' (Horst and Grabska, 2015: 10).

Ignorance studies

As Gross and McGoey (2015) concluded in their seminal handbook on ignorance studies some years ago, the insight that ignorance is socially constructed is no longer a novel one. It is time, they found, to move on from marveling about the fact that ignorance is constructed to exploring how and why it is constructed. This book contributes to such emerging epistemologies of ignorance that reflect on how best to examine and understand the production and sustainability of not-knowing or 'unknowledges' in several ways (Sullivan and Tuana, 2007). My main contribution to ignorance studies concerns the conceptual framework outlined in the Introduction and sophisticated in Chapter 6. In putting the notion of ambiguity centre stage, the book challenges residual dichotomous understandings of knowledge and ignorance that at times still implicitly underpin ignorance studies (Bailey, 2007). The strategic value of not-knowing, I show, often lies not in the flat absence of knowledge but in its uncertainty and unpredictability.

My approach seeks to move away from the disciplinary fragmentation of the relatively young field of ignorance studies. It does so by suggesting a concrete, operationalized framework. The concept of institutional ambiguity is not a new one, but the operationalization furthered here, which takes cues from refugee studies by focusing on informality, liminality, and exceptionalism, gives the idea of institutional ambiguity new substance. My framework offers explicit handles on where and how to look for it and how to study it comprehensively, linking domains and levels of governance that are often investigated separately. Rather than researching, for instance, ambiguous legal categorizations, practices of non-recording, spatial informalities, and temporal uncertainties on a case-by-case basis, the framework employed here allows for an analysis that links different manifestations of institutional ambiguity.

The idea of institutional ambiguity puts forward a systematic and comprehensive approach to locating and describing instances of unpredictable and uncertain governance. The related concept of a politics of uncertainty engages with the possibly strategic dimensions of such ambiguity by interrogating how empirical instances of informality, liminality, and exceptionalism come to be and persist. By investigating different categories of behaviour in concrete settings and moments, the concept of a politics of uncertainty goes beyond construing ambiguity as a result and manifestation of not-knowing. Drawing on critical policy studies and Foucauldian work on governance, it links (not-)knowing to (not-)acting. It thereby suggests that studying what people do and do not do is a helpful way to approach the far more elusive question of what people know and do not know that is central to ignorance studies.

Through these dual concepts of institutional ambiguity and the politics of uncertainty, the book speaks to key debates in the literature on strategic ignorance. Central to this is the way in which my framework and analysis allow for differentiation, showing that institutional ambiguity is never a generic reality, but crucially varies on spatial and temporal dimensions and for different societal groups. These differentiations, moreover, do not emerge by chance but are produced through patterns of inaction and partial and arbitrary action. Such production, crucially, itself occurs through actors that relate and interact in a hybrid – as in fragmented and often inconsistent – manner that complicates the attribution of particular manifestations of ambiguity. But, although complicated, my book shows that such attribution is now and then possible through carefully contextualized analysis.

This relates to another central concern of scholars working on socio-political ignorance: the question of intentionality. As discussed in detail in Chapter 6, apart from explicit 'confessions,' it is extremely challenging and problematic to assess the possibly deliberate nature of not-knowing. Yet lack of evidence is not the same as evidence that something does not exist (McGoey, 2019: 142). And as my case-studies have illustrated, linking specific outcomes for specific groups – in terms of informality, liminality, and exceptionalism in the domains of status, shelter, and representation – to specific behaviour of specific authorities – in terms of inaction and partial and arbitrary action – and the stated as well as unstated objectives of these authorities – in terms of politics and economics – offers a way to make visible and credible the strategic dimensions of ambiguity and uncertainty. Since inaction and arbitrary action are contingent more often than they are strategic, this is not a plea for a purely functionalist reading of institutional ambiguity. Rather, it suggests an analytical toolkit for those interested in teasing out the aspects of ambiguity that are strategically pursued. This take on strategy is not limited to or centred on deliberate planning for ambiguity. Rather, it denotes the opportunistic toleration, elaboration, or appropriation of informality, liminality, and exceptionalism. It thereby underpins McGoey's (2007: 228) conception of the rationality of ignorance as a more situated legitimation of inaction or ambiguous action that goes beyond an economistic equation of rationality with self-interest (Friedman, 2005).

This concerns the dialectic between agency and structure that is fundamental to ignorance studies. The cases explored in this book have shown institutional ambiguity to be a governmentality that is produced by the mutual constitution of political structure, here referred to as hybrid political order, and political agency, explored as a politics of uncertainty. Hybrid order breeds a politics of uncertainty, which in turn props up hybrid order. This interpretation of institutional ambiguity also links the two constitutive analytical strands in the field of ignorance studies: imposing ignorance on others on the one hand and maintaining or feigning one's own ignorance on the other hand. These two dimensions of socio-political not-knowing can be largely separate processes but, my analysis suggests, more often are intricately related. Defensive and offensive ignorance go hand in hand (McGoey, 2019). Professing or protecting that which one does not know (and does not want to know) often inevitably manufactures the not-knowing of others, depriving them of potential sources of information. Similarly, while imposing ignorance on others often requires knowledge on what these others should not know, it also means that having this knowledge should be hidden or denied. In revealing the productive aspects of not-knowing in Lebanese refugee governance, the book contributes to ignorance studies' quest to put the phenomenon of not-knowing on the map as a process rather than an attribute, 'an active accomplishment requiring ever-vigilant understanding of what not to know' (Gross and McGoey, 2015: 5; see also Frye, 1983 in Sullivan and Tuana, 2007: 2).

By engaging with these questions of imposing, feigning, and maintaining ignorance, we enter the realm of knowledge and power. My empirical analysis draws on and in turn sophisticates the new perspectives on power in relation to epistemic politics that ignorance studies offers (Mallard and McGoey, 2018). Exploring when and where and how institutional ambiguity follows from lack of political will to govern more consistently and how this relates to a lack of capacity to govern in a comprehensive and comprehensible way makes visible and complicates processes of domination (Lemke, 2000: 7). It allows for a critical reading of institutional ambiguity, which can be a manifestation of failure but also of violence (Ansems de Vries and Guild, 2019). In Lebanon, Carpi (2019) has compellingly shown, state liminality should not be mistaken for neutrality. It is a deliberate stance that allows violent neglect and renders passivity a form of enmity. As Tapscott (2017) shows, institutionalized arbitrariness might be a way for 'weak' states to be powerful, but our understanding of agnotological power as a form of violence should not be limited to so-called weak states (Davies, Isakjee and Dhesi, 2017). Inaction and ambiguous action amount to structural violence and shift biopolitics to necropolitics in governance dynamics in the Global North as well (Eule et al., 2018: 237).

A crucial concern for those studying socio-political ignorance is whether institutional ambiguity is a form of disorder or whether it constitutes a different order (De Waal, 2019). My analysis suggests it is both. The projection and production of disorder through imposing and feigning ignorance makes this disorder a given for some and an instrument for others. This is never absolute or static. Controlling knowledge through imposing ignorance means that some people, namely those who can choose to maintain and feign their ignorance, understand a particular institutional setting better than others. This distinction is always only partial and temporary, however, as was illustrated by the fact that state authorities in different localities and operating on different bureaucratic levels or under different mandates have vastly different understandings of the same policies and practices.

My analysis shows that institutional ambiguity can nevertheless attain hegemonic properties. This might seem counterintuitive in light of the Lebanese state's often proclaimed weakness and fragmentation. Dominance, however, here does not denote the coercive strength of individual state agencies, but rather the inescapability of the organizing logic of the Lebanese hybrid order and the politics of uncertainty that flourishes within it. Institutional ambiguity is often reproduced by those suffering from it. Following Hall (1988: 44 in Wedeen, 1999: 11), 'it becomes the horizon of the taken-for-granted: what the world is and how it works, for all practical purposes. . . [and sets] the limit to what will appear as rational, reasonable, credible, indeed sayable or thinkable' (see also Scott, 1985: 326). Refugees themselves, their representatives or authorities, and those humanitarian organizations claiming to help them have creative ways to deal with and at times subvert institutional ambiguity, but they are implicated in it as well (Cullen Dunn and Cons, 2014: 102), a situation that Ismail (2006: xxxv) has captured as 'the mutual ensnarement of rulers and ruled.'

The dual nature of ignorance as a form of domination and a form of contention and contestation is of great significance to ignorance studies (Bailey, 2007; Mathews, 2008; Parnell, 2000; Sullivan and Tuana, 2007; Raj, 2000). My analysis connects strategic forms of uncertainty to widely recognized realities of socio-economic and political vulnerability and marginalization. This shows that such precarity is a component of a yet more encompassing and more nefarious institutional ambiguity (Van Kooy and Bowman, 2019). This also means that coping with such manufactured vulnerability often reproduces ambiguity. This complicates our understandings of (possibilities for) resistance. It opens up new ontological approaches to forms of resistance that are 'silent,' 'everyday,' and/or non-overtly politicized (Bayat, 1997; Scott, 1985). Most crucially, it drives home the inherent co-constitution of oppression and resistance not just practically or politically, but epistemologically.

Positionality and future research

The nature of academia as a knowledge-generating business is in special need of reflection when questions of knowing and not-knowing are objects of investigation. Empirically studying not-knowing is fraught with inherent complexities. Most crucial of these is the question of whether something merely seems ambiguous to the researcher but is legible to those working with and under it, or whether ambiguity extends beyond the researcher's perceptions. Clearly, there is a lot I do not know (for sure) about refugee governance in Lebanon. This is so for various reasons, many of which will elude me; ignorance, after all, 'is often ignorant of itself' (Code, 2007: 227). It is so because of my background and the restrictions this entails in terms of social and linguistic access and psychological and cultural comprehension; because of the restrictions placed on my research in terms of access to the field (see Mencütek, 2019: 14; Lindberg and Borrelli, 2019); and because of the limitations of my professional and theoretical conditioning, which may, for instance, harbor residues of methodological nationalism and sedentarist analytical schemes regardless of attempts to shed these.

Thankfully, what I did not know was not the object, but rather an instrument of research, always put into critical conversation with what was unknown, uncertain, or inconsistent to my interlocutors, who were all crucial stakeholders in Lebanon's refugee governance. My account highlights the value of starting off from the experiences of those on the 'receiving end' of governance and 'study up' from there, exploring what is, or might be, known by whom under which conditions. Silence and ambiguity in the data then become manifestations of 'knowledge that fails to travel,' and the investigation of what obstructs such 'travel' turns into the researcher's core mission (Mathews, 2008: 490). Applying this approach offers several handles to, as Rappert and Balmer (2015: 330) propose, 'locate ignorance and its implications squarely within institutional practices.'

As many of my interlocutors also pointed out to me, this requires a degree of speculation, of 'what-if' history, that allows us to explore potential alternative scenarios (Alcoff, 2007). While this can never produce 'proof,' it can yield innovative understandings of knowledge economies. Considering that one can never indisputably prove what anyone else 'truly' thinks, this may be the next best approach to venture the examination of the minds of others that is uncomfortable but unavoidable in studying knowledge and ignorance (Gross and McGoey, 2015: 373). Being attuned to the possibility of a politics of uncertainty also reminds us that aspiring to academic closure and ironing out inconsistencies in research supply chains risks limiting our understanding of the workings of power (Goode, 2016; Desai and Tapscott, 2014: 6). Studying institutional ambiguity entails embracing confusion as a 'productive irritation' (Sedlacko and Dahlvik, 2017: 2).

In the analytical journey that followed from this embrace, I took to heart the mission of critical academia to challenge the dominant perspectives that contribute to oppression. But much like the creative contention of refugees might entrench the ambiguity that marginalizes them, critiques of dominant discourses may end up reinforcing them (Ahmed, 2006; Faist, 2018; Horst, 2018). This especially regards the basic fact that I have focused my analysis on Lebanon. Despite my explicit reflections on how institutional ambiguity also permeates refugee governance in the Global North, this might nevertheless give credence to the idea that chaos, uncertainty, and disorder are unique features of governance in the Global South. As also acknowledged in the book's Introduction, my research demarcations risk obscuring how Lebanon's (non-)policies are shaped by transnational migration regimes and the dominance of, in this case, European organizations within it. Rather than validating European discourses that depict regional host countries as impertinent and unruly, my account of the strategic dimensions of institutional ambiguity in Lebanon's refugee governance points to the need for a critical interrogation of the geopolitical parameters that incentivize this particular politics of uncertainty.

The potential of a 'critical' approach to backfire extends to the risk that in my effort to reveal the oppressive dynamics of strategic institutional ambiguity, I might have trespassed on interlocutors' 'right to silence' (Poland and Pedersen, 1998: 300; Bakewell, 2008; Landau, 2014). Refugees face a 'moral economy of data sharing' that primes them to share information and perspectives with humanitarians and researchers even though such 'shareveillance' has done very little to improve their lives (Halkort, 2019: 322). Despite my best efforts to avoid this, I might have compromised the coping mechanisms of those trying to navigate such oppression, which are equally dependent on informality, liminality, and exceptionalism. This touches on complex ethical considerations about researchers', but also practitioners', 'right to know' and their interventions in and co-optation of the knowledge economies of refugees and other societal actors involved in refugee governance.

The analysis presented in this book, inevitably shaped by personal, professional, and pragmatic considerations, thus reveals forms of institutional ambiguity, but may end up construing new epistemic and ethical ambiguities. It should, as such, be read as an explorative work that extends explicit invitations for future research in various directions. This includes an exploration of the linkages between statist and humanitarian regimes of ambiguity. It regards the extension and sophistication of the conceptual framework proposed based on empirical research beyond the confines of Lebanon, hybrid orders, or refugee communities. It concerns the cultural and societal dimensions of structural denial and ignorance that go beyond the more straightforward political aspects of strategic ambiguity. In particular, the insights furthered in this book can be enriched and nuanced by a more explicit focus on the experiences, perspectives, and considerations of political authorities themselves. Organizational ethnographies of relevant state agencies – which were beyond the scope of the current research – would shed more light on what the state itself can know (Mathews, 2008: 485; Mountz, 2010) and on the quotidian bureaucratic dynamics of assemblage and outsourcing that facilitate strategic ambiguity and diffuse responsibility (Eule et al., 2018: 196).

Political implications

Academic contributions are in themselves political interventions, as they have the potential to change how we see the world. The political implications of my analysis thus concern, first of all, what we research. Ignorance studies shows that to understand the workings of power we need to trace what is not known, what is not said, and what is not done in addition to our usual focus on the information that is shared, the initiatives that are started, and the policies that are made. This requires caution towards 'evidence-based' and 'policy-relevant research.' Being attuned to dynamics of strategic ambiguity and the related processes of imposing, feigning, and protecting not-knowing reminds us that the questions that political leaders or policy-makers do not want to ask or be asked are often the most relevant to understand dominant governmentalities (Bakewell, 2008; Baldwin-Edwards, Blitz and Crawley, 2019; Scheel and Ustek-Spilda, 2019).

The political relevance of my conceptual contributions does not just regard the questions we ask, but also the way we conceive of answers to them. As Fiddian-Qasmiyeh et al. (2014: 6) drive home: 'The field [of refugee studies] needs to remember that when it comes to the question of how to best ameliorate conditions, the right conclusions are often those that the powerful least want to hear.' A key example of this is the often narrow understanding of policy success or failure. My analysis confirms extant insights that where policies fail with respect to their publicly stated aims, they may well be considered successful with regard to more private or partisan objectives (Castles, 2017; Chabal and Daloz, 1999; Heyer, 2019; Verdeil, 2018). Addressing such 'failures' then is, as my case-studies have illustrated, not just a matter of building capacity or providing resources. It is equally crucial to shed the fiction of a coherent state that can be apprehended as a consistent actor and to engage with the more elusive question of political will of the various agencies that comprise state systems. The need to come to terms with the potential functionality of dysfunction revives the recurring demand of critical scholars for a political rather than a technical perspective on governance, development, and policy-making (Ferguson, 1994).

It also means a fundamental reconsideration of what 'counts' as policy. When I asked him whether I was correct in understanding that there had been no new policy to deal with the Syrian refugee presence in the country since 2014, a member of the Inter-Ministerial Committee tasked with overseeing the response to the Syrian refugee crisis commented: 'No *written* one, yes.'[6] Policy, he clarified, was not expressed in a single document or statement, but was rather the de facto sum of all the 'bits and pieces' of communication by the relevant institutions. It is such 'undeclared policies' that ask for our scrutiny (Atallah and Mahdi, 2017: 33). Policy and practice, in this way, are even more intimately related than often assumed (Yassin, Stel and Rassi, 2016).

Embracing the political dimensions of what is often regarded through a humanitarian lens means that we have to concern ourselves not just with the outcomes of policies, but with the intentions behind them. This book has abundantly chronicled how challenging this sometimes pyrrhic attempt to 'prove the existence of something for which the very ability to evade detection is a key criterion of success' can be (McGoey, 2012: 559). As a regional refugee response coordinator poetically reflected on his engagement with policy-makers: 'No matter how much we talk, there is a lot of smoke.'[7] But it has also shown that exploring the interests and drivers of specific instances of institutional ambiguity is essential in locating responsibility when it comes to refugee governance (Code, 2007: 228).

To turn to policy-makers' million-dollar question: what should we do faced with ambiguous refugee governance? At first glance, this may seem straightforward. If the problem is ambiguity and uncertainty, the solution should lie with promoting and demanding transparency, responsiveness, accountability, and those other traits of 'good governance.' This seems at times to be taken up by the international community which, in the Global Compact for Migration (2018: 12), called for strengthening 'certainty and predictability in migration procedures.' Challenging ambiguity by a simple 'call for clarity or precision,' however, is illusory (Aradau, 2017: 338). It is exactly because much of the lack of these things is strategic in many ways that they are so tenacious and that voicing the intention to reverse them appears ritualistic. Conceiving of policy recommendations, in this light, may be naïve at best and delusional at worst.

Any attempt towards formalizing the commitments and regulations of host states in terms of refugee status, shelter, and representation will need to take into consideration the interests behind their currently ambiguous nature. My case-studies suggest that a concrete starting point in breaking the vicious circle of uncertainty and repression could be to support the development of collective, public, and expressly political representation structures for refugees that are officially acknowledged and substantially capacitated to speak for refugee communities (Chatty, 2016; Horst, 2018; Stel, 2017). However complicated and problematic this may be, counterbalancing the repressive effects of institutional ambiguity should start with a more direct sense of representation beyond the humanitarian agencies, governmental bodies, and NGOs and civil society organizations that claim to work on behalf of refugees, but can hardly be held accountable by them (Silverman, 2008: 11 in Hanafi and Long, 2010: 135; Fiddian-Qasmiyeh, 2016; see also Malkki, 1996). Returning to the vignettes with which I opened this book, refugees' 'ignorance' is not a form of inferior intellectual capacity, recalcitrance, or laxness. If refugees 'don't get it,' this is often because they are not supposed to get it. Taking seriously their collective political representation might help to remedy the uncertainty and paralysis imposed on them.

A truly political reading of forced displacement that is cognizant of strategic ambiguities requires more reflexive forms of engagement with refugee governance. Instead of responding to knowledge gaps with routine data production, approaches to refugee governance need to question not merely what we do not know but why we do not know it. Addressing these questions also entails accounting for the ways in which the political decisions of the Global North facilitate and uphold the repressive politics of uncertainty that refugees face in the Global South. The political consequences of dynamics of imposed and feigned and maintained ignorance underscore that we have to confront our own deliberate not-knowing. This includes the violent conflicts that produce refugees and the geopolitics that determine refugee flows (Horst, 2018: 445). As Agier (2008: 3, 36) has proposed, one of the most tenacious foundations of the structural marginalization of refugees is 'our own ignorance of it'; a willful ignorance that prescribes the desperations that refugees face as 'other people's horrors, other people's exclusions' that do not concern us.

The politics of uncertainty described for Lebanon in this book is crucially rooted in and indicative of that country's political order, but it is also enabled by other countries' inaction. Europe has embraced the idea of shelter – now progressively rebranded as 'protection' or even 'perspective' – in the region as its foundational paradigm for refugee governance. It is keen on outsourcing refugee governance but does not care to understand how the governance it outsourced actually works or does not work. In fact, this outsourcing is dependent on maintaining an idealized fiction about ordered and benevolent refugee governance in regional host countries despite overwhelming empirical evidence to the contrary (Faist, 2018). These realities – whether it is looking away from the complications of the often celebrated 'self-settlement' of refugees in contexts bereft of any form of refugee protection or whether it is buying into the curtailing of access to livelihoods as a form of protecting refugees' rights to return, to give just two of the more blatant examples – amounts to 'unwelcome knowledge' that is avoided or denied (Cohen, 2011: xiii).

This sheds a problematic light on the routine championing of 'resilience' in engagement with regional refugee hosting countries (Mouawad, 2017). Europe's dependence on Lebanon's capacity to cope with the entirely disproportionate number of refugees it is 'asked' to host leads it to cherish anything that reeks of stability. Efforts to help Lebanon respond to the Syrian refugee crisis have in this way reinforced the country's status quo that only works for its oligopolistic elites (Geha, 2016; Hazbun, 2016: 1053; International Crisis Group, 2015). Rather than threatening the sovereignty of fragile states, as the conventional wisdom suggests, the regional governance of refugee 'crises' may further entrench the power positions of those that have made the ensuing institutional ambiguity work for them.

Strategic institutional ambiguity in the 'region' and its marginalizing effects exist by the grace of the strategic ignorance of the 'international community' (Faist, 2018; Horst, 2018). Refugees often speak of themselves as the 'forgotten ones' (Chabaan et al., 2010: 7).[8] Such reflections concern the 'cognitive dissonance' of formal political actors as well as their constituencies, who partake in this 'deliberately cultivated ignorance of the privileged' (Sullivan and Tuana, 2007: 3). This willful ignorance allows refugees to be made invisible and forgotten despite crisis-peaks of hypervisibility and naturalizes marginalization and oppression as a seemingly inevitable result of displacement (Fiddian-Qasmiyeh, 2016: 457; see also Agier, 2008: 8; Griffiths, 2013: 279). In response to this, with Code (2007: 219), I would argue for an epistemological understanding of responsibility in which we 'singly and collectively – indeed, singly because collectively – are responsible for what and how we know.' This might help to further question the protected obliviousness of and hence indifference to the systemic injustice that characterizes not just the Lebanese but the global refugee regime.

Notes

1 Author's interview with Lebanese human rights professional – Skype, 17 January 2018.
2 Interview – Zahle, 24 April 2018.
3 Author's interview – Skype, 12 March 2018.
4 Author's interview – Skype, 27 March 2018.
5 Author's interview with development analyst in Lebanon – Skype, 11 December 2017.
6 Author's interview – Skype, 30 January 2018.
7 Notes from interview with an international regional coordinator of the refugee response in the Bekaa for an international humanitarian organization – Zahle, 10 April 2018.
8 Author's field notes – South Lebanon, 10 June 2014.

References

Achilli, Luigi and Lucas Oesch. 2016. 'Des Espaces d'Ambiguïté: Les Camps de Réfugiés Palestiniens en Jordanie.' *A Contrario* 2, no. 23: 17–36.

Agier, Michel. 2008. *On the Margins of the World: The Refugee Experience Today*. Cambridge: Polity Press.

Ahmed, Sara. 2006. 'The Non-Performativity of Anti-Racism.' *Meridians: Feminism, Race, Transnationalism* 7, no. 1: 104–126.

Alcoff, Linda Martín. 2007. 'Epistemologies of Ignorance: Three Types.' In *Race and Epistemologies of Ignorance*, edited by Shannon Sullivan and Nancy Tuana, 39–58. Albany: State University of New York Press.

Al Masri, Muzna, Marianna Altabaa and Zeina Abla. 2016. *Informal Justice Mechanisms Used by Syrian Refugees in Lebanon*. Beirut: International Alert.

Ansems de Vries, Leonie and Elspeth Guild. 2019. 'Seeking Refuge in Europe: Spaces of Transit and the Violence of Migration Management.' *Journal of Ethnic and Migration Studies* 45, no. 12: 2156–2166.

Aradau, Claudia. 2017. 'Assembling (Non-)Knowledge: Security, Law and Surveillance in a Digital World.' *International Political Sociology* 11: 327–342.

Atallah, Sami and Dima Mahdi. 2017. *Law and Politics of 'Safe Zones' and Forced Return to Syria: Refugee Politics in Lebanon*. Beirut: Lebanese Center for Policy Studies.

Atallah, Sami, Georgia Dagher and Mounir Mahmalat. 2019. *The CEDRE Reform Program Needs a Credible Action Plan*. Beirut: Lebanese Center for Policy Studies.

Atme, Cybele. 2019. 'Finnovation: The Case of Financializing Humanitarian Interventions in Lebanon.' MSc thesis, University of Amsterdam.

Bailey, Alison. 2007. 'Strategic Ignorance.' In *Race and Epistemologies of Ignorance*, edited by Shannon Sullivan and Nancy Tuana, 77–94. Albany: State University of New York Press.

Bakewell, Oliver. 2008. 'Research Beyond the Categories: The Importance of Policy Irrelevant Research into Forced Migration.' *Journal of Refugee Studies* 21, no. 4: 431–453.

Bakewell, Oliver. 2014. 'Encampment and Self-Settlement.' In *The Oxford Handbook of Refugee and Forced Migration Studies*, edited by Elena Fiddian-Qasmiyeh, Gil Loescher, Katy Long and Nando Sigona, 127–138. Oxford: Oxford University Press.

Baldwin-Edwards, Martin, Brad K. Blitz and Heaven Crawley. 2019. 'The Politics of Evidence-Based Policy in Europe's "Migration Crisis".' *Journal of Ethnic and Migration Studies* 45, no. 12: 2139–2155.

Bauman, Zygmunt. 1993. *Modernity and Ambivalence*. Cambridge: Polity Press.

Bayat, Asef. 1997. 'Un-Civil Society: The Politics of the "Informal People".' *Third World Quarterly* 18, no. 1: 53–72.

Best, Jacqueline. 2012. 'Bureaucratic Ambiguity.' *Economy and Society* 41, no: 1: 84–106.

Biehl, Kristen Sarah. 2015. 'Governing Through Uncertainty: Experiences of Being a Refugee in Turkey as a Country for Temporary Asylum.' *Social Analysis* 59, no. 1: 57–75.

Blundo, Giorgio. 2006. 'Dealing with the Local State: The Informal Privatization of Street-Level Bureaucracies in Senegal.' *Development and Change* 37, no. 4: 799–819.

Blundo, Giorgio and Pierre-Yves Le Meur, eds. 2009. *The Governance of Daily Life in Africa: Ethnographic Explorations of Public and Collective Services*. Leiden: Brill.

Borgmann, Monika and Lokman Slim. 2018. *Fewer Refugees, More Refugeeism*. Beirut: Umam Documentation and Research and Institut for Auslandsbeziehunger.

Borrelli, Lisa Marie. 2018. 'Using Ignorance as an (Un)conscious Bureaucratic Strategy: Street-Level Practices and Structural Influences in the Field of Migration Enforcement.' *Qualitative Studies* 5, no. 2: 95–109.

Boswell, Christina. 2009. *The Political Uses of Expert Knowledge: Immigration Policy and Social Research*. Cambridge: Cambridge University Press.

Bully, Dan. 2014. 'Inside the Tent: Community and Government in Refugee Camps.' *Security Dialogue* 45, no. 1: 63–80.

Canning, Victoria. 2018. 'Border (Mis)Management, Ignorance, and Denial.' In *Ignorance, Power and Harm. Agnotology and the Criminological Imagination*, edited by Alana Barton and Howard Davis, 139–162. Cham: Palgrave Macmillan.

Caprioglio, Carlo, Francesco Ferri, and Lucia Gennari. 2018. 'The Taranto Hotspot: Unveiling the Developments of EU Migration Management Policies.' *Border Criminologies* 11 April.

Carpi, Estella. 2019. 'Winking at Humanitarian Neutrality: The Liminal Politics of the State in Lebanon.' *Anthropologica* 61: 83–96.

Castles, Stephen. 2017. 'Migration Policies are Problematic – Because They Are About Migration.' *Ethnic and Racial Studies* 40, no. 9: 1538–1543.

Chabaan, Jad, Hala Ghattas, Rima Habib, Sari Hanafi, Nadine Sahyoun, Nisreen Salti, Karin Seyfert and Nadia Naamani. 2010. *Socio-Economic Survey of Palestinian Refugees in Lebanon*. Beirut: American University of Beirut.

Chabal, Patrick and Jean-Pascal Daloz. 1999. *Africa Works: Disorder as Political Instrument*. London: The International African Institute (in Association with James Curry, Oxford and Indiana University Press, Bloomington and Indianapolis).

Chatty, Dawn. 2016. 'Refugee Voices: Exploring the Border Zones Between States and State Bureaucracies.' *Refuge* 32, no. 1: 3–6.

Chimni, B.S. 1998. 'The Geopolitics of Refugee Studies: A View from the South.' *Journal of Refugee Studies* 11, no. 4: 350–374.

Chomsky, Noam. 2012. 'Plutonomy and the Precariat: On the History of the U.S. Economy in Decline.' *The Huffington Post*, 8 May.

Code, Lorraine. 2007. 'The Power of Ignorance.' In *Race and Epistemologies of Ignorance*, edited by Shannon Sullivan and Nancy Tuana, 213–230. Albany: State University of New York Press.

Cohen, Stanley. 2011. *States of Denial: Knowing About Atrocities and Suffering*. Cambridge: Polity Press.

Cullen Dunn, Elizabeth and Jason Cons. 2014. 'Aleatory Sovereignty and the Rule of Sensitive Spaces.' *Antipode* 46, no. 1: 92–109.

Czajka, Agnes. 2012. 'Discursive Constructions of Palestinian Refugees in Lebanon.' *Comparative Studies of South Asia, Africa and the Middle East* 32, no. 1: 238–254.

Darling, Jonathan. 2017a. 'Acts, Ambiguities, and the Labour of Contesting Citizenship.' *Citizenship Studies* 21: 727–736.

Darling, Jonathan. 2017b. 'Forced Migration and the City: Irregularity, Informality, and the Politics of Presence.' *Progress in Human Geography* 41: 178–198.

Das, Veena and Deborah Poole, eds. 2004. *Anthropology in the Margins of the State*. Oxford: James Curry.

Davies, Thom, Arshad Isakjee and Surindar Dhesi. 2017. 'Violent Inaction: The Necropolitical Experience of Refugees in Europe.' *Antipode* 49, no. 5: 1263–1284.

De Genova, Nicholas P. 2002. 'Migrant "Illegality" and Deportability in Everyday Life.' *Annual Review of Anthropology* 31: 419–447.

De Genova, Nicholas P., ed. 2017. *The Borders of "Europe": Autonomy of Migration, Tactics of Bordering*. Durham: Duke University Press.

De Waal, Alex. 2019. 'Wild Power: Exploring Vocabularies of Political Disorder.' Paper presented at the workshop Democracy and Disorder: Political Unpredictability, Illiberal Governance and Prospects for Democratic Voice, Geneva, 2–4 May.

Desai, Deval and Rebecca Tapscott. 2014. '*Tomayto Tomahto*: The Research Supply Chain and the Ethics of Knowledge Production.' *Humanity Journal Online*, 4 December.

Diken, Bülent and Carsten Bagge Laustsen. 2005. *The Culture of Exception: Sociology Facing the Camp*. London: Routledge.

Edwards, Alice and Laura van Waas, eds. 2014. *Nationality and Statelessness Under International War*. Cambridge: Cambridge University Press.

Eule, Tobias G., Lisa Marie Borrelli, Annika Lindberg and Anna Wyss. 2018. *Migrants Before the Law: Contested Migration Control in Europe*. Cham: Palgrave Macmillan.

Faist, Thomas. 2018. 'The Moral Polity of Forced Migration.' *Ethnic and Racial Studies* 41, no. 3: 412–423.

Fakhoury, Tamirace. 2017. 'Governance Strategies and Refugee Response: Lebanon in the Face of Syrian Displacement.' *International Journal of Middle East Studies* 49: 681–700.

Ferguson, James. 1994. *The Anti-Politics Machine: Depoliticization and Bureaucratic Power in Lesotho*. London: University of Minnesota Press.

Fiddian-Qasmiyeh, Elena. 2016. 'Refugees Hosting Refugees.' *Forced Migration Review* 53: 25–27.

Fiddian-Qasmiyeh, Elena, Gil Loescher, Katy Long and Nando Sigona, eds. 2014. *The Oxford Handbook of Refugee and Forced Migration Studies*. Oxford: Oxford University Press.

Franck, Anja. 2019. 'Laughable Borders: On the Everyday Absurdity of Border Enforcement.' Paper presented at the IMISCOE international conference Understanding International Migration in the 21st Century: Conceptual and Methodological Approaches, Malmö, 26–28 June.

Freeman, Richard and Steve Sturdy, eds. 2014. *Knowledge in Policy: Embodied, Inscribed, Enacted*. Chicago: University of Chicago Press.

Friedman, Jeffrey. 2005. 'Popper, Weber, and Hayek: The Epistemology and Politics of Ignorance.' *Critical Review* 17, no. 1–2: 1–58.

Frye, Marilyn. 1983. *The Politics of Reality: Essays in Feminist Theory*. Trumansburg: Crossing Press.

Geha, Carmen. 2016. 'The Syrian Refugee Crisis and Lebanon's Endemic Deadlocks: Trading Reform for Resilience.' *Middle East Institute*, 17 March.

Ghaddar, Sima. 2017. *Lebanon Treats Refugees as a Security Problem – And It Doesn't Work*. New York: The Century Foundation.

Gibney, Matthew. 2014. 'Political Theory, Ethics and Forced Migration.' In *The Oxford Handbook of Refugee and Forced Migration Studies*, edited by Elena Fiddian-Qasmiyeh, Gil Loescher, Katy Long and Nando Sigona, 48–59. Oxford: Oxford University Press.

Glasius, Marlies. 2018. 'What Authoritarianism Is . . . and Is Not: A Practice Perspective.' *International Affairs* 94, no. 3: 515–533.

Global Compact for Safe, Orderly, and Regular Migration. 2018. https://refugeesmigrants. un.org/sites/default/files/180713_agreed_outcome_global_compact_for_migration.pdf

Goode, J. Paul. 2016. 'Eyes Wide Shut: Democratic Reversals, Scientific Closure, and the Study of Politics in Eurasia.' *Social Science Quarterly* 97, no. 4: 876–893.

Griffiths, Melanie. 2013. 'Living with Uncertainty: Indefinite Immigration Detention.' *Journal of Legal Anthropology* 1, no. 3: 263–286.

Gross, Matthias and Linsey McGoey, eds. 2015. *Routledge International Handbook of Ignorance Studies*. London and New York: Routledge.

Guazzone, Laura and Daniela Pioppi. 2012. *The Arab State and Neo-Liberal Globalization: The Restructuring of State Power in the Middle East*. Reading: Ithaca Press.

Gupta, Akhil. 1995. 'Blurred Boundaries: The Discourse of Corruption, the Culture of Politics, and the Imagined State.' *American Ethnologist* 22, no. 2: 375–402.

Hagan, Maria. 2018. 'Disassembling the Camp: The Politics of Policing Exiles in Calais, France.' MSc thesis, University of Amsterdam.

Hagan, Maria. 2020. 'The Contingent Camp: Struggling for Shelter in Calais, France.' In *Structures of Protection? Rethinking Refugee Shelter*, edited by Tom Scott-Smith and Mark E. Breeze. Oxford: Berghan Books.

Hagmann, Tobias and Didier Péclard. 2010. 'Negotiating Statehood: Dynamics of Power and Domination in Africa.' *Development and Change* 41, no. 4: 539–562.

Halkort, Monika. 2019. 'Decolonizing Data Relations: On the Moral Economy of Data Sharing in Palestinian Refugee Camps.' *Canadian Journal of Communication* 44: 317–329.

Hall, Stuart. 1988. '"The Toad in the Garden": Thatcherism Among the Theorists.' In *Marxism and the Interpretation of Culture*, edited by Cary Nelson and Lawrence Grossberg, 35–74. Urbana: University of Illinois Press.

Hanafi, Sari. 2008. 'Palestinian Refugee Camps in Lebanon: Laboratories of State-in-the-Making, Discipline and Islamist Radicalism.' Unpublished document.

Hanafi, Sari and Taylor Long. 2010. 'Governance, Governmentalities, and the State of Exception in the Palestinian Refugee Camps of Lebanon.' *Journal of Refugee Studies* 23, no. 2: 134–159.

Hazbun, Waleed. 2016. 'Assembling Security in a "Weak State": The Contentious Politics of Plural Governance in Lebanon Since 2005.' *Third World Quarterly* 37, no. 6: 1053–1070.

Heyer, Karl. 2019. 'Function Through Failure? Ambiguity, Incoherence, and Discretion in Migrants' Arrival and Reception in South Italy.' Paper presented at the Royal Geographic Society annual conference, London, 30 August.

Horst, Cindy. 2018. 'Forced Migration: Morality and Politics.' *Ethnic and Racial Studies* 41, no. 3: 440–447.

Horst, Cindy and Katarzyna Grabska. 2015. 'Introduction: Flight and Exile – Uncertainty in the Context of Conflict-Induced Displacement.' *Social Analysis* 59, no. 1: 1–18.

Hourani, Guita and Eugene Sensenig-Dabbous. n.d. *Migration Patterns in the Global South, the Middle East and North Africa as a Reflection of Policy Alternatives in the*

Field of Security, Labour Market and Social Welfare Planning. Cologne: Global South Studies Center.

Hughes, Sarah. 2019. 'Illegibility as Governance: Implications for Resistance within the UK Asylum System.' Paper presented at the IMISCOE international conference Understanding International Migration in the 21st Century: Conceptual and Methodological Approaches, Malmö, 26–28 June.

Hull, Matthew S. 2012. *Government of Paper: The Materiality of Bureaucracy in Urban Pakistan*. Berkeley: University of California Press.

Ilcan, Suzan, Kim Rygiel and Feyzi Baban. 2018. 'The Ambiguous Architecture of Precarity: Temporary Protection, Everyday Living and Migrant Journeys of Syrian Refugees.' *International Journal of Migration and Border Studies* 4, no. 1–2: 52–70.

International Alert and Lebanon Support. 2017. *Security that Protects: Informing Policy on Local Security Provision in Lebanese Communities Hosting Syrian Refugees*. Beirut: International Alert and Lebanon Support.

International Crisis Group. 2015. *Lebanon's Self-Defeating Survival Mechanisms*. Brussels: International Crisis Group.

Ismail, Salwa. 2006. *Political Life in Cairo's New Quarters: Encountering the Everyday State*. Minneapolis: University of Minnesota Press.

Joseph, Gilbert M. and Daniel Nugent, eds. 1994. *Everyday Forms of State Formation: Revolution and the Negotiation of Rule in Modern Mexico*. Durham: Duke University Press.

Kalir, Barak. 2014. *The Deportation Mess: A Bureaucratic Muddling of State Fantasies*. Oxford: Border Criminologies.

Kalir, Barak. 2017. 'State Desertion and "Out-of-Procedure" Asylum Seekers in the Netherlands.' *Focaal* 77: 63–75.

Kalir, Barak. 2019. 'Dep001artheid: The Draconian Governance of Illegalized Migrants in Western States.' *Conflict and Society: Advances in Research* 5: 19–40.

Kalir, Barak and Katerina Rozakou. 2016. '"Giving Form to Chaos": The Futility of EU Border Management at Moria Hotspot in Lesvos.' *Society and Space*. https://www.societyandspace.org/articles/giving-form-to-chaos-the-futility-of-eu-border-man agement-at-moria-hotspot-in-lesvos

Kalir, Barak and Willem van Schendel. 2017. 'Introduction: Nonrecording States Between Legibility and Looking Away.' *Focaal – Journal of Global and Historical Anthropology* 77: 1–7.

Katz, Irit. 2016. 'Camp Evolution and Israel's Creation: Between "State of Emergency" and "Emergence of State".' *Political Geography* 55: 144–155.

Kosmatopoulos, Nikolas. 2011. 'Towards an Anthropology of "State Failure" Lebanon's Leviathan and Peace Expertise.' *Social Analysis* 55, no. 3: 115–142.

Landau, Loren B. 2014. 'Urban Refugees and IDPs.' In *The Oxford Handbook of Refugee and Forced Migration Studies*, edited by Elena Fiddian-Qasmiyeh, Gil Loescher, Katy Long and Nando Sigona, 139–150. Oxford: Oxford University Press.

Lemaire, Léa. 2014. 'Islands and a Carceral Environment: Maltese Policy in Terms of Irregular Migration.' *Journal of Immigrant and Refugee Studies* 12, no. 2: 143–160.

Lemaire, Léa. 2019. 'The European Dispositif of Border Control in Malta: Migrants' Experiences of a Securitized Borderland.' *Journal of Borderlands Studies* 34, no. 5: 717–732.

Lemke, Thomas. 2000. 'Foucault, Governmentality, and Critique.' Paper presented at the Rethinking Marxism conference, Amherst, 21–24 September.

Lenner, Katharina. 2016. *Blasts from the Past: Policy Legacies and Memories in the Making of the Jordanian Response to the Syrian Refugee Crisis*. Florence: European University Institute.

Lenner, Katharina. 2019. 'Beyond Methodological Nationalism: Ambiguity, Translation and Assemblages in Forced Migration Policy.' Paper presented at the Royal Geographic Society annual conference, London, 30 August.

Lindberg, Annika and Lisa Marie Borrelli. 2019. 'Let the Right One In? On European Migration Authorities' Resistance to Research.' *Social Anthropology* 27, no. 1: 17–32.

Lund, Christian. 2006. 'Twilight Institutions: Public Authority and Local Politics in Africa.' *Development and Change* 37, no. 4: 685–705.

Mallard, Grégoire and Linsey McGoey. 2018. 'Constructed Ignorance and Global Governance: An Ecumenical Approach to Epistemologies of Power.' *The British Journal of Sociology* 69, no. 4: 884–909.

Malkki, Liisa M. 1995. 'Refugees and Exile: From "Refugee Studies" to the National Order of Things.' *Annual Review of Anthropology* 24: 495–523.

Malkki, Liisa M. 1996. 'Speechless Emissaries: Refugees, Humanitarianism, and Dehistoricization.' *Cultural Anthropology* 11, no. 3: 377–404.

Mathews, Andrew. 2008. 'State Making, Knowledge and Ignorance: Translation and Concealment in Mexican Forestry Institutions.' *American Anthropologist* 110, no. 4: 484–494.

Mazzola, Francisco. 2019. 'Mediating Security – Hybridity and Clientelism in Lebanon's Hybrid Security Sector.' In *Hybrid Governance in the Middle East and Africa: Informal Rule and the Limits of Statehood*, edited by Ruth Hanau Santini, Abel Polese and Rob Kevlihan. London: Routledge.

McGoey, Linsey. 2007. 'On the Will to Ignorance in Bureaucracy.' *Economy and Society* 36, no. 2: 212–235.

McGoey, Linsey. 2012. 'The Logic of Strategic Ignorance.' *British Journal of Sociology* 63, no. 3: 553–576.

McGoey, Linsey. 2019. *The Unknowers: How Strategic Ignorance Rules the World*. London: Zed Books.

Memişoğlu, Fulya and Asli Ilgit. 2017. 'Syrian Refugees in Turkey: Multifaceted Challenges, Diverse Players, and Ambiguous Policies.' *Mediterranean Politics* 22, no. 3: 317–338.

Mencütek, Zeynep. 2019. *Refugee Governance, State and Politics in the Middle East*. London: Routledge.

Menkhaus, Ken. 2006. 'Governance in the Hinterland of Africa's Weak States: Toward a Theory of the Mediated State.' Paper presented at the annual meeting of the American Political Science Association, Philadelphia, 30 August–2 September.

Migdal, Joel S. 2001. *State in Society: Studying How States and Societies Form and Constitute One Another*. Cambridge: Cambridge University Press.

Minca, Claudio, Danica Šantić and Dragan Umek. 2019. 'Managing the "Refugee Crisis" Along the Balkan Route: Field Notes from Serbia.' In *The Oxford Handbook of Migration Crises*, edited by Cecilia Menjívar, Maria Ruiz and Immanuel Ness, 445–464. Oxford: Oxford University Press.

Mitchell, Timothy. 1990. 'Society, Economy, and the State Effect.' In *State/Culture: State-Formation After the Cultural Turn*, edited by George Steinmetz, 76–97. Ithaca: Cornell University Press.

Mouawad, Jamil. 2017. *Unpacking Lebanon's Resilience: Undermining State Institutions and Consolidating the System?* Rome: Instituto Affari Internazionali.

Mountz, Alison. 2010. *Seeking Asylum: Human Smuggling and Bureaucracy at the Border.* Minneapolis: University of Minnesota Press.

Nawyn, Stephanie J. 2016. 'Migration in the Global South: Exploring New Theoretical Territory.' *International Journal of Sociology* 46, no. 2: 81–84.

Nielsen, Morten. 2007. 'Filling in the Blanks: The Potency of Fragmented Imageries of the State.' *Review of African Political Economy* 34, no. 114: 697–708.

Norman, Karin. 2005. 'The Working of Uncertainty: Interrogating Cases on Refugees in Sweden.' *Social Analysis* 49, no. 3: 195–220.

Norman, Kelsey P. 2019. 'Inclusion, Exclusion or Indifference? Redefining Migrant and Refugee Host State Engagement Options in Mediterranean "Transit" Countries.' *Journal of Ethnic and Migration Studies* 45, no. 1: 42–60.

Obeid, Michelle. 2010. 'Searching for the "Ideal Face of the State" in a Lebanese Border Town.' *Journal of the Royal Anthropological Institute* 16: 330–346.

Oesch, Lucas. 2015. 'The Ambiguous Encampment of the World.' *Jadaliyya*, 11 December.

Oesch, Lucas. 2017. 'The Refugee Camp as a Space of Multiple Ambiguities and Subjectivities.' *Political Geography* 60: 110–120.

Olivier de Sardan, Jean-Pierre. 2008. *Researching the Practical Norms of Real Governance in Africa.* London: Africa Power and Politics Programme.

Öner, N. Asli Şirin and Deniz Genç. 2015. 'Vulnerability Leading to Mobility: Syrians' Exodus from Turkey.' *Migration Letters* 12, no. 3: 251–262.

Oomen, Barbara, Moritz Baumgärtel, Sara Miellet, Elif Durmus and Tihomir Sabchev. 2019. 'Strategies of Divergence: Local Authorities, Law and Discretionary Spaces in Migration Governance.' Paper presented at the IMISCOE international conference Understanding International Migration in the 21st Century: Conceptual and Methodological Approaches, Malmö, 26–28 June.

Parnell, Philip C. 2000. 'The Innovations of Violent Days: Ignorance and the Regendering of Power in the Philippines.' *Social Analysis* 44, no. 2: 15–29.

Peteet, Julie. 2005. *Landscapes of Hope and Despair: Place and Identity in Palestinian Refugee Camps.* Philadelphia: University of Pennsylvania Press.

Pinelli, Barbara. 2018. 'Control and Abandonment: The Power of Surveillance on Refugees in Italy, During and After the Mare Nostrum Operation.' *Antipode* 50: 725–747.

Poland, Blake and Ann Pedersen. 1998. 'Reading Between the Lines: Interpreting Silences in Qualitative Research.' *Qualitative Inquiry* 4, no. 2: 293–312.

Qvist, Martin. 2017. 'Meta-Governance and Network Formation in Collaborative Spaces of Uncertainty: The Case of Swedish Refugee Integration Policy.' *Public Administration* 95: 498–511.

Raeymaekers, Timothy, Ken Menkhaus and Koen Vlassenroot. 2008. 'State and Non-State Regulation in African Protracted Crises: Governance Without Government?' *Afrika Focus* 21, no. 2: 7–21.

Raj, Dhooleka Sarhadi. 2000. 'Ignorance, Forgetting, and Family Nostalgia: Partition, the Nation State, andRefugees in Delhi.' *Social Analysis* 44, no. 2: 30–55.

Ramadan, Adam and Sara Fregonese. 2017. 'Hybrid Sovereignty and the State of Exception in the Palestinian Refugee Camps in Lebanon.' *Annals of the American Association of Geographers* 107, no. 4: 949–963.

Rappert, Brian and Brian Balmer. 2015. 'Ignorance Is Strength? Intelligence, Security, and National Secrets.' In *Routledge International Handbook of Ignorance Studies*, edited by Matthias Gross and Linsey McGoey, 328–337. London and New York: Routledge.

Rozakou, Katerina. 2017. 'Nonrecording the "European Refugee Crisis" in Greece: Navigating Through Irregular Bureaucracy.' *Focaal – Journal of Global and Historical Anthropology* 77: 36–49.

Sanyal, Romola. 2014. 'Urbanizing Refuge: Interrogating Spaces of Displacement.' *International Journal of Urban and Regional Research* 38, no. 2: 558–572.

Sanyal, Romola. 2018. 'Managing Through Ad Hoc Measures: Syrian Refugees and the Politics of Waiting in Lebanon.' *Political Geography* 66: 67–75.

Scheel, Stephan. 2019. *Autonomy of Migration? Appropriating Mobility Within Biometric Border Regimes.* New York: Routledge.

Scheel, Stephan and Funda Ustek-Spilda. 2019. 'The Politics of Expertise and Ignorance in the Field of Migration Management.' *Environment and Planning D: Society and Space* 37, no. 4: 663–681.

Schmidt, Katharina. 2019. 'Developmentalising Humanitarian Space The (Anti-)Politics of International Aid for Refugees in Jordan.' MSc thesis, University of Amsterdam.

Schuster, Liza. 2011. 'Dublin II and Eurodac: Examining the (Un)Intended(?) Consequences.' *Gender, Place & Culture* 18, no. 3: 401–416.

Scott, James. 1985. *Weapons of the Weak: Everyday Forms of Peasant Resistance.* New Haven and London: Yale University Press.

Scott, James. 2009. *The Art of Not Being Governed: An Anarchist History of Upland South Asia.* New Haven: Yale University Press.

Sedlacko, Michal and Julia Dahlvik. 2017. 'From Single Practices to State Aapparatuses: Knowledge Patterns and Hierarchies in Asylum and Environmental Policy.' Paper presented at the European Consortium on Political Research General Conference, Oslo, 7–10 September.

Serhan, Waleed. 2019. 'Consociational Lebanon and the Palestinian Threat of Sameness.' *Journal of Immigrant and Refugee Studies* 17, no. 2: 240–259.

Silverman, Stephanie J. 2008. 'Redrawing the Lines of Control: Political Interventions by Refugees and the Sovereign State System.' Paper presented at Dead/Lines: Contemporary Issues in Legal and Political Theory, Edinburgh, 28 April.

Slater Tom. 2012. 'The Myth of "Broken Britain": Welfare Reform and the Production of Ignorance.' *Antipode* 46, no. 4: 948–969.

Slominski, Peter and Florian Trauner. 2018. 'How Do Member States Return Unwanted Migrants? The Strategic (Non-)Use of "Europe" During the Migration Crisis.' *Journal of Common Market Studies* 56, no. 1: 101–118.

Stel, Nora. 2015. 'Lebanese-Palestinian Governance Interaction in the Palestinian Gathering of Shabriha, South Lebanon – A Tentative Extension of the "Mediated State" from Africa to the Mediterranean.' *Mediterranean Politics* 20, no. 1: 76–96.

Stel, Nora. 2016. 'Languages of Stateness in South Lebanon's Palestinian Gatherings: The PLO's Popular Committees as Twilight Institutions.' *Development and Change* 47, no. 3: 446–471.

Stel, Nora. 2017. 'Governing the Gatherings. The Interaction of Lebanese State Institutions and Palestinian Authorities in the Hybrid Political Order of South Lebanon's Informal Palestinian Settlements.' PhD dissertation, Utrecht University.

Stel, Nora. 2018. 'Exporting Institutional Ambiguity in Refugee Governance: How Lebanon's Politics of Uncertainty Mirrors EUrope's Politics of Exhaustion and Abandonment.' Paper presented at the European International Studies Association's annual conference A New Hope: Back to the Future of International Relations, Prague, 15 September.

Steppputat, Finn and Ninna Nyberg Sørensen. 2014. 'Sociology and Forced Migration.' In *The Oxford Handbook of Refugee and Forced Migration Studies,* edited by Elena

Fiddian-Qasmiyeh, Gil Loescher, Katy Long and Nando Sigona, 86–98. Oxford: Oxford University Press.

Stierl, Maurice. 2019. 'Migrants Calling Us in Distress from the Mediterranean Returned to Libya by Deadly "Refoulement" Industry.' *The Conversation*, 7 February.

Suárez-Krabbe, Julia and Annika Lindberg. 2019. 'Enforcing Apartheid? The Politics of "Intolerability" in the Danish Migration and Integration Regimes.' *Migration and Society* 2, no. 1: 90–97.

Sullivan, Shannon and Nancy Tuana. 2007. *Race and Epistemologies of Ignorance*. Albany: State University of New York Press.

Tapscott, Rebecca. 2017. 'The Government Has Long Hands: Institutionalized Arbitrariness and Local Security Initiatives in Northern Uganda.' *Development and Change* 48, no. 2: 263–285.

Tazzioli, Martina. 2017. 'Containment Through Mobility: Migrants' Spatial Disobediences and the Reshaping of Control Through the Hotspot System in the Mediterranean.' *Journal of Ethic and Migration Studies* 44, no. 16: 2764–2779.

Tekin, Beyca Ç. 2019. 'A Reappraisal of EU-Turkey Cooperation on Migration Management: The Unintended Consequences.' In *Refugee Crises and Migration Policies: From Local to Global*, edited by Gökçe Bayindir Goularas, Işıl Zeynep Turkan and İpek Edanur Onel, 45–61. Lanham: Lexington Books.

Tuckett, Anna. 2019. *Rules, Paper, Status: Migrants and Precarious Bureaucracy in Contemporary Italy*. Stanford: Stanford University Press.

Van Kooy, John and Dina Bowman. 2019. ' "Surrounded with so Much Uncertainty": Asylum Seekers and Manufactured Precarity in Australia.' *Journal of Ethnic and Migration Studies* 45, no. 5: 693–710.

Verdeil, Éric. 2018. 'Infrastructure Crises in Beirut and the Struggle to (Not) Reform the Lebanese State.' *Arab Studies Journal* XVI, no. 1: 84–112.

Vianelli, Lorenzo. 2017. 'Governing Asylum Seekers: Logistics, Differentiation, and Failure in the European Union's Reception Regime.' PhD thesis, University of Warwick.

Wedeen, Lisa. 1999. *Ambiguities of Domination: Politics, Rhetoric, and Symbols in Contemporary Syria*. Chicago: University of Chicago Press.

Whyte, Zachary. 2011. 'Enter the Myopticon: Uncertain Surveillance in the Danish Asylum System.' *Anthropology Today* 2, no. 3: 18–21.

Yassin, Nasser, Nora Stel and Rima Rassi. 2016. 'Organized Chaos: Informal Institution Building Among Palestinian Refugees in the Maashouk Gathering in South Lebanon.' *Journal of Refugee Studies* 29, no. 3: 341–362.

Index

Abbas, Mahmoud 164
Achili, Luigi 102, 108
accountability 4, 22; and arbitrariness
   67, 112; calls for more 168; and elite
   collaboration 33; and eviction processes
   106; and hybridity 44; and institutional
   ambiguity 46, 109, 191; lack of 37,
   86; measures 168; mechanisms to
   produce 90; sabotage of 224; and
   unaccountability 14, 90, 105, 112, 135
adhocracy 197
Agamben, Giorgio 10
agency and structure 7, 20, 205–206, 227
Agier, Michel 9, 232
agnogenesis 187–188
agnotology 188, 206, 227
Ahmed, Sara 79
ALEF 67
Allan, Diana 125, 159
Alliance of Palestinian Forces 131, 165
Alliance (*Tahaluf*) 131; *see also Tahaluf*
allotment, logic of 46
Al-Natour, Souheil 134
Al-Saadi, Yazan 92
Amal Party (Lebanon) 39, 167–168
Amal militia 124, 154
ambiguity 4, 179; and curfew practices
   104; definition of 8; epistemic 230;
   existential 107; legal 5; policy 13,
   61, 63; and political power 30, 34;
   statistical 148n39; status 127; utility of
   200–204; and vulnerability 145; *see
   also* institutional ambiguity; spatial
   ambiguity; strategic ambiguity
ambiguous action 12–14, 68, 137, 192,
   199; *see also* inaction and ambiguous
   action

ambiguous space 72; refugee settlements
   as 11, 193; *see also* gray space
Amnesty International 62, 202
amnesty law 132
Anderson, Ruben 4
Arab Deterrent Force 56
Arab states 122, 128
Arab Summit 122
Aradau, Claudia 187
Arafat, Yasser 122
Armenian community 87
arrest *see* refugee, arrests of
Atallah, Sami 43, 91, 106, 111, 192

Baalbaki, Noor 36, 38, 43, 48
Baban, Feyzi 4, 219
Balmer, Brian 229
Barjas, Elham 99, 110
Batruni, Catherine 37
Baumann, Hannes 34
Bauman, Zygmunt 9
Bayat, Asef 170
Beer, Robert 171, 181n41
Beirut 109; Mar Elias camp 118, 168;
   Palestinian settlements in 154; PLO in
   124, 167; political elites in 153
Beirut Port Authority 45
Bekaa, the 7, 69; coordination in 109,
   234n7; mayors in 110, 206n11; Syrian
   refugees in 99, 106–107, 112–114; *see
   also* Central Bekaa
Bekaa province 68
Bekaa Valley 17, 99; refugee camps in 66
benign strangulation 121, 133–136
Bergh, Sylvia 48
Bidinger, Sarah 61
Biehl, Kristen Sarah 3

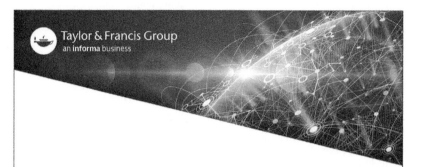